**LIBRARY OF CONGRESS**

Published by University Press of Mississippi,
in association with the Library of Congress

Jackson

DRAWN TO PURPOSE

AMERICAN WOMEN ILLUSTRATORS
AND
CARTOONISTS

MARTHA H. KENNEDY
FOREWORD BY CARLA D. HAYDEN

The Library of Congress gratefully acknowledges support from The Alfred Bendiner Foundation for this publication and from the Swann Foundation for Caricature and Cartoon for the accompanying exhibition.

www.upress.state.ms.us

Designed by Peter D. Halverson
Design concept by Michael Shveima

The University Press of Mississippi is a member of the
Association of American University Presses.

First printing 2018
∞

Library of Congress Cataloging-in-Publication Data

Names: Kennedy, Martha H. (Martha Hoeprich), author.
Title: Drawn to purpose : American women illustrators and cartoonists /
Martha H. Kennedy.
Description: Jackson : University Press of Mississippi, in association with the
Library of Congress, 2018. | Includes bibliographical references and index. |
Identifiers: LCCN 2017032089 (print) | LCCN 2017033179 (ebook) | ISBN
9781496815934 (epub single) | ISBN 9781496815941 (epub institutional) |
ISBN 9781496815958 (pdf single) | ISBN 9781496815965 (pdf institutional) |
ISBN 9781496815927 (cloth : alk. paper)
Subjects: LCSH: Illustrators—United States—Biography. | Women illustra-
tors—United States—Biography. | Cartoonists—United States—Biography. |
Women cartoonists—United States—Biography.
Classification: LCC NC975 (ebook) | LCC NC975.K46 2018 (print) | DDC
741.6092/2 [B] —dc23
LC record available at https://lccn.loc.gov/2017032089
British Library Cataloging-in-Publication Data available

To the memory of my mother,
Muriel B. Hoeprich (1922–2016),
and the artists featured in this book—
all kindred spirits in aspiring to and striving
for purpose in their lives

CONTENTS

FOREWORD

In 1949, a critic who thought he was being complimentary noted that "There is nothing about Anne Mergen's style of drawing to indicate that she is a woman." His notion to indicate that she is a woman." His notion that anything in her work indicating she was female would mark it as inferior was a typical line of thought. Mergen, who had been part of the *Miami Daily News*'s Pulitzer Prize–winning team years earlier, was by then a long-established and well-respected political cartoonist. She was among the few women in her line of work at the time, but she was part of that much larger community of artists who, as women, had to prove themselves exceptionally worthy of any recognition they received.

As the first woman to serve as Librarian of Congress, I am especially pleased with the release of *Drawn to Purpose*, as it features the works of many women who were the first to achieve recognition in male-dominated fields. Nearly 150 women who worked in fine arts, cartooning, and illustration are represented here. Since these artists strived to be recognized for their creative achievements rather than their gender, it may seem odd that *Drawn to Purpose* should focus only on women, but as cartoonist Liza Donnelly points out, "the risk of 'ghettoizing' women is one worth taking if it gives us the opportunity to discuss women's rights, freedom, and why there are so few women in this field."

Drawn to Purpose brings together a remarkable sampling of book illustrations, posters, industrial design, courtroom sketches, comic strips, political cartoons, and art for magazines and newspapers produced by women over a 150-year span. The startling array of imagery, technique, and points of view on display is compelling. I was struck by how all of these works relate to the written word, either amplifying a text or incorporating language into the artwork itself. As a kid who read everything, I pored over the illustrations just as much as the accompanying words. Images can make reading more meaningful and more memorable. On those occasions when you can't remember the title of a book, it seems you can always recall what was on the cover.

Here at the Library of Congress, the nation's first federal cultural institution, our collections comprise more than 165 million items, including original works of fine and illustrative art. The Library is honored to preserve this material for the public and for future generations to study and be inspired by. With the publication of *Drawn to Purpose*, we offer a tantalizing glimpse of these holdings. I invite you to visit the Library, either in person or online at www.loc.gov, to explore the collections and wherever your imagination takes you.

Carla D. Hayden
Librarian of Congress

PREFACE

I very earnestly believe . . . that there
should be no sex in Art . . . I am pointing,
I know, to a millennium at least . . . when
the term "Women in Art" will be as
strange sounding a topic as the title
"Men in Art" would be now.
—CECELIA BEAUX, 1915'

Clearly, Cecelia Beaux objected to being called a "woman artist." She was a leading light among American portrait painters, and in 1895 became the first woman to teach at the prestigious Pennsylvania Academy of Fine Arts. Twenty years would pass before another woman—Violet Oakley, an acclaimed muralist and illustrator—would join her on the faculty. At that rate, Beaux's estimated thousand-year timetable seemed right on schedule. Indeed, "women in art" is a story of incremental progress, and every now and then, someone makes a great leap forward.

As in nearly every other professional field, women pursuing careers in fine art, illustration, or cartooning encountered limitations in training, permitted subject matter, and adequate work environments. These obstacles and restrictions, largely imposed by men but also resulting from larger societal pressures, kept all but the most resilient women from advancing in the arts. Many labored in the shadows and on the margins as skilled assistants, practicing their craft and gradually gaining footholds in their chosen fields. From the mid-nineteenth century into the early twentieth, most of these women moved forward with little or no recognition. More than any other thread, women pushing back against social and industry impediments forms a major strand in the history of women in illustration and cartooning. The gradual broadening of subjects that women treated came to parallel new opportunities for education and professional employment. In contrast, the later twentieth and early twenty-first centuries have seen greater numbers of women—some of them household names—produce work that became and remains sought after by mainstream and alternative outlets.

In this overarching survey, *Drawn to Purpose* tracks historical trends, and both celebrated and little-known artists are featured here, as are types of artwork that have not received sustained attention. Although illustration and cartoons/comics are usually recognized as visually distinct from each other, the two are often interrelated. Among those who practice and study these art forms, some regard cartooning and comics as subsets of illustration. The illustrative arts also share a particularly close relationship with the fine arts, and many artists included in this book have worked in more than one medium and genre. In presenting a critical mass of works, *Drawn to Purpose* elucidates selected examples of art within the context of their creators' lives and the times in which they lived. Thus, the book aims to be a history, a resource, and a springboard to spur research on these artists and others in the field while underscoring the Library of Congress's vast collections in furthering this endeavor.

Drawn to Purpose was inspired by, and is based on, original art in the Library's Prints and Photographs Division (P&P) and enhanced by published materials from the Rare Book and Special Collections Division, the Serials and Periodicals Division, and the General Collections. Since 1870 P&P has collected American graphic art through US copyright deposits, gifts, and purchases. In building its collections, P&P seeks to meet the research needs of Congress and researchers by maintaining significant examples of the nation's visual culture. The division also makes its resources freely accessible to its reading room visitors and through its catalog, onsite and online exhibitions, and a robust web presence.

By many measures, women have become leaders in the world of contemporary illustration, producing best-selling works, winning top prizes, and becoming industry powerbrokers, a far cry from when they fought to get into print or to gain entry into the very organizations that would later honor them with major awards. Women who become illustrators and cartoonists represent a special breed of artist and form a self-selected sisterhood. Taking pencil, pen, or brush to paper, burin or needle to plate, litho pen to stone, or digital pen to pad, they ply their tools toward multiple ends—to tell stories, to entertain, to cause laughter, to enlighten, to persuade, to assert opinion, to earn a living. All of these artists are moved, even impelled, by a creative drive, by commerce, and often by necessity to create art that, in their minds and ours, fulfills a purpose.

CHAPTER 1

GOLDEN AGE ILLUSTRATORS

Howard Pyle and Mary Hallock Foote likely never crossed paths but they each put their charcoal- and ink-stained fingers on the quandary that challenged many talented women seeking careers in illustration. Pyle, perhaps the greatest illustration instructor of his time, taught at the Drexel Institute in Philadelphia and later his own school of il- lustration. Far from discouraging all women in his classes, Pyle believed that some were capable of producing illustration art equal to that created by their male peers. Further, he agreed that a woman had the right to pur- sue a career, but he also shared the widely held view that a woman could not sustain a marriage while also meeting the deadlines and high standard of work required of a pro- fessional illustrator.[3]

Given longstanding social pressure on most women to marry, it took exceptional determination on the part of even highly talented, motivated women to pursue ca- reers in the visual arts. The expectation of marriage, along with biases against their gender in art training and employment, hampered many aspiring artists. Others deliberately chose not to marry. Foote did marry and numbered among those who fulfilled roles in two spheres, professional and domestic, forging successful careers and private lives as wives and mothers. Many a sister illustrator, however, found that she needed to sacrifice one role for the other.

Whether she married or not, an art education was critical to an illustrator's professional development, as it helped expand opportunities for exhibition, commissions, and networking. In the 1890s, the Cooper Union, the New York School of Applied Design for Women, and the Philadelphia School of Design for Women offered courses intended for single women seeking vocational training.[4] Many, however, sought more rigorous training in the fine arts, which the Pennsylvania Academy of Fine Arts (PAFA) provided. For women, access to such a curriculum increased incrementally in the nineteenth century. During the 1840s, women could not study in the same classes as men at PAFA, although in 1844 the board of directors passed a resolution granting women "the exclusive use of the statue gallery for professional purposes . . . during the hours of 10 to 11:00 [am] on Monday, Wednesday, and Friday."[5] By 1856, with female enrollment increasing, women were allowed to study from casts in classes with men. They later gained unrestricted access to the sculpture gallery once the male statues had been covered with strategically placed fig leaves.[6] As of 1860, women could also attend lectures on anatomy, but unlike their male peers, they were not allowed to draw from live, let alone nude, male models.[7] Consequently, a number of women organized their own classes off campus, posing for one another clothed or sometimes half-draped. The academy later quietly added "Ladies' Life Classes" to the curriculum, and for many years life courses continued to be segregated.[8] In one notorious instance, Thomas Eakins, a professor of drawing at PAFA, was forced to resign in 1886 after he used a nude male model in a class with male and female students.[9]

For a number of aspiring illustrators, men and women, Pyle proved to be a crucial part of their art education. He taught a class at Drexel and went on to offer special summer classes at Chadds Ford, outside of Philadelphia, from 1898 to 1903 to select students, including such successful artists as Elizabeth Shippen Green, Jessie Willcox Smith, and Violet Oakley.[10] The Society of Illustrators, founded in 1901 by a group of male practitioners, recognized that some women were as worthy as men for membership, and elected Green and Florence Scovel as associate members in 1903. The following year saw Oakley, Smith, and May Wilson Preston welcomed as associate members,[11] but it was not until the 1920s that the society allowed women full membership.[12]

THE GOLDEN AGE

Despite the obstacles, American women illustrators increased in number and visibility beginning in the second half of the nineteenth century. As illustrated newspapers, literary magazines, popular periodicals and prints, and books played an increasingly important role in culture and society, skilled women artists contributed significantly to the narrative, documentary, comic, and satirical imagery that enlivened such widely disseminated publications. In addition to advancing storylines, these artists created images that demonstrated how female roles in society were changing. At the same time, subject matter considered acceptable for women artists—children, family, and fashion—was also gradually broadening. The growth of the middle class in post–Civil War America brought with it increased leisure time and social mobility, both factors that enlarged and enhanced women's experiences beyond the purely domestic world of home and child-rearing. In time women earned commissions to illustrate popular adult literature, including romances in short story and novel formats, as well as literary classics.

The Golden Age of Illustration spans the years from about 1880 to 1930 and coincides with a period when publishing flourished and illustrated magazines and books streamed into the homes of middle- and upper-class Americans. The post–Civil War era gave rise to enormous growth in industry and transportation, expansion of the middle and upper classes, and, with the spread of public schools nationwide, greater educational opportunities and higher literacy rates. These trends, combined with a notable increase in leisure time, produced great demand for illustrated publications. Readers eagerly sought image-filled

GOLDEN AGE PREDECESSORS

The often hidden and little-known work created by women for America's early print publishing houses set the stage for and possibly inspired the excellent work and broad recognition achieved by women illustrators who emerged during the Golden Age in the late nineteenth century. These establishments, initially concentrated in Boston, Philadelphia, and New York, primarily produced commercial and documentary lithographs, such as depictions of Civil War battles and appealing scenes of domestic life. Many of these illustrations went uncredited. The Pendleton lithographic establishment in Boston employed a number of women to assist in the complex lithographic process, in which drawings are made on polished limestone treated so that image areas retain ink and non-image areas repel it, and are then transferred to paper.[19] It is unlikely that female employees actually worked in the shop, however, because prevailing social norms did not encourage women's employment.[20] In Philadelphia, print publishers were renowned for producing some of the finest hand-colored lithographic book illustrations, and skilled women executed most of the coloring.[21] By the mid-nineteenth century, several women, trained at the Philadelphia School of Design for Women (now Moore College of Art), were also working as lithographers.[22]

While the contributions of these early lithographers and colorists generally remain obscure, one woman did win at least some name recognition. Trained by a professional artist, Frances Flora ("Fanny") Bond Palmer (1812–1876) emigrated from England with her husband, Edmund Seymour Palmer, and in 1844 the couple established a lithography business in Manhattan. The business failed, but its acquisition in 1851 by Nathaniel Currier opened new opportunities for Palmer, who rapidly became one of the most prolific and skilled artists for the legendary Currier & Ives firm.[23] During the 1850s she produced several pastoral series, including *American Farm Scenes* (1853), *American Country Life* (1855), and *American Winter Scenes* (1854). She also created two prints that became icons of American visual culture: *Across the Continent, Westward the Course of Empire Takes Its Way* (1868) and *The Rocky Mountains, Emigrants Crossing the Plains* (1866). This seems all the more remarkable considering that Palmer reportedly never traveled west of Hoboken, New Jersey, and lived in Brooklyn during the

Fig. 1.1. Fanny Palmer. The Valley of the Shenandoah, 1864. Lithograph, hand colored. Published by Currier & Ives.

years she worked for Currier & Ives. Like other commercial artists, she probably used photographs and published drawings of actual sites to create her works, including such Civil War subjects as *The Valley of the Shenandoah* (1864) (fig. 1.1) and *Cumberland Valley from Bridgeport Heights Opposite Harrisburg, PA* (1868).[24]

In addition to creating some two hundred lithographs she is known to have worked on many more that were issued anonymously. From 1862 to 1867 Palmer reportedly produced all but one of the still lifes published by the firm and is also believed to have made many of its anonymous fruit and flower prints.[25] Her employers' commercial interests and ideological convictions most likely determined the choice of subjects she handled. Unfortunately, Palmer left no known papers revealing her own opinions on the breadth of subjects she was assigned or how she might have regarded the ways in which women were being depicted. Even so, she stands out as a commercial artist who employed a broadly appealing mix of factual observation, artistic convention, and knowledge of other artists' published treatments of similar or related subjects. As Currier & Ives expert Ewell L. Newman observed, "It is likely that during the latter half of the nineteenth century more pictures by Mrs. Fanny Palmer decorated the homes of ordinary Americans than those of any other artist, dead or alive."[26]

works that offered articles of general interest, humor, self-improvement, poetry, and fiction in short and long form, as sources of enlightenment and entertainment. During its popular peak, illustration was a distinctive art form tied primarily to storytelling, informative texts, and advertising. Among the many aspiring artists who pursued careers in the field, those who became celebrated in their time included women, but hardly any of them, male or female, attained fame that lasted. Howard Pyle, Charles Dana Gibson, N. C. Wyeth, and Maxfield Parrish number among the few that are still remembered—all men.

Despite the broad appeal and cultural importance of illustration, its status as an art form remained unsettled during much of its Golden Age and after it waned.[13] Even among illustrators themselves, opinions varied as to the significance and proper place of illustration in the art world. Could it be regarded as a type of fine art, or, because such artwork was usually created for commissions involving text, must it be considered essentially commercial? During the last third of the nineteenth century, such well-known figures as Winslow Homer, Edwin Austin Abbey, John La Farge, and Howard Pyle all trained in art schools, worked actively in illustration, and helped elevate "the reputation of illustration from the level of a craft to that of a fine art."[14] Such respect, however, was short-lived among purists. In the 1890s, many more magazines were supported by advertising, which some viewed as leaving a commercial taint on the artwork inside.[15] Another factor affecting the status of illustration was "the perceived feminization of the field."[16] Despite the fact that the profession attracted large numbers of men, it was even more popular among women. This trend contributed to some art schools, including the Pennsylvania Academy of Fine Arts and the National Academy of Design, to resist offering courses in illustration.[17]

Despite the unresolved status of the art form, the Golden Age of Illustration brought forth visually compelling works of art executed in a variety of realist styles by many extremely accomplished artists. Such work "is usually viewed as a last vestige of representational painting" that preceded the growing use of photography in periodicals and the rising tide of modernist styles in painting and drawing.[18]

Stars of the Golden Age

At the peak of the Golden Age of American Illustration, numerous talented illustrators were producing thousands of drawings.[27] These included many dazzling works of art that were generally narrative, furthering the arc of a story or documentary, providing a visual record based on observation, or both. Mary Hallock Foote, Alice Barber Stephens, Elizabeth Shippen Green, and Jessie Willcox Smith won recognition from their peers, publishers, and the public rivaling that enjoyed by their male counterparts. Foote, Stephens, and Green explored and illustrated a range of subjects, including news and travel reportage, adult romances, and literary classics that extended well beyond children's literature. Smith and Maginel Enright Barney, who focused on children's literature, produced a high volume of work of exceptional quality. The little-known Jessie Gillespie became an acclaimed silhouette artist. Other women were recognized for their mastery of different specialties in or related to illustration.

Born into a Quaker family near Milton, New York, on the Hudson River, Mary Hallock Foote (1847–1938) would produce much of her work grounded in direct observation of her surroundings. Her family encouraged her artistic talent, and in 1864, just before her seventeenth birthday, she entered one of the earliest and most distinguished professional art schools for women, the Cooper Union School of Design in New York City. There she studied figure drawing and design, receiving prizes for her work. Foote later regarded two of her teachers there as mentors. Doctor, painter, and sculptor William Rimmer, who taught human anatomy and botany, undoubtedly contributed to Foote's ability to draw the human figure. Although there is no record of Foote studying wood engraving with William J. Linton, he likely provided her with helpful guidance in design for illustration.[28] Foote also began what became a lifelong friendship with sister student and aspiring painter Helena De Kay, who married Richard Watson Gilder, future editor of *Scribner's Monthly* and *Century Illustrated Monthly Magazine*. These professional and personal relationships combined with her exemplary record as a student proved critical in generating professional

Fig. 1.2. Mary Hallock Foote. "Packing" Water at Bush Tunnel. Ink, wash. Published in *Scribner's Monthly*, February 1878.

opportunities for her as an illustrator—and later as a writer—primarily of stories about life in mining camps and the American West.

Foote won and completed full-page assignments during the early 1870s for such magazines as *Appleton's Journal*, *Scribner's Monthly*, and the art journal *Aldine*. Between 1874 and 1877, she also worked with Hudson River School painter Thomas Moran and others to illustrate special gift editions of books by Nathaniel Hawthorne, Henry Wadsworth Longfellow, and John Greenleaf Whittier and was praised by reviewers for her rendering of the human figure and sense of design. Her career was well established by 1876 when she married an adventurous young mining engineer, Arthur De Wint Foote, who had won her over with his work

ethic, his ambition, and his potential to make valuable contributions to his field.[29]

Foote's career underwent a gradual transformation after her husband's work led the couple to relocate permanently in the West, establishing homes in Colorado and Idaho before settling finally in California. Their first stop in the Golden State was New Almaden, site of an extraordinarily successful quicksilver mine. "We kept house in that redwood-lined cabin just one year and a month [1876–1877]," wrote Foote. "A son was born to us there and prospered the first four months of his existence; then we shut the door on its little histories and never saw the place again. . . . We were in a camp of labor, yet not of it. On the last hill above us the Mexican camp was the home of a more barren and hopeless poverty even than that which we had at our elbow . . . we lived in the face of all that natural beauty, conscious in our souls of an overhanging mass of helplessness and want."[30]

Despite working under physically challenging conditions, raising three children, and being far removed from eastern publishing centers, Foote managed to continue producing and publishing well-composed, technically accomplished illustrations. Publishers sent her wood engravers blocks that she drew on and returned, and in addition to "the daily walk for exercise and in search of backgrounds" she also developed as a writer.[31] That she had household help in the form of "Lizzie, the maid we had imported from the East," made possible what otherwise might have been impossible. As Foote recalled, those unaware of her profession and ambition "must have wondered what on earth we needed of a maid in that little box of a cabin we were going to and what 'the wife' was 'able for' anyway."[32]

Gilder commissioned Foote to write and illustrate essays and articles documenting her experiences, thereby affording her an exceptional opportunity as a pioneering woman illustrator of the American West. Two drawings based on firsthand observation, *"Packing" Water at Bush Tunnel* and *"Dump" at the Great Eastern Tunnel* (figs. 1.2 and 1.3), published in *Scribner's Monthly*, February 1878, well represent her early work in the West and her meticulous drawing technique.

Among her best known illustrations is a series of eleven full-page wood engravings entitled "Pictures of

Fig. 1.3. Mary Hallock Foote. "Dump" at the Great Eastern Tunnel. Ink, wash. Published in *Scribner's Monthly*, February 1878. These This drawing and fig. 1.2 were completed during the Footes' time at New Almaden Mine, in the Santa Cruz Mountains, south of San Francisco. Both accompanied her article, "A California Mining Camp," in the magazine.

Fig. 1.4. Mary Hallock Foote. A Pretty Girl in the West. Graphite, wash. Published with Foote's essay, "The Pretty Girls in the West. Pictures of the Far West.—X" in *Century Illustrated Monthly Magazine*, October 1889.

the Far West," each accompanied by her own descriptive text, published in *Century* magazine in 1888–1889. In one drawing, *A Pretty Girl in the West* (fig. 1.4), Foote depicts a young guitarist entertaining a visiting gentleman. In this charming scene, each appears pleased to be in the other's company within the enclosed space of an outdoor porch, yet by positioning the figures sitting far apart, not making eye contact, and amid receding pillars to emphasize the sense of distance, Foote expertly conveys a feeling of restraint. This feeling is underscored by her accompanying essay, which describes how eastern girls out west attract admirers and risk encouraging romantic expectations that neither party can meet. In a later work, *Between the Desert and the Sown* (fig. 1.5), Foote depicts a lone young woman walking along an irrigation ditch. This finely crafted drawing is among the works that serve as windows into the artist's own and often isolated situation in the vast, sparsely settled expanses of western landscape—and that reflect her quest to maintain and nurture her identity as a cultivated gentlewoman.

Her vivid depictions of mining scenes, Mexican laborers, Pacific coast scenery, and women coping in frontier settings, published in both fiction and nonfiction works, are grounded in her direct experience of western life. Further, she penned sixteen volumes of fiction, some of which she illustrated. Foote reached a huge audience during her three decades of artistic activity, and she also won the admiration of critics and her peers. Artist William J. Hayes and illustrator William Allen Rogers, who called Foote "one of the most accomplished illustrators in America," made a pilgrimage to her home in Leadville, Colorado, in 1879.[33] Joseph Pennell, master printmaker, illustrator, and writer, also asserted, "I find that Mary Hallock Foote was one of our best illustrators."[34] When Foote was selected as a member of the New York Fine Arts Committee for the World's Columbian Exposition in Chicago in 1893, the honor signaled major recognition of the quality and impact of her work.[35]

Meanwhile, most professional illustrators were based in the East, and within a constellation of talented, Philadelphia-based women active during the Golden Age, Alice Barber Stephens (1858–1932) and Elizabeth Shippen Green (1871–1954) stand out as particularly distinguished. Stephens, born on a farm near

Fig. 1.5. Mary Hallock Foote. Between the Desert and the Sown. Ink, wash. Published in "Conquest of Arid America," by William E. Smythe, *Century Illustrated Monthly Magazine*, May 1895.

Salem, New Jersey, drew from an early age. "I had done many child drawings in the beginning, old people and the very simple working people . . . and got my models from life," she recalled late in life. "I touched only now and then society types."[36] Around 1869, she began taking classes at the Philadelphia School of Design for Women. A full-time student by 1873, she studied with the noted English engraver John Dalziel. While still a student, she honed her technique so well that she began to publish wood engravings of artists' illustrations in *Scribner's Monthly*.[37]

Desiring to draw her own work, Stephens enrolled for the 1876–1877 term at PAFA. Studying with Thomas Eakins, she learned new naturalistic techniques that required painting rather than drawing in depicting the nude (female) model. Eakins may also have taught Stephens photography, which she used as a tool for learning about design and lighting effects. One of Eakins's best students, she was entrusted with

engraving several of his works (fig. 1.6, *Biglin Brothers Turning the Stake*, ca. 1880).[38] In 1879 she painted *Women's Life Class*, which she engraved on wood and saw published as an illustration for a story on art schools in Philadelphia in the September issue of *Scribner's Monthly*.[39]

From 1878 on, Stephens contributed to many other publications, including *Century Illustrated Monthly*, *Cosmopolitan*, *Collier's Weekly*, *Ladies' Home Journal*, and *Country Gentleman*, sometimes producing both her own original drawings and the accompanying wood engravings required for publication. Working herself almost to exhaustion, she made the transition, by 1884, from wood engraver to illustrator. In 1885, she showed her drawings to Charles Parsons, *Harper's* art editor, and subsequently became a regular illustrator for that widely circulated magazine. It is notable that Stephens, unlike many sister illustrators, did little illustration of literature for children. The fact that she

Fig. 1.6. Alice Barber Stephens. The Biglin Brothers Turning the Stake, after painting by Thomas Eakins. Photomechanical print (after wood engraving). Published in "Spring Hereabout" by Clarence Cook, *Scribner's Monthly*, June 1880.

Fig. 1.7. Alice Barber Stephens. Selma Threw Herself at Full Length on the Ground, 1899. Watercolor. Published in "Three Chapters" by Gertrude Blake Stanton, *Cosmopolitan*, April 1895.

entered oil paintings in the annual exhibition of the Philadelphia Academy of Fine Arts every year from 1884 to 1890 underscores her professional ambition. Personally and professionally, it was an exciting era for Stephens, who felt the influence of W. T. Smedley, Charles Dana Gibson, Edwin Austin Abbey, and Howard Pyle.[40] "Abbey was Prince and King without a doubt," she later noted. "It was thrilling to watch new sets of drawings come out in *Harper's*. . . . I came in contact with these people and feel that I owe them much, but I hope that the direct contact with nature was my greatest teacher."[41]

Stephens traveled in Europe during 1886 and 1887. Even while trying to recover from her frantic working pace of previous years, she toured Italy and Holland, studied in Paris at the Académie Julian under Tony Robert-Fleury and at the Académie Colarossi, and exhibited two works at the 1887 Salon. Following her return home, she taught drawing, painting from life, crayon portraiture, and illustration at the Philadelphia School of Design. In 1890, the year that she married the painter Charles Hallowell Stephens, she won the Mary Smith Prize, a $100 award made annually to a woman artist resident at PAFA. Three years later, she had a son and received a Diploma of Honorable Mention at the World's Columbian Exposition for her skill in teaching drawing and portrait painting from life. A popular, devoted instructor, Stephens also shared a

studio from 1899 to 1903 with her student and protégé Charlotte Harding (1873–1951).[42]

With the rise of halftone printing technology in the 1890s, Stephens moved toward a softer, less linear approach to drawing, using charcoal, oil, and a combination of charcoal and wash. Several of the beautiful illustrations she created in 1895 show her maturing style. *Selecting Miniatures, Old Store, Bailey, Banks, Biddle, Philadelphia* (published as *Buying Christmas Presents*, fig. 1.8) demonstrates her increasingly sophisticated technique. The boldly diagonal composition of this scene that prominently features women as consumers reveals the influence of photography, while the still life in the foreground is done with painterly bravura. Her illustration for a short story, also created in 1895 (fig. 1.7), shows the two female protagonists enjoying the outdoors, one painting at an easel. The palette of lighter colors, more fluid brushstrokes, and

Fig. 1.8. Alice Barber Stephens. Selecting Miniatures, Old Store, Bailey, Banks, Biddle, Philadelphia, 1895. Watercolor, gouache. Published as Buying Christmas Presents, *Harper's Weekly*, December 14, 1895.

use of light effects indicate the influence of impressionism on the artist.[43]

In 1897, another landmark year for Stephens, the *Ladies' Home Journal* commissioned her to provide six cover illustrations portraying different types of the "American Woman," her work to alternate with women drawn by Charles Dana Gibson, then and now considered a leading light among the era's illustrators. Her commission reflected the spirit of the time, marked by the emergence of the "New Woman," a social phenomenon described by writers in the 1890s and early 1900s as an independent, often well-educated, young woman poised to enjoy a more active role in the public arena

than women of preceding generations. The Gibson Girl created by Gibson was widely regarded as the visual ideal of the New Woman and while he often highlighted her beauty and social skills, he also featured her talents and interests in his work.[44]

Although both Gibson and Stephens were associated with this new social type, Stephens herself was a living example of the New Woman in that she pursued her interests and developed her talent with great success. The cover art she created for this assignment shows strong stylistic affinities with her 1895 illustration of the woman selecting miniatures. That same year Stephens, along with Emily Sartain, director of

A CLUB OF THEIR OWN

When Emily Sartain and Alice Barber Stephens established the Plastic Club in March 1897, they provided a platform for female artists' professional development similar to the clubs where male artists gathered. Such an organization was sorely needed, and the club fulfilled its promise "to promote a wider knowledge of art and to advance its interest by means of exhibitions and social intercourse among artists."[46] Blanche Dillaye, a founding member and first president of the organization,[47] suggested the organization's name because the term "plastic" refers "to any work of art unfinished, or in a 'plastic' state," and can also refer "to the changing and tactile sense of painting and sculpture."[48] Open to women in any branch of the visual arts, the club initiated an ambitious schedule of activities, including lectures, classes, teas, and exhibitions of work by members as well as other female and male artists.[49] Illustrators Elizabeth Shippen Green, Jessie Willcox Smith, Violet Oakley, cartoonist Grace Drayton (see chapter 2), portraitist Cecelia Beaux, and photographer Eva Watson were among its many members. The Plastic Club first admitted men as members in 1991.[50]

Fig. 1.9. Alice Barber Stephens. She Bent Down over the Dead Monk, 1900. Oil. Published in *The Marble Faun* by Nathaniel Hawthorne, Houghton, Mifflin & Co., 1900.

the Philadelphia School of Design for Women, co-founded the Plastic Club, an organization for women artists based in Philadelphia. With her husband, Stephens was also a founding member of the Fellowship of the Pennsylvania Academy of Fine Arts.[45]

Stephens's career began to peak when she was in her forties, and her illustrations for *Middlemarch* by George Eliot and *John Halifax, Gentleman* by Maria Mullock Craik won a gold medal at the 1899 Exposition of Women's Work at Earl's Court in London. Her drawings for both books demonstrate her talent for depicting key moments or situations in a narrative that reveal or deepen the reader's understanding of the characters and relationships between them. She also skillfully delineates the sometimes elaborate interior settings in which notable scenes take place, yet manages not to allow the details and scale of such settings to overshadow the main focus on interactions between figures or a single figure's expressive effect.[51] Similarly impressive drawings for Nathaniel Hawthorne's gothic romance, *The Marble Faun* (1900), often cited as Stephens's finest book illustrations, were awarded a bronze medal at the Exposition Universelle in Paris. In skillfully composed scenes depicting Rome's elaborate architectural settings, Stephens keeps the dramatic focus on the protagonist, Miriam, who is shown in affecting attitudes of grief (fig. 1.9). These exceptionally accomplished drawings underscore

Stephens's strong ability to evoke the complex psychological drama central to leading works of fiction of her time. They also bring to mind Stephens's own words: "The true illustrator . . . must have the facility of the actor and novelist as well as the artist."[52]

In 1901, exhausted from overwork and family responsibilities, Stephens again traveled to England and Europe to recuperate and visit art museums. This time her husband and nine-year-old son accompanied her during a fifteen-month vacation. On her return she illustrated Louisa May Alcott's *Little Women* and short stories in *Harper's, McClure's,* and *Women's Home Companion* well into the 1910s.

During American involvement in World War I, Stephens refrained from painting, telling a reporter she did not think it worthwhile to create "pictures in the midst of destruction," although she did respond to a request from Charles Dana Gibson, then head of the Division of Pictorial Publicity for the wartime Committee on Public Information, to make posters in support of the war effort.[53] She may have created what was informally titled *Somebody Has to Raise Everything You Eat, Do Your Share* (fig. 1.10) at Gibson's behest.[54] Published in the November 1917 issue of *Red Cross Magazine* with the caption "The Gospel of Effort," it was one in a series of six poster designs by such prominent illustrators as Howard Chandler Christy, Coles Phillips, and Neysa McMein.[55] Stephens's bold, side view of a strong young woman focused on hoeing for the common good reflects the series theme of "Waste Not, Want Not" and has a heroic, even propagandistic aspect completely appropriate for a wartime home-front poster.

By 1926, Stephens ceased working in illustration, feeling that her style was out-of-step with postwar trends in the art form. Three years later, the Plastic Club held a retrospective exhibition of her work, saluting her artistic achievements. Prolific and highly skilled, Stephens gave visible form to a remarkable variety of memorable figures, many of them showing women in a wide range of pursuits that challenged the assumptions of her time. To what degree she could encourage, select, and shape her assignments as an illustrator cannot easily be determined. It is certain, however, that this accomplished artist and teacher left a rich legacy, not only through her art, but also

Fig. 1.10. Alice Barber Stephens. Somebody Has to Raise Everything You Eat, Do Your Share, 1917 or 1918. Crayon. Published in *Red Cross Magazine,* November 1917.

through her assistance to other artists, particularly women.

Younger than Stephens, the trio known as the Red Rose Girls—Elizabeth Shippen Green (1871–1954), Jessie Willcox Smith (1863–1935), and Violet Oakley (1874–1961)—also became distinguished Golden Age women illustrators. Green's earlier work in particular is similar in style and theme to that of her two close friends and other women in the field, but as her career unfolds her work gains uniqueness in scope, quality, and originality.

Born into an old Philadelphia family, Green was encouraged in her artistic interests by her father, who had worked as an artist-reporter during the Civil War. Following a private school education in Philadelphia, she studied at PAFA (1889–1893) with two accomplished painters, Thomas Anshutz and Robert

Fig. 1.11. Elizabeth Shippen Green. Gisèle, 1908. Watercolor, charcoal. Published in "The Dream" by Justus Miles, *Harper's Magazine*, October 1908.

Years later, she elaborated much further on Pyle's influence, noting that "in my own experience, it seems to me that he did not so much teach me to draw but how to interpret life. . . . He taught me, I might say, what philosophy of life I may possess."[56]

Beginning in 1900 Green and her two friends shared studio homes, mostly at the Red Rose Inn and later at Farm Hill, both outside Philadelphia. The three, joined by their friend Henrietta Cozens, had the farm refurbished and dubbed it Cogslea. The large living and studio spaces, the gardens and countryside, and the companionship allowed each of the artists to flourish. This communal living and working arrangement lasted for fourteen years—an unusual lifestyle choice at the time that benefited all. However unconventional, the arrangement accorded with Pyle's view that women should not combine matrimony and a career, an opinion that Smith echoed: "A woman's sphere is as sharply defined as a man's . . . If she elects to be a housewife and mother—that is her sphere and no other . . . If on the other hand she elects to go into business or the arts, she must sacrifice motherhood in order to fill successfully her chosen sphere."[57]

In 1901 Green won an exclusive contract as an illustrator with *Harper's Monthly*, an achievement that instantly elevated her into the ranks of such famous illustrators as Edwin Austin Abbey (1852–1911) and Pyle, her illustrious former teacher. Like many women illustrators of the time, Green depicted women and children but only concentrated on those subjects early in her career. She collaborated with Smith, for example, on *The Child, A Calendar* (1902), whose popularity boosted the reputations of both artists. In *The Mistress of the House*, a series specially commissioned in 1905, she fashioned a romanticized vision of domestic life featuring a beautiful young mother in surroundings similar to those depicted in paintings by Mary Cassatt (1844–1926). That same year, Green won the Mary Smith Prize awarded by PAFA for the best painting by a woman, published some of her finest illustrations in the book *Rebecca Mary*, and had more than forty drawings published in *Harper's*.

In her work for *Harper's* and other publications, Green often portrayed men and women in diverse dramatic situations, milieus, and moods. Throughout her career, in depicting characters in various historical

Vonnoh. While studying at the Drexel Institute (1894–1896) under Howard Pyle, she met Smith and Oakley, with whom she established lifelong friendships. Short, witty, extroverted, and willing to share her good humor, Green, like her sister comrades in art, pursued her own work with great diligence and seriousness.

Only eighteen when she published her first drawings in the *Philadelphia Times*, Green, like Stephens, took on professional assignments while still a student. She advanced from making pen-and-ink drawings of women's fashions and illustrations for children's stories to creating line and halftone illustrations for *St. Nicholas, Women's Home Companion*, and the *Saturday Evening Post*. She credited Pyle with teaching her the importance of visualizing, then realizing, the dramatic moment key to illustrating a narrative text.

Fig. 1.12. Elizabeth Shippen Green. Life Was Made for Love and Cheer, 1904. Watercolor, charcoal. Published in "The Red Rose," *Harper's Magazine*, September 1904. Green's image well suits the spirit of the poem by Henry Van Dyke: "When each heart gives out its best, / Then the talk is full of zest: / Light your fire and never fear, / Life was made for love and cheer."

Fig. 1.13. Elizabeth Shippen Green. *Welcome, Said the Old Man, Will You Come with Us*, ca. 1910. Pen and ink. Published in "The Mansion" by Henry Van Dyke, *Harper's Magazine*, December 1910.

Fig. 1.14. Elizabeth Shippen Green. *Once More the Herald Set the Trumpet to His Lips and Blew*, 1911. Oil, watercolor. Published in "Tapestries of Twilight" by Richard Le Gallienne, *Harper's Magazine*, May 1911.

periods, she displayed unusual ability to capture moments of human interaction and incorporate complex landscapes into her drawings. In *Gisèle* (1908) (fig. 1.11), for example, she employs a pleasing decorative style to portray the beautiful heroine of a short story who fits the feminine ideal of her time. The young woman's meditative expression and posture convey a psychological state of readiness as she waits the arrival of the male protagonist in this Gothic tale of romance. In contrast, in *Once More the Herald Set the Trumpet to His Lips and Blew* (ca. 1911) (fig. 1.14), Green creates a far different mood. In illustrating a short story by Richard Le Gallienne, she uses a low vantage point to heighten the visual impact of the boldly silhouetted men on horseback set against a colorful sky. The dramatic effect in this period scene rivals classic works by Howard Pyle. Another example, a pen-and-ink drawing, *Welcome, Said the Old Man, Will You Come with Us* (ca. 1910) (fig. 1.13), demonstrates her ability to depict figures of varied ages, to suggest psychological engagement between them, and to incorporate complex landscapes into her compositions.

Life Was Made for Love and Cheer (1904) (fig. 1.12), a stunningly designed, richly detailed watercolor, contains allusions to both concrete and intangible elements vital to her as an artist and human being. In this complex composition Green depicts herself, her equally gifted colleagues and housemates Smith and Oakley, and other friends amid the blooming grounds of the Red Rose Inn. The title, a line from Henry Van Dyke's poem "Inscriptions for a Friend's House," published opposite the image in *Harper's Monthly*, mirrors the artist's positive approach to her life and work. As the critic Harrison S. Morris observed, "what refreshes and renews the half-tone reproductions of her drawings [and] gives them unaccustomed angles of vision and unusual aspects, is this feeling for the beauty of line showing through the denser masses."[58]

Green's marriage in 1911 to Huger Elliott, a professor of architecture, pulled her away from Cogslea, the home she and her parents shared with Smith and Oakley. About four years earlier, Elliott had met and befriended Green and her companions through George Woodward, the owner of Cogslea. With his lively wit and love of nonsense verse, the young architect developed a special bond with convivial, extroverted Green. He remained a frequent, welcome visitor at Cogslea, even after he proposed to Green, who knew she would be breaking an agreement with her friends if she accepted. She put him off, telling him she didn't want to burden him with the expense of caring for her parents. After both died, however, he would not wait any longer, so she decided to marry, which she found difficult, but took comfort in knowing her friends were in sound financial shape.[59] Neither sadness at leaving her close friends nor relocating to accommodate her husband's career prevented her from continuing to work. In the following years she was prolific, producing drawings for *Harper's* until the end of her contract in 1924, illustrations for numerous books including the 1922 edition of *Charles and Mary Lamb's Tales from Shakespeare*, cover designs for *Good Housekeeping* in the 1930s, graphic art for popular organizations and causes, and advertisements.

Ambitious and highly productive, Green established a unique place as one of the most sought-after women illustrators of popular literature during the Golden Age of American Illustration. Though little known today, perhaps because so much of her work was disseminated in magazines, she remains an important figure in the world of illustrative art, not only because of her impressive body of work, but also for her willingness and drive to put her work before the public. Her aesthetic achievements, unusual versatility, and imaginative approaches to illustration helped conceptually stretch the possibilities for younger, similarly ambitious and talented female artists.

Children's Book Illustrators

Another of the Red Rose Girls, Jessie Willcox Smith, was one of the most successful and acclaimed children's book illustrators of her time. Others recognized for their work in this specialty include Maginel Wright Enright Barney, Fanny Young Cory (Cooney), and Katherine Pyle. Though long overshadowed by her famous brother Howard, Pyle became a prolific author and illustrator of children's books.

Although Jessie Willcox Smith was a native of Philadelphia, that mecca of the illustrative arts, she initially showed no interest in exploring this area of study. After graduating from high school in Cincinnati, she obtained a job there as a kindergarten teacher, but soon found the work difficult and unfulfilling.[60] While taking drawing lessons, she discovered her latent artistic talent and returned to Philadelphia in 1884, enrolling in the School of Design for Women.[61] She quickly realized that she needed more rigorous instruction and promptly transferred to the Pennsylvania Academy of Fine Arts, where Thomas Eakins was among her teachers. Smith published her first drawing in 1888 in *St. Nicholas*, a popular monthly magazine of literature for children, and obtained a post in the advertising department of *Ladies' Home Journal*.[62] Still motivated to pursue further training, Smith gained a place in Howard Pyle's inaugural illustration class at the Drexel Institute in 1894. She shared the experience with such budding luminaries in the field as Frank Schoonover and Elizabeth Shippen Green.[63]

After Violet Oakley joined Pyle's class in 1896, Smith and Oakley immediately collaborated on illustrating an edition of Longfellow's *Evangeline*, published in 1897. In 1903 Smith won the Mary Smith Prize for works exhibited at PAFA and collaborated with Green on a calendar, later published as *The Book of the Child*, which brought both artists national attention. Her reputation was enhanced the following year when she won a silver medal for illustration at the St. Louis International Exposition.

Smith's illustrated 1905 edition of Robert Louis Stevenson's *A Child's Garden of Verses* received praise not only for her superb craftsmanship but also deeper appreciation for the warmth and visual impact it projects. As one reviewer wrote at the time, "There is no better nor significant way to describe the irresistible charm of Miss Smith's work than to say its spirit is akin to that which pervades Stevenson's *A Child's Garden of Verses*."[64] Smith subsequently joined Green and Oakley in exhibiting works with the Society of Illustrators at the Waldorf Astoria in New York in 1907. She had already established a reputation as a first-class illustrator, highly regarded for her sympathetic

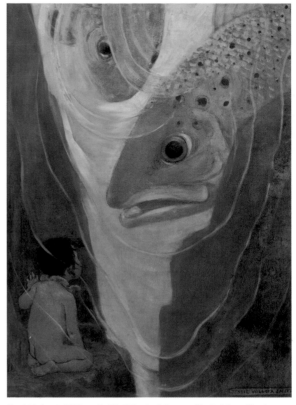

Fig. 1.15. Jessie Willcox Smith. He Looked Up at the Broad Yellow Moon and Thought That She Looked at Him, 1916. Charcoal, watercolor, oil. Published in *The Water Babies*, by Charles Kingsley, Dodd, Mead & Co., 1916.

Fig. 1.16. Jessie Willcox Smith. "Oh, don't hurt me!" cried Tom. "I only want to look at you; you are so handsome," 1916. Charcoal, watercolor, oil. Published in *The Water Babies*, by Charles Kingsley, Dodd, Mead & Co., 1916.

and appealing depictions of mothers, children, and babies, when she published *Dream Blocks* (1908), a series of delicate illustrations for a children's poetry collection by Aileen Cleveland Higgins. Her images for the delightful poems were critically acclaimed and widely circulated.[65] The exceptional empathy and understanding she displayed toward children in her illustrations led some to wonder if she had wanted a family of her own, but she expressed no regret about her own chosen path. Still, over time, she took on the financial responsibility for eleven children left orphaned by her relatives. Late in her career, with a sizable income, her friends dubbed her "The Mint," an affectionate term in recognition of her generosity.

In 1911, Smith won the Beck Prize at the Philadelphia Watercolor Club exhibit at the academy and exhibited works at the Rome Exposition. That year she and Oakley saw Green marry Elliott and leave Cogslea. Smith soon bought land nearby, built a new

home and studio, christened the place Cogshill, and moved in with her brother, aunt, and Henrietta Cozens. Smith continued working, winning a silver medal for watercolor at the Panama Pacific International Exposition in San Francisco in 1915.

Smith is perhaps best known for her illustrations for a 1916 edition of the Victorian children's classic *The Water Babies*, by the English Reverend Charles Kingsley. First published in 1863, this Victorian fairy tale, which became a bestseller in England and America, relates the story of Tom, a young chimney sweep, whose transformation by fairies into a "water-baby," or sprite, begins his journey into a state of happiness and spiritual redemption. Smith's frontispiece shows Tom trying to make sense of his plight: *He Looked Up at the Broad Yellow Moon and Thought That She Looked at Him* (fig. 1.15). This example and another scene in which Tom encounters huge fish (fig. 1.16) demonstrate Smith's imaginative powers in creating

Fig. 1.17. Maginel Enright Barney. [Mother, Daughter, and Swallows], ca. 1920. Watercolor, gouache. Published as cover, *Women's World*, July–August 1921.

Fig. 1.18. Maginel Enright Barney. [Boy Sitting in Top of Pine Tree], ca. 1927. Watercolor. Published in *Lost Village* by Alberta Bancroft, George H. Doran, 1927.

otherworldly scenes with dramatic yet realistic perspective as the engaging little sprite undergoes adventures and trials throughout this long fairy tale.

In 1917, Smith went on to publish the first of more than two hundred cover designs she eventually created for *Good Housekeeping*, replacing Coles Phillips, who had produced the magazine's covers for the previous five years. Her illustrated edition of *Heidi* appeared in 1922. By 1925 she began to increase her work in portraiture and devote less time to book and magazine illustration. In 1936, three years after her death, PAFA mounted a memorial exhibition of her work.

A shift toward lighter, purer hues and streamlined forms emerge in many illustrators' work by the 1920s. The work of artists who followed Smith reflected new trends in illustration for children. Technical improvements in printing technology, such as four-color engraving, and stylistic influences that included the

elegantly simplified forms so distinctive of Art Deco, Japanese prints, and modernist design, affected illustrators' composition and use of color. Fanny Young Cory (1877–1972) forged a peripatetic career path that later included cartooning. Born in Waukegan, Illinois, she moved to New York to study at the Art Students League and the Metropolitan School of Fine Art. Cory began publishing her work at an early age in *St. Nicholas Magazine*, and soon after that illustrated for *Century Magazine, Harper's Bazaar, Ladies' Home Journal,* and many others.[66]

Generally working in ink with wash or black watercolor, Cory demonstrated notable skill in depicting active, lively children, often with a touch of humor. She illustrated at least eleven books, including works by L. Frank Baum and Lewis Carroll, and several books she wrote herself for and about children.[67] With her career well under way, she moved to Montana, married rancher Fred Cooney in 1904, and raised three

Fig. 1.19. Jessie Gillespie. Desperation, Inspiration, Anticipation, Realization. Ink. Published in *Life*, March 3, 1915.

children. Her persistence in pursuing her profession in the West, far removed from major publishing outlets, recalls Mary Hallock Foote's similar determination early in her career in the late nineteenth century. In 1916, Cory briefly produced a single-panel cartoon, *Ben Bolt*, which did not last. She persevered, however, and eventually created successful comic features (see chapter 2). While not typical, Cory's career path bridged illustration and comic art, underscoring the interrelationship between the two popular art forms.

Maginel Wright Enright Barney (1877–1966) was born in Weymouth, Massachusetts, the youngest child of the Reverend William C. Wright and Anna Lloyd Jones. Maginel (her mother's contraction of Maggie Nell) was the younger sister of architect Frank Lloyd Wright, who early on encouraged her in drawing and painting. She attended the Art Institute of Chicago, where she met her husband, Walter J. ("Pat") Enright. They later moved to New York, where both became successful illustrators. After the couple divorced, Maginel married Hiram Barney, a lawyer, in 1923. Mainly using the name Maginel Wright Barney, she illustrated more than forty books, on her own or in collaboration with others between 1906 and 1965—including some that she wrote herself of childhood reminiscences.[68] From 1918 through 1940, she also created many dazzling cover designs for *Women's World*, as

well as illustrations and cover designs for many other magazines. Her cover design for *Women's World* (fig. 1.17) and her illustration for *Lost Village* by Alberta Bancroft (1927) (fig. 1.18) demonstrate qualities for which she was known—fresh, new clarity in composition and color, as seen in the pure colors and easily read figures in each drawing. The figure of the little boy amid the bold, irregular branches of the fir tree stands out, pulling the viewer's gaze into the intriguing scene.

"The Specialists"

Some women in the Golden Age staked out artistic real estate as specialists, go-to artists who filled niches left untouched by others—some even pursued the rarefied world of medical and scientific illustration. Jessie Gillespie (Willing) (1888–1972) produced silhouette art of a very high order—primarily for magazines and children's books.[69] In *Desperation, Inspiration, Anticipation, Realization* published in *Life*, November 3, 1915 (fig. 1.19), Gillespie shows the can-do New Woman emerging in four silhouettes. Static, withdrawn, and sedate on the left, she transforms through dress and outlook into a stylish figure striding forth on the right, buoyant and self-confident. She also created

Fig. 1.20. Jessie Gillespie. [Young Woman in White Dress with Fan, Contemplating Goldfish in Ornate Fishbowl], between 1910–1920. Gouache and lead white.

Fig. 1.21. Jessie Gillespie. Panta-loons. Ink, graphite, watercolor. Published in *Evening Star Sunday Magazine*, October 25, 1914.

Fig. 1.22. Ethel Reed. Albert Morris Bagby's New Novel *Miss Traumerei*, 1895. Color poster. Published by Lamson, Wolffe & Co., 1895.

Fig. 1.23. Ethel Reed. The Boston Sunday Herald—Ladies Want It, February 24, 1895 or 1901. Color lithograph. Published by Boston Eng. Co.

eye-catching advertising art (fig. 1.20), commercial work that she, like many other female illustrators, found to be an important source of income. Her series of female figures in pantaloons was an amusing visual riff (fig. 1.21) on a new fashion trend and highlighted the varied activities attracting women in the 1910s. Ethel Reed (1874–1912) became best known for her stunning poster designs. Japanese prints and Art Nouveau inspired her typically boldly patterned, colorful works. She often depicted young girls or women with lilies or poppies, visual motifs then regarded as erotically charged or exhibiting delicate, feminine qualities. Flamboyant and beautiful, she at times used herself as a model.[70] One of her posters may be a self-portrait (fig. 1.23), showing a young woman in profile reading the *Boston Sunday Herald*. In another poster (fig. 1.22), stylized yellow chrysanthemums in the foreground set off the graceful lines and form of a young woman

at a piano. These and her other poster designs prominently featuring female figures fit the era of the New Woman, whose presence as a participant in the performing arts and as a consumer of published materials was gaining increased visibility. Beset by a troubled romantic life and health problems that included deteriorating vision, Reed forged a brilliant but too-brief career. Along with Will Bradley and Edward Penfield, she was a leading figure in the burgeoning field of poster illustration.

Another specialist, Margaret Armstrong (1867–1944), pursued a highly successful career as an innovative book designer. Influenced by the arts and crafts movement and the work created by William Morris at the Kelmscott Press, Armstrong incorporated her own stylized drawings of flowers as important elements in many of her designs. She and her sister Helen also occasionally drew the floral designs that

Figs. 1.24 and 1.25. Margaret Armstrong. Book binding designs for *The Valley of Vision* by Henry Van Dyke, Charles Scribner's Sons, 1919, and *Pippa Passes* by Robert Browning, Dodd, Mead & Co., 1900.

Figs. 1.26 and 1.27. Margaret Armstrong. Book binding design and title page for *Candle Lightin' Time* by Paul Laurence Dunbar, Dodd, Mead & Co., 1901.

were key visual elements of her books' title pages (figs. 1.24–1.27). Armstrong later created hundreds of delicately drawn western wildflowers based on direct observation, and in collaboration with botany professor J. J. Thornber, published the authoritative *Field Book of Western Wildflowers* (1915).

Two other artists, Alice Stewart Hill (1850–1896) and Grace Spafford Whiting (1881–1964), whose work

chronologically brackets Armstrong's *Wildflowers*, reflect varying approaches to this esoteric art form. Hill developed a strong interest collecting and depicting wildflowers in the Pikes Peak area when her family moved to Colorado Springs in 1874. Building on previous training, she sought further instruction in Chicago and at the National Academy of Design in New York, specifically in painting flowers.[71] On her

Figs. 1.28–1.30. Alice Stewart Hill. Selections from *The Procession of Flowers in Colorado,* published by Roberts Brothers, 1886–1888. Watercolor.

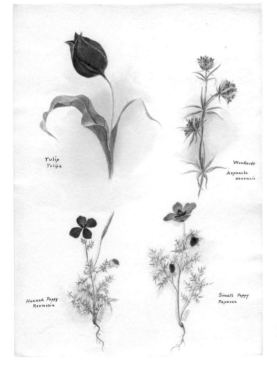

Fig. 1.31. Grace Spafford Whiting. Tulip, Tulipa; Woodruff, Asperula arvensis; Horned Poppy, Roemeria; Small Poppy, Papaver, 1931. Watercolor.

Fig. 1.32. Helen West Heller. Prairie Child. Woodcut. Published in *Migratory Urge*, F. J. Meine, 1928.

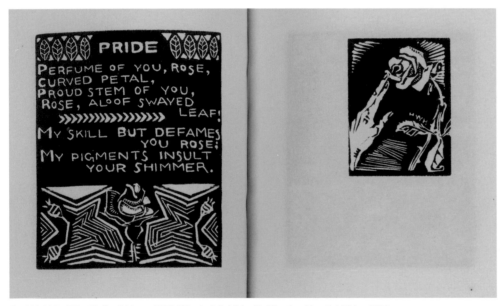

Fig. 1.33. Helen West Heller. Pride, ca. 1925. Woodcut. Published in *Migratory Urge*, F. J. Meine, 1928.

return, Hill sold her artwork, taught art for several years, and befriended several writers who included her work in their books.[72] Most notably, author Helen Hunt Jackson, who was known nationally for *Ramona* and *A Century of Dishonor*, bequeathed Hill the rights to a chapter about Colorado wildflowers from her book *Bits of Travel at Home*. Hill illustrated that text and published it as *The Procession of Flowers in Colorado* (1885), an eye-catching combination of letter press printing and hand illumination. In each one of the hundred printed copies, numbered and signed by the artist from 1886 to 1888, the text appears positioned consistently, but placement of the illustrations, all executed in watercolor by hand, vary from copy to copy. Even the signature varies, since Hill married during the latter part of the book's production. The fresh colors, carefully observed detail, exemplary artwork, and sensitive illustration placement are seen in figures 1.28–1.30, and the illuminated initial on the first page of text hearkens back to traditional medieval book design.[73]

The enduring appeal of such documentary art is also found in the work of Grace Spafford Whiting, who began painting flowers in the Holy Land in the 1930s. A member of the American Colony, a Christian utopian society that formed in Jerusalem in 1881, she and her sister Bertha Spafford Vester both created watercolors of native flora in the area (fig. 1.31). Whiting often noted in ink or watercolor both the Latin and familiar English names of flowers. Unlike Bertha, who published a small collection of flower illustrations in 1962, Grace seems not to have had any of her work published, even though she remained productive into the early 1960s.

The work of Helen West Heller (1872–1955) exemplifies another compelling, specialized approach to illustrating the natural world. Too little known as a fine artist and illustrator, Heller melded her own poetry within or opposite small, exquisite woodcuts in her limited edition book *Migratory Urge* (1928). Her romantic, personal *Prairie Child* (fig. 1.32) conveys the ecstasy of experiencing a particular landscape at night. *Pride* (ca. 1925) (fig. 1.33), paired with an image of a hand reaching to touch a delicate rose petal, is an ode to the superiority of nature's beauty over its artistic representation. Although Heller's work stands far apart from the kind of documentary drawings of Armstrong, Hill, and Whiting, her inspired depictions of the natural world faithfully document her response to it.

⬳

Many successful women illustrators of the Golden Age and their immediate predecessors pursued fine art training, yet demonstrated through their work and careers strong dedication to the principal aims of illustration: visually enhancing or elaborating upon fictional and nonfictional narrative texts, as well as devising imagery for advertisements. Their exemplary work provides glimpses of women's perceptions about their changing roles in society, signaling a collective consciousness of the New Woman. Selected examples show how these artists began to bridge the space between home and the wider world. As they gained footholds in commerce, art, and nonconformist fashion, they themselves came to model the spirit of growing independence and self-confidence characteristic of the New Woman. Within the parameters of conventional illustration outlets, some women expanded the range of "appropriate" female subjects and messages, whether purposely or not. With enviable technique and willingness to work extraordinarily hard for many years in established channels, the illustrators of this era paved the way for later women to create work that was more daring in theme and visual impact. Meanwhile, the New Woman was claiming fresh territory in the nation's newspapers, where female cartoonists had begun making their mark.

CHAPTER 2

EARLY CARTOONISTS

FROM CUTE AND CLEVER TO CAREER WOMEN

[Grace] Drayton drew children who were almost always five years old, dimpled, encased in baby fat, and given to lisping and baby talk . . . the sort of kids who'd automatically evoke reactions like ''Just adorable'' from maiden aunts.

—RON GOULART, popular culture historian, describing early cartoonist Drayton's comic strips[1]

She [Brenda Starr] was already a reporter when the strip started [in 1940], but she was sick and tired of covering nothing but ice-cream socials. She wanted a job with action, like the men reporters had.

—DALE MESSICK, cartoonist, describing the eponymous heroine of her comic strip[2]

Worlds apart and more than thirty years between their debuts, the little girl and kitten characters invented by Grace Drayton provide a revealing contrast with Brenda Starr, the glamorous reporter created by Dale (Dahlia) Messick. The extreme character differences highlight the challenges women faced as they tried to break into newspaper comics. Just as they faced resistance to depicting anything that exceeded the spheres of domesticity and pleasant landscapes, so they were limited to a short list of acceptable subject matter when it came to cartoons and comic strips: cute babies, children, and animals. Although male cartoonists certainly portrayed children in early comic strips, they also found publishing outlets for a broader range of characters and subjects.[3] Consider, for example, such strips as Frederick Burr Opper's *Happy Hooligan* (1900), about the misadventures of a tramp, and his *Alphonse and Gaston* (1902), starring two hapless but extremely polite Frenchmen, or

SEZ YOU

Winsor McCay's *Dream of the Rarebit Fiend* (1904), which featured a changing cast of mostly adult characters. During the 1930s, Messick, though, endured rejection after rejection of her strips with strong female protagonists before finding a publisher—during World War II.

THE RISE OF THE COMIC STRIP

The American newspaper industry was highly competitive and rapidly evolving at the turn of the twentieth century, when Drayton and her contemporaries sought to get their comics published. The US population doubled between 1870 and 1900, the number living in cities tripled, and the number of daily English-language newspapers quadrupled to nearly two thousand. Total circulation shot up from 2.6 million to 15 million.[4] Newspaper, book, and magazine publishing flourished as American literacy rates significantly increased between the Civil War and World War I. Newspapers, in particular, offered not only serious news but also welcome entertainment in sports coverage, human-interest stories, advice columns, women's features—and comics.

Competition among leading urban newspapers was intense in the 1890s. The emerging medium of comics played an important role in the keen rivalry between the *New York World,* owned by the enterprising Joseph Pulitzer, and the *New York Journal,* which belonged to relative newcomer William Randolph Hearst. Both Pulitzer and Hearst developed Sunday multipage color comic supplements, important components of their ongoing quest to win the most readers. What became one of the first enduring American comic strip characters, the Yellow Kid, aka Mickey Dugan, made his first appearance in a color panel titled "At the Circus in Hogan's Alley," on Sunday, May 5, 1895, in Pulitzer's *World.*[5] Created by staff cartoonist Richard Felton Outcault, this bald street urchin, clad in a yellow nightshirt, quickly became popular and was such a potentially valuable asset in boosting circulation that Hearst soon enticed his creator and other staff to leave Pulitzer and work for him. (Pulitzer countered by hiring George Luks, destined for Ashcan School fame, to continue *Hogan's Alley* in *his*

paper.)[6] Hearst encouraged Outcault to develop the Yellow Kid from a gag panel into a comic strip feature with all the elements commonly associated with the medium, including sequential panels, speech balloons, and character and story development.

The number and variety of Sunday newspaper comics blossomed in the early twentieth century. *Mr. A. Mutt Starts in to Play the Races*, by the sports cartoonist Bud Fisher in the *San Francisco Chronicle* on November 17, 1907, marks the debut of the first successful daily comic.[7] Hearst's paper was among the first to reprint its comic features in booklet form, thus offering a precursor to the modern comic book, which did not appear until the 1930s.[8] National and regional newspaper syndicates also became more powerful during this era. Syndicates sold writing and artwork, such as comics, to newspapers and other media, and by spreading the cost of expensive features among as many corporate subscribers as possible, numerous publications nationwide could afford to carry a wide selection of strips. Comic strip and political cartoon artists generally benefited from having their work syndicated, but as will be seen, women often found it difficult to gain syndication for their work. The obstacles they faced included fierce competition among cartoonists generally, a short list of themes deemed acceptable for comic strips by women, and outright discrimination by male editors. To get over this last hurdle, some women used masculine or ambiguous names when submitting their work for consideration.[9]

From about 1917 into the 1920s, a period that included American women's organizational leadership and service in World War I, and women at last winning the vote, comics by both male and female cartoonists gradually came to reflect the changing roles of women as many of them sought fulfilling activity outside the home. Popular imagery reflecting these changes began somewhat earlier, with the appearance of the New Woman in the 1890s, but the theme expanded with depictions of women campaigning for suffrage, a cause supported by many (but not all) women cartoonists, and, in the 1920s, of flappers, such as those drawn by Nell Brinkley and Virginia Huget. Not until the late 1930s and 1940s, however, were women able to successfully introduce comics with heroines who focused on careers and adventures outside the home, as seen in the work of Jackie Ormes and Dale Messick. Both labored for years to win syndication and reasonable distribution for their strips.

Creating and sustaining a successful comic strip was not just a matter of artistic ability; the most successful women cartoonists also developed the necessary entrepreneurial skills to thrive in such a competitive field and earn livings from their art. Several artists developed paper dolls as supplements or part of their comic features. Some, like Rose O'Neill, of Kewpie doll fame, and Marge Henderson Buell, creator of Little Lulu, created spin-off products that brought them lucrative returns. Others, such as Fanny Young Cory, also plied their drawing skills in illustrating books written by others, and occasionally, volumes they themselves had written. Versatility and willingness to take on work outside cartooning often proved essential not only to success but survival.

CUTE CHILDREN AND ANIMALS RULE

When Rose Cecil O'Neill (1874–1944) had a comic strip published in the 1896 September issue of *Truth Magazine*, it may have been the first published example of the genre by a woman.[10] O'Neill introduced her signature cherubic characters, the Kewpies (who supposedly came to her in a dream), in the *Ladies' Home Journal* in 1909 and four years later patented her Kewpie doll, which, combined with additional spin-off products, made her famous and very wealthy. Her charming creations quickly evolved from initially slim beings into rounder forms expressive of their kind and generous natures.[11] The strip eventually appeared in other magazines as well, running for more than twenty years. She also produced more than seven hundred drawings for *Puck*, the leading American humor magazine of her day (see chapter 5).

A nine-panel comic, published October 12, 1935 (fig. 2.1), humorously depicts the Kewpies preparing to celebrate Halloween by convincing others that ghosts exist. This lushly drawn, mature example not only demonstrates the endearing qualities of the Kewpies, but also the whimsical, imaginative features

with which O'Neill endowed them and their fanciful world of Kewpieville. The lengthy, extremely detailed handwritten notes to her colorist, "Miss Hess," regarding appearance of the panels attest to O'Neill's strong devotion to getting details right and making every effort to see her artistic vision realized. "Dear Miss Hess—I'd like to experiment with rich moonlight in this," began one such set of extensive instructions. "I'm sure you will know how to make it a success.—Moonlight in Panels 5, 6, 7, 8, 9, 10, 11, 12. I suppose we'll have to leave our Kewpies pink as usual, or they might be lost. . . . Daylight scene. Rich blue sky, fading into pink above trees. Cream ground. Lavender shadows. Foliage rich green over black. Plain flowers pink. Ruffled flowers blue outside rim, orange centers . . . Scootle's dress white with yellow flowers. Suitcase orange with coloured and white labels. Gus the Ghost pale blue with lavender ends on his streamers. Katy Kewp's petticoat blue blue. Johnny Kewp's belt vermillion. . . . Pale green toad."[12]

Although best known for the Kewpies, O'Neill stands out as unusually prolific and multitalented within an already select sisterhood of artists. Born in Wilkes-Barre, Pennsylvania, to parents with strong artistic and literary backgrounds but limited means, O'Neill grew up mainly in Omaha, Nebraska, in a home rich with books, storytelling, and humor, and attended Catholic and public schools intermittently—all of which nurtured her imagination and talents for artistic pursuits. Over the course of her professional life, which she spent mainly in New York with periodic sojourns to the family home in Bonniebrook, Missouri, the twice-divorced O'Neill created an estimated fifty-five hundred drawings.[13] These included illustrations for novels (including her own), fine art drawings that were exhibited in Paris and New York, and advertising assignments. With this huge volume of work, she was the main support of her family and a sometimes overly generous helpmate to others.

O'Neill's ample, mischievous Kewpies possessed an appeal similar to that seen in comics by other women of the era, especially Grace Drayton, whose Campbell Kids soup ads and popular comic strips featured cute children. Drayton (1877–1936) was born Viola Grace Gebbie in Philadelphia, the third of six daughters to art publisher George Gebbie and Mary

Fig. 2.1. Rose O'Neill. Kewpies. "And in Foozleville they don't believe in ghosts!" October 12, 1935.
Ink over graphite underdrawing with scraping out and paste-on.

Jane Fitzgerald, a devout Catholic.[14] She studied at the Philadelphia School of Design for Women under Robert Henri and with the painter Clifford P. Grayson at the Drexel Institute of Art, Science and Industry in the 1890s. Her pursuit of art training sets her apart from most of her peers, such as Nell Brinkley and Rose O'Neill, who were essentially self-taught. At the tender age of eighteen she sold a cover drawing of a girl and her cat to *Truth* magazine. She married her first husband, Theodore E. Wiederseim, in 1900.

Her first comic strip, *Naughty Toodles* (1903), featured a cute little girl, and later that year became *The Strange Adventures of Pussy Pumpkins and Her Chum Toodles*. In 1904 Drayton made her first drawings for streetcar ads for what became her best known creation, the Campbell Kids. She continued producing her charming landmark characters for the soup company for the next thirty years.[15] In a Campbell's presentation piece created ca. 1910 (fig. 2.2), the round-faced, pink-cheeked little girl, smiling, and looking upward, projects a charm that Drayton deployed in varied forms and settings time and after time.

Her wide-eyed types appeared in many comic creations, including *The Adventures of Bobby Blake and Dolly Drake in Storyland*, a strip written by her sister Margaret Gebbie Hays, in 1905–1906. From 1908 to 1911, she drew and wrote *Dotty Dimples* on an erratic schedule, and for the next four years she collaborated again with her sister to publish *The Turr'ble Tales of Kaptin Kiddo*, which was distributed by the North American Syndicate.[16] Along with famed women illustrators of the Golden Age, she became a founding member of the Plastic Club (see chapter 1). Her involvement in this and other arts organizations furthered her efforts to develop her talent and potential to earn income outside the comics. As early as the 1890s and into the twentieth century, she produced paintings of beautiful young women. The *Saturday Evening Post* published some of these works, which were executed in a manner similar to illustration art by Charles Dana Gibson and Harrison Fisher. This lesser-known side of Drayton's work demonstrates that her artistic aspiration extended well beyond cartooning.

Undeterred by strong disapproval of divorce in her day, she left her first husband and married her

Fig. 2.2. Grace Drayton. Campbell's Soup Kid presentation piece, ca. 1910. Watercolor, ink.

second, W. Heyward Drayton III, in 1911. (She would divorce him in 1923, but continue to use the Drayton surname for the rest of her career.) As Grace Drayton she revived her earlier comic *Dimples* for the Hearst Syndicate, and it ran from 1913 to 1918.[17] An exemplary Sunday page (fig. 2.3), "I hope you have made good New Year's Resolutions," December 26, 1915, shows Drayton's talent for humorous narrative involving child characters. Dimples, who has curly hair, an appealing round face, and a lisp, epitomizes the popular notion of "cute" reflected in the work of many women who succeeded in the realm of comic strip art from the 1910s into the 1930s.

Drayton also illustrated a number of children's books and short poems written by her sister for *Youth's Companion* magazine. From 1916 to 1922 she produced Dolly Dingle paper dolls for the *Pictorial Review*, which also sometimes ran them under such

Fig. 2.3. Grace Drayton. Dimples. "I hope you have made some New Year's resolutions," December 26, 1915. Ink over pencil with scraping out and paste-on.

variant titles as *Dolly Dimples* and *Dotty Darling*. She faced a discouraging downturn late in her life when her Sunday comic *Dolly Dimples and Bobby Bounce* was canceled in 1932. Mustering her creative energies, she began her last and most famous comic in 1935, a successful collaboration with writer Ed Anthony, entitled *The Pussycat Princess*. The following year, she suffered a fatal heart attack at the age of fifty-nine. The fact that Anthony and the artist Ruth Carroll continued the strip until 1947 confirms that Drayton's final creation had lasting appeal.

Meanwhile, Edwina Dumm (1893–1990) created one of the most successful, long-running animal-character strips thanks to the antics and charm of Tippie the dog. Born in 1893 in Upper Sandusky, Ohio, Frances Edwina Dumm was a shy, tomboyish young girl who loved to draw and play outside with her brother Robert. Her father, Frank Edwin Dumm, was an actor turned newspaperman. Perhaps his background and her stated desire in grade school to be an artist led her to choose newspaper cartooning because, as she once said, "there were a lot more newspapers in Ohio than art galleries."[18] She found the illustrations in Mark Twain's *Huckleberry Finn* and *Tom Sawyer* inspiring, and the male characters in these classics likely shaped her comic strip *Cap Stubbs and Tippie*.[19]

In 1911 the family moved to Columbus, Ohio, where Edwina completed high school. Although her family supported her sense of independence and dream of pursuing a career as an artist in New York, her father advised her to develop a backup plan to support herself. Accordingly, she took business classes in high school and worked as a stenographer for the local board of education while completing the Landon Correspondence School course in cartooning.[20]

When the short-lived *Columbus Monitor*, a weekly newspaper, began publication in 1915, Dumm submitted work and was hired as a staff artist, contributing illustrations, political portraits, editorial cartoons, and preparing a page of reportage and comment called "Spotlight Sketches." She thus became perhaps the first woman in the country employed as an editorial cartoonist. In this capacity, she addressed various regional and national issues, including women's suffrage, which she supported. Her work first appeared August 7, 1915, and her first signed cartoon appeared

on November 27, 1915. When the paper shifted to daily publication in July 1916, Dumm adjusted her output as needed.[21] During her time at the *Monitor*, she also occasionally drew a comic strip entitled *The Meanderings of Minnie*, which featured a tomboy and her dog, and it was this work that foreshadowed her future, unusually long-lived success. Soon after the *Monitor* folded in 1917, Dumm left for New York City.

After sending samples of her drawings to the George Matthew Adams Syndicate, she went to see Adams, who had been sufficiently impressed by her drawings of dogs that he asked her to do a strip about a boy and his canine companion. *Cap Stubbs and Tippie* debuted in 1918 as a daily and proved so successful that within six months Dumm was earning a living from it.[22] Beginning in 1934, she produced a Sunday feature, titled simply *Tippie*, that was first syndicated by George Matthew Adams and later by Hearst's King Features until 1963.[23]

Dumm's comic is commonly recognized as the first continuity strip by a woman, a major achievement. In drawing upon her childhood memories and a keen observation of her own dogs, she brought a special warmth and authenticity to her creation. One of her many exemplary strips, published July 2, 1944 (fig. 2.4), captures the vicissitudes of a dog's life particularly well. Her fully developed drawing style, loose and airy yet form-defining, was also well suited to capturing the antics and energy of her characters caught in the often humorous incidents of daily life.[24] The longevity of Dumm's comic certainly attests to the regard in which it was held.[25]

Being a woman in a field so dominated by men seems not to have given Dumm any great pause as she pursued her career with confidence and independence. After a long struggle for membership, she joined Hilda Terry and Barbara Shermund as the first women admitted to the prestigious National Cartoonists Society in 1950. (The organization reportedly resisted admitting women because if they attended meetings, "the men would not be able to curse.")[26] Renowned critic Alexander Woollcott was so taken with Dumm's comic that he engaged her to illustrate his book about three dogs, *Two Gentlemen and a Lady* (1928). Those drawings undoubtedly attracted the attention of Woollcott's friends at the original

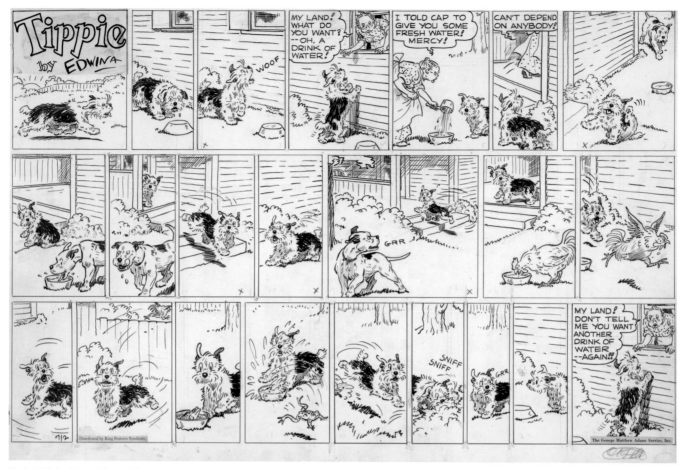

Fig. 2.4. Edwina Dumm. Tippie. [Thirsty dog, Tippie, trotting to water bowl], July 2, 1944. Ink brush with blue pencil and opaque white over graphite underdrawing, with overlay and paste-ons.

Life magazine. For that publication, Dumm created another series, this one about a little dog named Sinbad, which was subsequently published in two books, *Sinbad, a Dog's Life* (1930), and *Sinbad, Again!* (1932).[27] She also illustrated short verses written by her brother, the writer Robert Dennis Dumm, in a daily newspaper panel about another dog, this one named Alec. Prolific and resourceful, Dumm illustrated other authors' works as well, including *Flush of Wimpole Street and Broadway* by Flora Merrill (1933), and her depictions of Tippie also inspired songs written by her friend Helen Thomas. After her retirement from comics in 1966, Dumm illustrated children's books and painted portraits in watercolor.

CHARACTERS YOUNG AND FRESH, OLD AND SEASONED

Martha Orr and Marge Henderson Buell launched features within a year of each other. Each strip rose rapidly in circulation and contributed notably to the development of the genre. Their characters remained in the domestic sphere, but each cartoonist introduced a strong female character of lasting popularity.

A Philadelphia native, Marge Henderson (Buell) (1904–1993) saw her first cartoon published at the age of sixteen in the *Philadelphia Ledger*, a major coup for the precocious and talented teenager. In addition to the *Ledger* syndicate, she also drew for *Life*, the *Country Gentleman*, *Judge*, and *Collier's*.[28]

At twenty-three, she published her first comic, *The Boy Friend*, a single-panel cartoon that ran with her syndicate.[29] The *Saturday Evening Post* hired her in 1934 to draw a weekly cartoon with a female character to replace Carl Anderson's *Henry*, which King Features had acquired. Such a rapid rise for a cartoonist in a mainstream outlet like the *Post* was truly exceptional.

The following year, she married Clarence Addison Buell but continued with her career, publishing her first *Little Lulu* feature, the comic that would become her most enduring creation. Appearing in the *Post* from December 1935 until 1948, Lulu (fig. 2.5) was a lively little girl with corkscrew curls, a self-confident upright posture, and feisty demeanor, whose independence and adventures, in contrast to younger characters, such as Dimples, won her a host of fans.

When *Little Lulu* proved a huge hit, Buell oversaw what became a vast array of spin-off projects and products. Eventually, she delegated the writing and drawing to several other cartoonists. Irving Tripp and later John Stanley are credited with the writing and layout of the comic book *Little Lulu*, first published by Dell Comics in 1945,[30] and Woodrow Wilson "Woody" Kimbrell drew the newspaper strip from 1950 to 1964.[31] Stanley is credited with naming Lulu's friend Tubby Tompkins, rendering Lulu as a more assertive character, and developing storylines that feature ongoing strife between Lulu and her male playmates (figs. 2.6–2.7). Lulu appears more than mischievous, truly resourceful, and even feminist, managing to get the better of the boys every time.[32] Even though Buell no longer drew or wrote *Little Lulu,* she maintained ownership, and the later manifestations of Lulu continue the spirit of the original. Not only did Lulu star in comic books and animated cartoons, but she also served as an advertising mascot for Kleenex.[33] Buell oversaw a merchandising empire that included Little Lulu dolls, lunch boxes, clothing, puzzles, and toys. According to her son, she was "most pleased . . . at being an entrepreneurial success as a woman cartoonist."[34] When she finally sold *Little Lulu* to Western Publishing in 1971, Buell relinquished the rights to it and retired.

Buell's lively, feisty girl character made her mark in the field and inspired several imitations, none of which, however, won as long-lasting affection and popularity.

Fig. 2.5. Marge Henderson Buell. Little Lulu. [At the barber shop], 1942. Ink and watercolor over graphite underdrawing. Published in the *Saturday Evening Post*, September 12, 1942.

Martha Orr (Hassel) (1908–2001) created an unusual female protagonist in *Apple Mary*, but one still very much a figure of the traditional female sphere. Orr's character, however, brought the wise, elderly woman into the realm of comic strips, a figure that endured but also evolved with the times. Orr was born in Hillyard, Washington, the third of six children. Her mother was a homemaker and her father a lumber broker. Her uncle, Carey Orr, a Pulitzer Prize–winning political cartoonist for the *Chicago Tribune*, recognized her artistic talent and paid for her training at the Art Institute of Chicago.

Not long after she completed her schooling, Orr began drawing *Apple Mary*, which debuted October 29, 1934. It was syndicated (perhaps being the niece of Carey Orr helped) and quickly became a hit.[35] The strip centered on a gray-haired woman who sold fruit

Fig. 2.6. Marge Henderson Buell. Drawn by Woody Kimbrell. Little Lulu. "Fellers, I make a motion that we let Lulu and Annie join our tree house club," January 25, 1958. Woody Kimbrell drew Little Lulu between 1950 and 1964. Ink, graphite, and colored pencil.

Fig. 2.7. Marge Henderson Buell. Drawn by Woody Kimbrell. Little Lulu. No Girls Allowed, May 17, 1958. Ink, graphite, and colored pencil.

on street corners. She, her family, including her disabled grandson, Dennie, and friends were all poor and sympathetic, as they sought to make the best of difficult times and overcome the machinations of con men and petty thieves. Many other strips that emerged during the 1930s offered Depression-era readers modes of escape from social and economic woes. Some, such as *Little Miss Muffett*, featured orphan children. Others, including *Secret Agent X-9* (1934) and *Terry and the Pirates* (1934), offered exciting adventures. *Apple Mary*, in having an older woman as its protagonist, was rather unusual, but the social conditions in Orr's comic resonated with many readers. In one Sunday feature from October 9, 1939 (fig. 2.8), "It's funny, every time a little work appears around here, all the men disappear," Orr presents a homey, domestic episode that befits the era. By then

Orr had recently had her first child, and she sold the strip to devote more time to her own family. She then moved with her husband, Henry, from Chicago to Kenilworth, Illinois, where they had three more children. Although Orr had a studio in her home and continued to draw, she never created another comic strip.

Most sources identify *Apple Mary* as the precursor of the long-running strip *Mary Worth,* whose protagonist, a well-meaning older woman, evolved into a figure rather different from but not unrelated to Orr's creation. That comic inspired the film *Pocketful of Miracles* (1961) with Bette Davis. *Apple Mary* stands as a Depression-era classic, whose central theme focused upon coping with economic hardship with dignity and kindliness as embodied in the heroine herself.[36]

Fig. 2.8. Martha Orr. Apple Mary and Dennie. "It's funny, every time a little work appears around here, all the men disappear," October 9, 1938. India ink over graphite underdrawing.

Fig. 2.9. Nell Brinkley. [Uncle Sam's Girl-shower], 1918. Crayon, charcoal, and ink over graphite, with opaque white and overlay.

FLAPPERS IN ACTION

Long before women nationwide gained the right to vote with the Nineteenth Amendment in 1920, many competed successfully with men for business jobs that required skills in using typewriters, telephones, and accounting machines.[37] In the 1920s, women appeared primarily as flappers and office workers in comic strips, and it was male artists who first portrayed women in the workplace. Such characters, typically young and attractive, usually worked as stenographers for fashion executives or manufacturing moguls. *Somebody's Stenographer* (1918) later shortened to *Somebody's Stenog* by Alfred E. Haymond, featured Cam O'Flage, who more than stood out as a tall, long-legged blonde woman.[38] That strip preceded two of the most popular strips featuring young working women, *Winnie Winkle the Breadwinner* (1920; later shortened to *Winnie Winkle*) by Martin Michael Branner, and *Tillie the Toiler* (1921) by Russ Westover.

Nell Brinkley (1886–1944) created her own feminine ideal, the "Brinkley Girl," who figured actively in serial stories published in the *New York Journal* and other newspapers. The Brinkley Girl, likely modeled in part on her creator's appearance, had curly hair, wide-set eyes with long lashes, and often wore clothing with decorative patterning and folds. She emerged during an era when a number of illustrators fashioned their own American ideals of feminine beauty, inspired in no small part by the success of Charles Dana Gibson's revolutionary Gibson Girl. Brinkley's serial illustrated newspaper stories during the last year of World War I. Her strip and others by women cartoonists that featured flappers signal a more free-spirited tone in comics that probably reflects the increasing presence of women in public spaces. Others, however, continued producing established types of comics in traditional modes.

Brinkley's unfinished drawing, "Uncle Sam's Girl-shower," 1917 (fig. 2.9), shows a bevy of beauties floating into Washington, DC, eager to support the

Fig. 2.10. Virginia Huget. Molly the Manicure Girl. "Exercise is making a new girl out of me, Molly . . . ,"
August 28, 1928. India ink over pencil, with blue pencil.

Fig. 2.11. Virginia Huget. Molly the Manicure Girl. "Yes, Molly, they're fine looking chaps, but how in
the world can you tell them apart?" August 23, 1928. Ink and blue pencil over pencil with paste-on.

war effort, only to face a severe housing shortage. In this and many of her serial stories, Brinkley avoids using frames, an element associated with traditional comic strip format. Instead, she artfully arranges vignettes in relation to one another such that they effectively tell the story of idealistic young women seeking to help their country. She develops this approach further in series that follow, mostly Sunday full-color pages that are regarded as comics.[39] Brinkley's distinctive, fine-lined drawing style was influenced by Art Nouveau and inspired a number of imitators including cartoonists Peggy Prentice and Juanita Hamel, and most famously, Dale Messick.

Prolific cartoonist and illustrator Virginia (Clark) Huget (1899–1991) furthered the flapper cause as well. She was born in Dallas, Texas, the youngest of three children of Sarah and William Clark, a civil engineer. She married her childhood sweetheart Coon Williams Hudzietz and attended the Art Institute of Chicago. When she sold her first comic, *Gentlemen Prefer Blondes,* to the Bell Syndicate in 1926, she changed her married name to the more French-sounding Huget, possibly to avoid postwar anti-German prejudice. In naming her strip, she may have been influenced by Ralph Barton's illustrations for Anita Loos's best-selling book of 1925 of the same title. Huget reportedly drew the comic for only a few weeks after which Phil Cook took over; why she was replaced is not known.

Huget quickly went on to create several Sunday newspaper magazine cover color comic strips as well as daily black-and-white comic strip features.

WEAPONS DRAWN
World War II and Women in Comics

World War II pulled an unprecedented number of women—some three million of them in the United States, many of them wives and mothers—into work outside the home for the first time, and their labor was recognized as vital to the war effort.[43] In the world of comics, too, as men departed to serve in the armed forces, women stepped into their places. The number of female cartoonists working in the comic book industry tripled in 1942 and remained high through the end of the decade. Few drew the superhero characters that had become enormously popular after Superman made his first published appearance in 1938. Instead, most of them were tapped to exercise their special talent for drawing female characters extremely well.[44] Wartime also saw the birth of women superheroes, including Wonder Woman in 1941, arguably the best known and most enduring. She was not the first, however. Two other major superheroines appeared earlier: *The Catwoman*, created by Bill Finger and Bob Kane in 1940, and *Miss Fury*, the first of her kind created by a woman, Tarpe (born June) Mills.[45] Clad in tight-fitting panther skin from head to toe, with only the lower part of her face showing, Miss Fury (aka socialite Maria Drake) pursued dangerous adventures involving Nazis. Miss Fury ran as a Sunday feature from 1941 to 1952, and briefly as a comic book.[46] Prior to *Miss Fury*, Mills had been drawing costumed heroes such as the Purple Zombie, the Daredevil Barry Finn, and the Cat Man since 1938.

In contrast with superheroines, quite a different female character emerged in the comic strips. Fashion designer Gladys Parker (1906–1966) based Mopsy, her eponymous, curly haired heroine, on her own appearance and portrayed her contributing to the war effort in varied capacities and uniforms—as a defense worker, a WAC, a WAVE, an army nurse, and member of the motor corps. *Mopsy* appeared daily, and later in a Sunday strip with accompanying paper dolls, running from 1939 to 1965.[47] (In 1943–1944, Parker also drew Russell Keaton's wartime comic *Flyin' Jenny*, which featured a blonde aviatrix.)[48] When Mopsy lost her job in 1947, her experience reflected postwar reality for many women who had contributed skilled labor during the war but were let go as defense work wound down and to make way for returning servicemen. The strip proved so popular that *Mopsy* comic books had a five-year run beginning in 1948.[49]

The former include *Babs in Society*, which debuted in 1927, centered on a spirited flapper working in a department store who inherited a fortune from her uncle Ebenezer. In 1928, in addition to the Sunday color comic *Flora's Fling*, Huget drew *Molly the Manicure Girl*, a black-and-white daily, and *Campus Capers*. It is notable that amid a number of comic strips by women that featured freewheeling, carefree flappers, Huget identified her flappers as job holders, although from the few surviving examples, she did not belabor the point.[40]

Two rare original examples of Huget's classic flapper strip, both from August 1928, show the blonde manicurist Molly and her brunette friend Gertie at the beach (figs. 2.10 and 2.11). In both examples, Gertie plays the foil to Molly, the shrewder, smarter character, and both examples display Huget's fine drawing, ability to create engaging characters, and breezy humor typical of the era. Two other cartoonists who popularized the flapper in their work also created comic strips that are similar in tone to Huget's: *Merely Margy* by John Held Jr. and *Polly Truffles* by Russell Patterson.

In 1929, Huget produced *Double Dora* and another color Sunday newspaper cover comic, entitled *Miss Aladdin*, which set forth its heroine's adventures in elaborate fairyland settings. She demonstrated further versatility in 1937 when she successfully imitated Percy Crosby's style while she drew his comic *Skippy* when his alcoholism kept him from meeting deadlines.[41] Huget took over Don Flowers's adventure strip *Oh Diana!* in 1944 and drew it in his manner, using

EARLY CARTOONISTS: FROM CUTE AND CLEVER TO CAREER WOMEN

her maiden name Clark, and changed it into a teen strip, a genre more popular in the 1940s.[42]

In addition to comic strips, Huget illustrated books including *Still More Boners from Classroom and Examination Papers* (1931) and *Prize Boners* (1932), and fiction stories distributed by Bell Syndicate. She also created Lux soap ads in comic strip format—one of which won first prize from the Art Directors League of New York City. Versatile and productive, Huget broadened the image of the flapper by identifying her as a young working woman, thus marking a small, but notable step forward for women cartoonists choosing to spotlight working women in their casts of characters. It would not be until the late 1930s that women cartoonists would succeed in introducing women characters seeking more adventurous kind of employment in the wider world beyond the office.

CAREER WOMEN IN THE COMICS

Late in the Great Depression, two milestone characters appeared in the comics: Torchy Brown, the intrepid young African American character determined to break into show business, and the red-headed newspaper reporter Brenda Starr, equally determined to cover hard news stories. The two shared a strong, positive outlook on life and persistence in pursuing their ambitions despite the economic and social climate of the times.

Jackie Ormes's comic strip *Torchy Brown in "Dixie to Harlem"* debuted May 1, 1937, in the *Pittsburgh Courier*, which also syndicated it. In its one-year run, Ormes relates the story of a spirited teenage girl from Mississippi who makes her way to New York City, where she works to win fame and fortune as an entertainer at the famous Cotton Club. Ormes primarily cultivated the smaller, specialized African American readership in historically black newspapers, but she, like so many women before and after her, faced challenges in gaining syndication and some measure of security from her work as a cartoonist. Not only was being female a disadvantage, but there were far fewer black newspapers available to showcase her work. Attempting syndication in a mainstream newspaper

at this time was simply not realistic.[50] Why Ormes stopped drawing for the *Courier* is not known, and no original drawings for her first comic seem to have survived.[51]

She was born Zelda Mavin Jackson (1911–1985) in Pittsburgh, Pennsylvania, to William Winfield Jackson, who owned and operated a printing business, and Mary Brown Jackson, a skilled seamstress. She grew up with an older sister and spent much of her time drawing. After her father was killed in an auto accident in 1917, Ormes's mother married Porter M. Simmons, who moved his new family to Monongahela, Pennsylvania. Although her schools offered no art classes, she persisted in teaching herself drawing, and she produced art for the high school yearbook.

After graduating in 1930, she moved to Pittsburgh, where she was hired to proofread for the *Pittsburgh Courier* and did freelance reporting on police beats, court cases, and somewhat unusually, boxing matches. In 1931 she married Earl Clark Ormes, a bank accountant, and five years later, following the death of their three-year-old daughter, Jacqueline, from a brain tumor, Ormes and her husband moved to his hometown of Salem, Ohio. She then made her first successful foray into cartooning with *Torchy Brown*.

Attracted by expanding opportunities for African Americans, the Ormeses moved to Chicago in 1942, where Jackie took classes at the School of the Art Institute. She returned to cartooning with the short-lived *Candy* (1945), a single-panel cartoon featuring a wise-cracking housemaid that appeared in the *Chicago Defender*. (Once she was well known for her work in the *Chicago Defender*, the *Chicago Tribune* tried to win her away, but she remained loyal to the *Defender*.)[52] She later introduced her longest-running comic, a weekly single panel, *Patty-Jo 'n' Ginger*. Syndicated by the *Pittsburgh Courier*, it ran from 1945 to 1956.[53] In this clever cartoon, she paired beautifully dressed sisters often interacting at home. The older one listens and reacts primarily through facial expressions. The younger one voices sharply worded gags that usually satirize society and politics and that protest racial injustice. "I write my own gag lines," she told an interviewer. "I tried buying gags but they never seem to fit."[54] Ormes also took an extremely active role in developing the Patty-Jo doll. Both the doll and

Fig. 2.12. Jackie Ormes. Torchy Togs, August 4, 1951. Comic book insert, *Pittsburgh Courier*.

cartoon character may well have been inspired by Ormes's only child, the daughter who died so young, and the doll is believed to be the first high-end black doll for children that was widely sold.[55]

Ormes's final comic, a Sunday strip, *Torchy in Heartbeats* (aka *Torchy Brown's Heartbeats*) represents in some ways a revival of her first comic, even as it ran simultaneously with *Patty-Jo 'n' Ginger*. Distributed by Smith-Mann Syndicate, it ran from August 19, 1950, to September 18, 1954,[56] and included *Torchy Togs*, a popular paper doll accompaniment (fig. 2.12). Compared with Ormes's first comic, her later *Torchy* demonstrates how far the artist had grown professionally. In her heroine's later incarnation, she appears similarly proactive in pursuing adventure and romance, and works as a nurse in at least two situations, but also highlights instances of a mature, independent woman engaged with serious issues of race and environmental pollution while also seeking true love.[57]

One example of her later work, dated August 4, 1951 (fig. 2.13), demonstrates her ability to create engaging characters, build drama, and advance a narrative. This

episode focuses on Torchy's romance with Earl, a gifted musician, and captures her growing realization of how central his career and talent are to him, despite his affection for her. Ormes perfected her drawing technique in her spot-on depictions of Torchy, whose changing emotions are registered in her facial expressions and gestures that play artfully within and across each frame.

In the 1960s, Ormes began suffering from rheumatoid arthritis, which limited her ability to draw and paint, a later-in-life interest. Despite this setback and her husband's death in 1976, she pursued other activities. She lent support to Chicago's DuSable Museum of African American History and was an honored guest at a special doll club event in Lincoln, Nebraska, in 1984. Ormes died of a cerebral hemorrhage on December 26, 1985. Although her original drawings are extremely rare, she contributed to the world of illustrative art with groundbreaking imagery of strong, career-oriented, articulate black female characters.

Much better known than Ormes, Dale (Dahlia) Messick (1906–2005) also faced enormous challenges

Fig. 2.13. Jackie Ormes. Torchy in Heartbeats. Torchy, in Love with Earl, August 4, 1951.
Comic book insert, *Pittsburgh Courier*.

in her efforts to syndicate her strips. Born in South Bend, Messick grew up in Hobart, Indiana, not far from Chicago, where she attended school irregularly. She began drawing comic strips in high school, from which she did not graduate until she was twenty. After studying art in Chicago one summer, she worked for greeting card companies there and in New York while continuing work on comic strip features.

Over more than a decade, Messick developed four comic strips, none of them accepted for publication. In contrast with the imaginary character and setting of *Mimi the Mermaid* (early 1930s), the other three featured working girls trying to make it in the big city: *Weegee* (mid-1920s), *Peg and Pudy: The Strugglettes* (mid-1930s), and *Streamline Babies* (late 1930s). Messick struggled in vain to get her engaging comics[58] published and syndicated, even purposely changing her name from Dahlia to the ambiguous Dale in an effort to overcome editors' biases against women cartoonists.[59]

Why was there so much resistance to Messick's early creations by male editors? When she sought

publication of her innovative comics, there were few women editors in newspaper publishing.[60] Messick's female predecessors had produced comics that featured children, animals, flappers, and kindly older women, all actors in lighter storylines. The very nature of Messick's Brenda Starr, a heroine engaged in action stories that sometimes involved physical danger as well as romance, invaded or encroached upon adventure story comics, a type that editors had long regarded as a male domain.[61] It is worth noting that during the years that Messick sought to get her working girls in print, her male counterparts produced male-centered adventure strips that became legendary, such as *Tarzan* and *Buck Rogers in the 25th Century A.D.* (1929), *Dick Tracy* (1931), and *Terry and the Pirates* and *Flash Gordon* (1934).[62]

As America moved closer to entering World War II, women entered the workforce in increasing numbers, and it seemed an opportune time for Messick to again seek publication of her strip featuring a strong heroine. Although her submitted sample strip was rejected by Captain Joseph Patterson, publisher of the *New*

York Daily News and chief of the Chicago Tribune–New York News Syndicate, his assistant Mollie Slott saw promise. She worked with Messick on a new submission, changing the heroine from a bandit to a news reporter.[63]

On June 30, 1940, Messick's groundbreaking creation *Brenda Starr Reporter* finally appeared as the first nationally syndicated comic strip feature by a woman. In creating her heroine, she drew inspiration from the red-haired actress Rita Hayworth and named her after Brenda Frazier, a glamorous debutante.[64] As Messick herself acknowledged, the elegantly rendered heroines of Nell Brinkley also exerted a crucial influence on Brenda's manner and appearance, an embodiment of style, poise, and spirit that won her longstanding admirers during decades of adventures.[65]

From the beginning, Brenda lobbies for exciting, newsworthy assignments, seeking scoops like her colleague (and admirer) Tom Taylor. Her taste for challenge and adventure leads to encounters with dangerous criminals, occasional romance, and intrigue. She pursues jewel thieves, seeks a missing fashion model, and investigates a mysterious heiress, among other adventures. Over the years, she is kidnapped and rescued several times, and falls in love with the mysterious inventor Basil St. John, whom she marries in 1976 and later divorces. Other supporting characters include her brusque editor Mr. Livewright, her pal and colleague Hank O'Hair, and cub reporter Pesky; their lively interactions with Brenda bring humor into the stories. In later decades, Brenda investigates an international drug ring,[66] is furloughed by her newspaper, and, on her return, discovers bloggers at work in the newsroom.[67]

Brenda Starr, which at its peak popularity ran in two hundred fifty newspapers, marks a milestone among comic strips created by women in that the heroine embodies a worthy female counterpart to the male protagonists of adventure strips produced by men. The character herself projects a strong appeal and entices the reader with potential intrigue (figs. 2.14, 2.15, and 2.16), and Messick's lush drawing technique in brush and ink evokes mood and conveys emotion.

For forty years Messick drew Brenda Starr in all of her strips, using assistants to draw cars, animals, and nature scenes. When she retired in 1980, Ramona Fradon continued drawing Brenda with Linda Sutter as writer; following this team effort, June Brigman took over drawing the strip in 1995 with Mary Schmich as writer. Brenda, who outlived her creator, made her final appearance on January 2, 2011. Messick had succeeded in creating a comic that drew a following equivalent in size and devotion to those attained by the most successful adventure strips by men. Messick's last comic strip, *Granny Glamour*, appeared in *Oakmont Gardens*, a weekly California magazine, when she was in her eighties.

⤳

The women who first broke into the early comics field had much in common with their sister artists working in illustration. Both groups found that publishers' predominantly male editors deemed most subjects as off limits for female artists, although the narrow range of acceptable newspaper comic strip characters and settings gradually broadened in the early twentieth century. These women also faced longstanding social pressure to lead conventional lives as wives and mothers when, in order to succeed in the comics, it was necessary that they venture beyond domesticity. Some cartoonists, like Edwina Dumm, chose not to marry, telling friends that she "had neither the domestic skills nor the interest for it."[68] Among notable cartoonists who did marry, an unusually high number divorced. O'Neill, Drayton, and Messick each divorced twice; Brinkley also ended her marriage.

Divorce brought strong social disapproval, even stigma, and represented an uncommon choice when these women pursued their careers. Each undoubtedly suffered as a result. Although the reasons varied for these failed marriages, the effort required to succeed in cartooning could exact a huge toll on their personal lives. Urgent and deadline-driven, cartooning exerted an unrelenting demand to create and produce; when combined with the economically precarious nature of the business, they were often under great personal strain. There was no job security. Even comic strips

Fig. 2.14. Dale Messick. Brenda Starr. "Ha! I guess I'll always have this inner excitement as I approach a new assignment—especially one of this kind!" May 17, 1958. Ink, graphite, and colored pencil.

Fig. 2.15. Dale Messick. Brenda Starr. Brenda Has a Visit from the Captain . . . , January 7, 1956. Ink, graphite, and colored pencil.

Fig. 2.16. Dale Messick. Brenda Starr. "This Basil St. John must be quite a man," August 13, 1965. Ink over pencil with blue pencil, scraping out and paste-ons.

that had run for years could be suddenly canceled. During the Great Depression, Drayton hit a low point, telling her assistant who had asked her for work, "I have no work and am almost down and out . . . I shall send for you if I get another 'job.' I feel so sad when I look at our empty studio. To add to my agony, I lost my . . . sister a few weeks ago. So I am now all alone and poverty stricken in heart as well as in pocket."[69]

In contrast with this sad scenario, others demonstrated a notable entrepreneurial flair. Brinkley, Buell, O'Neill, Ormes, and Messick all developed or promoted paper dolls of their characters, an especially popular form of merchandizing. O'Neill, Ormes, and Buell created actual doll versions as well. Some also won recognition from both their peers and their industry. Messick's *Brenda Starr* was named the "Best Story Strip" by the National Cartoonists Society in 1976, and in 1997 she received the Milton Caniff Lifetime Achievement Award from that same organization. These high honors from the very professional organization that had earlier rejected her and other women's repeated applications for membership mark hard-won progress in ongoing efforts to garner professional recognition.

CHAPTER 3

NEW VOICES, NEW NARRATIVES IN COMICS

In a way, I draw myself every day as Elly Patterson . . . each illustration is more than a likeness, it's a signature, a statement and a sentiment as well . . . I'm not the only one who draws caricatures of myself in my work every day . . . [and] researches and exposes the inner me through the faces I draw—to some extent we all do! With or without the mirror, we are reflected in our work.

—LYNN JOHNSTON, creator of the comic strip For Better or for Worse, 1998[2]

For nearly forty years, Marty would whisk through the *Chronicle* city room, delivering a weekly batch of cartoons with the same bounce as when she put on her first pair of saddle shoes. Marty really was Bobby Sox.

—WILLIAM GERMAN, editor emeritus, San Francisco Chronicle, describing Marty Links, creator of the comic feature Emmy Lou, 1976[1]

Nearly forty years separate the debuts of Marty Links's and Lynn Johnston's signature comic strips, yet the strong thread of personal experience—even autobiography—that informs and inflects these and other female cartoonists' work weaves through the postwar era into the present. This impulse to draw upon one's own life begins to surface noticeably in women's work during World War II, when many obtained training and opportunities that enabled them to portray an expanded range of characters in their comic art. Such advances in the field, however, slowed notably—even halted—in the postwar years. Many female cartoonists, like their counterparts in other industries, were urged to leave their jobs so that men returning home from the war could take their places. Jackie Ormes, Dale Messick, and Gladys Parker were among those who did not leave, and they forged openings for succeeding generations of women to create new characters who reflected subtle as well as seismic changes in girls' and women's lives.

Male cartoonists, whose ranks had thinned nominally and temporarily during the war, reasserted themselves in the postwar comics industry, continuing to dominate adventure strips and also contributing to the family, romance, and soap opera genres. Leading characters at the time included aviator Steve Canyon by Milton Caniff and All-American families such as the Bumsteads by Chic Young. While Young drew upon his family life for material, he chose to emphasize themes and challenges that his readers also shared—the ups and downs of Blondie and Dagwood's daily life all treated with light-hearted, good-natured humor. Young's audience easily identified with his main characters thus ensuring the strip's success.[3] Women who broke into family-centered comics, however, tended to create narratives that used more personal and autobiographical voices. *For Better or for Worse*, *Stone Soup*, and *Sylvia* brought different perspectives on family life that diverged from those seen in crisis-free *Blondie*. Similarly, Links focused on a teenage girl's concerns more specifically in *Emmy Lou*, in contrast with the voices of Archie and his friends in Bob Montana's long-running comic.

The number of women creating comic strips and comic books gradually increased during the last half of the twentieth century, burgeoning in the twenty-first, particularly in the areas of independent and alternative comics and longer-form graphic narratives. Women have effectively utilized zines, minicomics, and web comics as proving grounds or means of launching their work. Web comics are being selectively collected by some institutions; those receiving highly positive responses from readers and peers are often published in print.

NEW VOICES FROM FAMILY-CENTERED COMIC STRIPS

When Martha Links introduced her comic *Bobby Sox* (later renamed *Emmy Lou*) in 1944, she joined a small number of cartoonists in capturing the travails of teenage girls, a popular genre that emerged in the early postwar years. "Teenagers"—as a distinct group with its own culture and identity—were an American postwar invention: the term itself had only been around since the early war years.[4] The subsequent boom in financial prosperity, material production, and mass media helped launch and sustain a teenage scene and attitude that thrived on burgers, came of age in cars, and consumed vast quantities of youth-minded pop culture. Whereas young children had long occupied real estate in the comics, in this new era teenagers staked out their turf as leading characters with entirely different concerns and storyline possibilities. Along with Links, two contemporaries, Hilda Terry and Linda Walter (and her husband, Walter Clark) also drew teen strips, *Teena* and *Susie Q Smith*, respectively,[5] as did Bob Montana, who drew *Archie*.[6] A generation later, male heroes, kids, and teens had to make room for women who came to dominate individual strips either as the featured family member or as an independent figure expressing previously overlooked sensibilities.

Martha "Marty" Links (1917–2008) grew up in San Francisco, and after just six months of study at the Fashion Art Institute—her only art training—she took a job painting murals in teen departments of the city's major stores.[7] When she was later hired to do fashion drawings for a major advertising campaign, the account executive dismissed her work as merely depicting "kids [who] look more like—like—bobbysoxers."[8]

In 1940, the *San Francisco Chronicle*'s Women's World department hired Links to do occasional cartoons, including a cartoon-style fashion page. She developed an idea for a character based on her own observations of what girls and boys were wearing while talking and interacting in soda fountains. In 1944, she launched *Bobby Sox*, a daily panel about Mimi, who, as a shorter and slightly older precursor to Emmy Lou, was described as a "precocious sub-deb with a flair for trouble."[9] Links's daughter at times served as a model for her comic, and she drew upon her own memories of adolescence as well.[10] The strip grew and evolved naturally from family life experiences and sustained an ever-youthful voice and perspective on growing up, a viewpoint that did not darken over time. Distributed by Consolidated New Features, her comic drew a loyal following. By 1946 Links had drawn more than six hundred cartoons, mostly about her teen characters, for the *Chronicle* and had signed with a syndicate. Five years later, Links renamed her comic *Emmy Lou* after realizing that bobby sox, the ankle-length socks worn with clunky shoes, were no longer in style. She also had begun a long collaboration with gag writer Jerry Bundsen. "As to the Sunday panels, these I dream up myself," she said, "and it is more work than everything else put together. I feel each idea is the last one I'll ever be able to eke out."[11]

In 1950 Links became one of the first women admitted to the National Cartoonists Society, shortly after Edwina Dumm, Barbara Shermund, and Hilda Terry succeeded in joining. (After Links became a member, all correspondence she received from the society was addressed to Mr. Links, even after she sent the organization an announcement of her first child's birth.)[12] By then, her single-panel dailies and half-page Sunday features had a national audience.[13] At its peak, *Emmy Lou* ran in nearly one hundred newspapers, and the *Chronicle* carried her comic for more than thirty-five years.[14]

Links worked hard, drew ten hours each day, and raised three children. Although she thought gender did not matter in practicing cartooning as a profession, the impact of constant deadlines on one's personal life certainly did. "Your life, your vacation—all revolve around that deadline . . . if you work hard, you can take a few days off now and then. But I must say that in order to take a six-week trip, I've almost literally had to get a year ahead with my cartoons."[15]

Several panels (figs. 3.1–3.3) project the innocent, amusing charm that is typical of Links's comic. While Emmy Lou, like most teenagers, is largely absorbed with her own issues, she also expresses concern for her boyfriend Alvin's welfare in a later panel (1964) set in a soda shop, in which she warns him not to aggressively pursue tips. Fun-loving, yet conscientious, the style-conscious Emmy Lou appears in a variety of casual outfits. Through her cast of endearing characters, the lively Emmy Lou, her baffled father, sweet mother, and always hungry boyfriend, Alvin, Links captured the anxieties and innocent delights of teenage girls in their social and family relations during the immediate postwar era.

Fig. 3.1. Marty Links. Emmy Lou. "What a nightmare!" February 17, 1951. Ink, opaque white, graphite, blue pencil.

The stable world of Emmy Lou eventually contrasted sharply with that of the turbulent late 1960s and early 1970s. The socially and politically divisive issues that marked these decades, including American involvement in the Vietnam War, the sexual revolution, the civil rights and women's movements, seemed a world apart from Emmy Lou's milieu. Long after Links's children reached adulthood, she felt that her cartoon no longer represented teens, and she ended *Emmy Lou* in 1979. She then began producing ceramic sculptures, worked for Hallmark as an illustrator for greeting cards, and retired at the age of eighty-two.

Nearly two generations after Links, Lynn Johnston (b. 1947) created a strip that was also grounded in family life, but it projected a new and mature female point of view, that of mother and wife. Johnston (née

"BUT MOM, ALL I DID WAS COME HOME ON TIME, CLEAN MY ROOM AND DO MY HOMEWORK. WHAT MAKES YOU THINK I HAVE A FEVER?!"

Fig. 3.2. Marty Links. Emmy Lou. "But Mom, all I did was come home on time," March 8, 1963. Ink, graphite, paste-on.

"GOLLY, ALVIN, YOU'D BETTER BE CAREFUL OR YOU'LL BE FIRED!"

Fig. 3.3. Marty Links. Emmy Lou. "Golly, Alvin, you'd better be careful," May 9, 1964. Ink, graphite, paste-on.

Ridgway) was born in Collingwood, Ontario, Canada. She enjoyed drawing and doodling as a young child, and her father, a jeweler, and mother, a calligrapher and bookkeeper, encouraged her to develop her artistic talent. Pursuing an interest in animation, she attended the Vancouver School of Art for two years then quit to take a job at a local animation studio.[16]

Following her marriage to a television cameraman and their move in 1969 to Ontario, she took a job training and working as a medical illustrator at McMaster University.[17] She described that time as "a wonderful five years of learning." When she became pregnant, she left her job to work at home. After her obstetrician challenged her to create some cartoons for the ceilings of his examination room, she produced eighty drawings that conveyed a humorous view of pregnancy. Not long after her son was born, Johnston and her husband divorced and she struggled working as a freelance commercial artist. She found a publisher for her doctor's office drawings, and her first book *David, We're Pregnant!* was published in 1973. Two successful sequels followed, *Hi Mom! Hi Dad!* (1977) and *Do They Ever Grow Up?* (1978).

Around the time her second title was published, she met her second husband, Roderick Johnston, a dental school student and pilot. He adopted her son and the two had a daughter. As the family prepared to move to northern Manitoba, editors at Universal Press Syndicate, impressed with her books, asked if she had interest in doing a daily comic strip. Johnston developed a strip featuring characters based largely on her own life and family, entitled *The Johnstons*, and submitted twenty examples to the syndicate.[18]

Expecting rejection, she was startled to receive a year-long development contract that allowed her to work on the strip before it was published. At the year's end, she signed a twenty-year contract, an especially long-term deal, and later secured the copyright to her strip.[19] Before it launched on September 9, 1979, Johnston changed the main characters' names and used editor Lee Salem's suggested title, *For Better or for Worse*. Some one hundred fifty papers had agreed to carry the strip (it would later appear in more than two thousand), becoming one of the most successful in modern comic strip history, running until 2008.[20] Johnston's characters, like those of Frank King's *Gasoline*

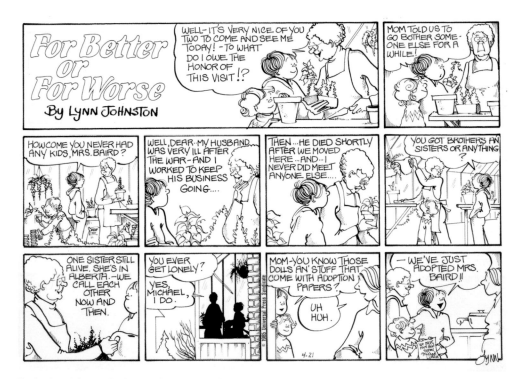

Fig. 3.4. Lynn Johnston. For Better or for Worse. "Well—it's very nice of you two to come and see me today!"
April 21, 1985. Ink over graphite underdrawing, with paste-ons.

Alley, age in real time, and develop ever-expanding circles of secondary characters. Johnston chronicled the ups and downs of the Patterson family, including wife and mother, Elly; her husband, John, a dentist; children Michael and Elizabeth, and later on, April. It is through the voice of Elly, the protagonist, that Johnston projects a strong female character's perspective on family life concerns and her own development as an individual.

Several examples demonstrate the scope of Johnston's themes and her remarkable ability to develop a cast of engaging characters that won her strip a huge and devoted readership. She captures the vicissitudes of many stay-at-home mothers in an early Sunday strip (fig. 3.5) with young Michael and Elizabeth squabbling over sharing space. Another Sunday strip (fig. 3.4) offers a heartening contrast that demonstrates the kids' gradual maturity. Within the traditional spatial limitations of the typical comic strip format, Johnston skillfully deploys her fluid drawing technique, natural dialogue, and carefully sequenced interaction between the children and an elderly neighbor. This well-realized strip references

Fig. 3.5. Lynn Johnston. For Better or for Worse. "Get over on your side!" February 20, 1983. Ink over graphite underdrawing, with paste-ons.

ideas such as the constant challenges of motherhood, neighborliness, loneliness, and compassion toward the elderly. It also portrays an elderly woman as an individual and not a stereotype.

Fig. 3.6. Lynn Johnston. For Better or for Worse. "So rather than get a job now, I'll pick up the credits I'm missing—and maybe get my degree!" November 19, 1980. Ink over graphite underdrawing with tonal film and paste-ons.

Fig. 3.7. Lynn Johnston. For Better or for Worse. "You ogled that girl, didn't you?" August 29, 1982. Ink over graphite underdrawing, with paste-ons.

Other examples bring out Elly's essentially optimistic and good-humored nature as well as her desire to pursue interests and talents outside the home (fig. 3.6); in the previous day's strip, Elly's husband, John, had suggested that she take belly dancing or gourmet cooking instead. Next to the character of Elly, their basically stable marriage remained fundamental to the healthy, long run of the strip (fig. 3.7). A devoted wife and mother, Elly retains her strong love of books and writing, leading her to venture outside her domestic roles to work in the town library and local bookstore. She eventually co-owns the latter and later sells it, on retirement.

Over the life of the strip, Johnston also bravely tackled sensitive topics such as death in the family, child abuse, and accepting the gay identity of a long-time friend.[21] The latter storyline, which Johnston had

been planning to do for a long time, played out over five weeks in 1993. It was both highly controversial and timely, as the United States debated whether to allow gay servicemen and women in the military. More than forty American newspapers asked Johnston's syndicate for alternate material or reruns, and nineteen canceled the strip.[22] In a letter to the *Chicago Tribune*, one reader wondered why "our favorite pastime—reading the comics—has to be tainted by sociological issues." Johnston certainly did not see the comics in that light. "The way the trend seems to be going, people are saying more important things now," she observed. "It's not just Dagwood can't make the bus. . . . life has never been more complicated than it is now." She took the negative criticism—and the praise—in stride, but the death threats were frightening. "I was prepared for some angry people," she recalled long afterward. "I think the one that hurt me the most was a woman who said 'I've just taken all your comic strips off my fridge' and that was, Ow! You took me off your fridge!"[23]

While her comic continued in the tradition established by *Gasoline Alley*, Johnston also notably broadened the thematic scope. By projecting the predominant, yet evolving voice of a mother and wife, and introducing challenging themes, Johnston made standout contributions to the art form of the comic strip. In 1985 she became the first woman and Canadian to receive the Reuben, the highest award given by the National Cartoonists Society. She also was the first woman to serve as its president (1988–1989), was nominated for a Pulitzer Prize in 1995, and inducted into the Canadian Cartoonists Hall of Fame in 2008.

Jan Eliot (b. 1950) created another type of long-running family strip, *Stone Soup*, which debuted in 1997. While it has features in common with Johnston's, Eliot's comic centers on the daily lives of a single, working mother and her two young daughters, an unusual combination of characters for this type of comic, but true-to-life for a growing number of family households.

Eliot married at eighteen and focused on ceramics at Southern Illinois State University before her two daughters were born. After her nine-year marriage ended, she began cartooning while working as a copywriter, graphic designer, and greeting card writer. Her

Fig. 3.8. Jan Eliot. Stone Soup. "Ahhh . . . Fairytales. How do they relate to modern life?" January 12, 1996. Ink with paste-ons.

Fig. 3.9. Jan Eliot. Stone Soup. "Can I take you to dinner?" September 23, 2007. Ink with paste-ons.

first comic strip, *Patience and Sarah,* was published in the *Willamette Valley Observer* in 1980–1981, and was the first to her knowledge that featured a single working mother.[24] Even so, her repeated efforts to win syndication brought only an offer too bleak to sign. She then pursued a career in graphic design, taking a job in the classified ad department of the *Observer,* and continued cartooning part-time.[25] Eliot's remarriage in 1988 brought her more emotional and financial support, enabling her to revisit cartooning with an idea for a new strip that featured two single mothers

and their children, a scenario that shares parallels with her years as a single mother.[26] Titling her comic *Sister City,* she persuaded the local Eugene, Oregon, paper, the *Register-Guard,* to publish it. During the five years it ran weekly, she again sought syndication, sending groups of drawings every six months over four years to the Universal Press Syndicate.

In 1995, her strip, renamed *Stone Soup* (figs. 3.8–3.9), became nationally syndicated.[27] She quit her day job and devoted herself full-time to cartooning. Her comic's focus on the family household of widowed mother, Valerie (Val) Stone; her two daughters Alix and Holly; her mother, Evie; her workplace; and her sister Joan, a divorced and single mother in the early years of the strip, was one of the few of its kind among family-centered strips, but one that mirrored the changed state of many American households. Milestone moments in the strip include the marriage of Joan and Wally, and more surprisingly, Val's marriage to Phil on July 25, 2015.[28] The latter marked a decisive moment for a strip long revered by readers devoted to a single mother protagonist and foreshadowed even bigger changes in the lives of the character and their creator.[29] "There's a certain momentum to these relationships . . . they eventually need resolutions," said Eliot.[30] The only notable backlash came from a small number of readers who were disturbed that Phil was multiracial and posted racist objections to the marriage online. Eliot, her editor, and many *Stone Soup* fans quickly rallied to have the offensive statements removed from the strip's website. Soon after, Eliot made the difficult decision to end the daily strip and continue only the Sunday feature.

From the Ranks of Single Working Women: Ack!

In the 1970s, Nicole Hollander and Cathy Guisewite created strong working women characters with distinctive, sometimes idiosyncratic voices and scenarios in their syndicated strips that ran for decades. Each spoke to a generation of career-minded women seeking to live comfortably and maintain good-humored perspectives on their lives in the not-so-welcoming working world.

Hollander was born in 1939 in Chicago to a labor activist and member of the carpenters union. She completed a BFA at the University of Illinois at Urbana-Champaign in 1960, then an MFA in painting at Boston University in 1966.[31] Married for a few years to Hungarian-born sociologist Paul Hollander, she was divorced in 1962, and thus pursued her career as a single woman.[32] While working in the late 1970s as the graphic designer for the feminist publication the *Spokeswoman*, Hollander occasionally added political illustrations. In 1976, she created *The Feminist Funnies*,

a comic strip in which she later introduced the character that became Sylvia.[33] With her trademark feather boa, open-heeled bedroom slippers and cigarette, Sylvia debuted in Hollander's first book of cartoons, *I'm in Training to Be Tall and Blonde* (1979). The book's success led Field Enterprises to distribute *Sylvia* as a daily comic strip.

The sharp, amusing thoughts and imaginings of Hollander's heroine shape and drive the comic, which has no action or storyline (figs. 3.10–3.11). The strip often has a feminist tone, frequently satirizes popular culture, and comments on timely political subjects as well as timeless themes in human relationships, and is one of the few to address women and aging. "I knew it was important," she said. "Since I was getting older and I always think whatever I'm feeling, at least a few others are feeling it too."[34] Sylvia, a stylishly coiffed stay-at-home mother and advice columnist, converses with her friends, her cats, space aliens, and her daughter. Recurring characters and themes, such as "The Woman Who Does Everything Better Than You," "The Woman Who Worries about Everything," "The Woman Who Lies in Her Personal Journal," "The Woman Who Is Easily Irritated," the "Fashion Cop," the "Love Cop," and "Alien Lovers," display Hollander's inventiveness and refined drawing.[35]

With the success of *Sylvia*, Hollander was one of a handful of women cartoonists whose work was published nationwide, enlivening the pages of eighty daily or weekly newspapers.[36] She published *Sylvia* collections, wrote and illustrated *Tales of Graceful Aging from the Planet Denial* (2007), collaborated with others as an author or illustrator on a wide variety of books, and illustrated children's books. Over the course of her career, she also developed a line of comics focused on cats, favored pets of both Sylvia and Hollander. In 2010, when the *Chicago Tribune* dropped *Sylvia* (and other strips that could not be easily reduced in size), her income dropped by half. Later that year, she and Alicia Eler launched a blog through which Hollander released new *Sylvia* strips. When she announced *Sylvia*'s retirement in 2012 ("Sylvia has retired from her comic strip and Dick Cheney got a new heart! Whew! What a week."), she blogged that the online experience had been more satisfying than she could have imagined.[37] Hollander continued to

Fig. 3.10. Nicole Hollander. Sylvia. "An estimated 100 million Americans spend $6.5 billion a year on vitamins, minerals and potions unregulated by the F.D.A.," January 12, 1998. Ink with paste-ons.

Fig. 3.11. Nicole Hollander. Sylvia. "The Woman Who Lies in Her Personal Journal." March 10, 1998. Ink with paste-ons.

write posts on current affairs and feature *Sylvia* strips from her archive, keeping her character's voice alive in cyber world.

Like Hollander, Cathy Lee Guisewite (b. 1950) emerged from the ranks of single working women to develop Cathy Andrews, another kind of female comic strip character, that, while certainly feminist at times, projects a gentler, more mainstream humor quite distinct from *Sylvia*. Born in Dayton, Ohio, Guisewite and her family moved to Midland, Michigan, where, as Guisewite describes it, "everyone attended church, PTA gatherings and Girl Scout meetings." After earning a degree in English at the University of Michigan in 1972, she worked as a copywriter for several Detroit-area advertising agencies and began drawing a simple cartoon figure with snatches of dialogue.[38] She sent these "explosions of frustration on paper" to her parents, and her mother suggested that they could be a comic strip. In 1976, the same year she moved into an executive-level position at W. B. Doner and Co., she won a long-term contract with Universal Press Syndicate and *Cathy* debuted.[39]

In her strip, Guisewite chronicled the travails and triumphs of a young, single career woman, focusing on workplace challenges, food, dieting, and Cathy's relationships with friends, men, and, especially, her mother. This groundbreaking strip was unapologetically autobiographical, and while the women's movement was well under way when *Cathy* premiered, no other comic featured a comparable female protagonist. Many readers identified with Guisewite's simply drawn, long-haired, wide-eyed character who shared her insecurities and famously uttered, "Ack!" in any number of annoying and stressful situations.

Fig. 3.12. Cathy Guisewite. Cathy. "It must be 100 in this room . . ." February 5, 1987. Porous point pen, tonal film overlay, opaque white with overlay and paste-ons.

Cathy's thoughts in the middle of a drawn-out business meeting (fig. 3.12) strike a chord with both sexes, and Guisewite uses brisk pacing and concise text to excellent effect. Comic tension mounts from frame to frame, Cathy's eyes widen as she shares her increasing discomfort in thought balloons. In several strips in the 1980s Guisewite explored gender issues in the workplace—including sexual harassment and maternity leave. When Cathy's boss, Mr. Pinkney, drunkenly made unwelcome advances, Cathy punched him in the nose. Another strip revolved around her friend who lost her position after just two weeks of maternity leave. During the 1988 presidential election, Guisewite had Cathy leaning toward Michael Dukakis over George H. W. Bush and several newspapers canceled her strip.[40] Overall, however, she rarely conveyed strong political stances, noting that her mother kept copies of both *Ms.* and *Bride* magazines and that "most women live somewhere between those two impulses . . . [and] believe a little of all of it."[41]

The strip enjoyed a remarkable thirty-three-year run, and at the height of its success it ran in more than fourteen hundred papers. In 1987, Guisewite won the first of three Emmy awards for her animated half-hour prime-time television show, *Cathy*.[42] Six years later she became the second woman to win the prestigious Reuben Award from the National Cartoonists Society, joining her colleague Lynn Johnston.[43]

In later years, there were fewer parallels between the comic and Guisewite's life, but two real-life events

inspired major storylines in the strip. Guisewite adopted a daughter in 1992 and later married a screenwriter. On the page, Cathy wed her longtime boyfriend Irving in 2005. "I never thought Cathy would get married," Guisewite said at the time. "And I also thought I would never get married. [Then] when I got married, people said, 'Oh, now the character's going to get married.' And I thought, no, this will really be where our lives separate. She'll go her way and I'll go mine. . . . But the truth is, now that I'm married and actually living with a man twenty-four hours a day, the wealth of material is too great to pass up."[44] The strip drew to a close in 2010, with Cathy announcing that she is expecting, and Guisewite opting to spend more time with her teenage daughter and aging parents.[45]

Singular Voices

Among comic strip creators working in the late twentieth century, one searches hard to find women outside the mainstream of white, heterosexual women. In the 1980s–1990s, Barbara Brandon-Croft and Alison Bechdel emerged as two strong voices for underrepresented communities. Each addressed additional social and political themes that engage these groups and broader audiences as well.

Born in Brooklyn, New York, in 1958 to cartoonist Brumsic Brandon and Rita Broughton, Barbara Brandon was raised in Newcastle, Long Island. As a

Fig. 3.13. Barbara Brandon. Where I'm Coming From. "Yes, that's my N.O.W. literature you see on the coffee table," December 15, 1991. Ink, tonal film overlay, and opaque white over pencil.

child she colored in silhouettes and drew borders on *Luther*, her father's nationally syndicated strip about an inner-city child's experiences. She majored in illustration at Syracuse University, and after graduation in 1980 freelanced for the *Village Voice, Crisis*, and MCA Records in New York.[46] While a fashion reporter for the Retail News Bureau she developed the strip *Where I'm Coming From* in 1982. *Essence* magazine liked the feature, but hired her instead as a beauty and fashion writer. It was not until 1989, when she heard from her father that the *Detroit Free Press* sought to publish more work by black cartoonists, that her strip made its first published appearance. Until then, getting mainstream editorial attention had proven difficult. "I think really the sad truth is if an editor were to consider my strip they can, at a glance, see my black characters and not even read it," she said. "My guess is if you were to do a little duck or a little white kid in front of a computer that they'd at least read it."[47]

Influenced by her father's cartoons and Jules Feiffer's many *Village Voice* cartoons that featured talking heads, Brandon developed her comic around nine—then eventually twelve—single black female characters between twenty-one and thirty-five years of age who appear as talking heads. Brandon used that style "because that's where my characters' minds are," adding that women are "always summed up by our

bodies. I just want to give us some dignity."[48] The women discuss a variety of contemporary concerns among themselves, and sometimes they directly address the reader. Drawing on discussion with her friends and her own wide reading, Brandon addressed issues of gender, race, relationships, family, and politics. The strip received positive responses, although it also drew negative reactions: some felt that men were unfairly criticized and others found its tone too feminist.[49]

When the Universal Press Syndicate acquired *Where I'm Coming From* in 1991, Brandon became the first nationally syndicated black female cartoonist and soon published two well-received collections of her work.[50] But getting a syndication deal put Brandon in a "very strange place," she later observed, as if she had taken up the only available slot for her type of strip. "I often talk about how you feel good because you're a black woman and you are representing, but . . . I'm actually closing the door [for others]. It won't be until I'm out of the door that they're able to get in."[51]

Early on, Brandon's weekly strip (figs. 3.13 and 3.14) enjoyed a modest run in more than fifty newspapers, but she ended it in 2005.[52] Her client list had dropped to seven newspapers, about one-tenth of what a feature generally needs to remain profitable for its supporters.[53] Throughout the 1990s, though, her strip gave voice to contemporary black women's complex

Fig. 3.14. Barbara Brandon. Where I'm Coming From. "In 1492, Columbus sailed the ocean blue," 1992. Ink, tonal film overlay, and opaque white over pencil.

concerns as race and gender equity played into greater public discourse.

Born in Lock Haven, Pennsylvania, Alison Bechdel grew up in Beech Creek, Pennsylvania. Showing artistic talent at an early age, she was encouraged to develop her gifts by her parents, Bruce Allen and Helen, both English teachers at the local high school. Bechdel attended Simon's Rock of Bard College in Great Barrington, then transferred to Oberlin College for her junior and senior years, earning a BA in studio art and art history in 1981. While a junior she wrote to inform her parents that she was lesbian. Four months later, her father was struck by a truck and killed when crossing a road, his death probably a suicide.[54]

After graduating in 1991, Bechdel worked a variety of jobs in New York City, Hadley, Massachusetts, and Minneapolis. She first published her comic strip *Dykes to Watch Out For* in the alternative Soho newspaper *WomanNews* in 1983. Two years later the strip was syndicated and began appearing in alternative newspapers nationwide. In 1990 Bechdel quit her day job to work full-time on her strip. With its cast of appealing, mostly lesbian characters engaged in ongoing challenges of relationships and broad political concerns of the day, the feature won a sizable following in gay and alternative venues (figs. 3.15 and 3.16). The characters do not stand out as either feminine or feminist stereotypes, but varied, engaging, and memorable individuals whose lives reflect universal concerns. In this respect, she made a significant contribution to comic strips about women.

Even for those not familiar with Bechdel or her comic, her name is well established in the popular

zeitgeist. A strip from 1985 would later form the basis for what became widely known as the "Bechdel Test." As two characters walk to a theater together, one tells the other, "I only go to a movie if it satisfies three basic requirements. One, it has to have at least two women in it . . . who, two, *talk* to each other about, three, something besides a *man*." Over time, critics and commentators have applied the test to literature, television, and various popular media—not to mention *other* comic strips—as a quick way to gauge the presence of women and depth of their characters in a given work.

Bechdel's taste for commentary on contemporary issues reminds one of Hollander's similar inclination in *Sylvia*. Both incorporate political and social content with a high degree of sophistication and artistic skill, but Bechdel's strip, by virtue of its more expansive format, contains lengthier statements and discussion. "There are cartoonists who draw better than they write. I think I write better than I draw," she observed. But even after drawing her strip for more than thirty years, she still had to "work very, very hard at the drawing. It doesn't come naturally. My hope is that one day it will come more naturally, that I'll get out of my own way and I'll trust myself more."

Bechdel regularly published the strip in book collections, and four of her volumes won Lambda Literary Awards. In 2006, she published *Fun Home: A Family Tragicomic*, a memoir that focused on her father, who taught and ran a funeral home. The sensitively drawn and written volume won wide critical acclaim, and her work has been widely published, translated, and included in many anthologies. A musical, *Fun Home* (2015), based on her graphic memoir, opened on Broadway to great success, winning five Tony awards, including Best Musical.[55] Other cartoonists have also had musical and theatrical productions based on their comics created and performed on stage, yet Bechdel's overall stardom in the realm of theatrical adaptation based on her work has so far eclipsed that of most of her peers.

Bechdel named *Rhymes with Orange* by Hilary Price (b. 1969) as one of her favorite strips, and it's one that stands out in several respects. Price's innovative comic succeeds within the mainstream, but also holds appeal to those who favor clever, off-beat

Figs. 3.15. Alison Bechdel. Dykes to Watch Out For. "Body and Soul," 1992. India ink and whiteout over graphite underdrawing.

Figs. 3.16. Alison Bechdel. Dykes to Watch Out For. "Through a Glass, Hardly," 1993. India ink and whiteout over graphite underdrawing.

humor. When she debuted her comic with King Features Syndicate at age twenty-five, she was the youngest woman to have a syndicated newspaper comic, and it rapidly won a sizable following in a highly competitive field still overwhelmingly dominated by men.

Born in Weston, Massachusetts, the youngest of three children, she was described as an extremely inquisitive child by her father. She enjoyed writing and spent hours doodling on scraps of paper or telephone books. As a teenager, she interned at the daily newspaper in Falmouth, Massachusetts, during two

Fig. 3.17. Hilary Price. Rhymes with Orange. "Where Parallel Lines Don't Meet," September 21, 2010. Ink and graphite.

Fig. 3.18. Hilary Price. Rhymes with Orange. "Take Your Daughter to Work Day," June 8, 2015. Ink.

summers. Attending Stanford University, she majored in English literature, co-captained the ski team, and played soccer briefly on the varsity squad, before graduating in 1991. Prior to release of *Rhymes with Orange*, she wrote bank ads for an advertising agency in San Francisco.[56] As an admirer of simple, fine line drawing, Price was influenced by the work of greeting card artist Sandra Boynton, Dr. Seuss, Shel Silverstein, and *New Yorker* cartoonists Roz Chast, Sam Gross, and George Booth.[57]

Favoring a spare, thin-lined style, Price includes just enough descriptive detail in rendering figures and setting to set the tone for the scenario, and begins each strip with her trademark feature, a small title panel that sets the stage (figs. 3.17 and 3.18). She engages with an impressive range of contemporary topics in *Rhymes with Orange* that she handles with a remarkable variety of design layouts. Using a revolving cast of characters in varied scenarios, she creates visually and verbally amusing, often witty observations about

domestic life often as imagined from the perspective of cats and dogs. "I work with all present-day stuff," she said of her subject matter. "The well that I keep returning to . . . is anxiety, vulnerability and pet fur, and sometimes all three come together." Her strip is unusual in its characters' anonymity. "There's no named character, but there is an 'every person' who keeps popping up and . . . [over time] her hair has been combed, her shoes have been tied, and she has grown fingers. One thing, however, has remained constant: her U boobs. I never wanted to name her because I didn't want to affiliate her with a single personality . . . or to a family . . . or to an occupation . . . though this seems to be the secret to comic strip success. . . . I think what makes it different as a strip drawn by a woman is that women . . . often tend to be . . . wife or mother or working single girl . . . but there's not the tradition of the 'every woman' that stands for everybody in the same way that we understand the 'every man,' but that's what I'm shooting for."[58]

EXPOS AND COMIC CONS

What began as low-key gatherings run by teenagers in Detroit and Chicago and an "official" first comics convention in New York City in 1964 became, within a few years, a circuit of modest and major multiday events that draw hundreds of thousands of visitors. Comic conventions, held nationwide and around the world, offer space to see and exhibit art and opportunities for cartoonists and illustrators to network with peers and clients, meet fans, and compete for prizes. The larger cons long ago outgrew their origins, moving out of community halls and hotel ballrooms and into convention centers, where in addition to comics, other touchstones of popular culture are also featured, including film, television, games, technology, memorabilia, and more.

"I have mixed feelings on comic conventions," said comics and graphic novel artist Miss Lasko-Gross, nearly twenty years after her first visit to the mega event known as the San Diego Comic-Con International. "Depending on the specific show, they can be both extremely welcoming and overwhelmingly alienating." The tremendous success of comic cons and small press fairs has also altered the nature of these proceedings. "There has been some controversy about more explicit recruiting and headhunting done at cons," said another graphic novel artist, Jillian Tamaki. "There seems to be some tension between wanting people to have [professional] opportunities and trying to maintain the independent spirit of the events."[60]

Two particularly notable and contrasting annual gatherings are held on opposite sides of the country. The San Diego Comic-Con, started in 1970, quickly became the best known and largest annual gathering for the comics community. Three thousand miles away, the Small Press Expo, established in 1994 in Bethesda, Maryland, is, in the view of Lasko-Gross, among the "more cerebral conventions." Women have become an increasingly strong presence at these festivals, and for younger artists, attending them is helpful in breaking into the industry.[61] Tamaki "was selling comics on my website and physically dropping off copies at stores around New York [but] the cons were where I met fellow creators (we can be hermetic creatures) and also felt 'introduced' to the comic press."[62]

Lasko-Gross seconded the importance of cons given the lone-wolf nature of her career. "Talking with fans is psychologically important in a profession where so much time is spent toiling away in isolation," not to mention the benefit of "being inspired by all the amazing artists around you." She also found these events useful in figuring out how best to promote her work. "Like many young artists, I assumed 'talent' and 'good work' would surely bring people to me. [At the San Diego Comic-Con] there was so much enthusiasm for brands and movie/TV properties, but little foot traffic or love for the artsy-ghetto section where I was situated. . . . these kind of humiliating experiences are the most valuable teaching tools. Now when I attend a big mainstream show I have realistic expectations, a sales strategy and a shamelessly bold attitude for approaching anyone I'd like to meet."[63]

Another of Price's goals "is to inspire more women to join the field." She has taught gag writing workshops and is willing to look at people's work for critique.[59] Although Price creates many cartoons that focus on women and women's perspectives, and occasionally comments as a lesbian on relationships in her work, such issues do not dominate her output. Her capacity for seeing and conveying humorous perspectives on contemporary life is impressively broad and multifaceted, and even sometimes embraces the political.

COMIC BOOK ARTISTS

In contrast with comic strips, comic books are publications in book or magazine format that present a story or collection of stories in the form of extended comics. The first were offered as giveaway advertising premiums in 1933. By 1935, comic books often consisted of reprints of newspaper strips and original humorous or action-filled stories for children. Comic books soon embraced a wide range of subjects and also targeted adults. The publication of Superman comic strips in *Action Comics* No. 1, June 1938, spawned a proliferation of illustrated superheroes that also leapt from the printed page to a vast range of related products and merchandise. Comic books flourished during the World War II era, bringing titles about war and crime to soldiers stationed abroad, but a host of other comics also emerged and succeeded during the 1940s and 1950s. These included animal characters by Disney and Looney Tunes, detective and horror stories, and illustrated classics. Notable among those that successfully moved from comic strips to comic books was *Little Lulu*.[64] The new format also brought new job opportunities for female cartoonists, especially since most were adept at portraying new female characters, including several superheroines, who entered the mix of characters.

The mode of comic book production that prevailed in the late 1930s–1940s also proved more challenging for women. To be economically viable, comic book shops had to produce a high volume of publishable work, which required a team of collaborators and division of labor (including writers, cartoonist/illustrators, and highly skilled inkers, letterers, and colorists) in a bullpen setting. This work model, with variations, persisted for decades. Most such shops and comic book publishers were run by and staffed largely with men. Such working conditions were seldom inviting for women—and offered fewer opportunities for them to exercise some degree of autonomy let alone creativity than was possible in producing comic strips.

From the beginning and into the 1950s, comic books aroused controversy and criticism from educators, church and civic organizations, and mental health experts, including many who blamed the popular publications for juvenile delinquency. Prominent among the last, the psychiatrist Dr. Fredric Wertham sought to ban sales of comics to children. In his 1954 book *Seduction of the Innocent*, he described the violence, horror, and unwholesome sexual attitudes he found in comic books. He was alarmed by the "subtle atmosphere of homoerotism which pervades the adventures of the mature 'Batman' and his young friend 'Robin'" and worried that "Superman not only defies the laws of gravity," but "he gives children a completely wrong idea of other basic physical laws." Wonder Woman was even worse, as she "is always a horror

Fig. 3.19. Marie Severin. *The Incredible Hulk*. "Ring around the Rhino," published June 1968. Ink and whiteout over pencil with overlays and paste-ons.

type. She is physically very powerful, tortures men, has her own female following, is the cruel 'phallic' woman. While she is a frightening figure for boys, she is an undesirable ideal for girls, being the exact opposite of what girls are supposed to want to be."[65] He concluded that "In no other literature for children has the image of womanhood been so degraded."[66]

The efforts of Wertham and others prompted US Senate hearings in 1954 on the effect of comic books on children. Under pressure, the industry responded with self-censorship by creating the Comics Code Authority, which issued a seal of approval printed on comic books that had passed a prepublication review.[67] This dramatic step, however, could not prevent

Fig. 3.20. Marie Severin. The Sleeping Giant, 2001. Ink, whiteout, and paste-ons over graphite underdrawing plus eight production digital files. Story by Stan Lee, art and color by Marie Severin, letters by Ken Bruzenak. Published in *9–11: The World's Finest Comic Book Writers and Artists Tell Stories to Remember*, ed. Paul Levitz, DC Comics, 2002. Page three of three.

Superheroines, the Silver Age and Beyond

Even though the superhero genre enjoyed a boom time known as the Silver Age (1956–1969)—a period of tremendous creative, artistic, and commercial success—that same era marked an unfortunate retrenchment for superheroines. As more superhero books flooded the market, one did not need X-ray vision to see that the number of superheroines and female creators declined drastically in the postwar years. The once towering Wonder Woman appeared more feminized and the few other female characters, such as Lois Lane, "Superman's girlfriend," tended toward marriage rather than fighting injustice.[69] It would be decades before superheroines would win greater visibility and before the number of women drawing them would gradually increase.[70]

Against this backdrop, Marie Severin (b. 1929) quietly pioneered a path that helped both contemporary and younger counterparts gain entrée. Born on Long Island, Severin grew up in an artistic family, and her father was a designer for the fashion company Elizabeth Arden. Initially, she aspired to creating stained glass, and as a teenager she took cartooning and illustration classes for a few months and later attended Pratt Institute for all of one day.[71] Severin got her start in comic books in 1953 when her brother John helped her get a job as a colorist at Entertaining Comics (EC). She colored many of its classic titles, including horror comics. When she thought publisher Bill Gaines or editor Al Feldstein allowed graphic imagery that went too far, she colored the questionable panel dark blue, and thus earned a reputation for being the "conscience of EC."[72]

During the downturn in comics publishing in the late 1950s, EC cut back its titles to only the black and white *MAD* magazine. Severin also worked as a colorist for Atlas and Marvel and later freelanced as a commercial artist. Returning to work for the legendary Stan Lee at Marvel in 1964, she soon volunteered to draw a spread for *Esquire*, winning recognition and finally obtaining drawing assignments. She penciled *Dr. Strange* and *The Incredible Hulk*, the latter for which she is perhaps best known, as well as covers or pages

a serious recession in comic book publishing in the late 1950s, a time when even some major artistic talents simply disappeared or were forced to find other kinds of work. In addition to being displaced by male cartoonists after the war, this industry-wide slump added notably to difficulties female cartoonists faced in pursuing work in the field.[68]

Fig. 3.21. Anne Timmons. 9/17, 2001. Ink, porous point pen, opaque white, and blue pencil before lettering added. Story text by Trina Robbins. Published in *9–11, Artists Respond*, Dark Horse Comics, 2002.

for many other classic titles such as *The Amazing Spider-Man*, *Iron Man*, and *Daredevil*.[73]

"Had I been a guy with my talent, I would have been privy to a hell of a lot," she would later note, "but because I was a girl, I wasn't that interested. I didn't want that much stuff. It was a masculine world . . . I made out okay without feeling I was intruding. I was a woman in the industry, so I wasn't privy to all the fun these guys had. I didn't want to make a million dollars, I didn't have the ambition the guys did. I didn't have to provide the home. I'm a woman of the '40s and '50s. I didn't expect to be the boss."[74]

Between 1967 and 1969, Severin took a leading role in production of *Not Brand Ecch*, Marvel's self-lampooning comic book, and her contributions included writing, inking and penciling, and creating cover art. Her success with *Ecch* led to her work on other humor titles for the company. But it was her drawing for *The Incredible Hulk*, "Ring around the Rhino" (fig. 3.19) published in June 1968, that showcased her accomplished technique as a Silver Age artist. In this well-designed cover page, Severin plays varied sizes and types of lettering off one another, using italicized all caps for the series title, white all-capital letters for the story title, and contrasting black lettering for the

banner headline, "Hulk Captured!" Lines of large lettering balance well with visually arresting images below. Through strongly juxtaposed depictions of the Hulk, Severin spotlights his dual nature: on the left, he breaks through a wall; on the right, he appears dramatically shrunken, a slumped figure in police custody. More than three decades later, in "The Sleeping Giant: A Hitherto Undiscovered Aesop's Fable" (fig. 3.20), a comic book story created in response to the terrorist attacks of September 11, 2001, Severin's depiction of a rampaging elephant demonstrated her undiminished ability to depict large forms caught in moments of unleashed physical fury.

Following in the superhero-booted footsteps of Severin, Amanda Conner (b. 1965) excelled in the traditionally collaborative mode of the mainstream comic book world. She has depicted both male superheroes and a number of vivid, strong heroines. Born in Los Angeles, California, to parents who were both artists, she grew up in Florida and Connecticut—an avid comic book reader and wanting to be Wonder Woman—and attended the Joe Kubert School of Cartoon and Graphic Art, now known as the Kubert School, in Dover, New Jersey, from 1983 to 1985.[75] Conner began her career by illustrating small projects for

Fig. 3.22. Trina Robbins. Cover for *Wimmen's Comix*, no. 14, 1989.

Marvel Comics, Last Gasp, and Archie Comics, eventually drawing titles for Marvel that included *Yellowjack*, *Avengers West Coast*, *Barbie*, and *Gargoyles*.[76] "I like drawing superheroes," she has noted. "It's fun for me. I would still love to be a superhero, though, to put on some spandex and kick some butt."[77]

For Conner, her experience in comic books—particularly the testosterone-fueled realm of superheroes—differed considerably from other women, especially those from an earlier era. "Most of the guys in comics would love to have more women doing comic book work. There's definitely not anyone going, 'We don't want girls doing this.' They're going, 'Oh, please let there be more girls into the same thing I'm into.'" She has attributed the paucity of women illustrating comics partly as a financial concern. "Most women who go into illustration find out you can make a lot more money going into advertising. The girls who are smart and draw say 'Hey—I can make ten times as much money doing an ad.' It doesn't even occur to most of them to do comic book illustration."

During the 1990s she worked for Claypool Comics drawing the series "Soulsearchers and Company," then met Marvel editor and her future husband, Jimmy Palmiotti, who began to ink her work. She later drew the rebooted *Power Girl* series, featuring Superman's cousin, a character first introduced in the 1940s, in collaboration with Palmiotti. In 2010 she worked with Laura Martin to create the cover for Marvel's *Girl Comics*, a three-issue collection of new short stories by fifty-eight women. Some fans criticized the collection as a "ghetto" for women creators, but many of these artists had not been published by Marvel for many years.[78]

Anne Timmons, no stranger to the world of superheroines, also draws a variety of comics that include female subjects and educational titles. She was born in Milwaukie, near Portland, Oregon, in 1956 to parents who were teachers. Drawing from an early age, she completed a BFA in illustration and painting at Oregon State University, tried acting in San Francisco and Portland, then reconnected with drawing in 1994 by taking a class in sequential art at Pacific Northwest College. Attending the Comi-Con International in San Diego in 1996 led to her meeting comics writer, artist, and historian Trina Robbins, with whom she has collaborated on numerous projects.[79] From 2000 to 2006, the two co-created the award-winning *Go Girl*, a comic about Janet Goldman, a semiretired flying superheroine, and her similarly gifted teenage daughter Lindsay.

Timmons collaborated further with Robbins on graphic novel adaptations of *Northanger Abbey* by Jane Austen (2007), and other titles about Florence Nightingale, Hedy Lamarr, Elizabeth Blackwell, and Lily Renée. She has found these topics especially appealing, since "I enjoy drawing women in a realistic manner, and I also like drawing lavish costumes and settings. . . . This is partly from my training as a fashion illustrator, but also partly because many male artists just can't—or won't—draw realistic women!"[80]

Timmons employed her well-honed drawing and storytelling skills in a three-page story entitled "9/17" (fig. 3.21), that she illustrated and Robbins wrote for *9-11, Artists Respond*, a comics anthology. Page by page, each with neatly organized panels, the story of a brief encounter in a post-9-11 airport setting unfolds clearly and dramatically. Words are hardly necessary as the viewer reads the story through gestures, facial expressions, and the key visual clue, a photograph of the deceased son and his family.

UNDERGROUND COMIX AND ALTERNATIVE COMICS

"Underground comix" emerged in San Francisco in the 1960s and reflected new political and social consciousness fueled by the Vietnam War. Creators articulated satirical, rebellious critiques of cultural norms—often with biting humor—focusing on such subjects as drugs, psychedelia, sex, and conveying fury toward—and mockery of—authority. Highly varied in aesthetic approaches, rejecting the clichéd storylines and content of mainstream comics, this new strain of the art form circulated in underground newspapers, and small independent presses published associated comic books, usually found at more expansive news-stands and head shops. Some works, such as *Zippy the Pinhead*, soon became popular above ground. Underground comics gradually waned as "alternative comics" arose in the mid-1970s, similarly rejecting the formulaic models of mainstream comics, espousing instead the potential of comics as a means of artistic self-expression and exploration. Unlike underground comics that targeted a limited audience, alternative comics, though produced as self-published or small press works, sought a more general audience.[81]

Trina Robbins and Diane Noomin, both Brooklyn born, were part of the underground movement and stand out as key figures not only for their own creative output but for their vital roles as editors of significant anthologies. These collected works documented a critical era in comics history specifically and in women's history more generally. Although Robbins and Noomin responded quite differently to the cultural movement and ultimately pursued dissimilar career paths, each was attracted to the movement that centered largely in the San Francisco Bay area and moved there. Nearly two dozen other sister cartoonists also got involved.[82] Many found, to their disappointment, that men in the movement were not open to including their work in comics anthologies, nor did they

Fig. 3.23. Carol Tyler. Cover for *Wimmen's Comix*, no. 16, 1990.

project a spirit of community, and a number were producing work that was blatantly sexist. The women responded by drawing, writing, and publishing their own compilations, such as *Wimmen's Comix*, a nearly annual anthology published from 1972 to 1992 (figs. 3.22 and 3.23), and *Tits 'n' Clits*. Amid the plethora of diverse styles, types of stories, and narrative approaches exemplified, being female is a central concern, a unifying thread that runs through this rich body of work produced by more than two dozen women.

Robbins (b. 1938) grew up reading comics, drawing, and writing, so "What else [other than a cartoonist] could I have become?" (figs. 3.24 and 3.25). Her mother, a schoolteacher, encouraged her to develop her artistic abilities.[83] She attended Cooper Union and Queens College, married, had a daughter, worked in Los Angeles as a costume designer, divorced, and returned to New York to do an underground comic for the *East Village Other*, before heading west. Once there, she became a founding contributor and editor of *Wimmen's Comix*. Robbins continued working in

Figs. 3.24 and 3.25. Trina Robbins. *1969*, 1988. Ink. Published by Rip Off Press.

comics primarily as a writer and editor, often collaborating with other women in producing many well-received comics series and graphic narratives that featured female characters. She took on a critical role, however, when she turned to documenting and researching the history of sister comics artists. As a self-described "herstorian," she drew on her own collection of their work, in both original and published form, her interviews with creators, and her vast knowledge of the field in writing a number of comics histories. Her studies have been essential in preserving a record of contributions to the art form that could easily have been lost. The importance of her work in the history of comics cannot be overstated.

Noomin (b. 1947) grew up on Long Island, and completed a BA at the Pratt Institute. Following her move to San Francisco, she became an original contributor to *Wimmen's Comix*. In 1973 she created DiDi Glitz, an alter ego and riveting character (fig. 3.26).

Noomin chronicled DiDi's striving for glamor, romance, and fulfillment in exquisitely drawn stories that often dazzle with over-the-top drama, décor, and fashion. DiDi's overeating and weight struggles speak to many women's preoccupation with body image. In the underground comics scene, she stood out as both especially idiosyncratic and as a landmark figure. This conflicted character came on stage in 1980 when a San Francisco–based theater group produced *I'd Rather Be Doing Something Else: The DiDi Glitz Story*. Designing the costumes and stage sets, Noomin also contributed to the book and lyrics.

As the underground movement waned in the early 1990s, younger cartoonists sought new viable outlets for their work, including self-syndication (selling one's work directly to newspapers) and publication in free alternative weekly newspapers. The latter, usually found in larger cities or college towns, relied on advertisements rather than paid subscriptions to stay in

Fig. 3.26. Diane Noomin. Didi Glitz. "A Blonde Grows in Brooklyn," 1989. Ink, watercolor.

business, and focused on in-depth local coverage. They also published unconventional, challenging comics not offered in most daily newspapers. Lynda Barry's *Ernie Pook's Comeek* and Nicole Hollander's *Sylvia* enjoyed long-lasting success in alternative publications.[84]

A multifaceted talent, Barry (b. 1958) worked as a painter, cartoonist, writer, illustrator, playwright, editor, commentator, teacher, and professor at the University of Wisconsin–Madison. Born in Richland Center, Wisconsin, Barry and her family moved to an ethnically diverse, lower-middle-class neighborhood in Seattle, where she and her brothers spent their formative years. Strained relationships with her parents, being biracial, and feeling an outcast made her childhood difficult. Her father, an Irish Norwegian meat cutter, and mother, an Irish Filipino immigrant who worked as a hospital janitor, separated and divorced during Barry's teenage years. She graduated from

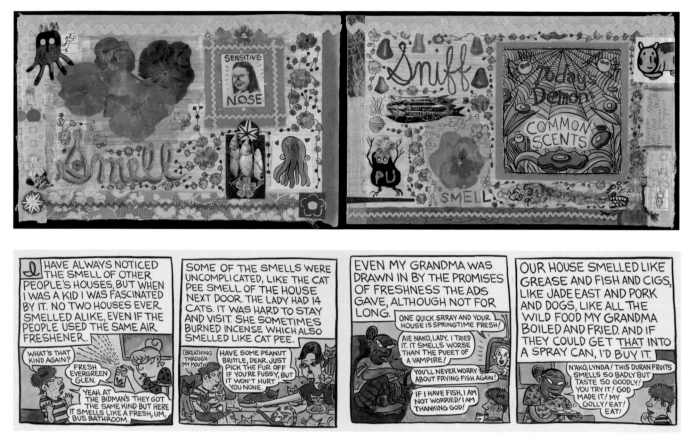

Fig. 3.27. Lynda Barry. Title and introductory pages for "Common Scents," 2002. Published in *One! Hundred! Demons!* Sasquatch Books, 2002.

Evergreen State College where she studied painting and writing and published some of her first comics. Barry contributed to *Wimmen's Comix*, but R. Crumb, rather than female underground cartoonists, was a major influence on her, mainly because he gave her "this feeling that you could draw anything." Still, she found his sexual subject matter disturbing.[85] Although she is known for *Ernie Pook's Comeek*, she also produced award-winning graphic novels.[86]

The opportunity to publish a weekly strip with the *Chicago Reader* in 1979 enabled Barry to earn a living through her comics. Originally entitled *Boys and Girls*, the strip initially focused on adult themes such as dating, relationships, and sex, although children sometimes appeared. As the title changed to *Ernie Pook's Comeek* over time Barry shifted from using pen to brush around 1984, and began to feature children.[87] Many of Barry's strips and other works involve characters in a Seattle-based family that include siblings Arna and Arnold Arneson and their cousins Marlys,

Maybonne, and Freddie Mullins, in addition to stories from her own life. The strip enjoyed a nearly thirty-year run until Barry retired it in 2008 as the number of weekly papers dwindled and there were "so few left that were still willing to print something as odd as my work."[88] Deeply committed to helping spark the creative potential in others as writers and artists, she taught workshops for years and later became a professor at the University of Wisconsin–Madison.

One of Barry's most innovative artistic breakthroughs is seen in *One! Hundred! Demons!* a work of "autobiofictionalography," the term she invented to describe its hybrid nature. The multilayered, multimedia approach she devised for this groundbreaking book is truly "a new comic art form and structure," one that has also been explicated as "scrapbooking the self" by comics scholar Susan E. Kirtley.[89] The original artwork incorporates textile collage and drawings in ink and watercolor. A look at several pages from one of the volume's stories, "Smell Sniff: Today's Demon:

Common Scents," demonstrates Barry's multifaceted approach and exuberant insight as she resurrects and transforms her youthful and keenly observed perspective on smells from her childhood. The title and introductory pages (fig. 3.27) feature collage elements that include colorful rick-rack and strips of floral patterned paper. These elements set off lettering and objects such as pressed pansies and drawn forms associated with less pleasant smells, including fish and the stylized form of what appears to be a Venus flytrap. The visual interplay between the collage and drawn vignettes set the tone for Barry's narrative musings. The labeled photograph of Barry as a young girl highlights her unusual sensitivity to smell.

On the first page of the story, she observes that each household has its own distinctive smell, "even if the people used the same air freshener." As she chronicles her olfactory impressions of various households she laments that even her beloved Filipina grandmother at one point succumbed to using fresheners that promised freshness, but ultimately rejoices in the distinctive scents of her family's cooking and colognes. Barry's light complexion and red hair contrast with her grandmother's darker coloring, and humorous exchanges between grandmother and granddaughter both underscore their strong bonds and move the story forward.

Barry, whose work reflects great variety in style and subject matter, stands out as singularly successful in many ways. When *Ernie Pook* ended, she turned to creating other innovative works, including *What It Is* (2008), *Picture This: The Near-Sighted Monkey Book* (2010), and *Syllabus: Notes from an Accidental Professor* (2014) in which she shares her meditations on and explorations in the creative processes of writing and drawing. These titles combined storytelling with how-to guidance through mixed-media technique. They are also part of an effort to answer the question "What is an image?" first posed to her by a college instructor when she was a nineteen-year-old student.

"Here's what I know about this question so far," she reported. "It's not a question that can be answered by just thinking or theorizing about it. It can only be answered through some sort of activity. 'What is an image' seems to have ten thousand answers and none of them are fixed. It changes as the nature of our attention and our needs change. An image has both steady and changeable qualities simultaneously, a place and time that is not in the same place and time as our own—though it must be accessed from our own place and time, and it seems to completely resist definition and explanation. I believe it will be a beloved mystery to me all my life."[90]

NARRATIVE ARTISTS GET GRAPHIC

The graphic novel is commonly recognized as a full-length story drawn in a comic strip style and published in book form, rather than as a serial or a periodical. Since comic studies emerged as an academic discipline in the 1970s, the term has generated considerable debate among scholars and practitioners of the art form. The publication of Will Eisner's *A Contract with God* (1978) and the Pulitzer Prize–winning *Maus* (1980) by Art Spiegelman helped spread greater use of the term, and the number of published graphic novels has also burgeoned. The terms "graphic narrative" and "graphic novel" are used interchangeably here and reflect the lack of strong consensus among those who study and create these works.

Several women who were born around the time the term "graphic novel" began showing up in print in the 1970s went on to successful careers as narrative artists who enriched and expanded the genre.

Raina Telgemeier, born and raised in San Francisco, enjoyed a steady diet of *Calvin and Hobbes* and *For Better or for Worse* on the comics pages and Baby-Sitter's Club books. In 1999, she moved to New York City to attend the School of Visual Arts, where she met her future husband, Dave Roman, a fellow student and aspiring cartoonist. After completing a BFA, she worked as an editorial assistant for a New York City publisher, but created and self-published minicomics on the side. Notice of her short story "Beginnings" by a Scholastic Publishing editor led her back to the Baby-Sitter's Club. She adapted four of the titles into graphic novel form, creating one hundred ninety drawings for each.

With publication of her first graphic novel, *Smile: A Dental Drama* (2010), Telgemeier achieved

Figs. 3.28 and 3.29. Raina Telgemeier. Minicomic for *Smile*, title page and double page spread. Photocopy, hand assembled. Self-published, ca. 2009–2010. *Smile* was later published by Scholastic.

widespread critical and popular success (figs. 3.28 and 3.29). Her autobiographical story about severely damaging her two front teeth, the subsequent surgery, wearing multiple sets of braces and a retainer with false teeth, all while coping with the routine challenges of adolescence, takes readers from middle school to high school. Her award-winning story struck a chord with young teens and tweens, an age group that found *Smile* true-to-life and riveting. With humor and honesty, the book dealt with finding her strengths and the sometimes painful reckoning with friends and classmates during her middle school years. Some critics regard *Smile* as a watershed moment for the genre in young adult literature. As Caitlin Rosberg of the A. V. Club observed, "*Smile* has inarguably changed the way many people look at comics, and the way the industry itself approaches audiences. It's not that there was no one else writing graphic novels for young women when *Smile* came onto the scene . . . but Telgemeier's incredible success legitimizes comics as suitable for YA literature and YA literature as suitable for comics."[91]

Two drawings (figs. 3.30 and 3.31) for *Claudia and Mean Janine* (2008) display Telgemeier's skills in storytelling and illustration. The sisters' contrasting personalities and abilities feature prominently in the story. Claudia, a member of the Baby-Sitter's Club and someone more devoted to drawing than to her classwork, often feels at a great disadvantage compared with her perfect sister. Janine, a straight-A student, studies constantly and devotes much of her time to working on her website. At a critical point in the story, Telgemeier depicts Claudia gradually retreating from her family. Virtually no words are needed to follow the progression of images. She employs her clean, spare style in depicting each character's sober face, giving the largest panel to Claudia finding comfort in her art.

Telgemeier also displays versatility in rendering settings that convey an engaging sense of place in her books. Her vista of San Francisco in *Smile*, shown from the elevated location of Twin Peaks, is a composite view that incorporates key landmarks of the Bay area landscape—the Oakland Bay bridge, Alcatraz and Angel Islands, and a long stretch of land along the East Bay. Her stunning views of desert landscape contribute atmosphere and a sense of immense desert distances traveled in *Sisters*, another graphic memoir.[92] Telgemeier's own family and life experiences have made for compelling, coming-of-age

Fig. 3.30. Raina Telgemeier. [Girl Begins to Paint as Others Use Telephones and Computer], ca. 2008. Ink, graphite, and blue pencil. Published in *Claudia and Mean Janine* by Ann M. Martin, Graphix, 2008.

Fig. 3.31. Raina Telgemeier. [Claudia and Children in Backyard], ca. 2008. Ink, graphite, and blue pencil. Published in *Claudia and Mean Janine* by Ann M. Martin, Graphix, 2008.

stories that resonate with both young adults and their parents. "My characters are all me, in a way," she says. "I have two sides to my personality that are sometimes at odds with one another: my over-the-top bustling enthusiasm about people and projects and ideas and experiences, and my anxiety and nerves and quiet side. I think most of the kids I write fall into one dominant version of these two ways of being. Callie (*Drama*, 2012) and Maya (*Ghosts*, 2016) are me at my most exuberant and extroverted. Cat (*Ghosts*, 2016) and Jesse (*Drama*, 2012) are bashful and introspective. And when I'm writing autobio, with myself in the leading role, I think you get the full spectrum."[93] Her appealing, authentic young heroines are a strong contribution to the graphic novel—and demonstrate the expanding possibilities of this evolving art form.

For Jillian Tamaki (b. 1980), who grew up in Calgary, Alberta, her background was somewhat of an anomaly among illustrators—she spent more time as a kid riding horses in the countryside than pursuing art. She did, however, hone her drawing skills by studying *Archie* comics and copying pictures of horses. In high school she developed a fascination for the Dadaists and Surrealists. With a longstanding interest in art history, she draws "a lot of inspiration from pop culture, classic illustration and design, contemporary art, art history, decorative arts, novels, folk art, and crafts."[94]

After graduation from the Alberta College of Art and Design, she worked at Bioware, a videogame company in Edmonton, and established her freelance illustration career in New York City before returning

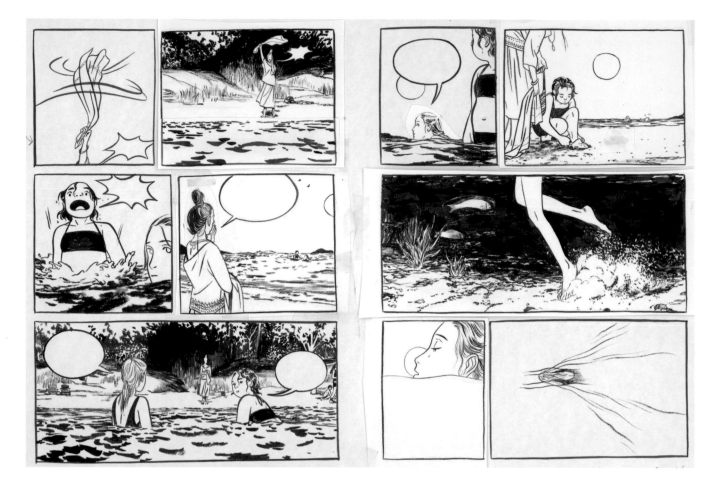

Figs. 3.32 and 3.33. Jillian Tamaki. [Scenes from *This One Summer*], 2013–2014. Ink, before lettering added.
Published in *This One Summer* by Mariko Tamaki and Jillian Tamaki, First Second, 2014.

Fig. 3.34. Lilli Carré. My Dreams Have Been Quite Strange Lately, 2010. Silkscreen. 58/80. Minicomic.

to Canada. She collaborated with her cousin Mariko Tamaki on the graphic novels *Skim* (2008), which won an Ignatz award for best graphic novel, and *This One Summer* (2014). Tamaki's drawings for *This One Summer*, set at a lake resort, reflect her strengths as a visual storyteller. Several threads run through the story that centers on two friends: the introverted Rose and the younger, boisterous Windy. Poised between childhood and adolescence, the two girls enjoy observing adults and older teens, lounging on the beach, swimming, and watching movies together. Tamaki captures their contrasting personalities and interpersonal dynamic in an underwater view on a double-page spread (fig. 3.33).[95] Amid the dark, watery depths, bubbles float around the girls' forms, Windy plunging and surging, Rose more languidly gliding and floating. In another drawing, with five panels (fig. 3.32),[96] Tamaki presents snapshot-like views of the girls in relation to the water.[97] Through such images, Tamaki evokes the peaceful atmosphere and poetic beauty of Awago Beach, the traditional location for the families' vacations.

In collaboration with her cousin, Tamaki creates believable young female characters based on her own experiences and imagination, and imbues her images with a strong sense of place. After visiting vacation cottages in Canada as part of her research, Tamaki combined her impressions with her own memories to inform her characters and give visible form to the overarching story. Tamaki's high level of artistry and empathy for her characters in conceiving and executing her imagery are notable contributions to the graphic narrative art form.

Working independently, Tamaki created the online comic *Super Mutant Magic Academy* (2010), which follows an unusual student body—some students actually have unusual bodies, including a girl with a lizard head and another with cat ears—who despite their eccentricities and the atypical nature of their high school, deal with normal teenage issues. Her characters convey rich personalities, such as the Bohemian-like performance artist Frances, who sports an ever-dangling cigarette from her lip and evokes a beyond-her-years wizened sensibility. After winning two Ignatz awards for best web comic, *Super Mutant Magic Academy* reversed a well-worn path in 2015 by going from the online world into a printed anthology.

Miss (Melissa) Lasko-Gross (b. 1977) and Lilli Carré (b. 1983) stand out from many others by virtue of the uniqueness and quality of their work. A minicomic by Carré (fig. 3.34), *My Dreams Have Been Quite Strange Lately* (2010), demonstrates the high artistic quality sometimes attained in this format, one that is typically handmade, self-published, small or

Fig. 3.35. Miss Lasko-Gross. Drawing of Henni for American Library Association poster, 2015. Ink, graphite.

her peers, she is exceptionally accomplished in several interrelated comic art media.

Lasko-Gross, in contrast, has focused her creative efforts primarily on comics and graphic narratives including two acclaimed autobiographical works, *Escape from Special* (2006) and *A Mess of Everything* (2009). In both she chronicles her uneasy path through childhood and adolescence, not shying away from her situation as a loner and outcast, bravely sharing unpleasant sides of her personality in episodic stories told through expressive imagery and succinct dialogue.[100] Her graphic novel, *Henni* (2015), departs from autobiography and features a girl-cat, a hybrid, eponymous heroine. A drawing of her protagonist (fig. 3.35) highlights Lasko-Gross's abilities to evoke key aspects of the narrative: Henni's curious, contemplative character and the mysterious, wooded landscape through which she wends her way through much of the narrative. Lasko-Gross's artful, thoughtful approach gives an intriguing and satisfying visual synthesis of her book. In *Henni*, she portrays her young adventurer coming to terms with forces of conformity and nonconformity in a process of discovery.[101]

Whether consciously or not, many graphic narrative artists mine and reflect to varying degrees their own life experiences, rather than working with pre-existing character types and storylines established by predecessors. Adolescence, with all the challenges it often entails—anxiety, vulnerability, confusion, rebelliousness, peer and parental relationships, and sexual identity—offers a particularly rich source. The authenticity of these artists' voices resonates with readers that include not only the usual pre-teen and teenage market, but also appreciative parents and other adult readers of contemporary comics. While fine art has long been revered as a means of speaking to human experience, the illustrative format devised and used by comic artists also demonstrates its powerful capacity to do the same.

of an unusual size, and shorter than a regular comic book.[98] In her two-sided comic with five folds and six panels, Carré narrates a young man's encounters with a woman on a bus. Through contrasting color schemes and voices that shift from the imagined dialogue of dreams to the man's solitary thoughts, the artist deftly evokes the separate yet interpenetrating states of dream and sometimes jarring reality. Carré, who describes herself as an interdisciplinary artist and illustrator, has published graphic novels, produced web comics, and created animated films.[99] Although she takes on a variety of creative projects, like many of

INTERLUDE

ILLUSTRATIONS FOR INDUSTRY

Whether drafting architectural elevations, sketching ideas for devices and decorations, designing furniture or textiles, or depicting new styles in fashion, those who give visible form to such creations rely on the same artistic abilities martialed by high-profile or brand-name illustrators. Perhaps it is because of the specialized or technical nature of such illustrations, or that other artists have themselves dismissed these designs as falling short of "true art," that many illustrators and their work are overlooked in art surveys, despite the role they have played in shaping the cultural environment.

Artists in industry usually bring both formal training and artistic sensibilities to their drawings, and have also experienced challenges as women working in fields that predominately employ men. (Maya Lin, whose design for the Vietnam Veterans Memorial won out over more than fourteen hundred other entries in a blind national competition, believed she would not have won if the selection committee knew her by name rather than by number.)[1] But there are also notable differences in the type of work they produce. In architecture and design, drawings must often meet rigid specifications and technical

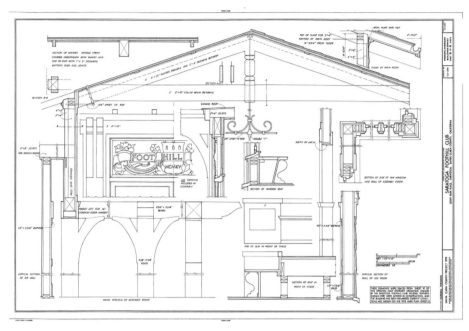

Fig. A. Julia Morgan. Sectional elevation and details, sheet 10, Saratoga Foothill Club, Saratoga, California, ca. 1914–1915. Traced by Barbara Friedman in 1978 for HABS CA-2014.

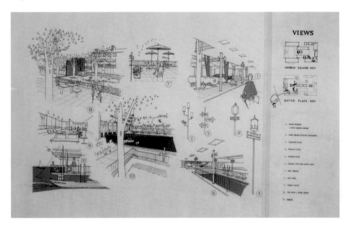

Fig. B. Chloethiel Woodard Smith. Apartment houses, Harbour Square, Washington, DC, between 1962–1969. Gouache on illustration board.

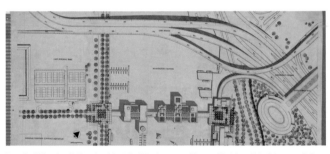

Fig. C. Chloethiel Woodard Smith. Washington Channel Bridge, Washington, DC, plan, 1966. Ink, graphite, and adhesive shading film on mylar.

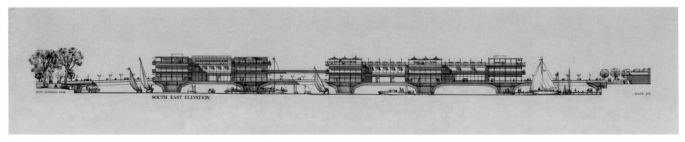

Fig. D. Chloethiel Woodard Smith. Washington Channel Bridge, Southeast elevation, 1966. Ink and adhesive shading film on mylar.

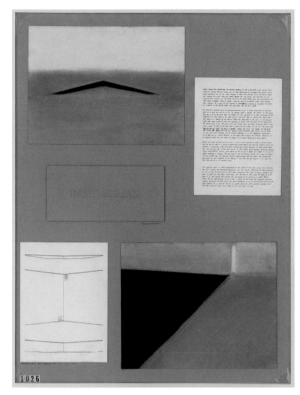

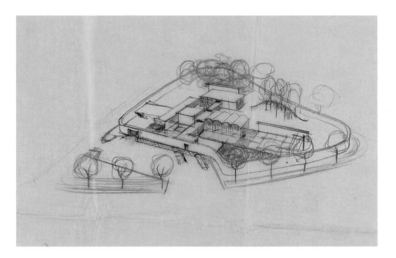

Fig. E. Maya Ying Lin. Panel 1 of 2, entry No. 1026, Vietnam Veterans Memorial Design Competition, 1981. Ink, graphite, colored pencil, and mixed media.

requirements, or give physical structure to an idea or concept. These artists usually draw to meet a client's specific desire—rather than their own—or through their illustrations they develop a visual, two-dimensional archetype of something meant to attract clients.

Julia Morgan, the first woman licensed to practice architecture in California, blazed a trail of blueprints for other women in the field, designing more than a thousand buildings between 1900 and 1950. In addition to her grand structures, including Hearst Castle, she helped shape California's Bay Area Tradition of vernacular architecture reflected in the aesthetic for small-scale buildings, such as the Saratoga Foothill Club (1915) (fig. A).[2] Decades later, another pioneering woman in the field, Washington, DC–based architect and planner Chloethiel Woodard Smith, headed up design projects for residential communities and the Washington Channel Bridge (figs. B–D).[3] In conceiving her prize-winning design for the Vietnam Veterans Memorial (1980–1981) (fig. E), Lin, a twenty-one-year-old Yale architecture student,

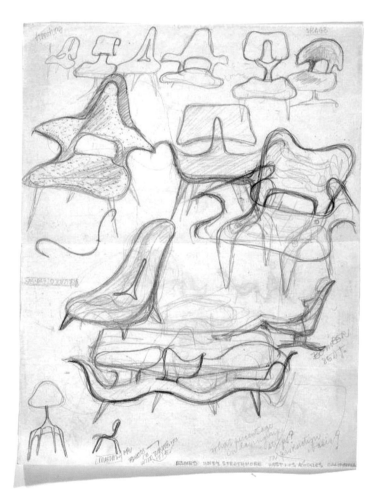

Figs. F and G. Ray Kaiser Eames. Detail of preliminary design sketch, Billy Wilder House project, 1949–1950. Graphite and colored pencil on tracing paper (top). [Design study for lounge chair, with sketches of various chair views], ca. 1948. Graphite (bottom).

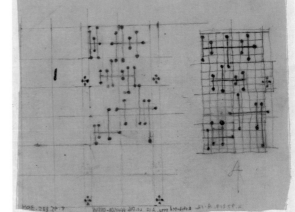

Figs. H and I. Ray Kaiser Eames. Collage design for Eames Office room, *An Exhibition for Modern Living*, Detroit Institute of Art, 1949. Graphite, paper, and photograph collage on paper (left). Abstract drawing for *Dot Pattern* fabric design, ca. 1947. Graphite on tracing paper (right).

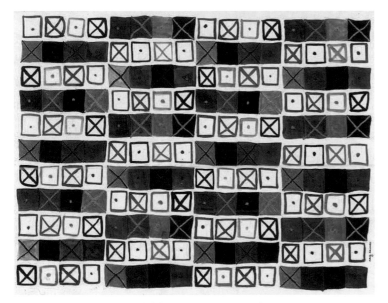

Fig. J. Ray Kaiser Eames. *Crosspatch* fabric design, 1945. Watercolor.

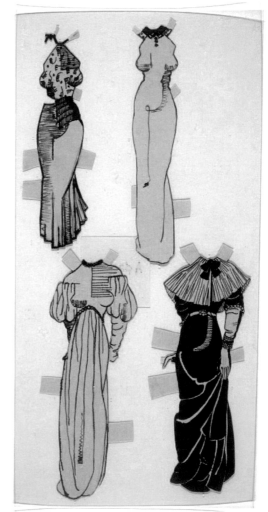

Fig. K. Ray Kaiser Eames. Four red floor-length dresses for a woman paper doll, ca. 1920–1952. Watercolor. Though known primarily for her home furnishing designs, Kaiser also had an interest in fashion.

Figs. L and M. Katherine Lamb Tait. Design for a stained glass window, Suffer the Little Children to Come Unto Me . . . , St. Luke's Church, Bridgeport, Connecticut, ca. 1930s–1940s. Graphite (left). Design for a stained glass window, The Rain Tree, ca. 1930s–1940s. Watercolor, graphite, ink (right). Tait, whose grandfather founded J & R Lamb Studios, began working as a designer there in the 1920s and rose to become head designer. She produced more than one hundred designs for stained glass, mostly of religious subjects.

created a monument that honors the many lives lost in the war and also identifies them as named individuals who are unified into a moving, visual whole. Her spare, beautiful design became a touchstone among memorials, inspiring architectural tributes that have followed.

Ray Kaiser and her husband, Charles Eames, formed a legendary professional partnership whose work in architecture and design transformed the everyday environment of mid-twentieth century America. As a trained architect, Charles took the lead on architectural projects, but Kaiser provided notable input as surviving sketches attest (fig. F). Kaiser's training as a painter imbued her with strong skills in developing designs for both three-dimensional and two-dimensional objects (fig. H). Both contributed to the furniture designs for which the couple is probably best known (fig. G). Most of the firm's drawings for textile designs indicate that she was the primary creator (figs. I and J). However, as the

public face of the Office of Charles and Ray Eames, Charles took credit for much, if not most, of the couple's collaborative work.[4] Architecture critic Joseph Giovannini observed that she was "Assumed to be only a nominal partner—the nurturing wife standing behind the great man—Ray Kaiser was marginalized in the perception of their work, a victim of common contemporary prejudices, which were perpetuated even through her obituaries in 1988. . . . Her career as a designer belonged to Charles."[5]

Other architects, designers, and technical illustrators, however, have succeeded in establishing careers that belonged solely to themselves. Morgan, Woodard Smith, and Lin stand out as notable success stories in that each influenced the development of a specific type of architecture or design. When Lin was in school in 1981, about a quarter of architecture students were women; thirty years later that figure had nearly doubled. In the arts, more than half of designers are women as are more than 20 percent of drafters in

Figs. N and O. Anna Marie Magagna. I'm So Stylish, 1970, and The Long Rope of Pearls, 1973. Ink, marker, gouache, pastel.
For ads run in the *New York Times.* A highly successful fashion illustrator, Magagna also published her work in *Vogue* and
Harper's Bazaar.

architecture-engineering firms. In the twentieth-first century, fashion illustration enjoyed a major revival through social media, as artists—primarily women—gained followings that led to commissions and clients.[6]

"Historically, the recognition of the significant roles and contributions of women in the fields of architecture and design often has been ignored or repressed," said Ford Peatross, founding director of the Center for Architecture, Design and Engineering at the Library of Congress. "This situation has changed dramatically for the better, although the road has not been an easy one. Many women architects and designers study and work on a more equal basis with their male counterparts, and head or define the work of internationally recognized firms and practices. This way was paved in part by the pioneering efforts of women like Julia Morgan, Katherine Lamb Tait, Ray

Eames, Chloethiel Woodard Smith, and Maya Lin. To the benefit of all, a heavy shroud of anonymity has been pulled back, allowing the brilliance of their work at last to shine through."[7]

CHAPTER 4

COMMENTATORS AND REPORTERS

Reflecting two sides of the same coin, editorial illustrators and artist-reporters produce drawings that are grounded in the real world. Both create images informed by their sharp observations of real situations, people, and actions, but each bends her or his skills to meet different goals. Editorial illustrators process their observations into imagery that is more interpretive and can appear literal or metaphorical, with the goal of illuminating their own understanding or commentary on the subject at hand for their viewers. Courtroom illustrators, among the best-known artist-reporters, operate under extreme time constraints to produce drawings that accurately capture and distill the crux of legal proceedings, generating artistic images in settings where cameras are banned. Close contemporaries Frances Jetter and Elizabeth Williams convey essential differences between the two kinds of nonnarrative, reality-based illustration that each practices. In general, practitioners of both types of illustration have pursued art training, employ styles that are representational, and aim to inform their viewers, but each also aims to transcend this goal.

30,000,000 IMMIGRANTS

Fig. 4.1. Bernarda Bryson Shahn. 30,000,000 Immigrants, ca. 1935. Lithograph. Note Ellis Island and the Statue of Liberty in the background.

Fig. 4.2. Bernarda Bryson Shahn. Miner (alternately known as Crippled Miner), ca. 1935. Lithograph.

One artist in particular, however, can be considered an American godmother to editorial and reportorial artists who followed, as she created artworks that incorporated aspects of both during a life that spanned the twentieth century. As an illustrator, printmaker, and painter, Bernarda Bryson (Shahn) (1903–2004) lived a remarkably eventful, productive, and long life. Born in Athens, Ohio, to Charles Harvey Bryson, editor and publisher of the *Athens Morning Journal*, and Lucy (née Weethee), a Latin professor, she began painting at a young age. Bryson's family background undoubtedly led her to develop interests in writing, history, and the "progressive social conscience" that characterizes much of her work. The fact that her maternal grandfather's house was a stop on the Underground Railroad is notable and likely informed thematic choices she later made.[3]

While working as a journalist, she interviewed Diego Rivera in 1933 about his murals for Rockefeller Center in New York City. She got more than a story when she met one of his assistants, the muralist Ben Shahn, who would go on to become a renowned artist himself. The two became devoted lifelong companions but did not marry until shortly before his death in 1969.[4] Bryson moved to New York in 1934 and made lithographs in the Graphics Division of the Public Works of Art Project (fig. 4.1). She also

became a founding member, president, and one of the spokespersons of the Unemployed Artists Union (later the Artists Union). The couple later moved to Washington, DC, and traveled across the country, documenting the lives of rural people during the Great Depression for the federal government's Resettlement Administration. Bryson made lithographs that reflected her perceptions of fellow citizens and demonstrated her keen powers of social observation, her high degree of artistry, and her own "progressive social conscience."

As a strong supporter of New Deal policies, Bryson was inspired by President Franklin D. Roosevelt's references to "a new frontier" in creating a lithographic series that referred not to geography but to human resourcefulness. She presented Rexford Tugwell, Roosevelt's undersecretary of agriculture, a proposal to tell "the continuing story of American—exploration, occupation and settlement of the frontier—then industrialized agriculture, division of the public domain—acquisition of mineral rights, depletion of the forests and the natural resources—waste." She proposed giving visible form to this idea in a book of thirty color lithographs, in which she would take "American society to task on issues such as slavery, labor, economics, and ignorance."[5] Tugwell approved the project.[6]

Bryson made notes and drawings while driving Shahn throughout the South and Midwest as he photographed the landscape and its people for the Historical Section of the Resettlement Administration,

Fig. 4.3. Bernarda Bryson Shahn. Arkansas Sharecropper and Wife, ca. 1935. Lithograph.

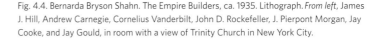

Fig. 4.4. Bernarda Bryson Shahn. The Empire Builders, ca. 1935. Lithograph. *From left*, James J. Hill, Andrew Carnegie, Cornelius Vanderbilt, John D. Rockefeller, J. Pierpont Morgan, Jay Cooke, and Jay Gould, in room with a view of Trinity Church in New York City.

"to provide a record of the faces and human costs of . . . people who might benefit from the relief programs."[7] Both talked with those they photographed or later portrayed. The subject in *Miner* (alternately known as *Crippled Miner* [fig. 4.2]) told them that he had suffered injuries on the job but had received no compensation until Roosevelt was elected president.[8] One sees a similar artistic approach in *Arkansas Sharecropper and Wife* (fig. 4.3). Bryson portrays them in an unsparing, forthright manner, much like her photographer-colleagues who were also documenting the effects of the Depression. Against the backdrop of their run-down housing and withered-looking crops on exhausted land, the man and woman wear worn clothing and expressions of discouragement; the advertisement for "666," a medical tonic for malaria, colds, and fever, reinforces an atmosphere of poor health and misfortune. She used Shahn's photographs and those of other photographers working for the Resettlement Administration, as well as her own notes and observations, in creating these works. Her distillation of poverty-stricken people makes this an exceptional series from the era. To most viewers, the image readily brings to mind Grant Wood's *American Gothic* (1930). Bryson, however, strongly maintained that she did not see the Wood's painting until well after she created the lithograph, which was based on a photograph by Shahn.[9]

One last example synthesizes aspects of form and content that are central to Bryson's overarching objectives for the project. In *The Empire Builders* (fig. 4.4), the same aesthetic is at work—vivid portrayals of figures against a revealing backdrop—but with the addition of lettering. She presents an imaginary group portrait of American financial leaders whose enterprises to a considerable degree hastened the end of the American frontier. Clad in sartorial splendor as befitting their elevated social standing, these titans of industry stand in a tastefully furnished Wall Street setting above the words "Those Christian men to whom God in his infinite wisdom has given control of the property interests of the country." (The line is attributed to George F. Baer, president of the Philadelphia & Reading Coal & Iron Company, when he faced a huge strike of 140,000 miners.) These words provide an ironic description of the self-contained and self-absorbed figures depicted. How Christian was the behavior of these empire builders in their quest to enrich themselves at the expense of public well-being?

Bryson sometimes combined titles with short texts in several other prints in the series, prompting viewers to think about the figures, their situations, and possible futures. This technique, and her plan to publish the images, clearly signals that she intended getting

Fig. 4.5. Bernarda Bryson Shahn. Louis Pasteur, ca. 1940. Ink.

Fig. 4.6. Bernarda Bryson Shahn. Diophantus [of Alexandria], ca. 1940. Ink.

her work and commentary greater distribution and exposure than exhibits in galleries would have offered. But her work on this project and own career stalled with the births of three children and her commitment to supporting Shahn's career. (She assisted him on two mural projects, including *Resources of America* for the Bronx, New York, Post Office in 1939.) Fortunately, a critical mass of lithographs and preparatory drawings from her project survived, and nearly sixty years later, Bryson and Jake Milgram Wien published a portfolio of the work in *The Vanishing American Frontier* (1995).

From the 1940s into the 1970s, Bryson drawings appeared in *Harper's*, *Fortune*, *Life*, *Scientific American*, and the *Atlantic Monthly*. Her portrayals of Louis Pasteur (fig. 4.5) and Greek mathematician Diophantus of Alexandria (fig. 4.6) display impeccably detailed, thin-lined drawing in ink. Showing Pasteur seated with a child gets at the enormous impact that his scientific discoveries, especially pasteurization, had on the health of children. Depicting Diophantus at work imaginatively references the idea of him laboring to

produce *Arithmetica*, the first work known to employ algebra in a modern way. Another drawing (fig. 4.7) published in *Life* in 1958 captures a modern sense of alienation among those in the postwar urban working world. It was not until the mid-1950s that Bryson turned to writing and illustrating children's books, crafting beautifully detailed images in a variety of styles and media that reflect her early exposure to subjects from antiquity.[10]

EDITORIAL ILLUSTRATORS

Editorial illustrators strive to fashion images that deliver a definite message, interpretation, or comment that sets it apart from more purely reportorial and documentary illustration. There is no one definition of editorial illustration, but the consensus holds that it usually accompanies text and may either visually state its contents or add another dimension to the writing that is not visible from reading it.[11] Illustrator Anita

Fig. 4.7. Bernarda Bryson Shahn. "I never want to sit behind a desk again, never want to live that vacant life which would glorify that total commitment to the job which seems to be a precondition for success," 1958. Ink. Published in *Life*, February 17, 1958.

Kunz adds that editorial illustration "also may visually incorporate the opinion of the artist. And because artists have a number of strategies and techniques at our disposal (i.e., distortion, color choice, referral back to previously produced artworks, etc.) the art can also serve to question, elaborate and even inspire a more visceral response to the text."[12] Such responses may be satirical and include caricature, for example. Since the late twentieth century, editorial illustration has evolved as an enlivening feature in magazines and newspaper op-ed pages.

Editorial illustrators reflect a fine art sensibility that generally differs from the aesthetics of political cartoonists. While subject to deadlines, editorial illustrators do not work under the same kind of pressures that cartoonists with daily deadlines and a higher volume of output must endure. Not surprisingly, for women in this field their works often convey strong points of view on women's status and related issues. Their work underscores the great broadening of expression that women pursued and experienced

since the Golden Age of Illustration. When considered collectively, editorial illustrations by Sue Coe, Anita Kunz, Whitney Sherman, and Melinda Beck can be seen to take up the strong thread of social observation and commentary that runs through the print series begun by Bernarda Bryson Shahn in the 1930s.

Sue Coe (b. 1951), a painter, illustrator, and printmaker known for works of scathing commentary on social injustice, grew up in a working-class family near Birmingham, England. Childhood influences, later reflected in her life and art, included her mother, an amateur artist who worked in a doll factory, her own job at a mothball factory, and the fact that the family lived near a hog farm and slaughterhouse. She attended the Chelsea School of Art, then pursued further art training as an illustrator at the Royal College of Art in London.[13] "My work and ideas never fit into the category of cartoonist, or fine artist, or even illustrator," she said, "so I had to create my own art world." She was quite taken by *L'Assiette au Beurre*,

Fig. 4.8. Sue Coe. Union Carbide, 1986. Graphite, gouache, wash.

Fig. 4.9. Sue Coe. Haiti, 1986. Graphite, gouache, wash, collage (letters). From *Police State* series.

an early twentieth-century illustrated French periodical in which artists focused on political topics and themes such as death or vivisection. "The work had the immediacy and urgency of journalism alongside the elegance of drawing," she said, which she found "enthralling."[14] When she came to the United States in 1972, Coe obtained newspaper assignments and her work also appeared in many issues of *Raw*, an influential comics anthology edited by Art Spiegelman and Françoise Mouly. Coe has contributed illustrations to many periodicals including the *New Yorker*, *Entertainment Weekly*, *Time*, and *Rolling Stone*. In creating editorial illustrations and "making pictures for other people's words," she thrived on the challenge of deadlines and "trying to outfox the corporation and get something edgy through the filter."[15]

A longtime advocate for animal rights, Coe also boldly addresses social and political inequality suffered by people and has long protested against American war policies. Using well-honed, fine-lined drawing skills, she executes her paintings and drawings in a

technically accomplished, realistic style described by one as "caricatured realism." Coe and her work exist in two spheres—illustration and fine art. In addition to exhibiting her work widely and often, she has continually sought to distribute it through news media, books, and exhibitions, and, unlike most established artists, to keep her art at affordable prices. Much of her work has been published collections that in varying degrees bear on the works selected for exhibit. The catalog for Coe's 1987 exhibition "Police State" includes informative commentary about each piece, which illustrated connections between corrupt government figures and capitalist entities.

The artist's concern for both humans and animals comes through in *Union Carbide* (1986), her graphic response (fig. 4.8) to the infamous leak of dangerous chemicals from the Indian subsidiary of the American firm Union Carbide Corporation in Bhopal, India, on December 3, 1984. When some forty-five tons of methyl isocyanate gas escaped from this insecticide plant, it drifted over heavily populated areas,

Fig. 4.10. Sue Coe. Bothatcher, 1986. Graphite, gouache, collage. From *Police State* series.

killing and gravely injuring thousands of people.[16] In her drawing, Coe depicts a helmeted figure wearing a grotesque gas mask and an armband with a skull and crossbones, a giant embodiment of omnipotent capitalist power as he sprays poison over the entire world and envelopes the helpless animals below. Note that the globe prominently features North and South America and not India, an indication of Union Carbide's pernicious reach.

In *Haiti* (1986) (fig. 4.9), Coe graphically references capitalists more explicitly, portraying them as vultures in mock business attire, one even sporting a top hat. Both bleed the island of its resources with their talons as a Haitian mother tries to drive them away with a broom.[17] Coe created this drawing soon after Haiti's president, Jean-Claude Duvalier, was overthrown following his brutal fifteen-year dictatorship that was backed by the United States. In her drawing, Coe points out that the forces that supported him and helped impoverish Haiti remain.[18] Her spare use of red in this instance, both literally and

symbolically, signifies the vital harm being done to Haiti, and heightens the searing effect of her dark imagery. She rarely uses red, typically favoring a somber, monochromatic palette of grays, blacks, and white.

Haiti and *Bothatcher* (1986) (fig. 4.10) are both part of a series entitled *Police State*, in which Coe strongly suggests that a "small coalition of big capital, state bureaucrats, threatened bourgeois property owners, and the security forces" are united against downtrodden members of society, such as workers, outsiders, and their supporters.[19] In *Bothatcher*, Coe indicts Britain's prime minister, Margaret Thatcher, and Pieter W. Botha, president of South Africa, for their positions on apartheid. Depicting them as a monstrous double-headed spider whose body sports a swastika, Coe labels the pair as fascist in a visual statement that is radical among artists of the time. Her use of collaged letters is particularly effective in this instance, for it highlights her verbal and visual inventiveness. This drawing exemplifies her ability to channel her moral outrage at Thatcher's refusal to impose sanctions against South Africa and Botha's intractable insistence on maintaining apartheid for as long as possible.

In *War* (1991) (fig. 4.11), Coe returns to a theme that has repeatedly engaged her. In this case, it is the Persian Gulf War that gives rise to one of her most powerful drawings. In front of a great mass of anonymous people in gas masks, grotesque yet also individualized, she depicts a single grieving figure robed in black, who appears female and whose face remains hidden behind her hand. Above the figures, the brilliant orange and yellow sky fairly screams with missiles and fighter jets that ominously streak and crowd the air space. Although tied to a specific, late-twentieth-century war and created for publication in the *Progressive*, this drawing projects timeless, universal associations with war. The bowed, sorrowful woman recalls similar figures portrayed by Käthe Kollwitz, and Coe's figures with gas masks remind one of those by Otto Dix and George Grosz. Coe's mourning figure with her pale, indistinct face also appears disquietingly skull-like, grieving not only for herself, but for all those behind her who are not yet dead, but might soon well be.

Spurred by specific events and trends, Coe also addresses the plight of women in strong graphic

Fig. 4.11. Sue Coe. War, 1991. Watercolor, graphite.

commentary. *Supreme Cruelty* (1991–1992) (fig. 4.12) addresses the conservativism of the Supreme Court following its ruling on *Planned Parenthood of Southeastern Pennsylvania v. Casey*. The case contested a set of burdensome restrictions on abortion enacted in Pennsylvania and challenged the *Roe v. Wade* (1973) decision.[20] Coe portrays justices as vultures balanced on a bare tree limb. The plurality that upheld Roe are perched closer to the tree trunk. Those dissenting are perched more precariously, further "out on a limb," so to speak.[21] Coe underscores her somber assessment by showing the tree growing roots in the shape of swastikas, hangers (symbolic of unsafe abortions), and bodies hanging from the tree, presumably victims of dangerous, illegal abortions. The bodies dangle beneath the dissenting justices. The red sun setting in the distance perhaps portends a narrowly averted state of darkness.

Considered one of the most scathing artists of her time, Coe practices her art with passion focused on specific contemporary events and issues and conveys palpable anger over the impact of human desire for power and control over other living creatures. The

strong, often disturbing visual effects produced by her work arises from her accomplished artistry and belies a fundamental optimism: that the process of witnessing specific, accurately detailed and identified injustices will suffice to inspire change.

Another creator of forceful graphic commentary, native New Yorker Frances Jetter (b. 1951) pursued fine art training and worked for many years in both editorial illustration and fine art. Like Coe, she is passionate about social justice, especially for the underrepresented, but her aesthetic and media preferences are quite different. Strongly influenced by German Expressionists, Jetter creates her illustrations as lino-cuts, a type of print that well suits her bold, linear style with emphatic use of black and white.

Jetter graduated in 1972 from the Parsons School of Design where she majored in photography, although she gravitated toward drawing and creating linoleum cuts when she began showing her work to art directors.[22] Beginning in 1974, her editorial illustrations on social and political issues began to appear in the *New York Times*, the *Washington Post*, *Time*, and elsewhere. Her work has been shown in venues across the United States and in Europe.[23]

Raised in a pro-union family of factory workers, Jetter has long believed that it's "workers against management . . . and that things aren't equal." She found editorial work appealing because it offered her the opportunity to "make the subject matter my own . . . pick parts that I could relate to. The whole idea of playing with things and turning them upside down and finding what the article really meant."[24] Fiercely independent and committed to expressing her own views in her own way even if it has led to rejection by editors, Jetter explains, "If too many people like one of my pieces, I'm immediately suspicious."[25]

She correctly anticipated rejection of one of her most controversial pieces, *The Republican Platform Against Choice* (fig. 4.13), which addressed division in the Republican Party about abortion. After submitting it, she began "'a much tamer piece which they [the editors] had within a couple hours.'" The *Village Voice* subsequently published her rejected print and she used it as the cover for her limited edition artist's book *The Reagan / Bush Years*, published in 1992. Despite the fact that Jetter created an alternate image,

Fig. 4.12. Sue Coe. Supreme Cruelty, between 1991–1992. Graphite, ink, and gouache.

she has worked to remain true to her principles in that she "accepts commissions only for theses that she personally supports."[26] Two other examples demonstrate her capacity to devise powerful visual metaphors in driving home her message. In *Remembering the Iraqi War Dead* (1991) (fig. 4.14), a huge hand from the upper right, possibly symbolic of some almighty power, opens from above to let fall cascades of tiny human skulls. Another illustration uses colanders as coarsening, destructive filters in a metaphor for censorship (fig. 4.15). She portrays this disturbing process in a tiered image that shows fulsome forms of books passing through the upper colander to emerge below as drastically reduced, miniaturized books that are further filtered through the colander head below, from which issue pitiful slips of paper, symbolic of simplified fragmentary thoughts. In *The Rehnquist Court* (1986) (fig. 4.16), the viewer meets rare Jetterian visual humor as a black robed figure beholds the US Supreme Court building, with a massive elongated column leaning to the right, like the leaning Tower of Pisa.

Steadfastly committed to illustration art and internationally acclaimed for her work in the field, Anita Kunz (b. 1956) began drawing at the age of five. Born in Toronto, she grew up in Kitchener, Ontario, Canada, and pursued art training at the Ontario College of Art. She began her career with a series of advertising illustrations for Del Monte Foods, but soon moved toward portraiture and editorial illustration. Through her academic training and exposure to concept-driven art by illustrators such as Coe, Russell Mills, and Marshall Arisman, she was inspired to make content and concept vital components of her art.[27]

From 1988 to 1990 Kunz produced the monthly illustrated endpaper for *Rolling Stone*. She went on to publish cover art and editorial illustrations for leading magazines, and the remarkable range of her work embraces political satire, witty caricature and portraiture, and commentary on economic, health, and social issues. Typically working in watercolor, ink, and occasional collaged elements, she has developed a singular, meticulous drawing technique and realistically detailed style informed by metaphor and imagination,

Fig. 4.13. Frances Jetter. The Republican Platform Against Choice, 1992. Lino-cut. After it was rejected by the *New York Times*, the piece appeared in the *Village Voice* and as the cover of Jetter's book, *The Reagan / Bush Years*, 1992.

Fig. 4.14. Frances Jetter. Remembering the Iraqi War Dead, 1991. Lino-cut. Published with article "A Moment for the Dead," by Lance Morrow, *Time*, April 1, 1991.

Fig. 4.15. Frances Jetter. Textbook Censorship, 1984. Lino-cut. Published with article "Who's on First: The Dumbing of America," by Nat Hentoff, the *Progressive*, February 1984.

Fig. 4.16. Frances Jetter. The Rehnquist Court, 1986. Lino-cut. Published with article "The Rehnquist Court: A Watershed," *New York Times*, June 22, 1986.

Fig. 4.17. Anita Kunz. Tugged, 2001. Water-color, gouache over graphite. Published in *Working Woman*, October 2001.

consistently producing work that is dazzling in technical accomplishment.

Like Coe, Kunz manifests strong interest in the status of women and issues that particularly affect them. She finds their modern quandary—multiple competing demands, expectations, and desires imposed by themselves and others—an especially engaging theme. Her editorial illustration *Tugged* (2001) (fig. 4.17), commissioned by *Working Woman* magazine, offers a thoughtful perspective on the fragmented nature of many women's existences. Tiny faces framed within the symbolic trappings of career and home responsibilities—a briefcase, cell phone, television, and office

block—embody multiple voices of conscience pulling on the figure's hair as she struggles to maintain an air of calm.

Kunz takes an ironic but not unsympathetic approach to her subject in *St. Hillary* (1993) (fig. 4.18). Her illustration illuminated a 1993 feature story for the *New York Times Magazine* about the First Lady, which discussed her views of virtue, politics, and the role of government in peoples' lives. Casting Clinton as St. Joan of Arc, Kunz employs the iconography of Old Master religious portraiture. Replete with halo, upward gazing face, and heroically clad in armor and sword, Kunz's figure of Clinton evokes the patience

Fig. 4.18. Anita Kunz. St. Hillary, 1993. Watercolor and gouache over graphite. Published with a feature article on Hillary Clinton in the *New York Times Magazine*, May 23, 1993.

Fig. 4.19. Anita Kunz. Vulture Capitalism, 2001. Watercolor, gouache over graphite. Published in *Forbes*, April 2, 2001.

Fig. 4.20. Anita Kunz. Hands, 1996. Watercolor, gouache, collage over graphite. Published with article about the global AIDs epidemic, in *Time*, December 30, 1996–January 6, 1997.

and passion of the martyred saint. Although created early in her tenure as First Lady, this symbolic portrait of her as a strong saint appears almost prescient and fitting in light of Clinton's attempt to develop an activist persona in her role then, and the officeholder that she became later. For a piece on investing in the business magazine *Forbes*, Kunz drew *Vulture Capitalism* (2001) (fig. 4.19) in the wake of many telecommunications companies' bankruptcies. The article addressed the practice of "vulture investing," or buying distressed debt securities in the hope of large profitable yields after a company is reorganized. Kunz takes her cue directly from the text and characterizes the investors as human-headed vultures with beak-like noses, wary expressions, and talons that greedily grasp buildings and bundles of currency. Her use of vultures resonates with historical tradition, recalling works by Coe and as far back as Thomas Nast in his graphic indictment of the Tammany machine.

Hands (1996) (fig. 4.20), a poetically expressive painting, is a conceptual response to an article about the global AIDS epidemic and possible treatments and cures for the disease. The viewer can easily infer

multiple meanings in this metaphorical image. Of varied sizes and color, the cluster of different hands underscores the point that AIDS afflicts people of all races and ages, eroding their self-reliance—as symbolized by each beseeching, outstretched hand. The miraculous rays of light toward which the hands expressively reach, however, signal hope for future treatments and cures.

With an international client base, Kunz stands apart from her peers by virtue of her distinctive style and the sheer range of subjects that she addresses.[28] Her paintings not only please, but also often transfix the eye and pull the viewer into a realm of visual metaphor that moves them to ponder the meaning of what is shown.

An award-winning illustrator, Whitney Sherman (b. 1949) is also a multifaceted artist, designer, educator, and lecturer. Born in New Jersey, she grew up in a creative family. She recalls, "My grandmother was an amateur painter, weaver, baker and seamstress, so she inspired me at a very early age, and my parents were very supportive." She completed a BFA in

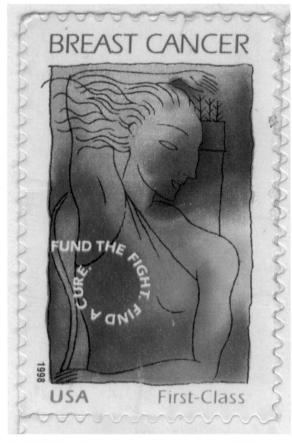

Fig. 4.21. Whitney Sherman. Breast cancer research stamp, 1998.

US Postal Service's first-issue breast cancer research stamp (fig. 4.21), which was the first semi-postal stamp (also known as a charity stamp) issued in the United States.[31] Each stamp was sold at a premium and thus collected money for research on breast cancer. Sherman coordinated with Ethel Kessler, the designer, and created the final art for the stamp, which makes a call for breast self-examination.[32] After many sketches, the decision was made to develop "the image of Artemis, the Greek goddess of the hunt, in line over a field of vibrant color. I struck on this idea of mythology to help represent a figure larger than any one nationality, race or age." Once Sherman had prepared a line drawing that showed "Artemis reaching back for her arrow [to strike the disease,]" the artist then realized that the goddess "was also mimicking the position taken when preparing to do breast self-examination." Rendered in flowing lines inspired by ancient Greek art, the half-figure contains circularly arranged lettering that reads "Fund the Fight Find a Cure" around one breast. Set on a vividly colored background, forms and message coalesce in a dynamic, yet self-contained design. The longest running issue in the US Postal Service, the stamp was later printed in several European countries and raised more than $78 million for research.[33] Although not an editorial illustration, Sherman's stamp artwork fulfills a vital, closely related purpose—to educate, inform, and potentially move viewers to take action.

In a drawing (fig. 4.22) for the 1994 Annual Report for the Robert Wood Johnson Foundation, she depicts a school playground from an elevated viewpoint, showing outlines for hopscotch, a basketball court, and children and adults active within space bounded by trees and bushes. The colorful, busy scene appears appealing at first glance. But very quickly, one sees that much is amiss. Larger figures ride bicycles with wheels that are collaged images of pills, colored capsules of drugs and additional pills ornament the trees and lie along the playground's edges. This drawing brings attention to the need for effective policies on drug-free school zones and the problem of schoolchildren having easy access to drugs. In another piece involving children's issues, Sherman created *Peer Isolation* (2006) (fig. 4.23) for an article on cyberbullying for *Teaching Tolerance*, the Southern Poverty

photography in 1971 at the Maryland Institute College of Art and soon began working in illustration.[29] During her career, she has developed an impressive list of clients that include mainstream newspapers, magazines, and book publishers, in addition to legal and health organizations, and leading institutions of higher education.[30]

Sherman typically begins her creative process with concise line drawing in graphite, enlarges and/or scans the drawing, then incorporates into the altered version varying combinations of media including pastel, gouache, ink, collage, paper, as well as digital color and digitally manipulated drawing. The results are illustrations that convey messages or ideas with layered meanings.

Like Coe and Kunz, Sherman has explored aspects of female identity in her work. Her interests in women's and health issues intersected strikingly in 1998 when she was commissioned to create artwork for the

Fig. 4.23. Whitney Sherman. Peer Isolation, 2006, printed 2013. Archival giclée print. The line art was drawn in graphite on vellum, scanned, and colored digitally. Published in *Teaching Tolerance*, Southern Poverty Law Center, 2006.

Fig. 4.22. Whitney Sherman. [Children Playing on a School Playground Surrounded by Drugs], 1993. NuPastel, ink, photocopy, and collage. The line art was drawn in graphite on vellum, enlarged and photocopied onto paper, colored with NuPastel chalks, ink added, and collage elements adhered with glue stick. Published as part of a series in the 1994 Annual Report for the Robert Wood Johnson Foundation.

Fig. 4.24. Melinda Beck. A Pilgrim in Paris, November 1, 2013. Giclée print. Published in the *New York Times*, November 29, 2013.

Fig. 4.25. Melinda Beck. Hate Speech, 2013. Giclée print. Published in *California Magazine*, December 1, 2013.

Fig. 4.26. Melinda Beck. Why Black Women Die of Cancer, March 1, 2014. Giclée print. Published in the *New York Times*, March 11, 2014.

Law Center's magazine. In her depiction of a dejected youth seated with his hands holding his head, a jagged pink form on the left appears to propel the black circles that revolve around the boy's head. The circles contain words pertaining to bullying and heighten the sensation of the victim's emotional pain. The line art drawn in graphite was scanned and loaded into Photoshop where it was colored digitally.

Another illustrator who combines computer and hand-done work in her art, Melinda Beck (b. 1966), was born and raised in New York City, to parents who were both artists. Beginning her art training early, she took classes in drawing and painting from the fourth grade through high school at the Art Students League. She also studied at the Philadelphia College of Art before attending the Rhode Island School of Design where she completed a BFA in graphic design in 1989.[34] Based in Brooklyn, New York, Beck recalls being unsatisfied early in her career at a corporate design firm. After her husband-to-be showed her portfolio to one of his clients, new assignment offers followed. She was eventually able to leave her full-time graphic design job to work on her own at home.

Beck's stylistic approach is always changing and developing, part of an effort to keep moving forward and not become bored. Her creative process begins with quick thumbnail sketches, including words. She also looks at art books for mental stimulation or inspiration.[35] Most of her work is born digital in its final form, although it often comprises layers that are hand-drawn, hand-produced (including woven string or wire forms), hand-lettered, scanned and colored or enhanced digitally. She works in several styles: silhouette, pen and ink, and graphic. She employs the third, that she terms graphic, in *A Pilgrim in Paris* (2013) (fig. 4.24), published with an opinion piece "The Lament of the Expatriate," by Patricia Druckerman in the *New York Times*. In this playful, whimsical image, Beck pokes gentle fun at the notion of Americans being radically changed or defiled by experience in the cosmopolitan city of Paris. Despite being wide-eyed and youthful, the visitor appears resolutely prim and pilgrim-like amid the picturesque playground of landmarks and quaintly decorative buildings.

Other editorial illustrations demonstrate how effectively Beck conveys strong social commentary in her unique silhouette style, which stems from a historical tradition of silhouette portraiture practiced by Charles Willson Peale in the eighteenth century. Working in this mode, Beck incorporates expressive silhouettes and frequently includes limbs or other body parts formed with wire or string, lettering by hand, and patterned borders. *Hate Speech* (2014) (fig. 4.25) graphically enhances an article entitled "You Can't Say That! Is It Time to Write the Epitaph for Epithets?" by Glen Martin for the spring issue of *California Magazine*. The title and searing imagery combine to drive home the message that hate speech is ugly and hateful. Beck constructs her illustration with visual layers of meaning. The central form, a silhouetted profile head, is riddled with holes through which an ominously red spiked snake-like form weaves in and out, emanating from a mouth filled with small, short, rodent-like teeth, as if to associate the line of red speech with the lowest of creatures. The border surrounding this troubling hybrid at first glance appears decoratively botanic, but a closer look suggests a crown comprising thorns, insects, and other signifiers of decay and destruction.

Beck employs her signature style to bold effect in work spanning her career. In an early example of her editorial work, *Racism/Sexism* (1991) (fig. 4.27), she uses an asymmetrical design, showing a young woman's face bisected diagonally, half white, half black.

Fig. 4.27. Melinda Beck. Racism/Sexism, 1991. Ink on scratchboard. Published in the *Village Voice*, 1991.

Executed in scratchboard and visually quite different from her later work, this illustration connects with aspects of Beck's future development. She remains attuned to racial inequality, for example, and incorporates symbolic forms more skillfully as narrative elements in her composition. In the stark *Why Black Women Die of Cancer* (2014) (fig. 4.26) a woman in silhouette, bent and ailing, sits on a stool amid a mass of snake-like tassels, emblematic of overwhelming obstacles or hurdles to be overcome in treatment, Beck comments pointedly that black women face greater challenges in pursuing treatment than white women.

Beck's early editorial illustration offers an instructive contrast with a later drawing, *Illustrating Illustration* (also titled *Just Another Day on My Desk*, from 2008) (fig. 4.28) for the Kilkenny County Council. Not only does it feature her silhouette style, it also underscores a notable aspect of her approach to

Fig. 4.28. Melinda Beck. Illustrating Illustration, June 1, 2008. Giclée print. Produced for Kilkenny County Council.

illustration—the use of found objects and words. Whitney Sherman chose to feature Beck's drawing on the cover of her book *Playing with Sketches* (2014) and describes her drawing as "a veritable instruction book for how [she] makes imagery from found objects, including vegetables, string, nuts, wire, paper tags, nails, tape, washers, and paper." If one begins reading the whole at the upper left, an attentive reader is rewarded with fascinating glimpses into Beck's creative process.

Jillian Tamaki, introduced in chapter 3 for her graphic narrative work, also creates editorial illustrations. In a standout example published in the *Guardian* (UK), entitled *Now & Then & When* (2008) (fig. 4.29), Tamaki converts the autobiographical, an innately personal art form, into a universal statement of the human female condition. She approached a time-honored theme in graphic art, the ages of a person from cradle to grave, from a partly autobiographical, partly speculative point of view. Within a two-panel horizontal, she depicted herself as a central, monumental figure, flanked by smaller full-length figures of herself getting progressively older. Her variation on the theme with figures in bathing

Figs. 4.29 and 4.30. Jillian Tamaki, Now & Then & When, 2008. Ink and graphite. Published in the *Guardian*, December 31, 2008. James Baillie. The life and age of woman, stages of woman's life from the cradle to the grave, ca. 1848. Lithograph, hand-colored. Tamaki harks back to and makes use of a centuries-old tradition that sets forth the stages of life conventionally experienced by women. Her depictions of herself in bathing suits at various ages are an amusing contrast between contemporary personal self-portrayals (including future imagined ones) and James Baillie's early nineteenth-century images of a generalized female figure. Seeing the two works side by side invites reflection on differing ways artists have approached the experience of being female—from a female perspective versus a male view, with humor and wit versus moralizing, generic versus personal.

CHAMPIONS OF BOOK CULTURE

Going beyond traditional book illustration and collected works, Sue Coe and Frances Jetter each developed a distinct type of book that features her artistic commentary on political and social issues. Although both provide online access to their art, maintaining a connection with book culture still matters: books offer an element of prestige and permanence and are part of a long cultural tradition. Their tangible, physical presence also provides a sense of value and pride in ownership. For Coe, "Books are the most important form for my work. . . . I am not as comfortable with words, but more comfortable with my words than anyone else's. Books can become reportage/visual journalism and show sequential images. . . . As soon as I could go feral, and start to make my own books, I did."[36]

Among Coe's many publications,[37] some released in tandem with solo exhibitions of her work, her earliest titles focus on the deaths of high-profile crusaders Stephen Biko and Malcolm X and social injustice.[38] She later turned her attention to the meat industry and conducted her own extensive investigations of slaughterhouses. This resulted in several books, including *Sheep of Fools* (2005) and *Cruel* (2012), each with a compelling cover design and graphic images of animals shown as beautiful beings, but also caught in the throes of horrible suffering as they are slaughtered.

Coe found success both inside and outside the world of fine art, but prefers making her art, especially prints and posters, accessible and affordable to many in book form. Having her art discussed and understood interests her far more than having it sold, and publishing affordable book collections further disseminates her work in an accessible and permanent format.[39]

Taking a different approach, Jetter has created handmade, limited edition artists' books, all executed in lino-cuts combined with letter press, to visually highlight themes that resonate with disturbing current events or trends but that also reference time-honored tropes. In *The Reagan / Bush Years* (1992), she sharply articulates her views on women's reproductive rights, censorship, and income inequality in bold, expressionist images, some of which employ historically inflected metaphors.[40] Jetter's monumental, large format book *Cry Uncle* (2009), with its accordion-fold pages that extend some forty feet when opened, powerfully decries specific practices of torture (fig. 4.31).[41] This and other books by Jetter are works of art unto themselves, part of a lineage tracing back to the Renaissance works of Albrecht Dürer. In her *Street of Booksellers* (2012), which uses a carved wooden ribcage for the cover, she invokes the voices of deceased poets to mourn the destruction wrought by a car bomb that exploded on al-Mutanabbi Street, where Baghdad's book vendors congregated.

Coe publishes carefully designed book compilations of her art accompanied by thoughtfully written text by herself or others. Jetter treats books as art objects that, while few in number, are more accessible than her stand-alone prints. For both artists, the very act of publication underscores their underlying motivation to share their views in a tactile, meaningful way with an audience beyond those who can view their original art firsthand in galleries and museums.

Fig. 4.31. Frances Jetter. *Cry Uncle,* 2009. Accordion-fold book of lino-cuts with text, over forty feet long unfolded.

Fig. 4.32. Marilyn Church. Jean Harris Trial, 1981. Colored pencil and water-soluble crayon on ochre paper.

suits, related vignettes and speech balloons, presents an updated counterpart to the demure figures and texts of artistic precedents seen in popular historical prints (fig. 4.30). Tamaki's rendition is all the more poignant for using herself as the subject and creating her drawing while in the flower of her own youth.

COURTROOM ILLUSTRATORS: DRAWING THE DRAMA

On trial for murder, defendant Jean Harris, elegantly attired and coiffed, loses her composure after a revealing letter she wrote to Dr. Herman Tarnower is read in court (fig. 4.32). Marilyn Church homed in on this pivotal moment in the sensational high-profile 1980 case, creating in short order strong likenesses of prosecutor George Bolen, Judge Russell Leggett, and Harris, but

also suggesting some empathy for the former school headmistress as she lowers her head, pulling her hands toward her chest as if to shield herself. What can be a life-changing moment on the witness stand for one person might also be just another day at the office for the veteran courtroom sketch artist. Charged with creating objective visual records under tight deadlines, courtroom illustrators depict astutely observed legal proceedings while striving simultaneously to make these scenes visually compelling pictures, portraying key players at moments of high drama.

Courtroom illustrators form a small, select group that includes a high proportion of women and occupies a unique part of the documentary and reportorial tradition. Nell Brinkley, one of America's earliest known women in cartooning (see chapter 2), was assigned to cover an especially sensational court case, the second trial of Harry Thaw for the murder

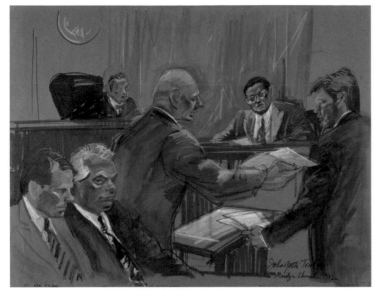

Fig. 4.33. Marilyn Church. John Gotti Trial, 1992. Colored pencil, graphite, felt tip pen, and water-soluble crayon on ochre paper.

Fig. 4.34. Marilyn Church. John Gotti Trial, 1992. Colored pencil, felt tip pen, and water-soluble crayon on ochre paper.

after the "circus" atmosphere that resulted from press coverage of the Lindbergh trial two years earlier. Consequently, a whole new genre opened for artists who could draw quickly and accurately under pressure. Not surprisingly, many courtroom illustrators who trained as fine artists did not intentionally pursue this niche specialty; instead, news editors wanting to enhance their legal reportage sought them out. Most of these artists work with newspaper and television reporters who indicate what kind of imagery is most desired for visual coverage. As Sara Duke, curator of Popular and Applied Graphic Art at the Library of Congress, noted, changes in policy and budgets has made it more difficult for courtroom artists to make a living at it. "As television becomes less willing—or able—to pay for illustrators, the artists either work fewer days per trial, the media uses a 'pool' artist (meaning that one artist enters the courtroom and all of the media outlets use the resulting drawings), or the trial is covered by photographers outside the courtroom. Expedient or not—it definitely changes how people learn about trials from the media."[43] Conditions for drawing also vary from case to case, as it is the presiding judge who decides where artists sit and work, but whether parked in the front or back row, these illustrators create recognizable portrayals and, ideally, visually capture the atmosphere. Since drawings must be finished the same day they are created for news media use, the artist's ability to quickly execute well-designed, easily read drawings with telling details in appearance, expression, and attitude is essential.

Marilyn Church (b. 1941) was born in Flushing, New York, the third of five children. Her father, a urologist, and her mother, a nurse, urged her to pursue a more conventional career path than art. As a compromise with her mother, she entered Pratt Institute's School of Fashion Design, but found it "too constricting" and an alternative, art education, proved equally dissatisfying. In 1959 she completed a BFA at Pratt. Robert Richenburg, an abstract expressionist painter, was one of her professors. After years as a freelance illustrator and graduate student, a lawyer suggested that she try courtroom illustration. She followed up, attending the trial of a Queens, New York, district attorney accused of misconduct. Sitting behind other

of famed architect Stanford White, in January 1908. Brinkley, then only twenty-one years old, joined veteran journalist Dorothy Dix as the only two women of the press on site. Brinkley's portraits of Thaw's famous and beautiful wife, Evelyn Nesbitt Thaw, who was the real center of public fascination, ran in the *New York Evening Journal* for the duration of the trial.[42]

In 1937, news cameras were banned from federal courtrooms, and many state courts followed suit

Fig. 4.35. Pat Lopez. Whitewater, Little Rock, ABC News, Clinton Testimony, April 28, 1996. Colored pencil.

artists, Church became engrossed as she drew. She later commented, "That's when I said, 'I can do this. This is great.'"[44] She would later find that, "Of all the different kinds of illustration I have done, the courtroom, with its high drama of history-making decisions, the skilled performances of attorneys, and always the challenge of same-day deadline, offers the most exciting and rewarding experience of my career."[45]

By 1976, Church identified herself as a courtroom artist as well as an illustrator and painter, and during a career of some thirty-six years, she chronicled major trials for the *New York Times*, ABC, and other outlets. Her courtroom art has featured both the famous and infamous, including subway vigilante Bernard Goetz, former boxer Rubin "Hurricane" Carter, "Dapper Don" Mafioso John Gotti, and celebrities Martha Stewart, Woody Allen, and Mia Farrow.[46] According to Church, "The principal players have to be recognizable, and the drawing has to be organized so that a viewer can understand it in three seconds on television. Since

there is never enough time to include every feature, each drawing is a compromise. I'm forced to choose whether to create an exact portrait, emphasize the scope of the courtroom, zero in on some expressive gesture, or include the judge's reaction."[47]

Two of her drawings from notable cases highlight the challenges in courtroom art. The trial of Jean Harris for the murder of Dr. Herman Tarnower, best-selling author of *The Complete Scarsdale Medical Diet*, in White Plains, New York, entailed the story of a woman scorned. Harris, the elegant, poised head-mistress of the Madeira School in McLean, Virginia, had been romantically involved for fourteen years with Tarnower when she was displaced by a younger woman and "became a surrogate for every discarded wife, every aging girlfriend, and every middle-aged woman who has watched her mate drift into the orbit of a younger lover."[48] As Church commented, "During the trial, I found it difficult to reconcile the two Jean Harrises. I saw the one who ran the elite girls' prep

Fig. 4.36. Pat Lopez. Abu Ghraib, Graner, January 2005. Colored pencil.

complained to her that she had not depicted the boss's hairline accurately, and on another day, Gotti himself gestured to her, pointing to his neck, which she understood to mean as a warning, "Don't draw my neck fat anymore. I'm watching you."[51]

Patricia Ann Lopez (b. 1954) came to American courtrooms by a circuitous route. Born into a military family, Lopez grew up in Bavaria. While living abroad she traveled around Europe enjoying art museums and cathedrals. She pursued her artistic interests at Southwestern Oklahoma State University, graduating with a degree in art education and commercial art in 1979.[52] Soon afterward, an Oklahoma City television station hired her to cover the ten-month *Silkwood v. Kerr-McGee* trial. Union activist and laboratory technician Karen Silkwood had died in 1974, and her family sued the chemical company for damages; the jury awarded them $10 million. During the trial Lopez met artist Howard Brodie, her idol, who was well known for his courtroom and war art. She recalls being embarrassed because the figures she drew were so "wooden," but Brodie told her she had talent and encouraged her to persevere.[53]

After an ABC-TV affiliate in Dallas hired her in 1985 solely to do courtroom work, her career advanced rapidly. Lopez covered many high-profile trials including the cases of Whitewater (fig. 4.35), Oklahoma City bombers Timothy McVeigh and Terry Nichols, the Waco Branch Dravidian Cult, Enron and Arthur Anderson, Matthew Shepherd's killers, and Abu Ghraib prison military personnel. The 1997 Oklahoma City bombing trials brought Lopez national recognition, and she donated her drawings to the Oklahoma National Memorial Museum, saying, "I did not want to sell this art for profit, because this trial was a part of Oklahoma and US history."[54]

For Lopez, "each drawing can take as little as 30 minutes," adding that her style is "representational and very realistic. . . . It does take more time and more effort, and because of that I've earned the right to take my time doing the drawings."[55]

Two drawings from her coverage of the Abu Ghraib trials at Fort Hood, Texas, in 2005, show other aspects of her approach to courtroom illustration. Her depiction (fig. 4.36) of Charles Graner Jr., formerly of the US Army, with his lawyer, Guy Womack, excludes

school . . . and the one who could cut the new mistress' clothing to shreds in a rage."[49] At that pivotal moment when a distraught Harris imploded, Church "could feel only empathy for . . . Harris. This drawing depicts a scene of complete humiliation for her. . . . Even the jurors seemed uncomfortable. I wanted to show her literally sinking into the witness stand."[50]

The 1992 case of John Gotti, head of the Gambino crime family, posed challenges of a different kind. While many of her drawings from the trial are riveting close-up views of Gotti, his lawyers, and key witnesses, Church also found vantage points from which to produce overall views. One such scene (fig. 4.34) shows Gotti and co-defendant Frank Locascio seated as lawyers Anthony Cardinale, John Mitchell, and Albert Krieger and Judge I. Leo Glasser listen to recordings. This scene effectively conveys the many legal personnel and amount of technical equipment used during the proceedings, in which tape-recorded evidence proved significant in the trial's outcome. Church captures Gotti's strong visual presence and watchful eye (fig. 4.33), incorporating details, such as his blow-dried hair and expensive clothing. She learned that Gotti knew which artists, reporters, and media outlets were covering his trial. His brother once details of setting, focusing entirely on bust-length likenesses: the men's serious expressions are striking even in profile, and Graner's powerful form dominates the whole, suggesting a strong, perhaps overbearing personality. In contrast, in the court-martial trial of Lyndie England, who was under Graner's command (fig. 4.37), England appears small and vulnerable, seated between lawyers Rick Hernandez and Captain Jonathan Crisp. Compared with Lopez's depiction of Graner, her rendering of England, while also realistic, emphasizes her much smaller physique and reminds viewers of her greater physical vulnerability amid officers above her in rank. To some degree viewers might read a slight hint of sympathy toward England. Despite suggestions of empathy on the part of Church and Lopez toward female defendants in complex cases, each illustrator managed to maintain an overall tone of neutrality that prevails in the bulk of their drawings.

Unlike most of her peers, Aggie Whelan Kenny is mostly self-taught, and began courtroom work in 1973.[56] Born in Worcester, Massachusetts, she pursued assignments across the nation, producing remarkable visual coverage of many well-known US Supreme Court cases for nearly three decades.

Hired to cover the 1974 trial of former US attorney general John Mitchell and former secretary of commerce Maurice Stans, who were charged with trying to prevent a federal investigation, she was seated so far from the proceedings that she used opera glasses. Despite the challenge, she produced illustrations of such high quality that she earned an Emmy for her work that appeared on *The CBS Evening News with Walter Cronkite*.[57] Among these drawings, her portrayal of FBI witness Mark Felt (fig. 4.38) demonstrates her ability to capture detailed likenesses. She carefully captioned her drawing, noting his name and the trial, years before Felt revealed his long-concealed identity as the Watergate scandal's intriguing secret informer, Deep Throat. This example highlights an ongoing challenge for her peers and herself "when there are often myriads of witnesses, you have to try to figure out who's important and who isn't. In this case, I certainly didn't know how important Mark Felt was."[58]

Elizabeth Williams (b. 1957) pursued a more typical career path on her way to the nation's courtrooms. A

Fig. 4.37. Pat Lopez. Abu Ghraib, England Court Martial, May 2005. Colored pencil.

Fig. 4.38. Aggie Kenny. Mark Felt at Mitchell Stans Trial, 1974. Pastel, watercolor, and graphite on blue paper.

native of upstate New York, she graduated from the Parsons School of Design in 1979.[59] Like Church, she had training in fine art and fashion illustration and early on, imagining "a glamorous career in fashion illustration. . . . Instead I was detoured into drawing courtroom scenes and images of mobsters and murderers and white collar criminals."[60] Williams began her career doing general publication illustration

Fig. 4.39. Elizabeth Williams. *Bernard Madoff Going to Jail after His Guilty Plea*, 2009.
Pastel and watercolor on tan paper.

assignments. The decline in art budgets, the rise of stock illustration, and the widespread use of Photoshop software adversely affected the market for her work, prompting her to try court illustration, which became a mainstay of her professional output. She tackled her first big case in 1984, the trial of John DeLorean, the American engineer famed for designing his eponymous DMC-12 sports car.[61]

Her courtroom drawings typically contain detailed depictions of key figures and setting that distinguish her work as particularly accomplished, despite her lament that she has too little time to craft pieces that she considers finished. She developed a well-honed "news sense," a feel for perceiving and rapidly drawing a defining moment in court proceedings. Williams, for example, was the only artist on the scene when Ponzi scheme perpetrator Bernie Madoff pled guilty and was sent away in handcuffs to jail (fig. 4.39). "I knew that was the moment everybody wanted to see. It wasn't a great drawing or anything, it was more like a great moment . . . you can't be so concerned about the artwork, you just gotta get it down . . . sometimes we send out stuff we're not so crazy about sending out."[62]

CHAPTER 5

COVERS
AND CARTOONS

You can't judge a book by its cover, but a magazine isn't so lucky—its personality is defined by its cover, and the rest of the magazine has to stand behind it.

—FRANÇOISE MOULY, cofounder of *Raw* magazine[1]

Many women illustrators in the late nineteenth and early twentieth centuries found outlets for their drawings in the pages of American magazines, and more rarely, on their covers. In a similar fashion, women cartoonists during this period, particularly those who specialized in humor or gag cartoons, appeared most often in the pages, but gradually had their work featured on covers. For thousands of magazines, cover art was the critical means of attracting readers. Even those who did not purchase magazines but saw them on newsstands, neighbors' coffee tables, or in waiting rooms were exposed to this vibrant platform and could hardly fail to notice covers designed to lure the eye and intrigue the curious. For artists, winning a cover assignment signified professional success, and cover art is commonly valued at more than twice the amount for drawings for internal pages.

Cover artists have identified themselves variously as cartoonists, or illustrators, or as both. This is fitting, given that cover art often incorporates features that are commonly recognized as characteristic of both

The best cartoons are exquisite explosive devices. When they are constructed just so, they produce an explosion (our laughter), but when they are not, they don't.

—DAVID REMNICK, New Yorker editor-in-chief[2]

art forms. Although photography and innovative typography transformed cover design beginning in the mid-1930s, cartoons and illustrated covers have never gone out of style.[3] With the burgeoning of illustrated magazine publishing in America in the late nineteenth century, cover designs came to provide visual identities, much like posters or calling cards, for magazines' contents. Female cartoonists and illustrators began to contribute to this art form as both the New Woman emerged and the suffrage movement grew.

MAGAZINES, A PUBLISHING PHENOMENON

After the Civil War the publishing industry expanded rapidly, injecting vigor and self-awareness into the nation's prospering economy. In the ensuing decades, the phenomenal growth in the number and variety of periodicals coincided with the "Golden Age of Illustration," as discussed in chapter 1. Compulsory public education prompted rising literacy rates and fueled the demand for a wide range of reading material, from the general to the esoteric. During this critical period, readers avidly sought magazines for self-improvement, entertainment, in-depth news coverage, instruction in daily living, and the like. Poised halfway between local newspapers and the world of books, magazines lack the immediacy of the former and depth of the latter, yet they held and still hold strong appeal as a convenient form of publication that introduces new ideas, explains current trends in a timely manner, and offers a national frame of reference.

Illustrated periodicals had become well established in the marketplace before the Civil War and such major early titles as *Leslie's Weekly* (1855–1922) and *Harper's Weekly* (1857) endured, but they did not always identify the artists whose work they published. Both appear to have published little if any work by women early on, but in the postwar years, some women illustrated fiction and poetry in *Harper's* titles. Considered more prestigious than newspapers by artists, magazines are typically printed on higher-quality paper, offer more opportunities for color printing, and their longer lead times commonly allow artists more time to create, produce, and finesse their work. Advances in color printing marked by development of the rotary color press in the 1890s and the increasingly visible role of advertisements in magazines brought more potential outlets for illustrators and cartoonists.

Titles intended to appeal mainly to men include *Puck* (1877–1918) and *Esquire* (1933 on); titles primarily for women, who had become dominant consumers in the marketplace, include *Good Housekeeping* (1885 on), *Ladies' Home Journal* (1883 on), *Women's Home Companion* (1873–1957), and *Family Circle* (1932 on). General interest titles encompassed the *Saturday Evening Post* (1898 on), the original *Life* (1883–1936) and *Vanity Fair* (1914–1936), and the *New Yorker* (1925 on). The latter two deliberately sought and attracted sophisticated, metropolitan clienteles.

The rise of photography and photojournalism, in addition to the development of half-tone printing in the 1890s, set in motion the gradual waning of illustration art in magazines. These factors combined with the growing use of typography as a key design element in periodicals would slowly but inexorably reduce the numbers of plum assignments for illustrators. It would take decades, however, before dwindling numbers of once high-profile magazines would abandon or cut back drastically on the use of cover art drawn by artists and cartoons in their pages. It is notable that such titles as *Time*, *Sports Illustrated*, *Ms. Magazine*, *Village Voice*, and, most significantly, the *New Yorker*, continue to publish cover designs and other art signed by illustrators; in addition, the *Washington Post* and the *New York Times* regularly publish credited works of art on their magazine covers, op-ed pages, and in review sections. E-zines and other online publications also proactively seek and publish work by illustrators.

The versatile Rose O'Neill was among the few women whose work appeared both in the pages and on the covers of a leading humor magazine, *Puck*. In the 1910s and 1920s, illustrator-cartoonists such as Ethel McClellan Plummer and Ann Harriet Fish created *Vanity Fair* cover designs that featured poised young women sporting the latest fashions and enjoying pastimes. Cover art by Alice Beach Winter and Ilonka Karasz for the radical leftist periodical the *Masses* depart from the former in tone and content, reflecting its more weighty interests, such as exploited workers and racism, which did not lend themselves to cheerful visual effects, as in the case of Winter's woeful child laborer.

In succeeding decades, Helen E. Hokinson, Alice Harvey, Barbara Shermund, Roberta MacDonald, and Dorothy McKay created numerous witty gag cartoons that showed women in domestic, social, and occasional workplace settings. These cartoonists' works enlivened the pages of mainstream magazines such as the *New Yorker*, *Women's Home Companion*, and *Esquire*. A few of these female cartoonists also had cover designs published. Contemporary cartoonists or illustrators Liza Donnelly, Victoria Roberts, Anita Kunz, Roz Chast, and Maira Kalman have broken into the ranks of those published in the *New Yorker*, but also found other notable outlets for their work.

EARLY ENTRIES

When Rose O'Neill made her way to New York City in 1893 to pursue her career, she blazed a well-drawn trail for women seeking a foothold in the competitive world of magazine illustration and cartooning. Lodging with the Sisters of St. Regis in New York, O'Neill was accompanied by two nuns when she first made the rounds of magazine publishing offices to sell her work.[4] She initially sold work to *Puck* and *Truth*, but soon found outlets in *Life, Ladies' Home Journal, Cosmopolitan, Harper's Bazaar*, and *Good Housekeeping*. Hard-working and astonishingly prolific, O'Neill produced more than seven hundred cartoons and other drawings for *Puck* alone over a period of eight years.[5] This was an impressive achievement for a woman working for the leading humor magazine and one whose readership was predominantly male.

Among O'Neill's stunning drawings for *Puck*, several convey her skeptical view of social relations between men and women. In one example, *His Full Name* (1900) (fig. 5.1), a timid census-taker queries the overbearing, pipe-smoking lady of the house who mocks her husband's claim as head of household. Her ample size visually reinforces the point. Among the hundreds of drawings O'Neill produced for *Puck*, quite a few surviving examples make fun of men.

Fig. 5.1. Rose O'Neill. His Full Name, July 1900. Graphite, ink brush. Published in *Puck*, August 8, 1900.

Fig. 5.2. Rose O'Neill. Signs, 1904. Black crayon and black ink over pencil, with opaque white on off-white wove paper. Published in *Puck*, August 17, 1904.

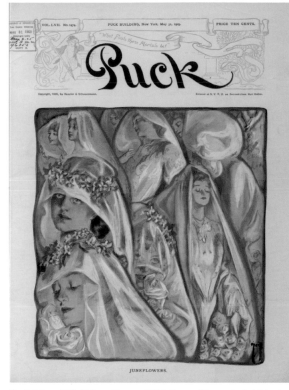

Fig. 5.3. Rose O'Neill. June Flowers, 1905. Chromolithograph. Published as cover, *Puck*, May 31, 1905.

In *Signs* (1904) (fig. 5.2), another typical example, a mother wisely counsels her daughter about a suitor.

O'Neill's distinctive, less than sunny perspective on courtship and marriage undoubtedly did not mirror prevailing social attitudes of the era, and possibly fed into the creation of *June Flowers*, a cover she created for *Puck* in 1905 (fig. 5.3). When she completed this seasonal design, she had divorced her first husband and begun a difficult second marriage, facts that likely shaped her approach. Some of O'Neill's brides appear subdued, and not joyful. Note the figure on the far right, whose downcast gaze and enveloped form could be read in more than one way. Her closed form and bland expression or mood could suggest maidenly modesty, or perhaps apprehension at possible constraints that marriage might impose.

O'Neill produced at least five cover designs for *Puck*. Another example that features female figures, *The Next Candidate for Statehood* (fig. 5.4), from the December 18, 1901, issue, invites a close look. She depicts the allegorical figure of Miss Columbia meeting a young girl in Hispanic dress, who represents the territory "New Mexico." Miss Columbia, personification of the United States, hands her a white dress typical of the era's feminine attire; it is labeled "Statehood" and contrasts with New Mexico's colorful ensemble. Columbia, in starred and striped drapery and Liberty cap, reinforces the idea of national identity, in contrast with the regional identity embodied by New Mexico. These visual clues suggest that New Mexico will need to sacrifice aspects of regional identity in order to become a state—a goal eventually achieved in 1912. O'Neill's depiction of Columbia as a dominant, allegorical figure accords with other cartoonists' and illustrators' portrayals of her in the early twentieth century. Given the largely political content of *Puck*, it is also likely that O'Neill was assigned this cover theme, rather than proposing it herself.[6]

Another cartoonist-illustrator, Brooklyn-born Ethel McClellan Plummer (1888–1936), published at least seven cover designs for *Vanity Fair* from 1914 to 1918. In her covers for the June 1914, August 1916, and May 1917 issues she employed a streamlined aesthetic, depicting stylish, flattened female figures defined by sophisticated use of bold lines, pattern, and color. Compared with the earlier Gibson Girl ideal, Plummer's young women in the 1914 cover (fig. 5.5) feature a slimmer, new model of American beauty. Her figures convey an awareness of themselves as fashionable, urban beings in their attitudes; their direct gazes communicate a poise and confidence that became hallmarks of the modern woman. This example offers an appealing invitation to *Vanity Fair*, then on the verge of becoming a leading magazine. More than a source for the latest fashions, the magazine attracted educated readers seeking intelligent, witty coverage of the latest in performing and visual arts, books, humorous writing, and sports. The other cover drawing features a young couple attending races (fig. 5.6).

Well known in her time, Plummer developed an unusually prominent professional profile. In addition to creating pro-suffrage artwork, she drew portrait sketches, painted, and produced drawings for *Vogue*, *Life*, *Women's Home Companion*, and the *New York Tribune*, and in 1925 she was the first woman to have a cartoon published in the *New Yorker*, although relatively few of her cartoons appeared there after that.[7] She exhibited in the 1910 landmark Exhibition of

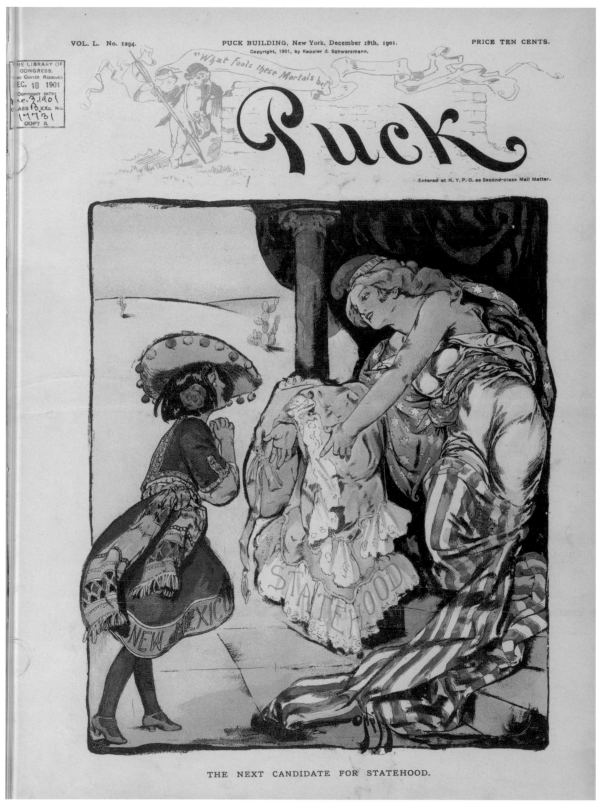

VOL. L. No. 1294.   PUCK BUILDING, New York, December 18th, 1901.   PRICE TEN CENTS.
Copyright, 1901, by Keppler & Schwarzmann.

"What fools these Mortals be!"

Puck

Entered at N. Y. P. O. as Second-class Mail Matter.

NEW MEXICO

STATEHOOD

THE NEXT CANDIDATE FOR STATEHOOD.

Fig. 5.4. Rose O'Neill. The Next Candidate for Statehood, 1901. Chromolithograph. Published as cover, *Puck*, December 18, 1901.

Fig. 5.5. Ethel McClellan Plummer, Vanity Fair on the Avenue. India ink, gouache, and watercolor over pencil. Published as cover, *Vanity Fair*, June 1914.

Fig. 5.6. Ethel McClellan Plummer. Couple at the Races. India ink, gouache over pencil. Published as cover, *Vanity Fair*, July 1916.

Independent Artists organized by Robert Henri and John Sloan, and the 1915 Exhibition of Painting and Sculpture by Women Artists for the Benefit of the Woman Suffrage Campaign in New York.[8] She also served as vice president of the Society of Illustrators and Artists. Sadly, her career ended prematurely with her sudden death of a cerebral hemorrhage at age forty-eight.

Another gifted artist of this period, Rita Senger (fl. 1915–1919), created striking cover designs for *Vanity Fair* and *Vogue* whose audiences were sophisticated and urban. One example, *Woman Dancing on the Shore* (1916) (fig. 5.7), projects a bold sensation of bodily freedom in keeping the New Woman. Wearing

a simple black dress, the lithe, young beauty glides to the left, her open form, streaming hair, and flowing scarf meld together, captured in a moment of motion. A caged bird in one hand, a flying bird alights on her other, visual elements that counter one another also reinforce a vision of freedom and release. Senger's boldly simplified forms with little modeling share traits in common with the forms utilized by other artists working in modernist styles, such as Plummer and Russell Patterson.

British-born Anne Harriet Fish (1890–1964) produced work for *Vanity Fair* during the 1910s that overlaps chronologically with that of Plummer and Senger. Building on the sophisticated urban women that are

Fig. 5.7. Rita Senger. Woman Dancing on the Shore, 1916. Gouache, watercolor over pencil. Published as cover, *Vanity Fair*, July 1916.

Fig. 5.8. Anne Harriet Fish. Dancing Couples, No. 1, 1920. Ink, watercolor, gouache, with painted overlays. Published as cover, *Vanity Fair*, March 1920.

particularly notable in Plummer's work, Fish created more than thirty cover designs for the magazine. Unlike Plummer and Senger, however, she continued creating vital cartoons and cover art well into the 1920s. These late works document a lessening social formality between the sexes as the twenties embraced a free-wheeling, carefree spirit.

Two dazzling cover designs, *Dancing Couples, No. 1* (March 1920) (fig. 5.8), and *Dancing Couples, No. 2* (March 1921) (fig. 5.9), demonstrate how Fish elaborates on the social experience of dance. In the first, formally dressed women and men press close together, torso to torso, faces close together, yet out-flung arms and legs across the space convey an exuberant joy in

freedom of movement. A year later, within a more defined nightclub setting, Fish depicts women and men more individualized in face, form, and fashion, as they exchange glances, both cool and flirtatious, while talking or dancing, some daringly close. This captivating world consisting predominantly of stylish, mostly happy couples highlights a new dynamic in social relations between the sexes. The piece displays Fish's extremely fine, lively yet controlled pen-and-ink drawing style, and bold use of color, both influenced by Art Deco. She also created elegant cartoon, caricature, and illustration drawings that were published in other American magazines including *Vogue, Harper's Bazaar*, and *Cosmopolitan*, as well as the British *Punch*.

Fig. 5.9. Anne Harriet Fish. Dancing Couples, No. 2, 1921. India and sepia inks, gouache, watercolor, silver paint, and pencil. Published as cover, *Vanity Fair*, March 1921.

Fig. 5.10. Anne Harriet Fish. The Art Shows. Ink. Published with "The Opening of the Social Season," in *Vanity Fair*, November 1917.

Fig. 5.11. Anne Harriet Fish. Careers for Our Girls: The High Flier, 1928. Watercolor, ink, and graphite. Published in *Cosmopolitan*, September 25, 1928.

Fish's *The Art Shows* (ca. 1917) (fig. 5.10) gives a breezy, satirical look at varied social types perusing sculptures on exhibit. Based on abbreviated facial expressions and figures' postures, reactions to artistic nudity range from mild shock to discomfort to earnest contemplation. The artist's views on suffrage are not readily determined, but many of her drawings feature spirited young women seeking adventure and achievement. Consider *Careers for Our Girls: The High Flier*, a double-page spread (fig. 5.11) published in *Cosmopolitan*, September 25, 1928, soon after Amelia Earhart became the first woman to fly across the Atlantic Ocean.[9]

The work of Plummer, Senger, and Fish in the 1910s offers an interesting contrast with cover designs by Alice Beach Winter (1877–1970). In her May 1912 cover (fig. 5.12) for the *Masses*, a radical leftist publication, Winter depicts a child worker's face, shown close-up, with the caption "Why must I work?" She employs her realist style to strong effect by offsetting the form of the child's face with her wide-eyed, wistful expression against a partial view of a factory in the background.

The compelling message of social concern for children's welfare has political ramifications and prefigures the kind of social observation and commentary on urban conditions that successors would find ways of incorporating into their cover art. Winter produced additional cover designs and illustrations for the magazine and served as its art editor until 1916.

Several years after Winter's child worker piece, Hungarian-born artist Ilonka Karasz (1896–1981) created quite a different type of image for the magazine's December 1915 (fig. 5.13) cover. The young artist's design of a lively dancer in modest yet exotic attire, drawn in a flattened, poster-like style, is one of several that feature dancers and other performing artists rendered in a similar aesthetic that the *Masses* published. It is interesting to reflect further on the apolitical nature of Karasz's fetching image. Not only was it commissioned by a magazine fueled by its political agenda, it was also published during World War I. In comparison with cover images by other female artists during this era, its removal from existing real-world experience is striking. This period marks a

Fig. 5.12. Alice Beach Winter. "Why Must I Work?" Photomechanical print. Published as cover, the *Masses*, May 1912.

Fig. 5.13. Ilonka Karasz. [A Dancer], 1915. Offset lithograph, color. Published as cover, the *Masses*, December 1915.

growing interest in publishing nonpolitical images at the magazine, owing in part to strong differences of opinion among artists about the purpose of their work in the publication.[10] The *Masses* published cartoons and other artwork by many artists who strongly influenced the course of American art and magazine publishing.[11]

Karasz would find success designing decorative arts, illustrating book covers and most notably producing artwork for the *New Yorker*, where she created 186 covers published from 1925 to 1973. The charming, well-designed imagery that she created for the magazine encompasses varied scenes of New York life, countryside pastimes, and seasonal themes, many of which have little or no relation to issue contents or strong social or political concerns. Underlying her well-constructed compositions is a rigorous, modernist design sensibility inflected by whimsical elements.

Nell Brinkley (1886–1944), often identified along with O'Neill as one of the two earliest American women cartoonist-illustrators, primarily drew serial comics

stories about beautiful, often heroic young women. One of her most enduring heroines, Golden Eyes, appeared on the cover of the *Seattle Sunday Times Magazine*, April 18, 1918 (fig. 5.14), to promote the sale of Liberty Bonds. Brinkley employs her characteristically fine-lined drawing technique, influenced by Art Nouveau aesthetic, in rendering the swirling folds of Golden Eyes's dress, cape, and signature curly hair blowing in the wind as she waves farewell, presumably to her departing soldier boyfriend. Bright-eyed yet sad, her stalwart figure embodied an active patriotism on the home front. This female cartoonist's drawing for a newspaper magazine cover represents a visually compelling example of its type.

The early twentieth-century depictions of female figures in cartoons and cover art shown here present mainly idealized or stylized images of women as allegorical or symbolic figures and urban sophisticates. Examples relating to social relations between the sexes also capture the gradual shifting toward greater freedom of expression for women artists—from brides to dancing in nightclubs. One exceptional example,

Fig. 5.14. Nell Brinkley. Golden Eyes with Uncle Sam, 1918. Watercolor, ink, gouache, and opaque white over graphite. Published as cover, the *Seattle Sunday Times Magazine*, April 18, 1918.

Winter's 1912 cover for the *Masses*, forecasts engagement with broad social issues such as child welfare by a future generation of women. On the whole, however, these examples present limited subject categories, which were likely determined by established editorial practices such as use of seasonal or holiday themes, general connections with magazine content, and other assigned topics.

THE *NEW YORKER* AND ELSEWHERE

One of the best known and beloved *New Yorker* cartoonists, Helen E. Hokinson (1893–1949), was born in Mendota, Illinois, the only child of Mary and Adolph Hokinson. Following early childhood in Moline and Des Moines, she and her family returned to Mendota in 1905. She first learned to draw from her father, a farm machinery salesman. In high school, she drew humorous sketches of classmates and teachers, carrying a sketchbook wherever she went. Following

graduation from Mendota High School in 1913, she completed a two-year program at the Chicago Academy of Fine Arts and attended the Art Institute of Chicago, studying fashion illustration, design, and cartooning.[12]

Living modestly in Chicago, Hokinson obtained assignments from art service agencies and department stores, and shared studio space with Alice Harvey, a friend and future cartoonist. Seeking further professional development, Hokinson moved to New York City in 1920, and Harvey joined her there the next year. While doing mainly fashion illustration for major stores such as B. Altman, John Wanamaker, and Lord and Taylor, Hokinson also began cartooning, and her comic "Sylvia in the Big City" was published for a few months in the *New York Daily Mirror*. In 1924 she and Harvey enrolled at the Parsons School of Art where she was strongly influenced by her teacher Howard Giles's instruction on Jay Hambidge's theory of dynamic symmetry. According to Hambidge, dynamic symmetry is "a method of obtaining regularity, balance, and proportion in design by diagonals and reciprocals to rectangular areas instead of by the plane figures of geometry, or by measurements of length units—such as the foot and meter—which have been used for the purpose for many centuries."[13]

Encouraged by Giles, Hokinson submitted a drawing to the *New Yorker* in 1925. Not only was it accepted, but the editors asked that she submit drawings weekly for possible publication. Thus began her long, successful association with the magazine. Her earliest cartoons had no captions, but editors later began to supply them. Recognizing Hokinson's keen powers of observation, humor, and graceful drawing technique, they suggested ideas to her and assigned her to cover various New York area events and venues.

In 1931 Hokinson created her first *New Yorker* cover, published her first cartoon collection, entitled *So You're Going to Buy a Book,* and met James Reid Parker. He became her cartoon collaborator, supplying ideas, situations, and captions. They also collaborated on *The Dear Man*, a monthly cartoon for the *Ladies' Home Journal*, and some advertising assignments. During the many years they worked together, Hokinson evolved her signature creations of heavyset, upper-class female characters that endeared themselves

Fig. 5.15. Helen Hokinson. "They're all staying for supper, Nora. Any inspirations?" ca. 1939. Ink brush and ink wash over graphite.

Fig. 5.16. Helen Hokinson. Reunion. "Remember that shy Alice . . .". Ink wash, collage. Published in the *New Yorker*, June 19, 1943, with a different caption.

to many readers for the rest of her career—and beyond. While admirers tended to regard these characters as a type of charming, kind, ingenuous woman given to short-lived enthusiasms, Hokinson thought of them as individuals.[14]

Two drawings (figs. 5.15 and 5.16) feature the kind of characters that Hokinson developed so well over the course of her career. In the former, the lady of the house enters the kitchen cheerfully addressing her disgruntled maid or cook; note the sink and counter filled with dirty dishes, a detail adding further irritation for the maid. Both drawings show off Hokinson's lush use of ink, ink washes, and delicate drawing of faces.

By the mid-1940s, Hokinson grew concerned that the women she drew were becoming misunderstood. She intended viewers to laugh with—rather than

at—them, so she began a campaign to defend and explain them. "I like my girls," she said. "They don't say anything I don't say. To me they aren't superficial women seeking culture in an easy way. A stupid woman making a stupid remark isn't humorous, but an intelligent woman making a confused remark sometimes is."[15] Some claimed that Hokinson was actually unaware that her drawings were humorous, "a legend that she herself enjoyed perpetuating," as if she were playing the intelligent but confused woman of her own cartoons.[16] On November 1, 1949, she was enroute to Washington, DC, to speak at the opening of the annual Community Chest drive, the type of cause easily associated with her characters, when her plane collided with another and plunged into the Potomac River. Everyone on board was killed. During her productive but too brief career, she produced more than eighteen hundred cartoons and sixty-eight cover designs for the *New Yorker*, a legacy that has inspired succeeding generations of cartoonists and appreciative readers.[17]

Hokinson's close friend Alice Harvey (Ramsey) (1894–1983) was also from Illinois, and she studied at the Art Institute of Chicago under Wallace Morgan. Harvey did illustrations for *Life, Judge, Woman's Day, McCall's,* and *Harper's Bazaar.* She began drawing for the *New Yorker* in 1925, the same year that Hokinson did. Harvey married, moved to Connecticut and soon started a family; she was among the first to draw about life with children for the *New Yorker.*[18] She also began drawing country scenes including horse shows, regattas, houses, and gardening. Hokinson, in contrast, continued with more urban subjects.[19] The two remained close friends, and both contributed to Lois Long's weekly *New Yorker* feature "On and Off the Avenue," a fashion column of candid criticism. And although they each drew cartoons about women, Harvey delved into the middle and working classes, tended to lampoon certain types, wrote her own captions, and used more pointed humor.[20] Cartoonist and scholar Liza Donnelly observes that they conveyed humor differently as well: Hokinson primarily through her drawing and Harvey more whimsically through ideas that were communicated verbally as seen in a 1930 work (fig. 5.18). In a later drawing (fig. 5.17), Harvey depicts a woman uninterested in what another woman, campaigning door-to-door, has to say.

More assertive than Hokinson, Harvey was occasionally asked by editors to rework some of her drawings. Partly in response to this, she wrote letters to *New Yorker* staff for cartoon ideas. In 1936, she drew *Sister Susie,* a short-lived comic strip for the *New York Daily News.* She continued working for the *New Yorker,* doing three cover designs but her work gradually disappeared from the magazine. A productive painter, she spent the rest of her life in Westport, Connecticut.[21] Harvey often argued about or refused to make changes to her work, including captions, when asked by editors to do so. She and editor Harold Ross exchanged letters that indicate a respectful clash of opinions that pitted his vision for the magazine against Harvey's desire to maintain her own artistic integrity. In a letter to him, she writes about the difference between illustration and humorous art

Fig. 5.17. Alice Harvey. "The woman who is running against you was here yesterday and seems very nice." Graphite, ink wash. Published in "An Ordinary Woman in Politics," by Anne Ellis, *Ladies' Home Journal,* April 1931.

Fig. 5.18. Alice Harvey. "But mother, you haven't lived yet!" Ink brush, ink wash over graphite underdrawing. Published in the *New Yorker,* March 15, 1930.

coming down "to a definition of terms. As a matter of fact—I hate always being humorous. What I like is being true—and knowing people and getting a thrill out of them and drawing it."[22]

Donnelly has suggested that a number of changing conditions, including editorial changes, from the blunt editorial style of James Geraghty, who became

Fig. 5.19. Barbara Shermund. "I'm sorry!" between 1945 and 1955. Watercolor, crayon, and ink and opaque white over graphite underdrawing.

the *New Yorker's* influential cartoon editor in 1939, to "the increased use of gagmen, and the possibility that these women . . . were unable or unwilling to reflect the new American sense of humor that was based on a growing acceptance of women in solely domestic roles" prompted a number of women to leave the field.[23] As women in many industries discovered in the postwar boom years, the New Woman and her similarly independent successors were encouraged to settle into home life once the nation had put the Depression and the war behind it.

Another successful cartoonist at the *New Yorker*, Barbara Shermund (1899–1978), was born in San Francisco to a mother who was a sculptor and a father who was an architect. Thus seemingly destined for an artistic life, she studied at the California School of Fine Arts and took classes at the Art Students League after she arrived in New York. She had her first cartoon published in the magazine in 1926 after beginning by doing spot drawings. From the beginning she cartooned about the New Woman, often making fun of her, and writing her own captions in a clear outspoken voice.[24] Her feminist tone set her apart from other cartoonists of the era. Early on, she used fluid brushwork to delineate her forms and skillfully applied washes. Particularly in her work for *Esquire*, she demonstrated accomplished watercolor technique, using vivid color effectively, and infusing forms with vitality.

Like Harvey, Shermund was urged by *New Yorker* editors to accept ideas from outside gag writers, and the faces of her women became more stylized, their comments less smart-alecky and more silly.[25] With the appearance of the men's magazine *Esquire* in 1933, Shermund found another outlet for her fluidly drawn cartoons, becoming a mainstay for the new publication. While taking a feminist tone in many of her drawings, Shermund does not avoid poking fun at members of her own sex. In a lively party scene from 1941 (fig. 5.21), the mix of smiling, drinking party-goers sums up the breezy, happy-go-lucky humor conjured in many of Shermund's cartoons. In another drawing that shows off her impressive technique in watercolor (fig. 5.19), ca. 1950, she depicts a disgruntled dog rolling his eyes at a would-be huntress's utter lack of skill. Spent shells littering the ground and birds escaping in flight drolly tell the tale. In a cartoon for

Fig. 5.20. Barbara Shermund. "Please make it snappy, Albert—I can hardly wait to refuse you!" 1960. Published in *Esquire*, 1960.

Esquire from 1960 (fig. 5.20), Shermund features a different kind of female, a humorously heartless young blonde responding to a marriage proposal, "Please make it snappy, Albert—I can hardly wait to refuse you!" This later example underscores Shermund's unabashed irreverence toward men and the institution of marriage.

Never at a loss for feisty or provocative images and words, Shermund made substantial contributions to the *New Yorker*, *Esquire*, and *Life* for years—her long-limbed, fashionably or scantily clad women frequently enlivened their pages. She also contributed a regular feature to King Features Syndicate and was illustrating

Fig. 5.21. Barbara Shermund. "Promise now. No thinking programs," 1941. Ink wash and ink.

long-lasting friendships with fellow students including Mary Pilblad, Susanne Suba, Arthur Getz, and Allela Cornell. Malman, along with Getz and Suba, went on to have work published by the *New Yorker*. Beginning in 1937 and for the next two decades, Malman created twenty-four *New Yorker* covers, an especially notable achievement given that she died when she was forty-eight.[28] She also created a modest number of cartoons and hundreds of spot illustrations for the magazine.

Malman's unusual style featured austere adult figures in dark clothing, often angular and sometimes ghostly in appearance. Children typically wear brightly colored clothing. During the World War II era, she particularly favored dark color schemes that imbued most of her cover designs with a rather somber tone, one that stands out from images by her peers. Given her familial connection with Britain, it is not surprising to see that several of her cover designs heightened awareness of the war's impact on civilians devastated by the Blitz. Her *New Yorker* cover (fig. 5.22) for June 30, 1945, published soon after Germany's surrender and in anticipation of the upcoming Fourth of July holiday, has a black background, but she softens the overall effect considerably by making the Declaration of Independence—then on display at the Library of Congress—the centerpiece. Figures in the foreground direct admiring gazes upward, their features reflecting a symbolic glow emanating from the founding fathers' ideals.

Meanwhile, Roberta MacDonald (1917–1999) and Dorothy McKay (1904–1974), both San Francisco natives, focused on cartoons rather than cover art. Both portrayed working women and their mid-twentieth-century cartoons provide interesting perspectives on women in the workforce. MacDonald came to New York City in 1941 after selling some cartoons to the *New Yorker* and married music critic W. H. Simon of the Simon & Schuster Publishing house three years later. She stands apart notably from many sister cartoonists in that she depicted women in the military and other jobs during World War II. While fairly conventional in her outlook, she poked fun at her own gender's preoccupation with maintaining attractive appearances and produced witty spoofs on gender relations, high-handed personalities, and the like.[29]

books by 1931. The prolific Shermund produced 597 drawings and eight cover designs that were published by the *New Yorker*, the last of which appeared in 1944.[26] She was among the first women admitted to the National Cartoonists Society (see chapter 3).[27] In addition to her work in the world of cartooning, Shermund exhibited her paintings and prints in a number of illustration art shows in New York City. Living the latter part of her life in a small house by the ocean, she died without having a collection of her vibrant cartoons published, which had been a longtime goal. Due to a newspaper strike at the time of her death, no fulsome obituary was published.

Another gifted cartoonist, Christina (Tina) Malman (Masters) (1911–1959), was born in Southhampton, England, and moved to the United States when she was two years old. She graduated from the Pratt Institute of Art in New York and while there formed

Fig. 5.22. Christina Malman Masters. The Declaration of Independence, 1945. Watercolor, pencil, collage. Published as cover, the *New Yorker*, June 30, 1945.

Using a thin, clean-lined style, MacDonald drew easily read compositions that sometimes consisted of visual sequences filled with many figures. A fine example of her sequential cartooning published in 1943 in the *New Yorker* (fig. 5.24) follows two women's visits to an employment agency. MacDonald uses visual humor skillfully and exclusively, juxtaposing contrasting female types and keeping the viewer guessing through the series. In another wordless cartoon published that same year (fig. 5.23), a wife in work clothes kisses her sleeping husband good-bye as she leaves for her job. Wearing overalls, work cap, and holding a lunch pail, she appears ready for physical labor. Many women worked in munitions factories or other defense facilities vital to the war effort. This example reflects

Fig. 5.23. Roberta MacDonald. [Wife Dressed for Work Kisses Sleeping Husband Good-bye], 1943. Ink, opaque white, and graphite. Published in the *New Yorker*, September 25, 1943.

Fig. 5.24. Roberta MacDonald. [Two Women at Employment Agency], ca. 1943. Ink and watercolor. Published in the *New Yorker*, May 1, 1943.

the tendency of the magazine during this period to publish cartoons that reference how the war affected Americans at home.[30]

From 1940 to 1952, MacDonald published more than a hundred drawings in the *New Yorker*, but as others experienced, in the postwar era less of her work was accepted and she grew frustrated and discouraged when communication with the magazine's editors brought no improvement in her situation. Geraghty, the *New Yorker*'s art editor, claimed that he never told her to stop submitting work or that it would fit better elsewhere, but insisted that he did tell her "she could make a fortune illustrating" books. She did go into that line of work successfully, although the fortune remained elusive.

McKay also portrayed women working in business settings in cartoons that were published in *Esquire*, but not in the *New Yorker*. Born Dorothy Jones, she began taking art classes at night at the California School of Fine Arts while still in high school, though her father, a minister, disapproved of her drawings of nudes that she brought home from class. She married cartoonist Donald McKay in 1922 and they moved to Greenwich Village in New York. Working as a secretary in advertising agencies during the day, she took classes at the Art Students League in the evening.[31] McKay drew constantly, filling many notebooks, and worked in a fluid drawing technique and made effective use of skillfully executed washes and watercolor, developing a style quite distinct from that of MacDonald.[32]

The *New Yorker* published only six of her cartoons from 1934 to 1936, but she found outlets for her work in other magazines including *Life*, *College Humor*, *Ballyhoo*, and *Forum*. Although she responded to requests from *New Yorker* editorial staff to edit and revise various drawings in attempts to produce the kind of work they were seeking at the time, she abandoned these efforts out of frustration by 1938. It is difficult to discern exactly why McKay was asked to revise her work many times and why, despite cordial, patient exchanges between her and editor Katherine White, so few of her cartoons were accepted. Replying to a complicated edit that seemed to allow no room for input from the artist, McKay wrote, "My confidence in pleasing The New Yorker Art Committee has just about gone. I admire the magazine and think you're

Fig. 5.25. Dorothy McKay. "Watch your language. I'm not on your board of directors," 1954. Watercolor. Published in *Esquire*, March 1954.

Fig. 5.26. Dorothy McKay. "I'm not the husband, I'm the father," between 1940 and 1960. Watercolor, graphite.

Fig. 5.27. Dorothy McKay. "The collection agency and I worked out a compromise satisfactory to both of us . . . you're to go to jail," 1954. Watercolor. Published in *Esquire*, November 1954.

swell, but when it comes to my work it is apparent that we don't agree as to what is funny."[33] Donnelly has observed that the humor there was gradually shifting toward "jokes aimed *at* women."

During these difficult years, however, and into the 1960s, she published many lively, technically accomplished cartoons in *Esquire*. In one example from 1954 (fig. 5.25), a secretary admonishes her startled-looking boss, "Watch your language. I'm not on your board of directors." Her trim, upright figure and indignant expression perfectly suit the caption, conveying assertiveness with humor. McKay's work experience as

a secretary surely shaped the amusing tone of this cartoon that also displays her well-honed watercolor technique and use of vibrant color. In another drawing the same year (fig. 5.27), she used well-designed settings and vividly realized male and female types for staging crisply worded interactions. Finally, in figure 5.26, she shows off a richly detailed setting and humor that was risqué for the era. It is interesting to compare McKay with a later cartoonist, Victoria Roberts (b. 1957), who in an example from 2003 (fig. 5.28) created a subtler and more ironic take on male-female relations a half century later.

NEW YORKER CARTOONS

Many a faithful reader unabashedly turns first to the magazine's cartoons when surveying a new issue. Over its storied history, the *New Yorker* has attracted, nurtured, and published work by many of the most renowned North American cartoonists and writers—and embraced work by international artists as well. By the late 1920s, not long after its launch, the *New Yorker* had already set itself apart from other magazines as artistically innovative by virtue of "its design, its aesthetic standards, and above all in the quality of its cartoons and drawings."[34] Founding editor Harold Ross and art director Rea Irvin are credited with establishing the magazine's revolutionary path. Both actively sought novel, up-to-date ideas and styles in design and drawings, especially in cartoons. Ross greatly preferred those that contained all or most of their humor and impact with little or no reliance on captions. This, along with his pressing for one-line captions, pushed cartoonists to produce sharp, crisp, concise work that eschewed time-worn tropes in the field.[35] As Lee Lorenz, former art and cartoon editor

for the magazine, noted, "The ideal *New Yorker* cartoon is the happy marriage of a distinctive style and an original point of view. A fortunate few are born with these gifts," adding advice from cartoonist George Booth's mother that "no matter what you're getting paid, give it plenty of oomph!"[36] Unquestionably, the magazine has done much to nurture and advance excellence in the art form, but not without great numbers of cartoonists receiving numerous rejections or undergoing painful edits to their work before having it accepted. Katherine White, a deeply influential senior editor specializing in fiction, often proved at times a key intermediary between the artists and the editors selecting cartoons. Despite White's good offices, however, some women eventually found that few of their drawings were being accepted. On the other hand, the warm relationship between White, Ross, and Helen Hokinson lasted many years. When Hokinson learned that cartoonist Peter Arno was paid more than she was, she promptly refused to submit any more cartoons until Ross rectified the situation. He did.[37]

Fig. 5.28. Victoria Roberts. "I'm treating you like a living deity for one day," 2003. Ink, ink wash. Published in the *New Yorker*, June 30, 2003.

TO AMUSE, ATTRACT, AND ALLURE: CONTEMPORARY ARTISTS

It is significant that Rose O'Neill and her cohorts gained entrée to this prestigious realm of cover design when they were relatively young. O'Neill was twenty-six years old when she published one of her early covers for *Puck* in 1901; Plummer was the same age when she published her 1914 cover for *Vanity Fair*; and Fish was just twenty-five when she produced the May 1915 cover design for *Vanity Fair*. In contrast, contemporary artists Anita Kunz was thirty-nine when she published her first *New Yorker* cover and Maira Kalman was forty-six; only Roz Chast was notably younger than her sister cartoonist-illustrators, breaking through at age thirty-two.

The general age difference between the groups raises the question: Why were women cartoonists in the early twentieth century notably younger and less experienced when they made their breakthroughs? When they began seeking publishing outlets, they encountered a plethora of possibilities and succeeded in winning assignments with periodicals either well established or destined to become leading exemplars of their types. High demand for illustrated magazines coupled with rapidly escalating numbers of them competing to survive may have made it easier for aspiring women cartoonist-illustrators to enter the field and win cover assignments. Their successors encountered stiff competition from male counterparts for plum assignments for far fewer periodical publications. Although women cartoonist-illustrators of today may find it more challenging to win cover art assignments than their predecessors, those who do pursue a broader range of subjects with far greater freedom. Three prominent women whose cover art supports this point are Roz Chast (b. 1954), Anita Kunz (b. 1956), and Maira Kalman (b. 1949). All three have produced impressive bodies of work, lengthy records of exhibitions that include international venues, received multiple awards and honorary degrees, and established high professional profiles that arguably equal or surpass those of their groundbreaking predecessors.

One of the leading cartoonists for the *New Yorker*, Chast has since 1978 had more than one thousand cartoons appear in the magazine. Two examples from her irregular series *Mixed Marriage* play off common or conventional wisdom about gender differences to comic effect, as in "Takes Two to Tango" (2008) (fig. 5.29*)*, and "A Quiet Evening at Home" (2002) (fig. 5.30). Using the trope of wives and husbands misunderstanding one another, Chast creates a humorous cartoon that also makes a pointed dig at the details seized upon in political reporting. She claims to be apolitical in her work and does not aim deliberately to make social commentary, but an undertone of political and social satire can be detected in some of her cartoons in the *New Yorker*. She is also particularly adept at creating cartoons that exploit common types of insecurities shared by many people, especially women. She addresses one of these—the problem of developing a sense of fashion that one finds comfortable and acceptable, in *Style* (2009) (fig. 5.31). In eleven panels she chronicles the fashion trials and tribulations of a girl who never wanted to look weird, but ended up feeling that way, resulting in anxiety and self-consciousness over fashion choices that lingered into adulthood. In addition to her cartoons, Chast has produced impressive cover designs, such as *April Fool* (fig. 5.32) from 2009, in which she spoofs American advertising and comments scathingly on one of the most devastating one-man scams of the early twenty-first century. Among colorful, delicately drawn vignettes, she offers candy bars that cause weight loss, "Vitamins That Make You Smarter," and culminates with an order form to send $25 million to Madoff Industries, a painful reminder of millions lost by clients of Ponzi-scheme-perpetrator Bernard Madoff. Chast here incorporates the kind of sharp social observations that typify her cartoons.

Chast was born in Brooklyn, New York, to parents who were educators—her father was a high school French teacher, and her mother an assistant public school principal. She began drawing as a child, with special awareness of cartoons and cartoonists published in the *New Yorker*. She took art classes while in high school at the Manhattan Art Students League and completed a BFA in painting from the Rhode Island School of Design. Not having much success in finding work as an illustrator, she began drawing cartoons and eventually submitted work to the *New Yorker*. Finding this a steady, effective platform for her work, she has

Fig. 5.29. Roz Chast. Mixed Marriage. "Takes Two to Tango," 2008. Ink, watercolor. Published in the *New Yorker*, October 13, 2008.

Fig. 5.31. Roz Chast. Style, 2009. Ink, watercolor. Published in the *New Yorker*, March 16, 2009.

Fig. 5.30. Roz Chast. Mixed Marriage. "A Quiet Evening at Home," 2002. Ink, watercolor. Published in the *New Yorker*, September 23, 2002.

Fig. 5.32. Roz Chast. April Fool, 2009. Watercolor and ink. Published as cover, the *New Yorker*, April 6, 2009.

published ten collections of her work and illustrated at least a dozen titles by other authors. She has also written and illustrated well-received children's books, but most notably, she created and published *Can't We Talk about Something More Pleasant?* her first graphic memoir about her parents, their aging and decline, and passing.[38] In 2015 she received the Reuben Award as Cartoonist of the Year, the most prestigious prize given by the National Cartoonists Society.

Anita Kunz's arresting cover caricature of Whoopi Goldberg (fig. 5.33) for the *Boston Globe Magazine* (September 13, 1992) captures the actress's larger-than-life personality by rendering her face as a large sculptural form that fills the pictorial field. Kunz inscribes Goldberg's locks with words that describe the actress's life and work. With care and ingenuity, Kunz pays tribute to Goldberg's achievements while visually reinforcing her identity as a proud African American woman, one who has joined the select ranks of those who become the subject of a cover story. Her portrayal celebrates an individual woman, not an allegorical or symbolic figure associated with past ideals distant from present concerns.

Kunz's compelling cover design entitled *Child Abuse* (fig. 5.34), for the January–February 1993 issue of *Ms. Magazine,* illustrated a harrowing article on ritual child abuse perpetrated by a satanic cult. By making a frightened naturalistic child the focal point in a vivid red and green color scheme, Kunz dramatizes the horrific danger to children posed by such cults. The surreal, nightmarish vision conjured by this artist demonstrates her remarkable ability to handle disturbing subject matter her predecessors would never have addressed. Her cover design for the *Washington Post Magazine,* entitled *Fear of Finance,* from 1991 (fig. 5.35) still retains the message and expressive effect it produced then. She depicts a cramped and fearful Everyman figure placed inside a constricting picture frame covered with symbols of financial obligations and material desires. Kunz produced this strong, conceptual work for an article on investors' ambivalence about investing for the future. Topics from the world of finance and business present her with some of her most challenging editorial assignments, but this example underscores the broad range of topics she addresses in her cover art.

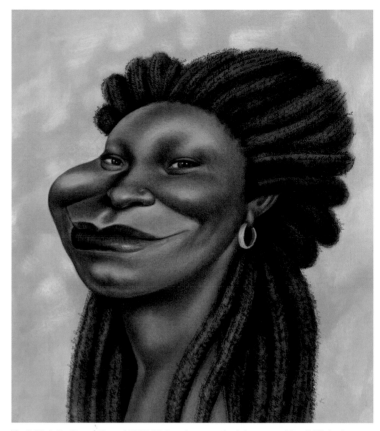

Fig. 5.33. Anita Kunz. Whoopi, 1992. Watercolor, gouache, ink over graphite. Published as cover, the *Boston Globe Magazine*, September 13, 1992.

In her July Fourth cover for the *New Yorker* in 2000, entitled *Climber* (fig. 5.36), Kunz depicts a generic mountaineer scaling the face of the Statue of Liberty, a symbol of American freedom. By depicting Lady Liberty cross-eyed at this affront, Kunz injects gentle humor into the image while also underscoring the audacity of such an assault. As the national holiday cover for America's leading magazine of culture and society, the image prompts the viewer to identify and reflect on issues appropriate for the day. These include the fragility of American freedom and the value that citizens attach to national symbols. In recalling the terrorist attacks of September 11, 2001, this cover design seems eerily prescient of national vulnerability to attack from seemingly anonymous persons.

Maira Kalman (née Berman) was born in Tel Aviv, Israel, and moved with her family to Riverdale, New York, in 1953, when she was four years old. As a child, she received a culturally rich upbringing with piano and dance lessons, visits to museums, and going to

Fig. 5.34. Anita Kunz. Child Abuse. Watercolor, gouache over graphite. Published as cover, *Ms. Magazine*, January/February 1993.

Fig. 5.35. Anita Kunz. Fear of Finance, 1991. Watercolor, gouache, and acrylic with collage. Published as cover, *Washington Post Magazine*, April 13, 1991.

concerts. After attending New York's High School of Music and Art, she enrolled at New York University, where she studied literature and pursued her interest in writing. There she met her future husband, Tibor Kalman, who was then a student in graphic design. After she graduated, she wrote very little and concentrated on drawing. She worked with her artistic husband when he became creative director of Barnes and Noble in the 1970s, and after he founded the graphic design firm M and Co, in 1986. She contributed to its output by designing record covers, textile designs, and movie titles. Beginning to explore children's books in the mid-1980s, she illustrated the lyrics to *Stay Up Late*, a song by David Byrne in 1987. She has gone on to write and illustrate children's books and publish collections of her own work. Her drawing style appears to draw upon such diverse influences as Matisse, Chagall, and folk art.

Beginning in 1995 she has contributed covers and pictorial features to the *New Yorker*. From 2006 to 2007 she wrote and illustrated a narrative journal of her life for the *New York Times* online, which was followed by a year-long exploration of American history and democracy beginning with the inauguration of President Barack Obama. Both were collected and published as illustrated volumes, *The Principles of Uncertainty* (2007) and *And the Pursuit of Happiness* (2010). In conjunction with her large solo exhibition that toured nationally, she published a companion volume, *Maira Kalman: Various Illuminations of a Crazy World* (2010), an engaging, colorful survey of her creative work.

Prolific, imaginative, and often quirky in her perspective, Kalman's ability to entertain both children and adults in her children's books sets her apart from many peers. She typically employs witty, stream-of-consciousness prose, visual puns and parodies, vivid colors, and an energetic drawing style. She believes that children's books should be more than comforting and nice, that they should inspire and take readers over the top in some way.[39]

A final example from the *New Yorker* features an unusual collaboration between two illustrators, a woman and a man—Maira Kalman and Rick Meyerowitz (b. 1943). As such it demonstrates how women have pushed creative boundaries in drawing cover art. In the wake of 9-11, she and Meyerowitz together developed their ingenious *New Yorkistan* cover (figs. 5.37 and 5.38) through jointly produced sketches and notes now preserved in the Library of Congress collections

Fig. 5.36. Anita Kunz. Climber, 2000. Watercolor, gouache over graphite. Published as cover, the *New Yorker*, July 3, 2000.

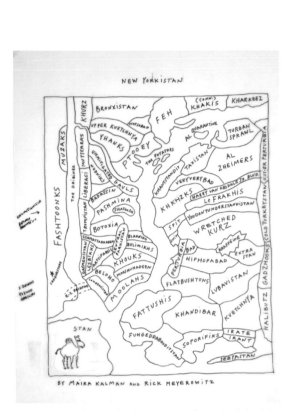

Fig. 5.37. Maira Kalman and Rick Meyerowitz. Close to final sketch for cover, 2001. Porous point pen, ink. Published as cover, the *New Yorker*, December 10, 2001.

Fig. 5.38. Maira Kalman and Rick Meyerowitz. New Yorkistan, print of art originally published as cover, the *New Yorker*, December 10, 2001.

(the first of the eleven preparatory works was drawn on a napkin). Other *New Yorker* cover artists have improvised on the idea of mapping New York, but this particular collaboration yielded exceptional results. In channeling their considerable knowledge of the city's neighborhoods and their own distilled experiences or impressions of these enclaves, Kalman and Meyerowitz invented pseudo-national names for numerous entities that suggest myriad cultural and global parallels. Their witty, imaginary placenames, coupled with clearly delineated districts within Manhattan, Queens, and Brooklyn, conjure humorous associations with the different ethnic, cultural, and socioeconomic populations that constitute much of the city. The artists seem to suggest that New York comprises so polyglot a population that the city can be considered a microcosm of the world fractured by multiple nations and national identities. Their inspired collaboration underscores the aesthetic scope and conceptual potential of cover art.

CHAPTER 6

CARICATURISTS AND POLITICAL CARTOONISTS

Probably the reason more [cartoonists] are left-leaning is because editorial cartoonists are by their nature non-conformists. We're irreverent and challenge convention, which isn't a conservative trait.
—Cartoonist ANN TELNAES, 2016[1]

I believe the risk of "ghettoizing" women is one worth taking if it gives us the opportunity to discuss women's rights, freedom and why there are so few women in this field of cartooning.
—Author and cartoonist LIZA DONNELLY, 2012[2]

Historically, caricature and political cartooning have proven particularly difficult specialties for women to enter. One finds few women who make either discipline the primary focus of their careers. Since the early twentieth century, however, women have made inroads as practitioners of these art forms—which are closely related. Caricature is described as an artistic representation in which the characteristic features of the original are exaggerated or debased, creating an inherently or unintentionally ludicrous effect. In political cartooning, the ability to create and incorporate strong caricatures into well-honed visual metaphors is vital. These cartoons consist primarily of one or more distinct illustrations, which convey an opinion about a political situation, with the aid of text captions and/or dialogue balloons and caricatures that often combine to produce a humorous effect. Like the long-standing tradition of political cartooning in America, caricature also has a lengthy history as a distinct specialty practiced in the form of stand-alone, popular works of art that feature figures of social, cultural, and political interest.

CARICATURISTS

Billing herself as "the only woman caricaturist," Kate Carew (1869–1961) claimed seniority in the modest-size line of those who would follow in this type of work. She began her career at the *San Francisco Examiner*, moved to New York in about 1896, and for years produced well-received illustrated interviews of such notable people as Mark Twain, Jack London, Sarah Bernhardt, and Theodore Roosevelt. Her elegantly drawn caricatures tended to compliment rather than ridicule her subjects. These pieces appeared in the *New York World*, the *New York Globe*, and the *New York Tribune*, and Joseph Pulitzer sent her to Europe in 1901 to do an interview series called "Kate Carew Abroad."[3] She settled in London in 1911, worked with the *Patrician* and the *Tatler*, and continued publishing in the *Tribune*.[4] She returned to America at the start of World War I and continued working until the late 1920s when her health and eyesight declined.[5] Little of her original art appears to have survived in publicly accessible collections, although reproductions can be found in many periodical archives. Her work has been cited as an early influence on her much younger brother, *New Yorker* cartoonist Gluyas Williams (1888–1982).[6] It may also have influenced, in indeterminate ways, the work of the women caricaturists who followed her.

Peggy Bacon (1895–1987), one of the few women in this field to receive recognition during her lifetime, initially had a career in painting in mind when she began her fine arts training. While studying at the Art Students League in New York, she began producing satirical drawings and in 1918 several appeared in *Bad News*, the school's humor magazine. The following year she published her first book, *The True Philosopher and Other Cat Tales*. Bacon both wrote and illustrated this collection of whimsical stories about the bonds between cats and their humans and the positive qualities of these animals that she adored. During the late 1920s and 1930s, Bacon produced biting, well-drawn caricatures of notable New York personalities, and exhibitions of these drawings drew critical, appreciative attention. Undoubtedly such notice of her work contributed to her receiving, in 1933, a Guggenheim Fellowship, which she used to create and publish a

Fig. 6.1. Peggy Bacon. Djuna Barnes, ca. 1935. Conté crayon pencil.

collection of caricatures of art world figures, entitled *Off with Their Heads!* (1934).[7] This highly successful work paired her visually stunning drawings and insightful commentaries and ensured her a lasting place as an important American caricaturist. Art historian Wendy Wick Reaves notes that by the time Bacon published these drawings, she "had honed her skills into a delicate balance between satiric distortion and affectionate mockery . . . [and the accompanying words] reveal the keenness of her observations and explain the meaning of her visual exaggerations."[8] This point is well taken in Bacon's original drawing of the lesbian writer Djuna Barnes (ca. 1934) (fig. 6.1), and the closely related caricature published in *Off with Their Heads!* Both show Barnes wearing a mannish jacket, beret-like hat, and exaggerated features.[9] The original drawing has a softer, more portrait-like quality than the version published in Bacon's book. The upswept hair and simplified, more boldly outlined lapels strengthen the impression of a dynamic, sharp personality. Bacon's accompanying published caption reinforces this impression: "An elegant head lifted

Fig. 6.2. Peggy Bacon. The Quest of Beauty, between 1936 and 1941. India ink and black crayon on off-white wove paper.

Fig. 6.3. Peggy Bacon. Professional Rival, between ca. 1940 and ca. 1950. Black ink with gray wash on off-white wove paper.

on a slender neck and long aristocratic body. Peach-blond hair with ripples in it, sharply tilted, scornful nose. Light eyes in shadowy hollows with a firm, bare gaze like a Siamese cat. Mouth forms an immobile ellipse, a trifle Hapsburg. Gives the effect of a solitary wading-bird, indifferent, poised and insulated, arrested in a long pause."[10]

Two additional drawings convey a humorous perspective on gender stereotypes. Bacon uses a delicate ink-and-crayon technique in *The Quest of Beauty* (ca. 1936–1941) (fig. 6.2), which shows an elegantly dressed woman studying finely modeled terracotta figurines, idealized feminine figures from antiquity. The woman's substantial, graceful form serves as a counterpoint to the miniature figures within the museum case. As she peers at the figures, she sees her reflection and raises her hand holding an open compact, its mirror inclined toward the figures, as if to offer them a chance to similarly view their own reflections and check their appearances. Perhaps Bacon intended this symbolic interaction between female figures across millennia as an invitation to the viewer to contemplate changing

notions of feminine beauty. In another caricature (ca. 1940–1950) (fig. 6.3), Bacon pokes gentle fun at the bohemian artist stereotype, possibly a generalized male counterpart to herself. She depicts her "professional rival" as a curly haired young man with a mustache and goatee, dressed casually, standing with a confident air on the street corner, holding a portfolio under his arm, with a briefcase at his feet. Where these original drawings by Bacon were published is unknown.

Off with Their Heads! brought Bacon numerous commissions for caricatures and a request from the *New Republic* for a series on Washington, DC, figures that was published in 1935.[11] She unfortunately lost interest in caricature and reportedly drew few afterward. "I couldn't stand getting under people's skins," she later explained. "The caricatures made them smart so."[12] For the next half century she worked as a book illustrator, wrote nineteen books of her own, and published drawings in numerous periodicals.[13] These included many children's books as well as a successful mystery novel *The Inward Eye* (1952).[14] Productive and generous through her career, Bacon frequently

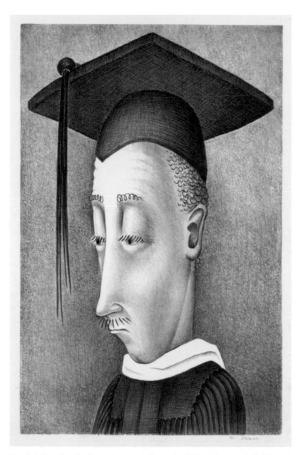

Fig. 6.4. Caroline Durieux. Academic Portrait, 1940. Lithograph. Published in *Caroline Durieux: 43 Lithographs and Drawings*, Louisiana State University Press, 1949.

Fig. 6.5. Caroline Durieux. Bourbon Street, New Orleans, 1943. Lithograph. Published in *Caroline Durieux: 43 Lithographs and Drawings*, Louisiana State University Press, 1949.

exhibited her work in New York, including more than thirty solo shows, and she taught at many art schools and universities over the course of her career. Through her body of diverse work including caricature, Bacon won general acclaim as one of America's most talented and prolific American women artists of the twentieth century. The caricatures she created constitute a singular contribution to the art form: the exceptionally high quality of her work, the sharp insights into the characters of her often famous subjects, and recognition she received from her peers mark a milestone for women in this specialty.

Less well known than Bacon, her contemporary, Caroline (Wogan) Durieux (1896–1989), also pursued fine art training and taught fine art. Throughout her career Durieux created satirical art that relied strongly on the power of caricature. Following graduation from Sophia Newcomb College in New Orleans, Durieux

studied painting at the Pennsylvania Academy of Fine Arts in Philadelphia (1917–1919), during which time she saw the work of nineteenth-century satirists such as Honoré Daumier, whose work proved a lasting influence.[15] Following her marriage to a New Orleans export-import businessman, Pierre Durieux, in 1921, she lived in Havana, Cuba, then moved in 1928 to Mexico City, which proved critical in her artistic development. During her years in Mexico, Diego Rivera and Howard Cook encouraged her to try lithography, and master printers Dario Mejia and George Miller instructed her in drawing on lithographic stones. Mejia printed her first set of twelve lithographs in 1932, the "Mexico Series," which was exhibited at the Weyhe Gallery in New York. In this body of work, Durieux critiqued the arrogance of ostentatious northern (i.e., Yankee) diplomats and businessmen who provided a questionable model for emerging middle-class Latin Americans.[16]

On her return to New Orleans in 1936, Durieux directed the Louisiana branch of the Federal Arts Project and taught art at Tulane University. In the more than thirty lithographs she created during the next ten years, she targeted particular social types and phenomena she knew well: pretentious academics and the idiosyncrasies of the Creole subculture's

Fig. 6.6. Caroline Durieux. Exit, 1944. Lithograph. Published in *Caroline Durieux: 43 Lithographs and Drawings*, Louisiana State University Press, 1949.

religious rituals and social gatherings.[17] In *Academic Portrait* (1940) (fig. 6.4), Durieux depicts an African American man in a mortarboard and gown; his downcast gaze and subdued expression, however, undercut the impression of authority or confidence that are commonly associated with members of academe. The subject of the portrait seems to project a sad awareness of self-delusion.[18] Durieux created the satirical *Bourbon Street, New Orleans* (1943) (fig.

6.5) at the request of museum curator Carl Zigrosser for his World War II–era *Artists for Victory* exhibit in New York.[19] In this lively nightclub scene, she portrays two young singers, both with features only slightly stylized, fully absorbed in their performance as soldiers look on appreciatively. Patterning of hair curls, clothing, and festoons of hanging lamps create linear rhythms that suggest the tempo of jazz tunes. In *Exit* (1944) (fig. 6.6), Durieux caricatures

Fig. 6.7. Aline Fruhauf. Nine Old Men, ca. 1936. Photomechanical print of original drawing. Fruhauf originally signed her drawing "Sue," which is visible in the upper right corner. Her image features caricatures of Supreme Court justices Louis Brandeis, Willis Van Devanter, Charles Evan Hughes, James Clark McReynolds, George Sunderland, Owen J. Roberts, Pierce Butler, Harlan Fiske Stone, and Benjamin N. Cardozo.

her subjects more sharply, pointedly contrasting an older woman and a younger one. Seated side by side in an audience, each pursues her own type of exit, the older one through sleep, the younger through rapt attention to what is on stage.

Durieux produced caricature art that focused on people of specific regions and cultures, particularly Mexico and Louisiana, forming a distinctive contribution to a genre that usually concentrated on public figures and celebrities. She also developed notable technical innovations in *cliché-verre*. In this process, a design is incised on a glass plate coated with an opaque substance then placed on photographic paper and exposed to light.[20] Although art galleries and museums showed her accomplished caricature prints, her work appears not to have been distributed widely in mass media outlets that were typically pursued, used, and perhaps more readily available to other caricaturists. The more limited dissemination of her work may reflect a deliberate decision on her part. Having trained as a fine artist who clearly immersed herself in detailed technical aspects of printmaking, perhaps Durieux wished to position herself unambiguously within the fine art world. If so, it might account for

the apparent rarity of her work in the popular media of her time.

Anita Fruhauf (1907–1978) and Irma Selz (1908–1977) both entered the field shortly after Bacon, whose success may have spurred them as close contemporaries to persist in caricature. While the two may have competed for assignments to some extent, they became friends. Fruhauf mentions Selz with respect and affection in her memoir, *Making Faces: Memoirs of a Caricaturist*.[21] Fruhauf particularly admired the work of painter and cartoonist Ralph Barton, whom she befriended as a young woman and who encouraged her artistic aspirations. From him she came to realize "that caricature was not only a respectable form of art but also a valuable way of documenting human beings."[22] This notion played into her work from the beginning. A native New Yorker, Fruhauf worked mainly in the world of art, music, literature, and theater, portraying performers and other artists, typically showing them with attributes of their talents or vocations. Beginning in 1927, her work appeared in the periodical *Musical America*, and was soon published in other outlets including New York newspapers.

Fig. 6.8. Aline Fruhauf. Raphael Soyer, 1937. Watercolor, graphite.

Fig. 6.9. Aline Fruhauf. Peggy Bacon, 1937. Watercolor and gouache.

Shortly after Fruhauf married biological scientist Erwin P. Vollmer in 1934, a print dealer asked her to do a series of drawings of legal figures that were inspired by nineteenth-century prototypes by British artists Ape and Spy; the drawings were then transformed into prints. One in the series, entitled *Nine Old Men* (ca. 1936) (fig. 6.7), depicting the justices of the Supreme Court, proved very popular.

Fruhauf then embarked on her *Artists at Work* series. Two examples from 1937 portray well-known artists Raphael Soyer (fig. 6.8) and Peggy Bacon (fig. 6.9). Each drawing demonstrates Fruhauf's sensitivity to her sitters' personalities with thoughtful posing and approaches. Note Bacon's upright posture, sharp nose, and gaze directed at the viewer; her alertness contrasts with the gentler, almost melancholy persona of Soyer. The brighter palette of blue and pink with accents of red and black in the former also contrasts with the

more subdued, subtle range of grayish-blue, beige, and muted black used for Soyer.

Fruhauf's move to Washington, DC, in 1944, when her husband was posted to the Naval Medical Center, affected her professional career.[23] The family's relocation brought loss of well-established professional contacts, networks, and cultural personalities more readily accessible in New York City. Raising two young daughters in a city less familiar to her may also have slowed her professional outreach. Nonetheless, she produced two new series of works about artists and music in Washington, which were exhibited in the city in 1950 and 1957, respectively.[24] Fruhauf's often whimsical line work and stronger focus on cultural rather than political figures show some commonality with Durieux. Fruhauf managed to have her work disseminated effectively in a variety of mass media publications.

Fig. 6.10. Irma Selz. Bill Mauldin—Democratic Candidate for Congress, 1956. Ink and whiteout over pencil.

Meanwhile, Selz left Chicago in the throes of the Great Depression, and became widely known as "New York's girl caricaturist"—a variation on Carew's self-given title—at a time when Miguel Covarrubias and Al Hirschfeld's linear styles were dominating and transforming the field. For the next two decades she was one of the most prolific creators of humorous graphic art, contributing great numbers of political and theatrical caricatures to more than fifty newspapers and periodicals as well as working for advertising agencies. In a drawing of Bill Mauldin as a youthful Democratic Party candidate for Congress in 1956 (fig. 6.10), Selz captures the strong, dynamic personality of the already famous, Pulitzer Prize–winning editorial cartoonist with bold, broad lines and areas of ink. Selz's concise linear style shares some similarities with the economic drawing style of Diana Denny, who entered the field in the mid-1940s.

Denny (1923–2015) studied at the Pennsylvania Academy of Fine Arts (BFA, 1945) and the University of Pennsylvania (MFA, 1946), then furthered her art education in Europe, winning two Cresson

fellowships. Inspired by her study of portraiture to explore political caricature she approached the news office of the *Philadelphia Record* in 1945 with seven caricature drawings. The paper purchased all of them. After she showed examples of her work to Edward Shenton, her instructor in illustration at PAFA, forty-nine were selected for exhibition in the print department as examples of a unique type of illustration. Newspaper reproductions were displayed with the original drawings in order to demonstrate how such work enhanced news stories. Denny explained that she not only studied pictures of her subjects—including General Douglas MacArthur and Winston Churchill—before drawing them, but also when possible, talked with their acquaintances and read all she could about them so that her depiction "will show the men inside and out."[25] The Indianapolis Museum of Art also mounted an exhibit of her drawings in 1946.[26]

As a staffer for the Scripps-Howard Newspaper Alliance from 1946 to 1961, Denny created a niche for herself as the company caricaturist, and her illustrations were often republished multiple times in many newspapers nationwide, with her work frequently appearing on the front page. Denny typically delineated the distinctive, defining features of her subject with a combination of bold brush-and-ink strokes and pen-and-ink lines that provided fine details indicating status. Her effective combination of bold outlines and defining detail is evident in her drawings of MacArthur (1946) (fig. 6.11) and Emperor Hirohito (1945) (fig. 6.12). Note the intricate description of their head gear, each with its row of decorative braid or distinctive layers of decorative borders crowned with national military symbols. She employs looser brushwork in her caricature portraits of Eleanor Roosevelt (ca. 1950) (fig. 6.13) and Maria Callas (ca. 1950) (fig. 6.14), creating impressive images of these impressive women. In the early 1960s, the responsibilities of life with a husband and three children in Washington, DC, led Denny to put a temporary hold on her professional life. She eventually joined John Sirica's Etching and Lithography Studio in Washington, where she learned and taught etching technique and printed artists' editions, and later established her own home studio.[27]

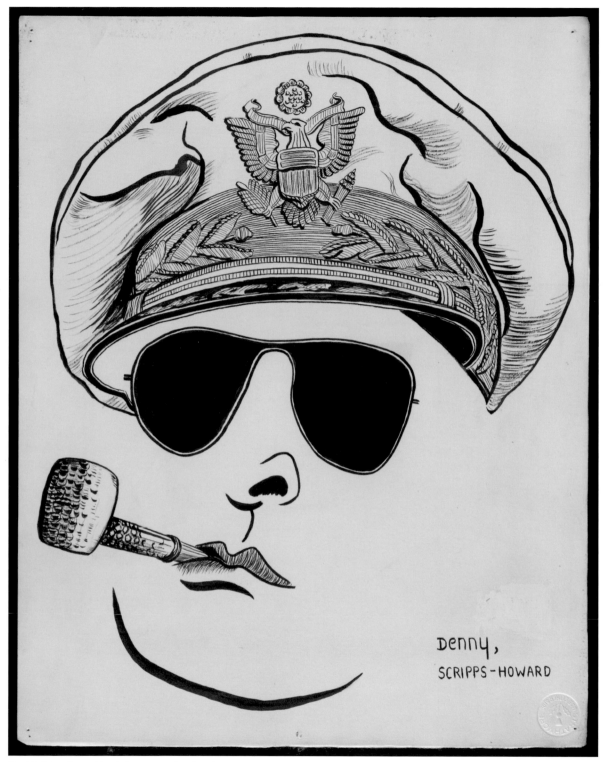

Fig. 6.11. Diana Denny. MacArthur, 1946. Ink and graphite.

Fig. 6.12. Diana Denny. Hirohito, 1945. Ink and graphite.

Fig. 6.13. Diana Denny. Eleanor Roosevelt, between 1945 and 1960. Ink over graphite underdrawing.

Fig. 6.14. Diana Denny. Maria Callas, between 1945–1960. Ink wash.

POLITICAL CARTOONISTS

Women have always found political or editorial cartooning the most difficult illustration specialty to break into, a field long considered "the ungentlemanly art."[28] Women who were pro-suffrage cartoonists and illustrators, such as Laura Foster (1871–1920), made historically significant contributions to the field by bringing attention to often-overlooked topics. Considered together, the work of women in political cartooning reveals varying degrees of engagement with women's status and rights, a gradual broadening of subjects addressed, and work that one cannot imagine any male cartoonist doing. The closely related terms "political cartoonist" and "editorial cartoonist" are used somewhat interchangeably here; it should be noted, however, that editorial cartoonists generally and historically denote those affiliated with specific newspapers, and many if not most of those active in the field are also nationally and internationally syndicated. Many political cartoonists work on a freelance basis, but they are also full-fledged, active members of the Association of American Editorial Cartoonists, which is widely regarded as the leading professional organization of cartoonists in this specialty.[29]

Edwina Dumm (1903–1990) is considered to be one of the first North American woman to be a political cartoonist. A strong supporter of women's suffrage, she also commented artistically on other issues of her day, including World War I, Prohibition, and the economy.[30] Following her graduation from high school in Columbus, Ohio, she completed the Landon Correspondence School course in cartooning and worked as a stenographer with the Columbus Board of Education. In 1915, the *Columbus Saturday Monitor* hired her as staff artist, and she contributed spot illustrations, portraits of politicians, and a weekly editorial cartoon. When the publication became the *Columbus Daily Monitor* in July 1916, her output increased significantly, and she sometimes drew a humor page called *Spotlight Sketches,* which included a comic strip (see chapter 2).[31] In an article about her in the March 1916 issue of *Cartoons Magazine,* the surprised writer noted that Dumm "interprets world events in real masculine cartoons."[32]

Fig. 6.15. Edwina Dumm. "It was a brave and noble act, my boy!" ca. 1916. India ink over graphite underdrawing.

A rare original political cartoon drawing by Dumm, titled *It Was a Brave and Noble Act, My Boy!* (fig. 6.15), was created during World War I. The young soldier sleeping peacefully on the lower left dreams that a senior officer is commending him for capturing the Mexican revolutionary commander Pancho Villa, who drew American ire by staging raids into the United States, as well as Mexican president Venustiano Carranza, both of whom are tied to a tree in the background. In fact, the American "Punitive Expedition" into Mexico led by General John Pershing failed to find, or even catch sight of Villa, and capturing Carranza was never one of its goals. She treated the subject of the failed mission humorously and imaginatively—as a case of unfulfilled dreams.[33]

After the *Monitor* ceased publication in 1917, Dumm left for New York City to pursue a career as an artist. Once there, her success working in comic strips, beginning with *Tippie,* led her away from editorial cartooning (see chapter 2). Decades would

Fig. 6.16. Laura E. Foster. Looking Backward, 1912. Photomechanical print.

a tripod, symbolic of fame, and looks back sorrow-fully, as Trina Robbins has written, at the "joy she has surrendered in her quest for the vote, a career, and success. The blooming flowers of domesticity, here, give way to withered branches as the woman climbs beyond her proper sphere. Even in 1912, many people, women and men, opposed women's suffrage, arguing that women were happiest with lives centered around home, marriage, and children."[34] Foster published nu-merous other cartoons in *Judge* and *Life* that more clearly affirm her pro-suffrage stance, and she was not alone. Lou Rogers (born Annie Lucasta Rogers, 1879–1952) produced emphatic pro-suffrage cartoons for *Ladies' Home Journal, Woman's Journal,* and the humor magazine *Judge*.[35] Nina Allender (1873–1957), another pro-suffrage cartoonist, continued her po-litical cartooning after passage of the Nineteenth Amendment, moving into other roles on behalf of women's rights.[36]

Rose O'Neill also drew suffrage cartoons that were published in *Puck*, a leading humor magazine aimed primarily at a male audience. In *Suffrage Kewpies* (1915) (fig. 6.17), her signature creations playfully but pointedly campaign for voting rights for their moth-ers. In her landmark book *Cartooning for Suffrage* (1994), Alice Sheppard contends that the emergence of the *Masses*, a leftist magazine whose editors and main contributors were generally supportive, coincid-ed with and influenced the use of cartoons drawn by American women to promote the cause.[37] By contrast, art historian Rebecca Zurier, in her study, does not find such correlation between the kind of cartoons produced by these women and the expression of ad-vocacy for suffrage, although she makes the point that the few women associated with the magazine actively participated in feminism. Cornelia Barns (1877–1970), one of the *Masses* editors, did address conditions of women's lives in her cartoons. Zurier contends, how-ever, that she did not convey strong social commen-tary in her work, but rather expressed pro-suffrage views by satirizing men's presumption of superiority as seen in cartoons such as *Anti-Suffrage Meeting: United We Stand!*[38] Another *Masses* editor and car-toonist, Alice Beach Winter (1877–1970), focused on children and the stark difference between the poor and the wealthy.

pass before another woman would enter the fray and succeed as a newspaper editorial cartoonist. While not associated with specific newspapers, Dumm's peers were women who similarly sought to earn livelihoods by drawing for newspapers and magazines. Given that women were essentially excluded from the political process until they won the right to vote and edito-rial cartooning is intended to comment on political matters, it is hardly surprising that Dumm was the only woman who was, by strict definition, an editorial cartoonist. Yet many women of Dumm's generation *were* activists who, along with some men, support-ed women's right to vote. Support for that cause was not universal among women, however. Even the pro-suffrage Foster produced a haunting cartoon, *Looking Backward*, that reflects ambivalence about this and other proposed or actual social changes in the early twentieth century (fig. 6.16). Published in *Life*, Foster's cartoon shows a woman ascending stairs topped with

Fig. 6.17. Rose O'Neill. Suffrage Kewpies, 1915. Photomechanical offset. Published in *Puck*, February 15, 1915.

In 1933 the *Miami Daily News* hired Anne Briardy Mergen (1906–1994) as editorial cartoonist, a challenging, prestigious position she held for more than twenty years, long before the second wave of the women's movement arose and gained momentum. Women's issues such as having a career and the right to equal pay, for example, do not figure in her work. In *Editorial Cartooning*, published in 1949, author Dick Spencer III offered the backhanded compliment that "There is nothing about Anne Mergen's style of drawing to indicate that she is a woman." He went on to praise "her bold, straightforward style" and her ability to do "pointed cartoons."[39] His statements bring to mind examples of Mergen's World War II–era cartoons such as *Abdication!* (fig. 6.18) in which she excoriates Adolf Hitler, by showing the devil abdicating his throne to the German dictator, who is carrying a sword labeled "Nazi murder factories."

Born in Omaha, Nebraska, in 1906, Mergen loved to draw as a child, and her parents, second-generation Irish immigrants, Frank and Elizabeth Briardy, encouraged her. After her father's death in 1926, she and her family moved to Miami. She worked at Burdine's department store a few years before relocating to Chicago with her mother and sister in tow so that she could pursue art training. For two years, she worked a day job and attended night classes at the American Academy of Art. Returning to Miami, she took a job drawing fashion ads at Burdine's and in 1932 married Frank Mergen and soon was raising two children.[40]

Fig. 6.18. Anne Mergen. Abdication! between 1939 and 1945. Ink, crayon, graphite.

Finding the advertising work boring and routine, Mergen began to develop a one-page fashion story centering on two cartoon characters, shopping in the exclusive stores in the Lincoln Road area of South Beach. She called it "Anne and Peg's Scrapbook," which advertised offerings from Burdine's and other shops, and submitted it to the *Miami Daily News*. The paper had her expand the feature to two pages and published it for three years. Intrigued that the paper had no editorial cartoonist, she drew her first political cartoon, which was about Prohibition, and the *News* published it in April 1933.[41] Using her art school education—which had not included cartooning—her experience in fashion illustration and a strong interest in current affairs, she trained herself and worked her way into becoming the full-time editorial cartoonist in 1936. Early in Mergen's career, when the *Miami Daily News* won a Pulitzer Prize in 1939 for its investigative

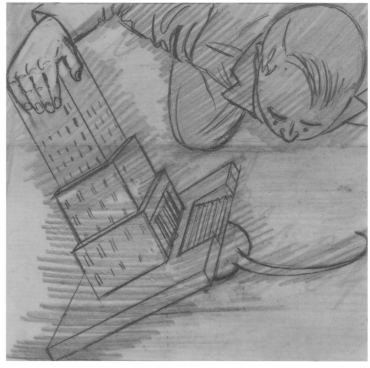

Fig. 6.19. Anne Mergen. [Charges of Graft and Corruption], 1938. Graphite. Sketch for the cartoon reproduced by *Editor & Publisher* when reporting Pulitzer Prize was awarded to *Miami Daily News* for its outstanding civic leadership.

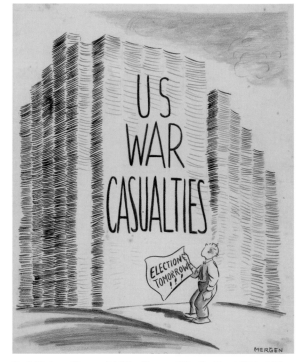

Fig. 6.20. Anne Mergen. A Million Reasons Why You Should Vote, 1941. Ink, crayon, and graphite.

reporting on the corrupt mayor and city commission in Miami's "termite administration," Hal Lyshon, the paper's editor, wired her saying, "Don't let anyone ever tell you it wasn't Mergen cartoons that won the Pulitzer today." A sketch (fig. 6.19) for one hard-hitting cartoon shows her ability to devise a strong visual metaphor that addressed corruption in city government.[42] Working in a spare, clear style, Mergen drew mostly in pencil with touches of ink, fashioning bold, eye-catching compositions that conveyed forthright messages. Throughout her career she maintained a consistently high level of technical skill, readable messaging, and artistic inventiveness in her work.

Feature stories about Mergen consistently underscored how well she managed to balance her dedication to her family and her work, stressing that she focused on her home and family as her daytime job and pursued her satisfying career in the evening. "I love my children and my husband and my work . . . and I find I have time enough for them all."[43] Such accounts undoubtedly oversimplify the situation, but Mergen's devotion to her family and her work

and ability to navigate both spheres of responsibility were remarkable during an era when managing both was not the prevailing social norm. How did she do it? Her daughter Joan Bernhardt recollected that her mother read multiple newspapers from across the nation, regularly listened to radio news programs, and would begin sketching in the afternoon in her studio. Her parents discussed her mother's ideas as she was drawing, and her father would pose if needed. After Mergen completed her final drawing, sometimes late at night, her father would deliver it to the newspaper office.[44]

One cannot help but notice that Mergen and Chicago native Herb Block "Herblock" (1909–2001), a close contemporary and fellow midwesterner, both addressed many of the same themes of civic welfare in their work. For example, Mergen's *A Million Reasons Why You Should Vote* (1941) (fig. 6.20) features an Everyman figure looking up at towering piles of papers labeled "US WAR CASUALTIES" as he holds a sign that says "Election Tomorrow!!!" In another example (fig. 6.21), Mergen challenges apathetic voters by

Fig. 6.21. Anne Mergen. What's Wrong with this Picture? between 1940–1952. Crayon and ink brush over graphite underdrawing.

Fig. 6.22. Anne Mergen. Giving Them Something To Think About, 1954. Ink, crayon, and graphite. Published in the *Miami Daily News*, April 14, 1954.

depicting a staggering number of people lined up for the circus, the Orange Bowl, and the theater while just two lonely voters appear at voting booths. The sense of moral urgency conveyed by these two cartoons is reminiscent of the tone taken by Herblock in cartoons such as 1942's *While Millions Die for the Right to Vote*.[45]

Mergen deemed adequate support for education, protection of the environment, racial desegregation, and health-related issues as vital to the civic good. In the 1940s, when her own two children were young and polio posed possible tragedy to thousands, many of her cartoons urged support for research to prevent and cure the illness. "Real happiness comes from an interest in the significant affairs of the world, of keeping abreast of the times, of being informed— and doing something about it," she said at the time.[46] When a polio vaccine was developed in the 1950s, she referenced the research that underlay the triumph in a cartoon that also celebrated this medical milestone (fig. 6.22). Mergen felt she had aided in some small way to victory over this terrible disease and took some satisfaction from her role.[47]

Once established as an editorial cartoonist, Mergen did not venture seriously into other types of illustration. Over more than twenty years, she produced more than seven thousand editorial cartoons for the *Miami Daily News*, as well as other Cox company newspapers such as the *Atlanta Journal*. Her cartoons were selected numerous times for reprint in the cartoons-of-the-week section in *Editor & Publisher*, one of journalism's leading magazines. Following the death of President Franklin Roosevelt, whom she greatly admired, she created two cartoons that Eleanor Roosevelt requested for the Hyde Park Library Museum.[48] Although Mergen retired in 1956, she continued to publish some cartoons on a freelance basis for another five years. In 1953, she received the Wendy Warren Award, a national honor given by *Today's Woman* magazine to an outstanding woman "who has added stature to woman's place in the world, achieved marked success in business, industry, science or the arts, or who has contributed to the community welfare through her activities and accomplishments."[49]

"IT'S FROM THE I.R.S.—IT SAYS, 'ALL INCOME, FROM WHATEVER SOURCE DERIVED...'"

Fig. 6.23. Etta Hulme. "It's from the I.R.S.—it says, 'all income, from whatever source derived . . .'" April 10, 1975. Crayon, ink, and opaque white over blue pencil and graphite underdrawing.

Etta Hulme's path to becoming a political cartoonist was neither rapid nor direct, despite an interest in cartooning that began in her teenage years. The daughter of a grocery store owner and a teacher, Etta Parks was born in 1923, in Somerville, Texas. After completing a degree in fine arts at the University of Texas, Austin, she worked in a Disney animation studio in California for two years, then produced commercial art and taught in an art school in San Antonio.[50] She relocated briefly to Chicago in 1949 to illustrate *Red Rabbit* comic books, an animal parody of cowboy comic hero Red Ryder.[51]

Returning to Texas, Hulme freelanced as an editorial cartoonist for the *Texas Observer* beginning in 1954. In 1972, she was hired as the full-time editorial cartoonist by the *Fort Worth Star-Telegram,* where she worked for more than thirty years.[52] Over her long career Hulme developed a distinctive, sharply humorous approach that gave a singular edge to her compelling visual commentary on what often proved to be central questions of her time. Though unabashedly liberal in her political orientation, she pulled no punches in lampooning excesses, foibles, and flaws in the actions and words of leaders in both major parties, as well as public institutions and organizations of all stripes.

Some of Hulme's recurring concerns include elected federal officeholders' blatant self-interest, inadequate gun control laws, insufficient concern for the environment, the high cost of advanced weaponry, ineffective response to sexual misconduct in the military, and inadequate oversight of CIA budgets. In one cartoon (fig. 6.23), she depicts her signature short, pudgy male figures as castaways on a desert island unearthing treasure. Their joy is interrupted by an ironic reminder from the IRS that income taxes are due and that it has the right to know about "all income, from whatever source derived."

In 1981, Hulme became the first woman to win the National Cartoonists Society Editorial Cartoon Award. Before winning the same award again in 1998, she served as president of the American Association of Editorial Cartoonists (AAEC). Pelican published a collection of her cartoons, *Ettatorials: The Best of Etta Hulme* (1998), and she was the subject of an acclaimed documentary, *Trailblazer: The Editorial Cartoons of Etta Hulme*, that when screened in 2004 at the annual meeting of the AAEC, received a standing ovation, a testimony to the esteem in which her peers held her.[53]

In the first decade and a half of the twenty-first century, two traumatic events related to the world of editorial cartooning sent waves of shocked disbelief around the world. Violent protests against cartoons showing the prophet Muhammed published by the Danish newspaper *Jyllands-Posten* on September 30, 2005, and the murder in Paris of five cartoonists working for *Charlie Hebdo* magazine by Islamic extremists on January 7, 2015, brought anguished and, in some cases, rapid reactions from many American editorial cartoonists, including Signe Wilkinson, Ann Telnaes, Liza Donnelly, and Jen Sorensen. Taking part in public programs, professional association discussions, writing commentaries, and/or creating cartoons about the role of cartooning in the face of conditions that became increasingly challenging, they expressed varying opinions about the tragedies while powerfully supporting freedom of speech. Wilkinson has been especially forthright, declaring that "We haven't learned much, except that we have given Jihadist Muslims the right to choose how and whether, here in America, the image of their prophet can be used in cartoons or anywhere else. This is a right [that] cartoonists, newspapers and social critics on all platforms do not extend to prophets or symbols of other faiths . . . If the devout do awful things in the name of their prophets, they shouldn't be surprised to see their prophets in cartoons, and we shouldn't be afraid to put them there."[54]

In Donnelly's view, "While we must be forceful, inflammatory images or words are not always the answer. Personally, I would probably not have accepted the assignment to draw Muhammed. But these decisions are intensely personal, and I defend wholeheartedly my colleagues' right to do so." When Telnaes moderated a panel on "Cartooning and Free Speech" at the 2015 annual meeting of the National Cartoonists

Society, she strongly and respectfully disagreed with colleague Garry Trudeau in her response to the Hebdo killings. While Trudeau decried the murders, he was also somewhat critical of the cartoonists' use of free speech in their work, whereas Telnaes stressed that their right to exercise free speech should be absolute and no matter how offensive their work, no cartoonists should have to worry about being killed for the ideas they express.[55]

Telnaes took—and illustrated—a resolute view on a related and similarly volatile issue after several communities on the French Riviera banned women from wearing full-length swimsuits known as burkinis. "Many saw the garment as an extension of the recent Islamic extremist attacks against France while opponents of the burkini bans claim it was just another example of Islamophobia from the Western world," she said. "I've frequently used the image of women being completely covered up, usually in a burka or niqab, to comment on the oppression in patriarchal societies. However, I believe the key is whether or not this is a free choice. Personally, I think a woman should be able to wear a paper bag on her head if that's what she wants to do. The problem isn't whether she chooses to wear a bikini or a burkini, the problem is when governments or religious institutions deny women their human and economic rights." Telnaes came to see this as a "push/pull situation" and produced an animated gif "with two men alternately pulling on or pulling off a niqab with a woman standing in the middle." She called it *Men: Stop Telling Women What to Wear*.[56]

Signe Wilkinson was born in Wichita Falls, Texas, to Quaker parents in 1950. After completing a BA in English at Denver University, she attended PAFA and later supported herself doing graphic design at the Academy of Natural Sciences and working as a stringer for regional newspapers. In 1982 the *San Jose Mercury News* hired her as a full-time editorial cartoonist; three years later, she moved to the *Philadelphia Daily News*, where she spent her career while contributing to other publications on the side. The year 1992 marked a landmark moment in the profession when she became the first woman to win the Pulitzer Prize for editorial cartooning.[57] The award committee highlighted her work on issues that particularly affected women and children, such as the military deployment of women

Fig. 6.24. Signe Wilkinson. "How can I make sure my child won't suffer from the wage gap between men and women?" 1988. Ink, blue pencil, and opaque white. Published in *Ms. Magazine*, November 1988.

Fig. 6.25. Signe Wilkinson. "Oh, I approve of arresting everyone who passes toxic substances to fetuses, and I mean . . . everyone!" 1989. Ink, blue pencil, and opaque white. Published in *Ms. Magazine*, November 1989.

Fig. 6.26. Signe Wilkinson. "The court's abortion decision is an affirmation of our progress in protecting human life!" April 20, 2007. Ink, opaque white, and graphite. Published in *Philadelphia Daily News*.

in the Gulf War and the closure of many small savings and loan institutions during a recession.[58] That same year she published *Abortion Cartoons on Demand*.

Wilkinson's talent for addressing serious questions with pointed humor is especially evident in cartoons she created for *Ms. Magazine* in the 1980s (figs. 6.24 and 6.25). In one she deals with lifelong pay inequality and in the other she addresses the irony of being judgmental toward others and overlooking greater threats. A strong advocate for the individual's right to privacy and for women's right to make choices involving reproduction, she criticizes and mocks public officials who threaten to compromise those rights (fig. 6.26). While she grapples with these weighty, divisive issues head on, she cleverly injects visual humor into her imagery. In the latter cartoon, a two-pronged critique, she shows the White House heavily weighted with an absurd number of security devices while President George W. Bush shouts from a window, reassuring a local gun shop owner that his privacy rights are protected (fig. 6.27).

Another woman to win the Pulitzer Prize for editorial cartooning, Ann Telnaes projects a powerful voice in support of equal rights, both at home and abroad. Telnaes was born in Stockholm, Sweden, in 1960 to a Norwegian father and a German mother and moved to the United States as a child. She earned a BFA in character animation at the California Institute of the Arts.[59] Early in her career, Telnaes did freelance work for Disney and smaller studios in Los Angeles and London. As one of the animators for *The Brave Little Toaster* (1987), she also worked in Taiwan for five months. While benefiting from this experience, she found the assembly-line work dissatisfying and sought more creative outlets. She worked for Disney Imagineering from 1987 to 1993 and also completed freelance assignments in humorous illustration and licensing work for Warner Bros.[60]

The controversial 1991 Senate hearings on Clarence Thomas's nomination to the US Supreme Court and the testimony of Anita Hill prompted Telnaes to produce a series of political cartoons that launched her career in the field. During the 1992 Republican National Convention, Telnaes's work began to be published regularly and she moved to Washington, DC, the next year. She tied for first place in a cartoon contest

Fig. 6.27. Signe Wilkinson. "Don't worry. Your privacy is protected by the Constitution," 2007.
Ink, opaque white, and graphite. Published in the *Philadelphia Daily News*, July 13, 2007.

sponsored by *Editorial Humor* magazine and won a contract with the North American Syndicate (then owned by King Features.) In mid-2000, she moved from the North American Syndicate to individual distribution with the Los Angeles Syndicate, which Tribune Media Services subsequently took over.

Entering the field somewhat later in her career than most political cartoonists, Telnaes quickly developed her distinctive, hard-hitting, and visually appealing style. Although primarily dedicated to political cartooning, Telnaes has explored a variety of outlets for her work. In 2002, she joined *Six Chix*, a daily comic strip produced weekly with five other women, each of whom contributed a Sunday strip every six weeks. She enjoyed this but found it difficult not to inject political issues into the strip and withdrew after a few years. Telnaes has shown her work in solo exhibitions, including "Pens & Needles: The Editorial Cartoons of Ann Telnaes" at the Newseum (2001–2002) and "Humor's Edge: Cartoons by Ann Telnaes" at the Library of Congress (2004), and her cartoons have also appeared in group shows.

One of Telnaes's Pulitzer Prize–winning cartoons (fig. 6.28) comments concisely, sharply, yet also humorously on the US Supreme Court decision on the 2000 presidential election, an event that raised widespread concerns about interference of the court in the political process. She conveyed her concern for the women of Afghanistan in *Aim Carefully, Please* (fig. 6.29). When this cartoon was drawn, US forces were preparing to attack Afghanistan in the wake of the September 11, 2001, terrorist attacks. Telnaes's cartoon addresses the particular vulnerability of Afghan women, whose movement and ability to be informed were severely limited. Telnaes comments, "At the time I was thinking, just be careful where you're aiming those bombs." Like many of her peers, Telnaes expressed concern about threats to individuals' civil rights in the face of increased security measures that became operative in the aftermath of September 11. Her concern to protect civil rights comes to the fore in *For the New Year I've Decided to Give Up Smoking, Drinking and My Civil Rights* (fig. 6.30). This drawing is another example of Telnaes's gift for

Fig. 6.28. Ann Telnaes. The Bush Decision, December 13, 2000. Ink brush over blue pencil and graphite underdrawing with opaque white.

Fig. 6.29. Ann Telnaes. "Aim carefully, please," 2001. Ink brush over colored pencil underdrawing and opaque white. Published by North America Syndicate, October 2, 2001.

communicating strong messages with visual grace and light humor.

A complement to Wilkinson's 2007 abortion decision cartoon can be seen in Telnaes's scathing piece *The "Partial Birth Abortion" Ban Signing Ceremony* (2003) (fig. 6.31). The smiling men who surrounded President George W. Bush as he signed the bill include Jerry Falwell, Attorney General John Ashcroft, and Senator George Allen. No women appeared in the widely distributed photograph of the signing. "The situation is so absurd that you don't have to do much," said Telnaes. "You're just showing what everyone who looks at the photo is thinking." Her wry take on the 2003 Massachusetts Supreme Court ruling that gay couples have the right to marry (fig. 6.32) makes the point that the traditional view of marriage between a man and a woman did much to demote some Americans to second-class citizenship. This particular drawing shows off her distinctively elegant, streamlined drawing style in a composition that achieves a perfect balance between main figures, setting, and decorative detail.

Among many recurring issues and themes that stand out in Telnaes's work are the status of women worldwide, freedom of expression, major failings of public figures, and the state of the environment. She also returned to her professional roots, producing animated editorial cartoons for the *Washington Post* website.[61] As a finalist for the 2011 Herblock Prize, an award for excellence in editorial cartooning that is bestowed annually by the Herb Block Foundation to commemorate the cartoonist's legacy, she won recognition for her editorial animations, which then marked another professional milestone for women in the field, as well as recognition for editorial cartoons in the form of animations.[62] The judges who bestowed this honor described her cartoons thusly: "Done with an elegant line in her singular style her cartoons are pithy, punchy and irreverent . . . timelessly classic" (Matt Wuerker); "in her tight exquisitely drawn animations, Ann lets her victims hang themselves with their own words" (Signe Wilkinson); further, her work charts "a new direction, capsulizing sound, movement and cartooning into an effective political message" (Harry Katz).[63]

Fig. 6.30. Ann Telnaes. "For the New Year I've decided to give up smoking, drinking, and my civil rights," October 28, 2001. Ink brush over pink pencil and graphite underdrawing with opaque white.

Fig. 6.31. Ann Telnaes. The "Partial Birth Abortion" Ban Signing Ceremony, November 6, 2003. Ink brush over blue pencil and graphite underdrawing with opaque white.

> SO, WHICH ONE OF YOU GETS TO ENDURE CENTURIES OF 2ND CLASS STATUS AND BEING LEGALLY CONSIDERED THE PROPERTY OF YOUR HUSBAND?

Fig. 6.32. Ann Telnaes. "So, which one of you gets to endure centuries of 2nd class status and being legally considered the property of your husband?" November 21, 2003. Ink brush over pink pencil and graphite underdrawing with opaque white.

In a profession that largely leans left, Lisa Benson's conservative take on politics makes her a notable exception. Like Telnaes, Benson came to editorial cartooning a little later than most of her colleagues and made her start in the field while raising her family. Born in La Jolla, California, she grew up in a family with creative siblings who encouraged her interest in drawing, painting, and ceramics. Interested only in art, she took every relevant class offered while attending Rim of the World High School near Lake Arrowhead. She always enjoyed the daily comics page, especially *Peanuts* by Charles Schulz and *Garfield* by Jim Davis. During the 1973 Watergate hearings, she discovered editorial cartoons, rushing home from school to see the latest Paul Conrad and Pat Oliphant cartoons.[64]

Uninterested in college, she moved to San Luis Obispo, worked for accountants, married an architect, then settled in Apple Valley, in the high desert of Southern California, and raised a family. During the recessions of the early 1990s, Benson contributed to family income by doing paste-up, ad design, and editorial cartoons for the monthly publication the *Senior Advocate*. In 1992, she sent a sample editorial cartoon to the *Victor Valley (California) Daily Press*. In response, the Opinion page editor hired her to do

two cartoons a week, and in 2007 the Washington Post Writers Group began syndicating her work.[65]

In her cartoons, Benson exhibits strong drawing skills characterized by use of massed forms, clearly organized compositions, fine lines in rendering details, and minimal lettering, all balanced within easily read works. In *Fiscal Sanity* (2009) (fig. 6.33), Uncle Sam searches in vain inside a cornucopia whose depths contain only one big continuously empty black hole, a metaphor for fiscal policies that appear empty of material promise. In *Social Security* (2010) (fig. 6.34), Benson's wide-eyed eponymous eagle perches precariously on a nest of flimsy paper IOUs and stares at the viewer as eggs slip away below, positing that this key entitlement program for retirees had become unsustainable. Benson has created fewer cartoons on women's issues than Telnaes and Wilkinson. It is clear from her work, for example, that she supports abortion rights, but she does not agree that federal funds should be used.[66] She is good natured about being among the few conservative voices in the field. "Just like Hollywood, conservatives are outnumbered by their liberal colleagues, [and] the same seems to be true for journalism. Much of the media leans to the left, so I'm guessing there's not much appetite for conservative views. If the nation is nearly split down the middle—half Republican, half Democrat—then I think editors are missing an opportunity to reach out to a good chunk of America."[67]

By the early twenty-first century, many news outlets in print, facing stiff online competition from other news sources, existed in precarious circumstances. To survive, papers made drastic reductions in staff, including editorial cartoonists, whose numbers have significantly diminished. Some cartoonists found outlets in alternative papers; others, like Telnaes, Donnelly, and Sorensen successfully shifted from working primarily in print to digital media.

Liza Donnelly identifies herself as a contract cartoonist for the *New Yorker* magazine, but she has built her career over thirty years by publishing her work in many other venues as well, including books. She focuses on culture and politics, particularly women's rights.[68] Two drawings exemplify her engagement with political topics. In one image (fig. 6.35), drawn in

Fig. 6.33. Lisa Benson. Fiscal Sanity, 2009. Ink. Published in *Victorville Daily Press*, November 18, 2009.

Fig. 6.34. Lisa Benson. Social Security, 2010. Ink. Published in *Victorville Daily Press*, March 17, 2010.

"NEXT SEMESTER, I WAS THINKING OF TAKING 'HOW TO AVOID RAPE,' BUT THE PRE-REQUISTS ARE 'HOW TO DRESS,' 'HOW TO BEHAVE,' AND 'HOW TO PLEASE.'"

Fig. 6.35. Liza Donnelly. "Next semester, I was thinking of taking 'How to avoid rape,' but the [prerequisites] are 'How to dress,' 'How to behave,' and 'How to please,'" 2010. Ink and wash.

"THIS ONE IS FOR COMPLETELY ERADICATING THE WORD 'PEACE' FROM MY VOCABULARY."

Fig. 6.36. Liza Donnelly. "This one is for completely eradicating the word 'peace' from my vocabulary," 2014. Ink, watercolor, and wash.

the wake of prominent news coverage about campus rape, a young woman discusses with her roommate the possibility of taking a course on "How to avoid rape," but then notes that prerequisites include courses on how to dress, behave, and please. In another work (fig. 6.36), a highly decorated male military official confides to a female guest that he received one of his award insignia "for completely eradicating the word 'peace'" from his vocabulary. As a charter member of an international project, Cartooning for Peace, Donnelly has created a number of cartoons as part of her commitment to international understanding through humor.[69] Her fluid drawing style and ability to evoke scenes with minimal details is evident in both these drawings, which appear at first to present breezy, lighthearted scenarios, but transmit serious messages.

Donnelly was born in 1955 and grew up in Washington, DC, so her engagement with political topics is not surprising. As a cultural envoy for the US State Department, she has traveled the world to speak on freedom of speech, cartoons, and women's rights, and her cartoons have also been exhibited internationally. In 2014, she delivered the commencement address at the University of Connecticut Graduate School, which awarded her an honorary doctorate in recognition of her contributions to the field.[70]

Jen Sorensen, born in 1974, was the first woman to win the Herblock Prize for her editorial cartoons. A native of Lancaster, Pennsylvania, her parents, both public schoolteachers, encouraged her interest in cartooning.[71] She drew cartoons for college publications while attending the University of Virginia, graduating Phi Beta Kappa with a degree in cultural anthropology. The *C-VILLE Weekly*, in Charlottesville, offered Sorensen a spot on the paper early in her career, and Sorensen soon began her own weekly strip, *Slowpoke*. In the years following the 2000 presidential election and the September 11, 2001, terrorist attacks, her work became more political. Winning a Xeric Award in 2000 enabled her to publish her first collection of strips, *Slowpoke: Café Pompous* (Alternative Comics) the next year, followed by additional collections. Sorensen's political cartoons are nationally syndicated and appear in alternative weekly newspapers, including her local weekly, the *Austin Chronicle*, as well as in

Fig. 6.37. Jen Sorensen. Great Moments in Equality, 2008. Ink over graphite.

national magazines and news websites, and she serves as comics editor for *Fusion*, a media company that is "both a cable channel and digital news outlet aimed at diverse young adults."[72]

Her work in multipaneled, alt-weekly format is carefully calculated, economical, and cleanly drawn and lettered. Cartoonists whom she mentions as attracting her interest in the alt-weekly genre include Tom Tomorrow, Ruben Bolling, Ted Rall, Lloyd Dangle, Ward Sutton, and Matt Groening.[73] Her customary four-panel format provides a platform that

enables her to provide some distilled background to the complex issues and commentaries she creates. While low key in responses to interview questions about being one of the few successful women political cartoonists, she is strongly concerned about the underrepresentation of women's voices in that field and in other very public conduits of information and opinion.[74] A notable number of her cartoons directly address unequal treatment of women in the workplace and public sphere. Consider *Great Moments in Equality* (2008) (fig. 6.37) in which she lampoons

Figs. 6.38 and 6.39. Jen Sorensen. The Prevailing Trend in Business Is Paying Nothing for Online Content, 2008. Ink over graphite; final art with color added digitally.

vice presidential candidate Sarah Palin, yet also uses her signature character Drooly Julie to make the point that Palin's candidacy is notable. As a younger voice in the field, she also grapples with the growing use of online platforms for political cartooning. *The Prevailing Trend in Business Is Paying Nothing for Online Content* (figs. 6.38 and 6.39) is her pointed commentary on this development. Sorensen's position at *Fusion* marks her most direct engagement with and commitment to date with electronic distribution of political cartoon commentary.

Collectively, women's voices in editorial cartooning from the past into the present reflect far more than the changing roles of women in society. Through emboldened voices and imagery, they have enlarged their power to create art that is not only honored by their peers, but more important, brings to the public strong, individually formed views about often divisive, controversial issues, visual commentary that helps shape opinions and illuminate the critically important political and social debates of their times. As Telnaes has said, "What I'm really striving for in my work is for it

to stand on its own years from now so that other generations can look at my editorial cartoons and get a sense of what people were thinking and talking about. In this sense, historical editorial cartoons are really comparable to art history. Studying art history is a wonderful way to learn about world history: through the artist's use of subject matter and technique the viewer gets a sense of the political and social climate of the time. Even how a piece of artwork is received by the public and critics tells you a great deal."[75]

ACKNOWLEDGMENTS

Writing a book-length survey of artworks created by women illustrators and cartoonists represented in the Library of Congress's Prints and Photographs Division gradually took shape as a dream and then became a goal I was eager to pursue. I could never have undertaken such a daunting project without substantial help and encouragement from colleagues, editors, friends, many of the artists featured in the book, and my family.

The Library's Publishing Office gave generous encouragement and support that were absolutely crucial to completion of the book. Many thanks go to the chief, Becky Clark, and talented editors Susan Reyburn and Margaret Wagner, who so skillfully, tirelessly, and patiently worked with me. Thanks, too, to editor Aimee Hess, image specialist Athena Angelos, and editorial assistant Hannah Freece for their thorough, critical work on text and image content.

I am deeply grateful to P&P chief Helena Zinkham, whose strong backing for this project has never wavered since I proposed the idea years ago. I cannot thank my supervisor Barbara Natanson and colleagues Beverly Brannan and Katherine Blood enough for reading and commenting on drafted chapters and discussing with me the lives and careers of many artists and their works. I also greatly appreciate my colleagues Sara Duke and Ford Peatross generously contributing insightful commentaries on women creators in specific areas of their expertise.

Further, I gratefully acknowledge the timely assistance of P&P's digital team headed by Phil Michel and Kit Arrington. I appreciate the careful cataloguing of many works by Karen Chittenden and accessioning thousands of newly added works by Bonnie Dziedzic. I tip my cap to conservators Holly Krueger, Heather Wanser, Julie Biggs, and Betsy Haude, who repaired and stabilized so many of the drawings found in these pages.

I extend warm thanks to Georgia Higley and Megan Halsband in the Serials and Government Publications Division and to Mark Dimunation and Eric Frazier in the Rare Book and Special Collections Division for finding and sharing treasures in their collections to include in this book, enriching and strengthening its visual impact. Exhibit director Cynthia Wayne, Interpretive Programs Office chief David Mandel, and exhibit designer Michael Shveima helped me sharpen my thinking about the narrative and design aspects of the whole project and I thank them.

The editors and talented specialists at the University Press of Mississippi, including Lisa McMurtray, Shane Gong Stewart, Pete Halverson, Vijay Shah, and Craig Gill, deserve special thanks for skillfully shaping, designing, and producing the final handsome volume.

I am also grateful to Leslie Long, the late Walt Reed, Roger Reed, Fred Taraba, Jan Grenci, and Brian Walker for sharing their knowledge about various artists and professional practices. It is a pleasure to acknowledge Warren Bernard, executive director of the Small Press Expo, who drew my attention to and shared his special knowledge about a host of talented cartoonists and illustrators. Thanks also to archivist, friend, and comics expert Michael Rhode for sharing many suggestions. Further, I greatly appreciate the strong, early support for the project from former colleagues Linda Osborne, Ralph Eubanks, and Jeremy Adamson.

To the many artists in this book, and the donors and dealers who have helped acquire examples of their work, I express enormous gratitude. Additional, heartfelt thanks to those who responded so helpfully and warmly to many requests for information and commentary. Their responses have been invaluable.

Last but not least, more thanks than I can express to my family, my husband, Dane, and my daughter Alene, for their steady encouragement and unfailing support.

NOTES

PREFACE

1. Quoted in Christine Jones Huber, *The Pennsylvania Academy and Its Women, 1850–1920* (Philadelphia: Pennsylvania Academy of Fine Arts, 1974), 6. Exhibition catalog.

CHAPTER 1: GOLDEN AGE ILLUSTRATORS

1. Howard Pyle quoted in Alice E. Carter, *The Red Rose Girls: An Uncommon Story of Art and Love* (New York: Harry N. Abrams, 2000), 44.

2. Mary Hallock Foote, *A Victorian Gentlewoman in the Far West: The Reminiscences of Mary Hallock Foote*, ed. Rodman W. Paul (San Marino, CA: Huntington Library, 1972), 101.

3. Carter, *The Red Rose Girls*, 52.

4. Michele Bogart, *Artists, Advertising, and the Borders of Art* (Chicago: University of Chicago Press, 1995), 30.

5. Huber, *The Pennsylvania Academy and Its Women*, 12.

6. Ibid., 12, 15.

7. Carter, *The Red Rose Girls*, 14–15.

8. Ibid., 14–15. Illustrator Alice Barber Stephens (1858–1934) memorably portrayed sister students working from a nude model in her 1879 painting, *Female Life Class*; see Huber, *The Pennsylvania Academy and Its Women*, 17.

9. "Thomas Cowperthwaite Eakins," *Benezit Dictionary of Artists, Oxford Art Online*. Oxford University Press, accessed May 9, 2016, http://www.oxfordartonline.com/subscriber/article/benezit/B00057005.

10. Henry C. Pitz, *Howard Pyle: Writer, Illustrator, Founder of the Brandywine School* (New York: Clarkson Potter, 1975), 227.

11. Bogart, *Artists, Advertising, and the Borders of Art*, 38.

12. "History of the Society," *Society of Illustrators*, accessed April 30, 2016, https://www.societyillustrators.org/history-society.

13. It is notable that until the early twenty-first century, most art historians gave little attention to the "Golden Age of Illustration" and illustration in general.

14. Bogart, *Artists, Advertising, and the Borders of Art*, 19.

15. Ibid., 20.

16. Ibid., 30.

17. Ibid., 30.

18. Michael Zakian, *Illustrating Modern Life: The Golden Age of American Illustration from the Kelly Collection* (Malibu, CA: Frederick R. Weisman Museum of Art, Pepperdine University, 2013), 9.

19. For descriptions of lithography, the print process developed by Alois Senefelder in the late eighteenth century, see Sally Pierce and Catharina Slautterback, *Boston Lithography, 1825–1880* (Boston: Boston Athenæum, 1991), 1–2; Marie-Stephanie Delamaire, *Lasting Impressions: The Artists of Currier & Ives* (Winterthur, DE: Winterthur Museum, Garden and Library, 2016), 10. Exhibition catalog.

20. Pierce and Slautterback, *Boston Lithography*, 5, 6, 170, 173. See also Helena E. Wright, *With Pen and Graver: Women Graphic Artists before 1900* (Washington, DC: National Museum of American History, Smithsonian Institution, 1995), 3–23.

21. Erika Piola and Jennifer Ambrose, "The First Fifty Years of Commercial Lithography in Philadelphia: An Overview of the Trade, 1828–1878," in *Philadelphia on Stone: Commercial Lithography in Philadelphia, 1828–1878*, ed. Erika Piola (Philadelphia: Pennsylvania State University Press in association with The Library Company of Philadelphia, 2012), 32.

22. Ibid., 21–22. Victoria Quarre and Lavinia Bowen have been identified as lithographers in Philadelphia during the 1850s and the Philadelphia School of Design for Women was established in 1844 and was training women as lithographers and periodical illustrators by the early 1850s, according to Piola and Ambrose.

23. Charlotte Streifer Rubinstein, "Fanny Palmer: The Workhorse of Currier & Ives," in *Fanny Palmer: A Long Island Woman Who Portrayed America* (Cold Spring Harbor, NY: Society for the Preservation of Long Island Antiquities, 1997), 9.

24. Ibid., 11. According to Rubinstein, Currier sent Palmer to Long Island in his carriage to sketch rural details and locations from nature that could be integrated into prints.

25. Charlotte Streifer Rubinstein, *American Women Artists from Early Indian Times to the Present* (Boston: G. K. Hall, 1982), 69.

26. Quoted in Rubinstein, "Fanny Palmer," 7; John Michael Vlach, *The Planter's Prospect* (Chapel Hill: University of North Carolina Press, 2002), 113.

27. Walt Reed mentions ca. 1880 as the advent of the "Golden Age" of illustration in *The Illustrator in America, 1860–2000* (New York: Society of Illustrators, 2001), 6. Others give the era a span of about fifty years, from ca. 1880 to 1930. See Bogart, *Artists, Advertising, and the Borders of Art*, 15; Zakian, *Illustrating Modern Life*, 8.

28. Sue Rainey identifies William Rimmer and W. J. Linton as instructors whom Foote identified as mentors during her time of study at the Cooper Union's School of Design for Women in "Mary Hallock Foote: A Leading Illustrator of the 1870s and 1880s," *Winterthur Portfolio: A Journal of American Material Culture* 41, nos. 2–3 (Summer/Autumn 2007): 102–3.

29. Foote, *A Victorian Gentlewoman in the Far West*, 101, 103. In describing the letters that she and her future husband exchanged as each established their careers, she juxtaposes the appeal of her own successes with her appreciation for his developing professional experience in mining and its potential importance.

30. Ibid., 125.

31. Ibid., 128.

32. Ibid., 124.

33. Quoted in Robert A. Taft, *Artist and Illustrators of the Old West* (Princeton, NJ: Princeton University Press, 1953), 172–73. Taft also mentions that Rogers and Hayes did not find Foote at home because she had accompanied her husband on a prospecting trip.

34. Joseph Pennell, *The Adventures of an Illustrator, Mostly in Following His Authors in America & Europe* (Boston: Little, Brown, and Company, 1925), 58.

35. Rainey, "Mary Hallock Foote," 139, note 208.

36. Ann Barton Brown, *Alice Barber Stephens: A Pioneer Woman Illustrator* (Chadds Ford, PA: Brandywine River Museum, 1984), 21.

37. Ibid., 8.

38. Stephens thought her finest wood engraving was a depiction of Tanagra figurines published in *Scribner's Monthly* 21 (April 1881): 924, LC-USZ62-85539. See also Brown, *Alice Barber Stephens*, 13.

39. Stephens later donated the painting to the Pennsylvania Academy of Fine Arts.

40. Fred Taraba, "Alice Barber Stephens: The First Famous Female Illustrator," in *Masters of American Illustration: 41 Illustrators & How They Worked* (St. Louis, MO: Illustrated Press, 2013), 395.

41. Brown, *Alice Barber Stephens*, 21.

42. Patricia Smith Scanlan, "'God-gifted Girls': The Rise of Women Illustrators in Late Nineteenth Century Philadelphia," *Nineteenth Century Gender Studies* 11, no. 2 (Summer 2015): 10.

43. Helen Goodman, "Alice Barber Stephens," *American Artist* 48, no. 501 (April 1984): 48.

44. For discussion of Charles Dana Gibson and his connection with the New Woman, see "The Gibson Girl as the 'New Woman,'" *The Gibson Girl's America: Drawings by Charles Dana Gibson*, 2013. Library of Congress, accessed March 8, 2017, https://www.loc.gov/exhibits/gibson-girls-america/the-gibson-girl-as-the-new-woman.html.

45. Brown, *Alice Barber Stephens*, 24–26.

46. Barbara MacIlvaine, "A History of the Plastic Club," *Plastic Club*, accessed March 9, 2017, http://www.plasticclub.org/history.html.

47. See biographical information about artist Blanche Dillaye, who originated the name for the Plastic Club, at "Blanche Dillaye," *Plastic Club*, accessed March 9, 2017, http://www.plasticclub.org/dillaye.html.

48. "About the Plastic Club," *Plastic Club*, accessed March 9, 2017, http://www.plasticclub.org/about.html.

49. Scanlan, "'God-gifted Girls,'" 13.

50. "About the Plastic Club," http://www.plasticclub.org/about.html.

51. See, for example, Stephens's award-winning illustrations from George Eliot's *Middlemarch* (New York: Thomas Crowell, 1899): [Dorothea busy in the old library,] LC-USZ62–54592, in which Stephens illuminates the relationship between Dorothea and her scholarly, older, husband, the Reverend Edward Casaubon. She portrays the two physically separated by tables and piles of books, showing the youthful, vigorous Dorothea standing and handling materials, in contrast with her sedentary, withdrawn husband at the back of the library; [Two women], LC-USZC2–415; and [Two men approaching women at tea table], CAI—Stephens, no. 41 (B size).

52. From "The Art of Illustrating," *Women's Progress*, November 1893, quoted in Taraba, "Alice Barber Stephens," 396.

53. Quoted in Brown, *Alice Barber Stephens*, 34.

54. The inscription "1917 or 18, for poster" appears on the verso.

55. See "'Waste Not, Want Not,' The Need For Conservation of Food as Seen by the Artists," *Red Cross Magazine* 10, no. 10 (November 1917): 517–23. Stephens's design is third in the series, 520.

56. Carter, *The Red Rose Girls*, 44.

57. Ibid., 52.

58. Harrison S. Morris, "Elizabeth Shippen Green," *Book Buyer* 24, no. 2 (March 1902): 114.

59. Carter, *The Red Rose Girls*, 131, 135, 157.

60. Ibid., 12. Sources differ as to whether Smith attended lessons given by a female friend or cousin. See also S. Michael Schnessel, *Jessie Willcox Smith* (New York: Thomas Y. Crowell, 1977), 18.

61. Schnessel, *Jessie Willcox Smith*, 17–18.

62. For more on this magazine, see "*St. Nicholas* Archives," *Online Books Page*, ed. John Mark Ockerbloom, 2017. University of Pennsylvania, accessed March 9, 2017, http://onlinebooks.library.upenn.edu/webbin/serial?id=stnicholas.

63. Margaret E. Wagner, *Maxfield Parrish & the Illustrations of the Golden Age* (San Francisco: Pomegranate, 2000), 21.

64. George Alfred Williams, "American Painters of Children," *Women's Home Companion* (September 1911): 14, quoted in Schnessel, *Jessie Willcox Smith*, 94.

65. Carter, *The Red Rose Girls*, 143.

66. Reed, *The Illustrator in America*, 96. Sara Duke, *Biographical Sketches of Cartoonists & Illustrators in the Swann Collection of the Library of Congress* (Arlington, VA: ComicsDC through Lulu.com, 2012), 60–61.

67. These works were *Our Baby Book* (1907), *Little Me: in picture and verse* (1936), and two collections of her comic strips, *Sonny Sayings* (1929) and *Little Miss Muffet* (1936).

68. Mary Jane Hamilton, "Nantucket in the Art of Maginel Wright," *Nantucket Historical Association*, accessed November 26, 2012, http://www.nha.org/history/hn/HN-summer07-wright.html. Originally published in *Historic Nantucket* 56, no. 3 (Summer 2007). Barney wrote and illustrated two interesting titles *Weather signs and rhymes* (1931) and *The Valley of the God-almighty Joneses* (1965), reminiscences of her childhood.

69. Roger Reed stated that Gillespie was "indeed world-class in the silhouette field," and shared a copy of a September 13, 1922, memo from Mr. G. G. Clark to Mr. Conway recommending Gillespie for an advertising job working on an Underwood account. Mr. Clark also described Gillespie as the "greatest silhouette artist in this country." E-mail from Roger Reed to the author, June 29, 2013.

70. Kelly Holohan and Donna Halpern, "Reed, Ethel," *Grove Art Online, Oxford Art Online*. Oxford University Press, accessed May 10, 2016, http://www.oxfordartonline.com/subscriber/article/grove/art/T2021958.

71. Edwin Bathke and Nancy Bathke, "Alice Stewart Hill, Colorado Springs' First Wild Flower Artist: Her Family & Friends," *Extraordinary Women of the Rocky Mountain West*, ed. Tim Blevins et al. (Colorado Springs: Pikes Peak Library District with the Colorado Women's Hall of Fame, 2010), 112–13.

72. Ibid., 115, 116.

73. See also James D. Van Trump, "'The Procession of Flowers in Colorado': A Note on a Picture Album Memorial to Helen Hunt Jackson," in *Huntia: A Yearbook of Botanical and Horticultural Bibliography* 1 (April 15, 1964): 25, 28, http://www.huntbotanical.org/admin/uploads/05hibd-huntia-1-pp25–32.pdf.

CHAPTER 2: EARLY CARTOONISTS: FROM CUTE AND CLEVER TO CAREER WOMEN

1. Ron Goulart, *The Funnies: 100 Years of American Comic Strips* (Holbrook, MA: Adams Publishing, 1995), 17.

2. Richard Severo, "Dale Messick, 98, Creator of 'Brenda Starr' Strip, Dies," obituary, *New York Times*, April 8, 2005.

3. Brian Walker, *The Comics: The Complete Collection* (New York: Abrams Comicarts, 2011), 10.

4. Ibid., 11.

5. Harry Katz, *Cartoon America: Comic Art in the Library of Congress* (New York: Abrams, 2006), 55. It should also be acknowledged that controversy among comics historians about the origin and role of Richard F. Outcault's Yellow Kid has abounded for years and is likely to continue, according to Walker, *The Comics*, 15.

6. Walker, *The Comics*, 11.

7. Ibid., 29. See also Ron Goulart, *The Encyclopedia of American Comics* (New York: Facts on File, 1990), 27–28.

8. "King Features History," *King Features*, accessed March 9, 2017, http://kingfeatures.com/about-us/king-features-history/.

9. See Trina Robbins's discussion in particular about Dale Messick's struggles for syndication, the perception of her adventure strip as invading male territory, and women changing their names to avoid bias. Trina Robbins, *Pretty in Ink: North American Women Cartoonists, 1896–2013* (Seattle: Fantagraphics Books, 2013), 63–64, 70, 110.

10. See an example of *The Old Subscriber Calls*, O'Neill's earliest comic, in Robbins, *Pretty in Ink*, 8–10. It is also mentioned in Linda Brewster, *Rose O'Neill: The Girl Who Loved to Draw* (Princeton, IL: Boxing Day Books, 2009), 61.

11. Helen Goodman, "Rose O'Neill (1874–1944)," *The Art of Rose O'Neill* (Chadds Ford, PA: Brandywine River Museum, 1989), 29; Reed, *The Illustrator in America*, 154; Duke, *Biographical Sketches of Cartoonists & Illustrators*, 229–30.

12. Quoted from the author's transcript of O'Neill's inscription on the October 12, 1935, strip.

13. Brewster, *Rose O'Neill*, 61.

14. William F. McGrath, "Grace Drayton, a Children's Illustrator Who Also Painted Young Women: A Biographical Sketch," *International Journal of Comic Art* 14, no. 2 (Fall 2012): 239–63.

15. Robbins, *Pretty in Ink*, 17.

16. Allan Holtz, *American Newspaper Comics: An Encyclopedic Reference Guide* (Ann Arbor: University of Michigan Press, 2012), 125, 134.

17. Holtz, *American Newspaper Comics*, 125.

18. Robert C. Harvey, "Dumm, Edwina," *American National Biography Online*, April 2003, accessed March 9, 2016, http://www.anb.org/articles/17/17-01675.html. Lucy Shelton Caswell, "Edwina Dumm's Biography," *Edwina Dumm*. Billy Ireland Cartoon Library & Museum, The Ohio State University, accessed March 9, 2017, https://cartoons.osu.edu/digital_exhibits/edwinadumm/biography.html.

19. Caswell, "Edwina Dumm's Biography."

20. Ibid.; Harvey, "Dumm, Edwina."

21. Caswell, "Edwina Dumm's Biography"; Harvey, "Dumm, Edwina."

22. Harvey, "Dumm, Edwina."

23. Holtz, *American Newspaper Comics*, 96; Goulart, *The Encyclopedia of American Comics*, 54; Harvey, "Dumm, Edwina." Tippie changed from a short-haired dog to a woolier one at the request of George Matthew Adams. He found the frisky dog Sinbad that Dumm had created for *Life* magazine so appealing that he asked her to replace the original Tippie with a breed resembling Sinbad. She responded by having Tippie get lost, then found by a crippled boy, who became so attached to the dog that when Cap found his pet, he couldn't separate the two. Cap then got a new wooly haired dog also named Tippie.

24. Harvey, "Dumm, Edwina."

25. Walker, *The Comics*, 358.

26. Robbins, *Pretty in Ink*, 96.

27. Both published in New York by Coward-McCann.

28. Glenn Collins, "Marjorie Buell, 88, Pioneer Cartoonist; Created 'Little Lulu,'" *New York Times*, June 3, 1993: D24.

29. Robbins, *Pretty in Ink*, 42, and Holtz, *American Newspaper Comics*, 81. *The Boy Friend* ran from June 25, 1925–1927.

30. For John Stanley's work on Little Lulu, see "John Stanley," *Lambiek Comiclopedia*, 2017, accessed February 23, 2015, http://www.lambiek.net/artists/s/stanley.htm.

31. Biographical information on Kimbrell from "Woodrow Wilson 'Woody' Kimbrell," *Find a Grave*, accessed February 23, 2015, http://www.findagrave.com/cgi-bin/fg.cgi?page=gr&GRid=71407872.

32. Robert C. Harvey, "Buell, Marjorie Henderson," *American National Biography Online*, 2002, accessed March 9, 2017, http://www.anb.org/articles/17/17-01668.html.

33. "Little Lulu," *Don Markstein's Toonopedia*, accessed June 8, 2015, http://www.toonopedia.com/lulu.htm.

34. Quoted in Harvey, "Buell, Marjorie Henderson."

35. Holtz, *American Newspaper Comics*, 255.

36. Judy Geater, "Lady for a Day (1933) and Pocketful of Miracles (1961) (Frank Capra)," *Movie Classics*, October 10, 2015, accessed March 9, 2017, https://movieclassics.wordpress.com/2015/10/10/lady-for-a-day-1933-and-pocketful-of-miracles-1961-frank-capra/.

37. Harry L. Katz and Sara W. Duke, *Featuring the Funnies: One Hundred Years of the Comic Strip* (Washington, DC: Library of Congress, 1998), 19. Exhibition catalog.

38. Holtz, *American Newspaper Comics*, 359, and Brian Walker, *The Comics before 1945* (New York: Harry N. Abrams, 2004), 118–20, 140–41, present dated examples and describe working girl and flapper strips in general terms.

39. Trina Robbins, ed., *The Brinkley Girls: The Best of Nell Brinkley Cartoons* (Seattle: Fantagraphics Books, 2009), 74–123. Note that in the serials that feature flappers, 1923–1930, Brinkley numbers vignettes that correspond with verses or texts by other authors. Robbins in fact describes these structured one-page Sunday features as comics.

40. Robbins, *Pretty in Ink*, 59.

41. Ibid., 40.

42. Duke, *Biographical Sketches of Cartoonists & Illustrators*, 160.

43. Barbara J. Harris, *Beyond Her Sphere: Women and the Professions in American History* (Westport, CT: Greenwood Press, 1978), 152.

44. Robbins, *Pretty in Ink*, 73, 74–80. Robbins describes a plethora of war era comic book titles that featured attractive, often daring female characters that were illustrated by such women as Ann Brewster, Jill Elgin, Barbara Hall, Fran Hopper, Lily Renée, and Ruth Roche. Among comic book companies that hired women in the 1940s, Fiction House, founded by Jerry Iger and Will Eisner, stood out as one publisher that hired more women cartoonists than the others.

45. Trina Robbins, *The Great Women Superheroes* (Northampton, MA: Kitchen Sink Press, 1996), 16.

46. Ibid., 16; "Miss Fury," *Don Markstein's Toonopedia*, accessed March 9, 2017, http://www.toonopedia.com/missfury.htm.

47. Robbins, *Pretty in Ink*, 76, 78–79.

48. "Flyin' Jenny," *Don Markstein's Toonopedia*, accessed March 9, 2017, http://www.toonopedia.com/flyinjen.htm.

49. Trina Robbins and Catherine Yronwode, *Women and the Comics* (Rolla, MO: Eclipse Books, 1985), 64.

50. Robbins, *Pretty in Ink*, 111. Only a few black male cartoonists "had managed to break the color barrier in comics during the first entire half of the [twentieth] century."

51. Twelve examples of Ormes's first comic strip from *Torchy Brown in "Dixie to Harlem,"* are reproduced from microfilm of the newspaper pages on which they appeared in Nancy Goldstein, *Jackie Ormes: The First African American Woman Cartoonist* (Ann Arbor: University of Michigan Press, 2008), 71–74.

52. Shelley S. Armitage, "Black Looks and Imagining Oneself Richly: The Cartoons of Jackie Ormes," *Polish Journal for American Studies* 7 (2013): 87.

53. Holtz, *American Newspaper Comics*, 304.

54. Goldstein, *Jackie Ormes*, 38.

55. Ibid., 3.

56. Holtz, *American Newspaper Comics*, 392.

57. Armitage, "Black Looks and Imagining Oneself Richly," 96, 99.

58. For an appealing example of Messick's unpublished comic *Streamline Babies*, see Robbins, *Pretty in Ink*, 60.

59. Ibid., 59.

60. Karen Greenspan, *The Timetables of Women's History: A Chronology of the Most Important People and Events in Women's History* (New York: Simon & Schuster, 1994), 330, 336, 338. Greenspan cites American women becoming newspaper editors and publishers only by the 1930s–1940s, listing Eleanor Medill Patterson taking over the *Washington Herald* as editor and publisher in 1930; Anne McCormick as the first woman on the editorial board of the *New York Times*, designated as "freedom editor" in 1936; Dorothy Schiff as New York City's first female newspaper publisher, publishing the *New York Post* in 1939. None of these women are mentioned as comics editors. Mollie Slott, who helped Dale Messick win syndication with the Chicago Tribune-New York News Syndicate, later worked as comics editor at the *New York Herald Tribune*, exactly when is not known. "Molly Levinson (Slott)," Geni, accessed March 30, 2015, http://www.geni.com/people/Mollie-Levinson/6000000000773107355.

61. Robbins, *Pretty in Ink*, 64.

62. Holtz, *American Newspaper Comics*, 376, 87, 124, 379, 152. See also entries for individual comic strip features by title in *Don Markstein's Toonopedia* online at http://www.toonopedia.com/#toons.

63. Robbins, *Pretty in Ink*, 63.

64. Ibid., 63.

65. Trina Robbins in Dale Messick, *Brenda Starr, Reporter: The Collected Dailies and Sundays, 1940–1946* (Neshannock, PA: Hermes Press, 2012), [11].

66. Goulart, *The Encyclopedia of American Comics*, 49.

67. "Comics: Brenda Starr, retired reporter," *Boston Globe*, December 20, 2010.

68. Harvey, "Dumm, Edwina."

69. Quoted in Robbins, *Pretty in Ink*, 56–58. Drayton's Sunday strip *Dolly Dimples and Bobby Bounce* had been canceled in 1932.

CHAPTER 3: NEW VOICES, NEW NARRATIVES IN COMICS

1. R. C. Harvey, "Hare Tonic: Mistress of Adolescent Angst, Girlish Laughter Division," *Comics Journal*, December 4, 2013, http://www.tcj.com/mistress-of-adolescent-angst-girlish-laughter-division/.

2. Robert C. Harvey, *A Gallery of Rogues: Cartoonists' Self-Caricatures* (Columbus: The Ohio State University Cartoon Research Library, 1998), 145.

3. Walker, *The Comics*, 352–55.

4. The *Oxford English Dictionary* (2nd ed., 1989) cites US origin and gives first use in 1941; *Webster's Ninth New Collegiate Dictionary* (1986) gives the year 1939.

5. Robbins and Yronwode, *Women and the Comics*, 77–78.

6. Walker, *The Comics since 1945*, 57.

7. Carl Nolte, "Martha Arguello—Bobby Sox, Emmy Lou Cartoonist Dies in San Rafael," *San Francisco Chronicle*, January 9, 2008, accessed November 5, 2012, http://www.sfgate.com/bayarea/article/Martha-Arguello-Bobby-Sox-Emmy-Lou-cartoonist-3298729.php.

8. Ibid.

9. Ibid.

10. Ibid. Links mentions using her memories as a source in a reminiscence in Allan Holtz, "News of Yore. Marty Links Tells Her Own Story," *Stripper's Guide*, February 5, 2008, accessed April 20, 2015, http://strippersguide.blogspot.com/2008_02_01_archive.html.

11. Ibid.

12. Robbins, *Pretty in Ink*, 96–97.

13. Robbins and Yronwode, *Women and the Comics*, 78.

14. Nolte, "Martha Arguello."

15. Links interview with Ed Mitchell for Cartoonist PROfiles, 1976, quoted in Harvey, "Hare Tonic: Mistress of Adolescent Angst."

16. "Lynn Johnston," *Contemporary Authors Online*, Gale, 2011. *Literature Resource Center*, accessed March 9, 2017, go.galegroup.com/ps/i.do?p=LitRC&sw=w&u=loc_main&v=2.1&id=GALE%7CH1000050938&it=r&asid=b514124c13d41f8a1b57982497c11ce7; Susanna McLeod, "Lynn Johnston, Creator of *For Better or for Worse*," *Cartoonists*, April 19, 2002, accessed March 9, 2017, http://www.thecartoonists.ca/Index_files/2002pages/TC%20-%20Lynn%20Johnston,%20Creator%20of%20For%20Better%20or%20For%20Worse.htm.

17. "A Little about Lynn," *For Better or for Worse*, accessed March 9, 2017, http://www.fborfw.com/behind_the_scenes/lynn/.

18. "Lynn Johnston," *Contemporary Authors Online*.

19. E-mail from Brian Walker to the author, November 16, 2016.

20. Heidi Ulrichsen, "Beyond *For Better or for Worse*," *Sudbury Northern Life*, October 22, 2014, http://www.northernlife.ca/news/lifestyle/2014/10/22-for-better-for-worse-sudbury.aspx; "Universal Press Will Syndicate 'For Better or for Worse,'" *Kansas City Business Journal*, July 27, 2004, http://www.bizjournals.com/kansascity/stories/2004/07/26/daily13.html.

21. In his entry for "For Better or for Worse," Don Markstein mentions Johnston including stories involving death, commenting that "the family's response has been both realistic and moving." See "For Better or for Worse," *Don Markstein's Toonopedia*, accessed October 22, 2012, http://www.toonopedia.com/forbettr.html.

22. Staci Kramer, "'Coming Out'—Many Say It Isn't a Funnies Matter," *Washington Post*, April 13, 1993: B5.

23. Ibid.; *The National*, CBC Television, Toronto, November 2, 2007, Segment 017.

24. E-mail from Jan Eliot to author, July 14, 2016, in which Eliot states that she knew of no other strip featuring a single mother at that time.

25. Biographical information taken from the following online sources: "About Jan," *Stone Soup by Jan Eliot*, accessed March 9, 2017, http://www.stonesoupcartoons.com/about-jan.html; Susanna McLeod, "Jan Eliot, Creator of *Stone Soup*," *Cartoonists*, November 12, 2004, accessed March 9, 2017, http://thecartoonists.ca/Index_files/2004pages/TC%20-%20Jan%20Eliot,%20Creator%20of%20Stone%20Soup.htm; "Festival Speaker 2015 Jan Eliot—Stone Soup," *Kenosha Festival of Cartooning*, 2015, accessed March 9, 2017, http://kenoshacartoonfest.blogspot.com/2015/02/festival-speaker-2015-jan-eliot-stone.html.

26. "About Jan," *Stone Soup by Jan Eliot*.

27. "Festival Speaker 2015 Jan Eliot—Stone Soup," *Kenosha Festival of Cartooning*.

28. Eliot says she thought long and hard about Wally and Joan marrying in the strip, in an interview with Suzanne Tobin of the *Washington Post*, October 24, 2003, http://www.washingtonpost.com/wp-dyn/articles/A59819–2003Oct21.html.

29. After much discussion, going back and forth on the question of Val marrying Phil, the event happily takes place: *Stone Soup*, July 25, 2015, http://www.gocomics.com/stonesoup/2015/07/25.

30. Dave Astor, "Some Comic Strips Not Set in 'Stone,'" *Editor & Publisher*, November 6, 2000, https://www.questia.com/magazine/1G1–66709343/some-comic-strips-not-set-in-stone.

31. "Speakers," *2004 Festival of Cartoon Art*, The Ohio State University, accessed March 9, 2017, https://cartoons.osu.edu/sites/FCA/2004/speakers.htm; "Nicole Hollander, Comics Creator," *Redirectify.com*, accessed March 9, 2017, http://www.redirectify.com/people/nicole-hollander.html.

32. "Nicole Hollander, Comics Creator," *Redirectify.com*.

33. "Nicole Hollander," *Lambiek Comiclopedia*, accessed March 9, 2017, https://www.lambiek.net/artists/h/hollander_n.htm.

34. E-mail from Nicole Hollander to the author, November 16, 2016.

35. Martha H. Kennedy, "Sylvia's World: Nicole Hollander Shares a Spicy Slice of Life," *Library of Congress Information Bulletin* 3, no.4 (April 2004): 66–67.

36. "Nicole Hollander," *Lambiek Comiclopedia*.

37. Robert C. Harvey, "The Iconic Sylvia Holland," *Rants & Raves*, April 27, 2012, accessed March 10, 2017, http://gocomics.typepad.com/rcharvey/2012/04/the-iconic-sylvia-holland.html.

38. "Cathy Lee Guisewite," *Encyclopedia of World Biography* 18, Gale, 1998. *Biography in Context*, accessed February 14, 2012, link.galegroup.com/apps/doc/K1631002749/BIC1?u=loc_main&xid=0690408d.

39. "Cathy Lee Guisewite," *Encyclopedia of World Biography*.

40. See newspaper articles that relate these controversies: Ben Fulton, "It's the End of the Line for 'Cathy,'" *Salt Lake Tribune*, September 28, 2010, http://archive.sltrib.com/article.php?id=11274425&itype=storyID; "Bush Ad Replaces Comic Strip," *New York Times*, November 4, 1988, http://www.nytimes.com/1988/11/04/us/bush-ad-replaces-comic-strip.html.

41. Fulton, "It's the End of the Line for 'Cathy.'"

42. "Cathy," *Don Markstein's Toonopedia*, accessed May 4, 2015, http://www.toonopedia.com/cathy.htm.

43. "Cathy Lee Guisewite," *Encyclopedia of World Biography,* and "Cathy by Cathy Guisewite," Andrews McMeel Syndication, accessed March 9, 2017, http://www.universaluclick.com/comics/strip/cathy.

44. Mark Voger, "Cathy Is Tying the Knot," *Seattle Times*, February 3, 2005.

45. Tom Heintjes, "The Cathy Guisewite Interview," *Hogan's Alley* 18 (April 24, 2012): http://cartoonician.com/cathy-guisewite-the-goodbye-girl.

46. Brandon studied illustration at Syracuse University, according to David Astor, "Where She Came from to Get Syndicated," *Editor & Publisher* 124, no. 47 (November 23, 1991): 38. She graduated in 1980, according to "Barbara Brandon Biography," *Biography.com*, April 2, 2014. A&E Television Networks, accessed March 9, 2017, http://www.biography.com/people/barbara-brandon-21320057.

47. Quoted in Kyle Norris, "Comics Crusader: Remembering Jackie Ormes," *All Things Considered* (Washington, DC: National Public Radio, broadcast July 29, 2008). Transcript accessed March 10, 2017, http://www.npr.org/templates/transcript/transcript.php?storyId=93029000.

48. Astor, "Where She Came from to Get Syndicated," 38.

49. Ibid., 38.

50. Walker, *The Comics since 1945*, 300.

51. Su-Jin Yim, "Ethnic Comic Strips a Tougher Sell in Shrinking Market," *Newhouse News Service*, December 4, 2001, https://search.proquest.com/docview/454663825?accountid=12084.

52. "Barbara Brandon," *Contemporary Black Biography* 3, Gale, 1992. *Biography in Context*, accessed February 2, 2012, link.galegroup.com/apps/doc/K1606000088/BIC1?u=loc_main&xid=85c7343a.

53. Tom Spurgeon, "Barbara Brandon-Croft Ending Strip," *Comics Reporter*, March 9, 2005, http://www.comicsreporter.com/index.php/barbara_brandon_croft_ending_strip.

54. "Alison Bechdel," *Contemporary Authors Online*, Gale, 2014. *Literature Resource Center*, accessed March 9, 2017, go.galegroup.com/ps/i.do?p=LitRC&sw=w&u=loc_main&v=2.1&id=GALE%7CH1000110903&it=r&asid=e357cd1ae27067ab8d7ce9e9c5933dfa; "Alison Bechdel Biography," *Encyclopedia of World Biography*, accessed March 9, 2017, http://www.notablebiographies.com/newsmakers2/2007-A-Co/Bechdel-Alison.html.

55. June Thomas, "Fun Home Won Five Tonys: How Did a Graphic Memoir Become a Musical," *Slate*, June 8, 2015, http://www.slate.com/blogs/outward/2013/10/08/fun_home_is_america_ready_for_a_musical_about_a_butch_lesbian.html.

56. Kelli Anderson, "Rhymes with Harpoonist," *Stanford Magazine*, May/June 1999, https://alumni.stanford.edu/get/page/magazine/article/?article_id=40671.

57. Hilary Price, "About," *Rhymes with Orange*, accessed March 9, 2017, http://www.rhymeswithorange.com/about.

58. "King Features: Celebrating 100 Years at the Library of Congress," webcast of panel discussion, Library of Congress, Washington, DC, May 22, 2015, accessed March 10, 2017, https://www.loc.gov/today/cyberlc/feature_wdesc.php?rec=6806.

59. Price, "About," *Rhymes with Orange*.

60. E-mail from Jillian Tamaki to the author, July 28, 2016; e-mail from Miss Lasko-Gross to the author, August 11, 2016.

61. In 2015, women won Ignatz awards in every category. See Andrew Wheeler, "Women Triumph at Ignatz Awards with Wins for Foster-Dimino, Goldstein, Carroll, Carre, and J. Tamaki," *Comics Alliance*, September 15, 2015, http://comicsalliance.com/ignatz-award-winners-2015/. Women also won seven awards, a notable number, of the 2015 Eisner awards. See Andrew Wheeler, "2015 Eisner Award Winners: Was This the Best Ever Year for the Eisners? (Hint: We Won an Award)," *Comics Alliance*, July 11, 2015, http://comicsalliance.com/eisner-winners-2015/.

62. E-mail from Jillian Tamaki to the author, July 28, 2016.

63. E-mail from Miss Lasko-Gross to the author, August 11, 2016.

64. See also Patrick Trimble, "Chronology of Comic Strips and Comic Books in America," Integrative Arts 10, Pennsylvania State University, accessed March 10, 2017, http://www.psu.edu/dept/inart10_110/inart10/striptime.html.

65. Fredric Wertham, *Seduction of the Innocent* (New York: Rinehart & Company, 1954), 34.

66. Ibid., 234.

67. See also Dr. Amy Kiste Nyberg, "Comics Code History: The Seal of Approval," *Comic Book Legal Defense Fund*, 2016, accessed July 15, 2016, http://cbldf.org/comics-code-history-the-seal-of-approval/. The Library of Congress holds the papers of Dr. Fredric Wertham and a finding aid can be found at http://rs5.loc.gov/service/mss/eadxmlmss/eadpdfmss/2010/ms010146.pdf.

68. Robbins, *Pretty in Ink*, 116–17; David Hajdu, *The Ten-Cent Plague: The Great Comic-Book Scare and How It Changed America* (New York: Picador/Farrar, Straus and Giroux, 2008), 328–29.

69. Carolyn Cocca, *Superwomen, Gender, Power, and Representation* (New York: Bloomsbury, 2016), 7–8.

70. Ibid., 9–14. Cocca traces incremental gains for superheroines, during the 1970s–1980s ("Bronze Age"), 1980s–2000s ("Dark Age" or "Modern Age"), and 2010s (new Golden Age or Dark Age continued?).

71. Katherine Keller, "The Chromatic Queen, Marie Severin," *Sequential Tart*, accessed March 10, 2017, http://www.sequentialtart.com/archive/may02/severin.shtml.

72. Steve Duin and Mike Richardson, *Comics between the Panels* (Milwaukie, OR: Dark Horse, 1998), 396.

73. Robbins, *Pretty in Ink*, 120, 124; and Dewey Cassell with Aaron Sultan, *Marie Severin: The Mirthful Mistress of Comics* (Raleigh, NC: TwoMorrows Publishing, 2012), 169.

74. Quoted in Duin and Richardson, *Comics between the Panels*, 396.

75. Russell Lissau, "WONDER WOMEN Here they come, crashing into the sexist stronghold of Superhero comic books. What do they want?!! What will they do?!!," *Daily Herald* [Arlington Heights, Ill.], February 22, 2000: 1.

76. Alex Heigl, "DC Comics Amanda Conner Talks about Her Work, Fantasy-Casting Power Girl, and Being a 'Woman in Comics,'" *People*, October 21, 2014, accessed December 16, 2014, http://www.people.com/article/amanda-conner-DC-comics.

77. Lissau, "WONDER WOMEN," 1.

78. Robbins, *Pretty in Ink*, 157.

79. Ibid., 165, 168, 175; Carol Cooper, "Pretty Persuasian," *Village Voice*, January 2, 2001, accessed March 23, 2015, http://www.villagevoice.com/2001-01-02/books/pretty-persuasion/; "About Me," *Anne Timmons, Illustrator*, accessed March 23, 2014, http://www.annetimmons.com/About_Me.html.

80. E-mail from Anne Timmons to the author, February 12, 2017.

81. M. Keith Booker, ed., "Underground and Adult Comics," *Encyclopedia of Comic Books and Graphic Novels* (Santa Barbara, CA: Greenwood/ABC CLIO, 2010), 654.

82. See the table of contents for Diane Noomin, ed., *Twisted Sisters 2: Drawing the Line* (Northampton, MA: Kitchen Sink Press, 1995), which contains comics by sixteen female cartoonists.

83. "Trina Robbins," *Authors and Artists for Young Adults*, 61, Gale, 2005. *Biography in Context*, accessed November 18, 2015, link.galegroup.com/apps/doc/K1603001324/BIC1?u=loc_main&xid=767771b3.

84. Robbins, *Pretty in Ink*, 148.

85. Susan E. Kirtley, *Lynda Barry: Girlhood through the Looking Glass* (Jackson: University Press of Mississippi, 2012), 4.

86. Ibid., 15–16; "Lynda Barry," *Wisconsin Institute for Discovery at the University of Wisconsin-Madison*, accessed March 10, 2017, http://wid.wisc.edu/profile/lynda-barry/.

87. Kirtley, *Lynda Barry*, 103.

88. E-mail from Lynda Barry to the author, December 11, 2016.

89. Kirtley, *Lynda Barry*, 148

90. E-mail from Linda Barry to the author, December 12, 2016.

91. Shea Hennum, J. A. Micheline, Caitlin Rosberg, and Oliver Sava, "Raina Telgemeier's Smile Signaled a Sea Change in Comics Still Felt Today," *A.V. Club*, June 19, 2016, http://www.avclub.com/article/raina-telgemeiers-smile-signaled-sea-change-comics-238414.

92. Raina Telgemeier, *Smile* (New York: Graphix/Scholastic Press, 2010), title page; Raina Telgemeier, *Sisters* (New York: Graphix/Scholastic Press, 2014), 174 and 197.

93. E-mail from Sheila Marie Everett (director of publicity, Scholastic), with quotation from Telgemeier, sent to author, December 16, 2016.

94. "FAQ," *Jillian Tamaki*, accessed July 6, 2015, http://www.jilliantamaki.com/faq.

95. Jillian Tamaki and Mariko Tamaki, *This One Summer* (New York: First Second, 2014), 160–61.

96. Ibid., 163.

97. Ibid., 80–81.

98. A minicomic is a small, creator-published comic book, often photocopied and stapled or with a handmade binding. These are a common inexpensive way for those who want to make their own comics on a very small budget, with mostly informal means of distribution. A number of cartoonists have started this way and gone on to more traditional types of publishing, while other more established artists continue to produce minicomics on the side. Minicomics are even less mainstream than alternative comics. See definition at ZineWiki, s.v. "minicomic," accessed November 23, 2015, http://zinewiki.com/Minicomic.

99. See Carré's website, http://lillicarre.com/, and Tom Spurgeon's interview of Carré for the *Comics Reporter*, August 2, 2009, http://www.comicsreporter.com/index.php/resources/interviews/21374/.

100. Kirtley, *Lynda Barry*, 12.

101. Hannah Means Shannon, "The Unintentional Rebel—Miss Lasko-Gross Discusses New Graphic Novel Plus Process Art," *Bleeding Cool*, December 19, 2014, accessed March 10, 2017, http://www.bleedingcool.com/2014/12/19/unintentional-rebel-miss-lasko-gross-discusses-new-graphic-novel-henni-plus-process-art/.

INTERLUDE: ILLUSTRATIONS FOR INDUSTRY

1. *Maya Lin: A Strong Clear Vision*, directed by Freida Lee Mock (American Film Foundation, 1994).

2. See Historic American Building Survey catalog record for the Saratoga Foothill Club in the Library of Congress Prints and Photographs Online Catalog, http://www.loc.gov/pictures/item/ca0980/.

3. Claire Aubin, "Chloethiel Woodard Smith," *School of Architecture & Allied Arts, University of Oregon*, accessed September 5, 2016, https://aaa.uoregon.edu/100stories/alumni/chloethiel-woodard-smith.

4. Joseph Giovannini, "The Office of Charles Eames and Ray Kaiser: The Material Trail," *The Work of Charles and Ray Eames: A Legacy of Invention* (New York: Harry N. Abrams in association with the Library of Congress and the Vitra Design Museum, 1997), 46.

5. Ibid., 46.

6. Amanda Kolson Hurley, "Would There Be More Women Architects if There Were More Women Developers?" *Architect*, September 17, 2012, http://www.architectmagazine.com/design/would-there-be-more-women-architects-if-there-were-more-women-developers_o; Daniel Davis, "Where Gender Inequity Persists in Architecture: The Technology Sector," *Architect*, October 28, 2014, http://www.architectmagazine.com/business/where-gender-inequity-persists-in-architecture-the-technology-sector_o; US Bureau of Labor and Statistics, *BLS Reports: Women in the Labor Force: A Databook*, February 2013, Table 11, pp. 29–31, http://www.bls.gov/cps/wlf-databook-2012.pdf; Eric Wilson, "In Fashion, Who Really Gets Ahead?" *New York Times*, December 8, 2005; Dhani Mau, "How to Make It as a Fashion Illustrator in 2015," *Fashionista*, March 30, 2015, accessed March 16, 2017, http://fashionista.com/2015/03/how-to-become-fashion-illustrator.

7. Ford Peatross, e-mail to the author, February 17, 2017.

CHAPTER 4: COMMENTATORS AND REPORTERS

1. Quoted in Jerelle Kraus, *All the Art That's Fit to Print (And Some That Wasn't): Inside the New York Times Op-Ed Page* (New York: Columbia University Press, 2009), 83.

2. Elizabeth Williams and Sue Russell, *The Illustrated Courtroom: 50 years of Court Art* (New York: CUNY Journalism Press, 2014), 15.

3. Margalit Fox, "Bernarda Bryson Shahn, Painter, Dies at 101," *New York Times*, December 14, 2004: A41.

4. Ibid.

5. See section on Bernarda Bryson Shahn in *New Growth: Recent Acquisitions in Caricature, Cartoon & Illustration.* A Caroline and Erwin Swann Memorial Exhibition, October 26, 1995–January 1996. Library of Congress, Washington, DC. Exhibition catalog, n.p.

6. Bernarda Bryson and Jake Milgram Wien, *The Vanishing American Frontier: Bernarda Bryson Shahn and Her Historical Lithographs Created for the Resettlement Administration of FDR* (Seattle: University of Washington Press, 1995), 2–3.

7. Ibid., 8.

8. Ibid., 35.

9. Ibid., 37.

10. Two of the earliest children's books that Bryson illustrated were *Alphabet for Joanna* by Horace Gregory (New York: Holt Rinehart Winston, 1946) and *The White Falcon* by Charlton Ogburn in 1955. These were followed by *Bright Hunter of the Skies* by Herbert Best (New York: Macmillan, 1961); *Shepherd of the Sun* by Ben Appel (New York: Ivan Obolensky, 1961); *Pride and Prejudice* by Jane Austen (New York: Macmillan, 1962); *The Return of the Twelves* by Pauline Clarke (New York: Coward-McCann, 1963); *Wuthering Heights* by Emily Brontë (New York: Macmillan, 1963); *Calendar Moon* by Natalia Belting (New York: Holt, Rinehard & Winston, 1964); *Mr. Chu* by Norma Keating (New York: Macmillan, 1965); *The Storyteller's Pack* by Frank R. Stockton (New York: Scribner, 1968); *The Grindstone of the Gods* by Carl Withers (New York: Holt, Rinehart & Winston, 1970). "Bernarda Bryson Shahn," *Contemporary Authors Online*, Gale, 2006. *Biography in Context*, accessed June 16, 2011, http://link .galegroup.com/apps/doc/H1000013411/BIC1?u=loc_ main&xid=7c649a29.

11. "Editorial Illustration," *Alex Greenhead*, October 8, 2012, accessed March 13, 2017, https://alexgreenhead.wordpress .com/2012/10/08/editorial-illustration/.

12. E-mail from Anita Kunz to the author, August 4, 2016.

13. Catherine M. Grant, "Sue Coe," *Grove Art Online, Oxford Art Online*, updated January 18, 2006. Oxford University Press, accessed January 23, 2012, http://www.oxfordartonline .com:80/subscriber/article/grove/art/T097653–2006–01–18.

14. E-mail from Sue Coe to the author, October 28, 2016.

15. Ibid.

16. For information on the accident, see *Encyclopedia Britannica*, s.v. "Bhopal Disaster," November 22, 2015, accessed December 28, 2015, http://www.britannica.com/event/Bho pal-disaster.

17. Timothy W. Luke, "Sue Coe: Developing the Present, Defining a World," *Shows of Force: Power, Politics, and Ideology in Art Exhibitions* (Durham, SC: Duke University Press, 1992), 171.

18. See verso of "Haiti" in Sue Coe, *Police State* (Richmond: Anderson Gallery, Virginia Commonwealth University, 1987), [second (reproduction) print in portfolio].

19. Luke, "Sue Coe," 170.

20. See summary of case at "Timeline of Important Reproductive Freedom Cases Decided by the Supreme Court," American Civil Liberties Union, accessed March 13, 2017, https://www.aclu.org/timeline-important-reproductive-free dom cases-decided-supreme-court.

21. For the justices' votes, see Chicago-Kent College of Law at Illinois Tech, "Planned Parenthood of Southeastern Pennsylvania v. Casey," *Oyez*, accessed March 13, 2017, https:// www.oyez.org/cases/1991/91–744.

22. Zina Saunders, "Frances Jetter Profile," *Zina Saunders*, February 15, 2010, accessed March 13, 2017, http://zinasaun ders.buglogic.com/?section=news&article=9810&d=true.

23. See Frances Jetter's website: "Biography," *Frances Jetter*, accessed March 13, 2017, http://fjetter.net/frances_bionew books.html.

24. Quoted in Saunders, "Frances Jetter Profile."

25. Ibid.

26. Kraus, *All the Art That's Fit to Print*, 83.

27. Martha H. Kennedy, "Canadian Counterpoint: Illustrations by Anita Kunz," an exhibition in the Swann Gallery for Caricature and Cartoon, September 4, 2003–January 3, 2004, Library of Congress, Washington, DC. Exhibition brochure, n.p.

28. Reed, *The Illustrator in America*, 433.

29. For biographical information for Sherman, see Michael Gibbs, "Artist Whitney Sherman," *Truly Amazing Women*, accessed March 13, 2017, http://trulyamazingwomen.com/ the-women/artist-whitney-sherman; "Whitney Sherman," *Stereohype*, accessed March 13, 2017, http://www.stereohype .com/765__whitney-sherman.

30. See Sherman's website for her bio and C.V.: "Biography," *Whitney Sherman*, accessed March 13, 2017, http://www .whitneysherman.com/bio. Her many clients listed include the *New York Times, Business Week, Forbes*, Random House, Henry Holt & Co, McGraw-Hill, Harlequin Press, St. Martin's Press, Tolleson Design, Pentagram, Ronn Campisi Design, Herman Miller, Warner Bros. Records, the Discovery Channel, Scholastic, Southern Poverty Law Center, the Red Cross, American Federation of Teachers, American Medical Association, American Social Health Association, Johns Hopkins Hospital, American Bar Association, the Robert Wood Johnson Foundation, other health organizations, Stanford University, Harvard University, Purdue University, and other institutions of higher education.

31. For information on Sherman's work on the breast cancer stamp, see "Whitney Sherman, Director," *Maryland Institute College of Art*, accessed March 13, 2017, https://www

.mica.edu/About_MICA/People/Faculty/Faculty_List_by_Last_Name/Whitney_Sherman.html.

32. The US Postal Museum defines "semi-postal stamp" as "a postage stamp bearing a higher-than-normal postage rate. The excess revenue was given to charity or some other cause." Arago Glossary, s.v. "semi-postal stamp," *Smithsonian National Postal Museum*, accessed March 13, 2017, http://arago.si/edu/glossary_s.html. For more on the collaboration between designer Ethel Kessler and Sherman, see "Semi-Postal: Breast Cancer Research Issue," *Smithsonian National Postal Museum*, accessed March 13, 2017, https://arago.si.edu/category_2048260.html.

33. Sherman gives her take on development of her artwork for the breast cancer stamp on her website at "Work: Breast Cancer Research Stamp," *Whitney Sherman*, accessed March 13, 2017, http://whitneysherman.com/index.php?/work/spStamp/.

34. Biographical information from *New Growth* exhibition catalog, 1995; Beck's website, http://melindabeck.com/; "Meet the Judges," *CMYK Magazine,* accessed August 1, 2014, https://www.cmykmag.com/judges/melindabeck.html; Beck, interview with the author, May 2014.

35. Beck, interview with the author, May 2014.

36. E-mail from Sue Coe to the author, October 28, 2016.

37. The following includes many major titles: *How to Commit Suicide in South Africa* (New York: Raw Books, 1983); *Paintings and Drawings* (Metuchen, NJ: Scarecrow Press, 1985): *X,* with text by Art Spiegelman, ed. Art Spiegelman and Francoise Mouly (New York: Raw Books, 1986); *Police State* (catalog), 1987*; Meat: Animal and Industry,* with Mandy Coe (Vancouver, Canada: Gallerie Publications, 1991); *Dead Meat* (New York: Four Walls, Eight Windows, 1995); *Dangerous Drawings: Interview with Comix and Graphix Artists*, with illustrator Robert Crumb, ed. Andrea Juno (Juno Books, 1997); *Pit's Letter* (New York: Four Walls, Eight Windows, 2000); *Bully!* with Judith Brody (Montreal: Drawn & Quarterly, 2004); *Cruel: Bearing Witness to Animal Exploitation* (New York: OR Books, 2011).

38. Deborah Feller, "Art Review: Sue Coe," *News and Views*, June 12, 2012, accessed March 13, 2017, http://www.deborahfeller.com/news-and-views/?p=1588. See also list of selected solo exhibitions: "Sue Coe," *Graphic Witness: Visual Arts & Social Commentary*, accessed March 13, 2017, http://graphicwitness.org/coe/coebio.htm.

39. Stephen F. Eisenman, "The Art and Politics of Sue Coe—Animal Rights as Anti-Capitalism," *Women's Caucus for Art Honor Awards 2015*, accessed June 8, 2016, https://www.nationalwca.org/LTAcat-pics/LTA/LTA2015.pdf; See also Susan Vaughn, "Making It: Staying True to a Unique Vision of Art," *Los Angeles Times*, April 1, 2001.

40. Faculty profile online: https://www.mica.edu/About_MICA/People/Faculty_List_by_Last_Name/Whitney_Sherman.html.

41. For more images of the book, see "Frances Jetter Books," *Frances Jetter*, accessed March 13, 2017, http://fjetter.net/francesjetterbooks.html. "Cry Uncle" won an Honorary Mention Award at the Pyramid Atlantic Book Arts Fair, Silver Spring, Maryland, 2010.

42. Trina Robbins, *Nell Brinkley and the New Woman in the Early 20th Century* (Jefferson, NC: McFarland, 2001), 9, 13.

43. E-mail from Sara Duke to the author, March 10, 2017.

44. Mark Hartsell, "Artist Marilyn Church: From Courtroom to Library, a Collection of Sketch Characters," *Library of Congress Information Bulletin* 70, nos. 1–2 (January–February 2011): 294.

45. Quoted in Susanne Owens, M. Jessica Rowe, and Barry M. Winiker, *Contemporary Courtroom Artists* (Syracuse: Lowe Art Gallery, College of Visual and Performing Arts, Syracuse University, 1976). 7. Exhibition catalog.

46. For a sample of courtroom drawings by Church that are held by the Library of Congress, visit http://www.loc.gov/pictures and search for "Marilyn Church."

47. Marilyn Church and Lou Young, *The Art of Justice: An Eyewitness View of Thirty Infamous Trials* (Philadelphia: Quirk Books, 2006), 8.

48. Ibid., 37.

49. Ibid., 37, 40.

50. Ibid., 39.

51. Hartsell, "Artist Marilyn Church," 298.

52. "Pat Lopez," *Fine Art America*, accessed March 13, 2017, http://fineartamerica.com/profiles/patlopezartworks.html.

53. Rosanna Ruiz, "Artist Highly Sought for Court Depictions: Sketch of Justice," *Houston Chronicle*, June 12, 2002.

54. "Pat Lopez," *Fine Art America.*

55. Ruiz, "Artist Highly Sought."

56. Williams and Russell, *The Illustrated Courtroom*, 11.

57. Ibid., 91.

58. Quoted in Elizabeth Williams, "Two Experts on Courtroom Illustration: Elizabeth Williams and Aggie Kenny," *ARTFCITY*, February 23, 2015, accessed March 13, 2017, http://artfcity.com/2015/02/23/two-experts-on-courtroom-illustration-elizabeth-williams-and-aggie-kenny/.

59. The Lineup Staff, "Behind the Scenes of America's Most Notorious Cases," *Lineup*, January 6, 2015, http://www.the-line-up.com/illustrated-courtroom/; Julie Shapiro, "Artist Captures the Sketchiest Character of All: Bernie Madoff," *Downtown Express* 22, no. 8, July 3–9, 2009, http://www.downtownexpress.com/de_323/artistcaptures.html.

60. The Lineup Staff, "Behind the Scenes."

61. Daniel Fitzsimmons, "Reporting by Drawing," *New York Press*, November 6, 2013, http://www.nypress.com/reporting-by-drawing/.

62. Williams, "Two Experts on Courtroom Illustration."

CHAPTER 5: COVERS AND CARTOONS

1. Françoise Mouly, "Introduction," *Covering the New Yorker: Cutting-Edge Covers from a Literary Institution* (New York: New Yorker Abbeville Press Publishers, 2000), 6.

2. *The Complete Cartoons of the* New Yorker (New York: Black Dog & Leventhal Publishers, 2004), 9.

3. Stephen Heller and Louise Fili, *Cover Story: The Art of American Magazine Covers, 1900–1950* (San Francisco: Chronicle Books, 1996), 15–16.

4. Helen Goodman, "Rose O'Neill (1874–1944)," in *The Art of Rose O'Neill* (Chadds Ford, PA: Brandywine River Museum, 1989), 11.

5. Ibid.

6. Likelihood that O'Neill was assigned cover design topics was discussed with Richard Samuel West, in author's conversation with him, April 29, 2013.

7. Liza Donnelly, *Funny Ladies: The New Yorker's Greatest Women Cartoonists and Their Cartoons* (Amherst, NY: Prometheus Books, 2005), 25–26.

8. Sources that list Plummer's participation in this exhibition and support for woman suffrage: Harry Ransome Center, The University of Texas at Austin, exhibitions website at http://norman.hrc.utexas.edu/bookshopdoor/signature.cfm?item=43#1; Alice Sheppard, *Cartooning for Suffrage* (Albuquerque: University of New Mexico Press, 1994), 226; David Saunders, *Field Guide to Wild American Pulp Artists*, accessed February 15, 2015, http://www.pulpartists.com/Plummer.html.

9. On June 7, 1928, Earhart became the first woman passenger to fly across the Atlantic Ocean. "Amelia Earhart." *Contemporary Heroes and Heroines*. Vol.1, Gale, 1990. *Biography in Context*. Web. June 26, 2013. She then flew across the continent departing August 31, 1928, from Rye, New York, to Los Angeles, and back. "Amelia Earhart completes first transcontinental flight in 1932," *New York Daily News*, August 26, 1932. http://www.newyorkdailynews.com/news/world/amelia-earhart-completes-transcontinental-flight-1932-article-1.2331880.

10. For an account of disagreements about the role and captioning of drawings for the *Masses* among the artists, writers, and editors of it, see Rebecca Zurrier, *Art for the* Masses: *A Radical Magazine and Its Graphics, 1911–1917* (Philadelphia: Temple University Press, 1988), 52–57, 154–56.

11. Elise Kenney, "Artists' Biographies," in *Art for the* Masses, 183. Zurrier, *Art for the* Masses, xv–xvi; Sheppard, *Cartooning for Suffrage*, 228.

12. "Helen Elna Hokinson," *Encyclopedia of World Biography* 23, Gale, 2003; Donnelly, *Funny Ladies*, 28.

13. "Jay Hambidge," *Dictionary of American Biography* (Charles Scribner's Sons, 1936). *Biography in Context*, link. galegroup.com/apps/doc/BT2310012030/BIC1?u=loc_main&xid=2616f34c.

14. "Helen Elna Hokinson," *Encyclopedia of World Biography*.

15. Donnelly, *Funny Ladies*, 108.

16. R. C. Harvey, "Helen E. Hokinson," *Comics Journal*, July 22, 2013, http://www.tcj.com/helen-e-hokinson/.

17. "A Look Back at: Helen Hokinson," *New Yorker Store Blog*, September 14, 2009, accessed April 26, 2010, http://blog.newyorkerstor.com/2009/09/14/helen-hokinson.

18. Donnelly, *Funny Ladies*, 38–41.

19. Ibid., 41.

20. Ibid., 44.

21. Ibid., 108.

22. Quoted in Ibid., 87.

23. Ibid., 109.

24. Ibid., 54–55.

25. Ibid., 64.

26. Michael Maslin, "Revisiting Barbara Shermund," http://michaelmaslin.com/index.php?mact=News,cntnt01,detail,0&cntnt01articleid=296&cntnt01returnid=15.

27. See Caitlin McGurk on Barbara Shermund, at http://library.osu.edu/blogs/cartoons/2012/03/27/womens-history-month-barbara-shermund-1899–1978/.

28. See list of pages with reproduced covers by Malman in index, *The Complete Book of Covers from the* New Yorker, *1925–1989* (New York: Abrams, 1989), 390.

29. Donnelly, *Funny Ladies*, 93–95.

30. Ibid., 98.

31. Ibid., 78–79. See also Chuck Thorndike, *The Business of Cartooning: The Success Stories of the World's Greatest Cartoonists* (New York: House of Little Books, 1939), 34.

32. Thorndike, *The Business of Cartooning*, 34.

33. Quoted in Donnelly, *Funny Ladies*, 81.

34. George H. Douglas, *The Smart Magazines: 50 Years of Literary Revelry and High Jinks at* Vanity Fair, *the* New Yorker, Life, Esquire *and the* Smart Set (Hampden, CT: Archon Books, 1991), 153.

35. Ibid., 153.

36. Lee Lorenz, "The Other Side of the Desk. Preface," in Donnelly, *Funny Ladies*, 17.

37. Harvey, "Helen E. Hokinson." www.tcj.com/helen-e-hokinson/.

38. For biographical information on Chast, see multiple sources: "Roz Chast," *Contemporary Authors Online*, 2007; Chast's website, http://rozchast.com/bio.shtml; Sky Dylan-Robbins, "At Home with Roz Chast," *New Yorker Online*, March 6, 2014, http://www.newyorker.com/books/page-turner/at-home-with-roz-chast; "Roz Chast: Cartoon Memoirs," *Norman Rockwell Museum*, on exhibition from June 6–October 26, 2015, http://www.nrm.org/digital/roz chast/.

39. For biographical information on Kalman, see multiple sources: "Maira Kalman," *Contemporary Authors Online*, 2012; Kalman's website, http://www.mairakalman.com/.

CHAPTER 6: CARICATURISTS AND POLITICAL CARTOONISTS

1. E-mail from Ann Telnaes to the author, December 17, 2016.

2. Liza Donnelly, "Cartoons by Women around the World Are a Needed Perspective," Forbes.com, August 17, 2012.

3. Robbins, *Pretty in Ink*, 21–22, 24. See also "Kate Carew," *Lambiek Comiclopedia*, November 11, 2006, accessed March 16, 2017, https://www.lambiek.net/artists/c/carew_kate.html; Edan M. Hughes, *Artists in California, 1786–1940*, 3rd ed., vol. 1 (Sacramento: Crocker Art Museum), 192; Doris O. Dawdy, *Artists of the American West*, rev. ed., vol. 3 (Athens: The Ohio University Press and Sage Book of Swallow Press, 1980), 71–72.

4. Pulitzer sent Carew to Europe in 1901 to work and she returned to settle in London in 1911. Barbara Schmidt, "Kate Carew, the Only Woman Caricaturist," *Twain Quotes*, accessed March 16, 2017, http://www.twainquotes.com/interviews/confessions.html.

5. "Kate Carew," *Lambiek Comiclopedia*.

6. Obituary, "Gluyas Williams, Cartoonist," *New York Times*, February 15, 1982.

7. Megan McShea, Finding Aid for Peggy Bacon papers, 1893–1973, bulk 1900–1936, Archives of American Art, Smithsonian Institution, 2006, http://www.aaa.si.edu/collections/peggy-bacon-papers-5832/more.

8. Wendy Wick Reaves, *Celebrity Caricature in America* (New Haven, CT: National Portrait Gallery, Smithsonian Institution in association with Yale University Press, 1998), 248–49.

9. Peggy Bacon, *Off with Their Heads!* (New York: R. M. McBride & Company, 1934), 87.

10. Ibid., n.p.

11. Reaves, *Celebrity Caricature in America*, 253.

12. Quoted in ibid., 253.

13. Liza Donnelly, *Funny Ladies: The New Yorker's Greatest Women Cartoonists and Their Cartoons* (Amherst, NY: Prometheus Books, 2005), 46–49. Donnelly comments insightfully on Bacon as a multitalented artist and asserts that her "most distinguished works were her caricatures."

14. McShea, Finding Aid for Peggy Bacon papers, 2.

15. Richard Cox, "Caroline (Wogan) Durieux (1898–1989)," in Jules Heller and Nancy G. Heller, eds., *North American Women Artists of the Twentieth Century: A Biographical Dictionary* (New York: Garland, 1995), 165–66.

16. Ibid., 165–66.

17. Ibid., 165–66.

18. Richard Cox, *Caroline Durieux: Lithographs of the Thirties and Forties* (Baton Rouge: Louisiana State University Press, 1977), 38.

19. Ibid., 39.

20. Durieux also, with help from university science professors, "invented the electron print, in which isotope drawings were exposed to photograph paper and printed by chemical means." See Cox, "Caroline (Wogan) Durieux," 166.

21. Aline Fruhauf, *Making Faces: Memoirs of a Caricaturist*, ed. Erwin Vollmer (Santa Barbara: John Daniel and Company, 1990), 61–62, 140.

22. Ibid., 43.

23. Obituary, "Aline Fruhauf," *New York Times*, May 28, 1978. It is interesting to note factors that played into Fruhauf's move to Washington, DC, include her husband's posting to the Naval Medical Center and the couple having two young daughters. Vollmer, "Editor's Preface," in Fruhauf, *Making Faces*, xxv, xxvii, xxviii. See also LuLen Walker, *Aline Fruhauf: The Face of Music II*, Charles Marvin Fairchild Memorial Gallery, Georgetown University, January 15–May 14, 2002, http://www.library.georgetown.edu/exhibition/aline-fruhauf-face-music-ii.

24. LuLen Walker, "Aline Fruhauf."

25. "News Caricaturist 'Arrives,'" *Washington Daily News*, Monday, October 29, 1945: 5.

26. "Past Exhibitions," Indianapolis Museum of Art, accessed September 7, 2015, http://www.imamuseum.org/exhibition/diana-denny-caricatures.

27. Diana Denny's daughter, Angela Kalmus, affirms that her mother taught etching at John Sirica's printmaking studio, probably in the 1970s. E-mail from Angela Kalmus to the author, November 13, 2015.

28. The Association of American Editorial Cartoonists website has biographical sketches on some 152 editorial cartoonists, only 14 of whom are women. Most are regular members, but a few are associate, retired, or student members. "Cartoonist Profiles," *Association of American Editorial Cartoonists*, http://editorialcartoonists.com/cartoonist/.

29. For an overview and basic information about the composition membership in the Association of American Editorial Cartoonists, see their website, http://editorialcartoonists.com/.

30. Caswell, ibid., http://cartoons.osu.edu/digital_exhibits/edwinadumm/biography.html.

31. Duke, *Biographical Sketches of Cartoonists & Illustrators*, 89.

32. Robbins and Yronwode, *Women and the Comics*, 33.

33. Caswell, "Edwina Dumm's Biography."

34. Ibid., 53.

35. Alice E. Sheppard, *Cartooning for Suffrage* (Albuquerque: University of New Mexico Press, 1994), vii, viii, xv–xxiv.

36. For a biographical sketch of Nina Evans Allender, see "Nina Allender," National Woman's Party at the Belmont-Paul Women's Equality National Monument, accessed March 16, 2017, http://nationalwomansparty.org/womenwecelebrate/nina-allender/.

37. Sheppard, *Cartooning for Suffrage*, 205.

38. Rebecca Zurier, *Art for the Masses: A Radical Magazine and Its Graphics, 1911–1917* (Philadelphia: Temple University Press, 1988), 101.

39. Dick Spencer III, *Editorial Cartooning* (Ames: The Iowa State College Press, 1949), 81.

40. Joan Bernhardt, Mergen's daughter, interview with the author, January 7, 2016.

41. Joan Bernhardt, interview with the author, January 7, 2016. See also Joan Mergen Bernhardt and Paul S. George, "Anne Mergen Bernhardt: Miami's Trailblazing Editorial Cartoonist," *South Florida History* 34, no. 3 (2006): 27–33.

42. Bernhardt and George, "Anne Mergen Bernhardt," 27–33.

43. Wylly Folk St. John, "'Mergen' Is a Woman," *Atlanta Journal Magazine*, September 2, 1945: 6.

44. Joan Bernhardt, interview with the author, January 7, 2016.

45. See image and catalog entry for "While millions die for the right to vote," by Herb Block, 1942, Library of Congress Prints and Photographs Online Catalog, LC-DIG-hlb-00459.

46. Patricia Bronte, "Anne Mergen Top Ranking Cartoonist, Daily News Star Is Rarity in Drawing Field," *Miami Daily News*, Wednesday, July 9, 1941.

47. Bernhardt and George, "Anne Mergen Bernhardt," 27–29.

48. Spencer, *Editorial Cartooning*, 83.

49. "Dr. Estelle Popham, Mrs. John Eisenhower, First Winners of Wendy Warren Award," *Stilwell Democrat-Journal*, October 22, 1953: 8.

50. Tim Madigan, "Etta Hulme, Acclaimed Star-Telegram Cartoonist, Dies," *Fort Worth Star-Telegram*, June 27, 2014.

51. Susanna McLeod, "Etta Hulme, Political Cartoonist," *Cartoonists*, May 31, 2002, accessed July 21, 2014. http://thecartoonists.ca/Index_files/f_j.htm.

52. Madigan, "Etta Hulme."

53. Ibid.

54. Michael Cavna, "A Year after the Hebdo Attack, Cartoonists Mull What's Changed," *Washington Post*, January 8, 2016: C1.

55. No transcript of the panel is accessible, but Telnaes's and Trudeau's disagreement was not resolved and is well expressed by Telnaes in the *Washington Post* and summarized by *Sacramento Bee* editorial cartoonist Jack Ohman in the following: Ann Telnaes, "Garry Trudeau's Dangerous Logic about Charlie Hebdo," *Washington Post*, April 20, 2015; Jack Ohman, "'Doonesbury,' Trudeau, Free-Speech Absolutists?" *Sacramento Bee*, May 1, 2015, http://www.sacbee.com/opinion/editorial-cartoons/jack-ohman/article20045709.html.

56. Ann Telanes, Tom Toles, and Michael Cavna, "How Three Editorial Cartoonists Took on 2016," *Washington Post*, December 17, 2016. Published on Medium.com, https://medium.com/thewashingtonpost/how-three-editorial-cartoonists-took-on-2016-d4154fe5b0fa#.zbn4qds6v.

57. "Cartoonist Profile: Signe Wilkinson," *Association of American Editorial Cartoonists*, accessed March 16, 2017, http://editorialcartoonists.com/cartoonist/profile.cfm/WilkiS/; "Signe Wilkinson," *GoComics*, accessed March 16, 2017, http://www.gocomics.com/signewilkinson.

58. *Editorial Cartoon Awards 1922–1997: From Rollin Kirby and Edmund Duffy to Herbert Block and Paul Conrad*, ed. Heinz-Dietrich Fischer and Erika J. Fischer (Munich: K. G. Saur, 1999), 273–76.

59. Martha Kennedy, "Ann Telnaes, Cartoonist: Singular in Style and Substance," in *Humor's Edge: Cartoons by Ann Telnaes* (San Francisco: Pomegranate in association with the Library of Congress, 2004), 13–19.

60. Ibid., 14.

61. "Portfolio," *Ann Telnaes*, accessed March 16, 2017, http://www.anntelnaes.com/portfolio/.

62. "2011 Prize Finalist, Ann Telnaes," *Herb Block Foundation*, accessed March 16, 2017, http://www.herbblockfoundation.org/2011-finalist. Note that Telnaes is the only one among Herblock Prize finalists and winners whose editorial animations have received this recognition: "Herblock Prize & Lecture," *Herb Block Foundation*, accessed March 16, 2017, http://www.herbblockfoundation.org/herblock-prize.

63. "2011 Prize Finalist, Ann Telnaes," *Herb Block Foundation*.

64. Stanford Chandler, "Insight: Editorial Cartoonist Lisa Benson," *Humor Times*, April 4, 2012, accessed March 16, 2016, http://www.humortimes.com/7819/insight-cartoonist-lisa-benson/.

65. Benson has received the following awards for her work: first place honors from the California Newspaper Publishers Association (under 75,000 circulation) in 2000, second place from the same in 2004, and second and third place from the Society of Professional Journalists' Inland Southern California Chapter. "Lisa Benson," *Cartoonist Group*, accessed March 16, 2017, http://www.cartoonistgroup.com/properties/benson/about.php.

66. See Benson's twenty-four cartoons relating to women's issues at http://www.cartoonistgroup.com/subject/The-Woman-Comics-and-Cartoons-by-Lisa+Benson%27s+Editorial+Cartoons.php. A search of cartoons on women's issues by Wilkinson and Telnaes on the same website, http://www.cartoonistgroup.com/search/cartoonist.php, yields 219 hits and 323 hits, respectively. Even given the fact that Wilkinson

and Telnaes have practiced political cartooning longer than Benson, the great difference in numbers is revealing.

67. E-mail from Lisa Benson to the author, December 14, 2016.

68. "About," *Liza Donnelly*, accessed September 28, 2015, http://lizadonnelly.com/bio.

69. Ibid.

70. Ibid.

71. See transcript of Sorensen's acceptance speech at "2014 Prize Winner, Jen Sorensen," *Herb Block Foundation*, accessed March 16, 2017, http://www.herbblockfoundation.org/her block-prize-winner/1072.

72. As part of this venture, Sorensen also mentions "Graphic Culture," "a collection of cartoons, comics, and longer-form graphic journalism pieces, as well as occasional animation and articles about cartoonists." See more at Jen Sorensen's website, http://jensorensen.com, and at "Graphic Culture," *Fusion*, accessed March 16, 2017, http://fusion.net/series/graphic-culture/.

73. "Featured Blog Partner: Q&A with Jen Sorensen," *Oregon News Network*, May 16, 2012, accessed March 16, 2017, http://www.oregonlive.com/news-network/index.ssf/2012/05/featured_blog_partner_qa_with_18.html.

74. Sorensen's acceptance speech, "2014 Prize Winner, Jen Sorensen," *Herb Block Foundation*.

75. Quoted in Brigid C. Harrison, "Interview with Ann Telnaes," *PS: Political Science and Politics* 40, no. 2 (April 2007): 234.

BIOGRAPHICAL SKETCHES

ABBREVIATIONS

ANB   American National Biography Online, http:///www. anb.org/articles/index.html.

Carter   Carter, Alice A. *The Red Rose Girls: An Uncommon Story of Art and Love.* New York: Harry N. Abrams, 2000.

Century of American Illustration   *A Century of American Illustration.* Brooklyn: Brooklyn Museum, 1972. Exhibition catalog.

Complete Book of Covers   *The Complete Book of Covers from the* New Yorker, *1925–1989.* New York: Abrams, 1989.

Donnelly   Donnelly, Liza. *Funny Ladies: The* New Yorker's *Greatest Women Cartoonists and Their Cartoons.* Amherst, NY: Prometheus Books, 2005.

Duke   Duke, Sara. *Biographical Sketches of Cartoonists & Illustrators in the Swann Collection of the Library of Congress.* Arlington, VA: ComicsDC through Lulu.com, 2012.

Falk   Falk, Peter. *Who Was Who in American Art.* Madison, CT: Sound View Press, 1999.

Fruhauf   Fruhauf, Aline. *Making Faces: Memoirs of a Caricaturist.* Cabin John, MD: Seven Locks Press, 1987.

Harvey   Harvey, Robert C. *A Gallery of Rogues: Cartoonists' Self Caricatures.* Columbus: The Ohio State University Cartoon Research Library, 1998.

Heller   Heller, Jules, and Nancy G. Heller, eds. *North American Women Artists of the Twentieth Century: A Biographical Dictionary.* New York: Garland, 1995.

Hess and Northrop   Hess, Stephen, and Sandy Northrop. *American Political Cartoons: The Evolution of a National Identity, 1754–2010.* Montgomery, AL: Elliott & Clark Publishing, 1996. First Transaction Edition, 2011.

Holtz   Holtz, Allan. *American Newspaper Comics: An Encyclopedic Reference Guide.* Ann Arbor: University of Michigan Press, 2012.

Hughes   Hughes, Edan Milton. *Artists in California, 1786–1940.* 2 vols. Sacramento: Crocker Art Museum, 2002.

Kovinick   Kovinick, Phil, and Marian Yoshiki-Kovinick. *An Encyclopedia of Women Artists in the American West.* Austin: University of Texas Press, 1998.

Lambiek   *Lambiek Comiclopedia,* https://www.lambiek.net/comiclopedia.html.

Larson   Larson, Judy L. *American Illustration, 1890–1925: Romance, Adventure & Suspense.* Calgary: Glenbow Museum, 1986.

Lightman   Lightman, Sarah, ed. *Graphic Details: Jewish Women's Confessional Comics in Essays and Interviews.* Jefferson, NC: McFarland, 2014.

Mantle Fielding   Opitz, Glenn B., ed. *Mantle Fielding's Dictionary of American Painters, Sculptors, and Engravers.* Poughkeepsie: Apollo Books, 1986.

Maslin   Maslin, Michael. New Yorker *Cartoonists from A to Z.* http://michaelmaslin.com/index.php?page=nyer-cartoonists-a-z.

Oxford Art Online   Includes *Grove Art Online* and the *Benezit Dictionary of Artists,* published by Oxford University Press, http://www.oxfordartonline.com/subscriber/.

Pettys   Pettys, Chris. *An International Dictionary of Women Artists Born be*fore 1900. Boston: G. K. Hall, 1985.

Philadelphia: Three Centuries   *Philadelphia: Three Centuries of American Art.* Philadelphia: Philadelphia Museum of Art, 1976. Exhibition catalog.

Reaves   Reaves, Wendy Wick. *Celebrity Caricature in America.* New Haven, CT: Yale University Press, 1998.

Reed   Reed, Walt. *The Illustrator in America, 1860–2000.* New York: Society of Illustrators, 2001.

Robbins   Robbins, Trina. *Pretty in Ink: North American Women Cartoonists, 1896–2013.* Seattle: Fantagraphics Books, 2013.

Robbins and Yronwode   Robbins, Trina, and Catherine Yronwode. *Women and the Comics.* Rolla, MO: Eclipse Books, 1985.

Rubenstein   Rubenstein, Charlotte Streifer. *American Women Artists from Early Indian Times to the Present.* Boston: G. K. Hall, 1982.

Samuels and Samuels   Samuels, Howard, and Peggy Samuels. *The Illustrated Biographical Encyclopedia of Artists of the American West.* New York: Doubleday, 1976.

Seaton   Seaton, Elizabeth G., ed. *Paths to the Press: Print-making and American Women Artists, 1910–1960*. Manhattan, KS: Marianna Kistler Beach Museum of Art, 2005.

Sheppard   Sheppard, Alice. *Cartooning for Suffrage*. Albuquerque: University of New Mexico Press, 1994.

Taraba   Taraba, Frederic B. *Masters of American Illustration: 41 Illustrators & How They Worked*. St. Louis, MO: Illustrated Press, 2013.

Thorndike   Thorndike, Chuck. *The Business of Cartooning*. New York: House of Little Books, 1939.

Wagner   Wagner, Margaret E. *Maxfield Parrish and the Illustrators of the Golden Age*. San Francisco: Pomegranate, 2000.

Walker   Walker, Brian. *Comics: The Complete Collection*. New York: Abrams Comic Art, 2011.

Williams   Williams, Elizabeth. "Two Experts on Courtroom Illustration: Elizabeth Williams and Aggie Kenny." *ARTFCITY*, February 25, 2015. http://artfcity.com/2015/02/23/two-experts-on-courtroom-illustration-elizabeth-williams-and-aggie-kenny/.

Williams and Russell   Williams, Elizabeth, and Sue Russell. *The Illustrated Courtroom: 50 Years of Courtroom Art*. New York: CUNY Journalism Press, 2014.

Zurier   Zurier, Rebecca. *Art for the Masses: A Radical Magazine and Its Graphics, 1911–1917*. Philadelphia: Temple University Press, 1988.

AHERN, MARGARET

b. 1921, New York; d. 1999, Wheaton, IL
Father: John McCrohan; mother: Margaret O'Connell
Harrison Art School; Chicago Academy of Fine Arts
Work includes: editorial cartoonist, *New World Newspaper* (later *Chicago Catholic*), early 1940s; monthly strips *Beano* (1948–1999) and *Angelo* (1951–1954) for *The Waifs Messenger*, monthly newsletter for Mercy Home for Boys and Girls, Chicago; best known for *Speck, the Altar Boy*, feature syndicated by National Catholic News Service (1954–1979); also drew *Our Parish* (1966–1978) under the pseudonym Peg O'Connell.
Sources: Lambiek; G. J. Zemaitis, "Margaret Ahern, 78, Cartoonist," *Chicago Tribune*, August 28, 1999.

ARMSTRONG, MARGARET NEILSON

b. 1867, New York; d. 1944, New York
Father: David Maitland Armstrong; mother: Helen Neilson; sister: Helen Maitland Armstrong, sometime collaborator
Educated privately by a British artist
Work includes: book cover designs for titles by Myrtle Reed, Henry Van Dyke; *Field Book of Western Wildflowers* (New York: C. P. Putnam's Sons, 1915) written in collaboration with J. J. Thornber (Professor of Botany, University of Arizona), which included five hundred illustrations in black and white, and forty-eight plates in color all drawn by Armstrong from nature; by ca. 1913, she focused on designs for her own books; wrote biographies of *Fanny Kemble: A Passionate Victorian* (1938), and *Trelawny, A Man's Life* (1940) and three murder mysteries; produced approximately 314 designs.
Exhibited at the 1893 World's Columbian Exposition in Chicago, won an award for her cover designs.
Sources: Kovinick, 405; Petteys, 780.

ARROYO, ANDREA

b. 1962, Mexico City
Self-taught visual artist with background in modern dance
Work includes: cover art for the *New Yorker*; editorial illustrations for the *International Herald Tribune*, *New York Times*, and the Center for Disease Control; illustrations for three children's books including *La Boda* (1996); *In Rosa's Mexico* (1996); *The Legend of the Lady Slipper* (1999).
Sources: ArtHaus, San Francisco gallery, http://www.arthaus-sf.com/artists/andrea_arroyo/; www.andreaarroyo.com.

AYER, MARGARET

b. 1894, Brooklyn; d. 1981, Castro Valley, CA

Father: Dr. Ira Ayer; mother: M. Louise Foster; husband: Alfred Babbington Smith, banker

Philadelphia Museum of Industrial Arts; private art instruction in Paris and Rome

Work includes: text and illustrations for six children's books and illustrations for fifty-two books, for both children and adults; a number reflect her travels abroad including two trips to Thailand in 1918–1919 and 1962–1963.

Member of Asia Society, Society of Illustrators, Women's National Book Association and Artist's Guild of New York.

Sources: Finding Aid, Margaret Ayer Papers, Special Collections & University Archives, University of Oregon, Eugene.

BACON, PEGGY (MARGARET FRANCES)

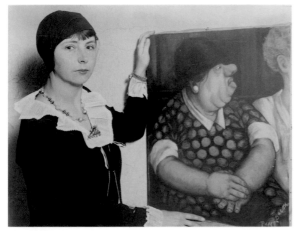

ca. 1930

b. 1895, Ridgefield, CT; d. 1987, Kennebunk, ME

Father: Charles Roswell Bacon, artist; mother: Elizabeth Chase, artist; husband: Alexander Brook, painter; two children

New York School of Fine and Applied Arts; Art Students League (1915–1920), studied with portraiture with George Bellows, painting with Andrew Dasburg, Kenneth Hayes Miller, John Sloan

Work includes: printmaker, caricaturist, painter, illustrator of more than sixty books; poet, teacher, author of children's books; *Lion-hearted Kitten* (1927); *Mercy and the Mouse* (1928); *Animosities* (1931); *The Terrible Nuisance* (1931); *Cat Calls* (1935); *Off with Their Heads* (1935); *Starting from Scratch* (1945); *The Good American Witch* (1957). Taught at the Art Students League 1935–1936, 1948–1952.

Exhibitions include: Alfred Stieglitz's Intimate Gallery (1928), three solo shows at the Downtown Gallery (1931–1934), and a yearlong retrospective at the National Collection of Fine Arts, Washington, DC (1975).

Awards include: Guggenheim fellowship (1935); American Academy and Institute of Arts and Letters Gold Medal for graphic art (1980).

Sources: Duke, 45; Heller, 247–48; John T. McQuiston, "Peggy Bacon, 91, Illustrator and Author of Gentle Satire," *New York Times*, January 7, 1987; Megan McShea, Finding Aid, Peggy Bacon papers, Smithsonian Institution Archives of American Art, 2006; *Oxford Art Online*; Seaton, 88–89; Reaves, 186–87, 247–53, 261, 276.

BARNEY, MAGINEL WRIGHT (ENRIGHT)

b. 1877, Weymouth, MA; d. 1966, East Hampton, NY

Father: Rev. William C. Wright; mother: Anna Lloyd Jones; brother: Frank Lloyd Wright; first husband: Walter J. ("Pat") Enright, illustrator; one daughter; second husband: Hiram Barney, lawyer

School of the Art Institute of Chicago, 1897

Work includes: illustrations for more than forty books, including *Hans Brinker or the Silver Skates* (1918); *Heidi* (1921); *The Lost Village* (1927); titles by L. Frank Baum, and text and illustrations for *Weather Signs and Rhymes* (1931); cover designs for *Women's World* (1918–1940) and other magazines; designs for posters for National War Garden Commission, 1919.

Exhibitions include: Art Institute of Chicago, 1905; Mary Steener Gallery, French & Company, New York City; solo exhibition of landscapes executed in needlework, Sagittarius Gallery, New York, 1962.

Sources: Falk, 212; Mary Jane Hamilton, "Nantucket in the Art of Maginel Wright," *Historic Nantucket* 56, no. 3 (Summer 2007); Reed, 165; Eugenia Sheppard, "Art or Craft," *New York Herald Tribune*, October 26, 1962: 15.

BARNS, CORNELIA (BAXTER)

b. 1888, Flushing, NY; d. 1941, Los Gatos, CA

Father: Charles Edward Barns, theater manager; mother: Mabel Balston; husband: Arthur S. Garbett, music critic; one son

Pennsylvania Academy of Fine Arts, studied with William Merrit Chase and John Twachtman; won two Cresson fellowships to travel to Europe in 1910 and 1913

Work includes: contributions to the *Masses*, 1913–1917, three years on its editorial board; contributing editor to the *Lib-*

erator, established in 1917; drew covers and illustrations for *Sunset* magazine and illustrations for the *Liberator* from 1918 to 1924; published "My City Oakland," daily editorial vignette in the *Oakland Post Enquirer* or *Oakland Tribune*; art editor and associate editor for *Birth Control Review*, also published cartoons in *Suffragist* and *Woman Voter*; contributing editor for the *New Masses*, 1925; illustrator for *New Masses* and *Good Morning*, 1926–1930.

Sources: Sheppard, 222; Zurier, 175.

BARRY, LYNDA

Self-portrait

b. 1956, near Richland Center, WI

Husband: Kevin Kawula

Evergreen State College (Olympia, WA), 1979

Work includes: cartoon strips *Girls and Boys*, *Ernie Pook's Comeek*, and *Modern Romance* in various publications including alternative newspapers, *Esquire*, *Village Voice*, *New York Times*, *Raw*, *Salon.com*, 1984–1989; *The Good Times Are Killing Me* (1988); *Come Over, Come Over* (1990); *My Perfect Life* (1992); *It's So Magic* (1994); *The Freddie Stories* (1999); *Cruddy: An Illustrated Novel* (1999); *The! Greatest! of! Marlys!* (2000); *One! Hundred! Demons!* (2002) won American Library Association's Alex Award; *What It Is* (2008) won Eisner Award for Best Reality Based Graphic Novel; *Picture This* (2010); *Blabber, Blabber, Blabber: Volume 1 of Everything* (2011); *The Freddie Stories* (new ed., 2011); *Syllabus: Notes from an Accidental Professor* (2014).

Associate professor with the School of Education's Art Department, University of Wisconsin–Madison. UW–Madison's first recipient of the Chazen Family Distinguished Chair in Art.

Exhibitions include: *Drawing Fast and Slow: The Compbook Art of Lynda Barry*, Madison Children's Museum, WI, 2015; *The Marlys Show*, Adam Baumgold Gallery, 2016; Drawn & Quarterly 25th Exhibit, Paris, 2016.

Awarded Milton Caniff Lifetime Achievement Award by the National Cartoonists Society, 2017

Sources: "Lynda Barry," *Authors and Artists for Young Adults* 54, Gale, 2004, *Biography in Context*; "Lynda Barry," *Wisconsin Institute for Discovery at the University of Wisconsin–Madison*, http://wid.wisc.edu/profile/lynda-barry/; "Lynda Barry Named UW–Madison's Distinguished Chair in Art," *Drawn & Quarterly*, https://www.drawnandquarterly.com/press/2016/11/lynda-barry-named-uw-madisons-distinguished-chair-art; Susan E. Kirtley, *Lynda Barry: Girlhood through the Looking Glass* (Jackson: University Press of Mississippi, 2012); Robbins, 136, 148, 150, 174–75.

BECHDEL, ALISON

Self-portrait

b. 1960, Lock Haven, PA

Father: Bruce Allen Bechdel, antiques dealer, English teacher, funeral director; mother: Helen Fontana, English teacher, actress

Simon's Rock of Bard College; Oberlin College, BA, 1981

Work includes: syndicated cartoon *Dykes to Watch Out For*, 1983–2008; 11 collections of *Dykes to Watch Out For*, 1986–2005; *The Essential Dykes to Watch Out For* (2008); *Fun Home: A Family Tragicomic* (2006); *Are You My Mother?: A Comic Drama* (2012); comics for *Slate*, *McSweeney's*, *Entertainment Weekly*, *New York Times Book Review*, and *Granta*; coedited *The Best American Comics*, with Jessica Abel and Matt Madden (2011).

Awards include: many Lambda awards for volumes of *Dykes to Watch Out For*; *Fun Home* was named one of the ten

Best Books of 2006 by *Time* magazine, won an Eisner Award for Best Reality-Based Work and Lambda Literary Award for lesbian memoir/biography, and was a finalist for the National Book Critics Circle Award; Guggenheim fellowship, 2012; MacArthur "genius" grant, 2014.

Sources: "Alison Bechdel," *Contemporary Authors Online*, Gale, 2014, *Literature Resource Center*; Alison Bechdel, "Introduction," *The Best American Comics 2011*, ed. Jessica Abel and Mat Madden (New York: Houghton Mifflin Harcourt, 2012), xiii–xviii; Hillary Chute, *Graphic Women: Life Narrative and Contemporary Comics* (New York: Columbia University Press, 2010); Robbins, 138, 148, 160–62; Judith Thurman, "Drawn from Life: The World of Alison Bechdel," *New Yorker*, April 23, 2012, 48–55.

BECK, MELINDA

b. 1976, New York
Husband: Jordin Isip, illustrator; two daughters
Rhode Island School of Design, BFA, graphic design, 1989
Work for clients including Anorak, Bloomberg Personal Finance, Boston College, Fit Pregnancy, Martha Stewart, *McSweeney's*, Neiman Marcus, Nickelodeon, Random House, *Rolling Stone*, Scholastic, Target, the *Boston Globe*, the *New York Times*, *Time*, *Print* magazine, Swiss Miss, *Urbis* magazine.
Exhibitions include: *New Growth: Recent Acquisitions . . .* , Library of Congress, 1995–1996; *Before or Since: Works by Melinda Beck & Jordin Isip*, Spur Gallery, Baltimore, MD, 2011; *Pixelated: The Art of Digital Illustration*, The New Britain Museum of American Art, 2012; *Melinda Beck & Julia Rothman: The Narrative Image*, ISB Gallery, Rhode Island School of Design, 2016.
Sources: "Member Spotlight—Melinda Beck, Illustrator," *Altpick.com*, June 14, 2004, http://altpick.com/spot/melinda_beck/index.php; *New Growth: Recent Acquisitions in Caricature, Cartoon & Illustration* (Washington, DC: Library of Congress, 1995), exhibition brochure; www.melindabeck.com.

BENSON, LISA

Self-portrait

b. 1958, La Jolla, CA
Husband: Gregory M. Benson, architect; four children
Work includes: paste-up, ad design, editorial cartoons for the *Senior Advocate* (early 1990s); editorial cartoonist for *Victory Valley (California) Daily Press* (beginning 1992); syndication with Washington Post Writers Group (beginning 2007).
Awards include: first place honors from California Newspaper Publishers Association (under 75,000 circ.) in 2000; second place from California Newspaper Publishers Association (under 75,000 circ.) in 2004; second and third place from Society of Professional Journalists' Inland Southern California Chapter (2005).
Sources: "Lisa Benson," *American Association of Editorial Cartoonists*, http://editorialcartoonists.com/cartoonist/profile.cfm/BensoL/; "Lisa Benson," *Washington Post News Service & Syndicate,* https://www.washingtonpost.com/syndication/cartoonists/lisa-benson/?name=lisa_benson&utm_term=.646a704aa20d.

BLANCHARD, MARTHA LEE

b. 1916, Toledo, OH; d. 1970, New York
Father: Samuel E. Blanchard; mother: Marie Cochran Har-
taugh worked as a reporter, columnist, reviewer for news-
papers; other relatives worked for newspapers
Studied art with Thomas Keane in Toledo
Work includes: fashion ads for Toledo department stores;
after move to New York, published single-panel cartoons
in the *New Yorker*, *Saturday Evening Post*, *Collier's*, *Punch*
(London), *This Week*, and illustrated *Dear Rabbi* (1968), a
humor book compiled by Bill Adler; collection of work,
Husbands and Lovers (1971).
Sources: "Martha Blanchard, Toledo Native Was Cartoonist,"
Toledo Blade, May 4, 1970: 18; Robbins, 42.

BOND, DOROTHY ANN

b. 1905; d. 1982
Secretary for an admiral during World War II, ca. 1939–1945
Work includes: *Life with the Navy* (1943), published under
pseudonym "Navy Nora"; daily panel titled *The Ladies*
(daily, 1945–1961; Sunday, 1945–1959) syndicated by John
F. Dille Co., then National Newspaper Syndicate; daily
strip *Chlorine* (daily beginning 1947; Sunday, 1946–1949)
for Dille Co. targeted secretaries, reportedly modeled on
Bond's own secretary Dee Mulvey; book collections *All
Men Are Dogs* (1950), *Let's Have a Baby* (1950).
Bond is described as "free-spirited," working in a slip and
high heels, by Mulvey, who worked for her in Chicago.
Bond billed herself in her books as "America's No. 1 Wom-
an Cartoonist."
Sources: "Biographical Files," *Billy Ireland Cartoon Library &
Museum, The Ohio State University Libraries*, https://car
toons.osu.edu/biographical-files; Holtz, 104, 229; Lambiek;
Robbins, 112–14; Robbins and Yronwode, 74, 77.

BRADSHAW, ANNETTE

Born in San Francisco, active 1920s
Work includes: cartoon panels *Feminisms* and *Her Problems*,
and fashion illustrations for newspapers in the 1920s, in
addition to writing and illustrating articles about fashion
and clothing. Worked for the Hearst syndicates 1920–1922,
published her work in such newspapers as the *Birmingham Age-Herald*, *Coshocton Tribune* (Coshocton, OH),
Evening News (Harrisburg, PA), *Great Falls Daily Tribune*
(Great Falls, MT), *Iowa City Press-Citizen*, and the *Washington Post*.

Described as a Brinkley imitator, she was among the first to
use a running title (i.e., title of her comic placed on the
upper left) and regularly use a gag punchline instead of
the more usual use of text. Owing to these practices and
her use of humor based on conversations between wom-
en, she is credited with paving the way for the popular
flapper strips of the 1920s.
Sources: Duke, 35–36; "Latest Creations in Women's Finery
Find Expression Thru Her," *Coshocton Tribune*, March 27,
1922: 3; Robbins and Yronwode, 20–21.

BRANDON-CROFT, BARBARA

b. 1958, Brooklyn
Father: Brumsic Brandon, cartoonist; mother: Rita Broughton
Syracuse University, majored in illustration
Work includes: freelance illustrator for the *Village Voice*, *Crisis
Magazine*, MCA Records, New York, 1980; fashion report-
er for Retain News Bureau, New York, 1981–1983; beauty
and fashion writer for *Essence* magazine, 1983–1989; strip
Where I'm Coming From first appeared in *Detroit Free
Press*, 1989; syndicated cartoonist, Universal Press Syndicate, 1991; strip ended in 2005 due to disinterest. Published
two well-received collections of her strip.
Strip centered on conversations between her all-female characters discussing issues that affect women. Only black
female cartoonist in a major syndicate during the run
of her strip.
Sources: David Astor, "Where She Came from to Get Syndi-
cated," *Editor & Publisher* 124, no. 47 (November 23, 1991);
"Barbara Brandon," *Contemporary Black Biography* 3, Gale,
1992, *Biography in Context*; Barbara Brandon, *Where I'm
Coming From* (Kansas City: Andrews and McMeel, 1993);
Barbara Brandon, *Where I'm Still Coming From* (Kansas
City: Andrews and McMeel, 1994); Lambiek; Sheila Rule,
"Popular Culture: The 'Girls' Talking, with a Black Per-
spective," *New York Times*, July 19, 1992.

BRINKLEY, NELL

ca. 1925

b. 1886, Edgewater, CO; d. 1944

Father: Robert Serrett Brinkley; mother: May French (Brinkley); husband: Bruce McRae III; son: Bruce

Work includes: editorial drawings for *Denver Post*, 1903; drew "pretty girls" for *Denver Times*, 1903; drawings and stories published in *New York Journal*, 1907; comics series *Golden Eyes and her Hero Bill* (1918–1919), *Kathleen and the Great Secret* (1920–1921), *Betty and Billy and their Love Through the Ages* (1921–1922).

Sources: Nell Brinkley, *The Brinkley Girls: The Best of Nell Brinkley's Cartoons from 1913–1940*, ed. Trina Robbins (Seattle: Fantagraphics, 2009); Trina Robbins, *Nell Brinkley and the New Woman in the Early 20th Century* (Jefferson, NC: McFarland, 2001); Robbins, 24, 26, 30–32, 34–35, 43, 64, 69, 105, 175; Robbins and Yronwrode, 12–14; Sheppard, 222.

BUELL, MARGE HENDERSON

b. 1904, Philadelphia; d. 1993, Elyria, OH

Father: Lyman Henderson, attorney; mother: Bertha Brown; husband: Clarence Addison Buell

Villa Maria Convent (or Academy), Malvern, PA

Work includes: syndicated newspaper *The Boy Friend* (1925–1927); *Dashing Dot* for magazines; the *Saturday Evening Post* hired her to do comic featuring a girl and *Little Lulu* appeared in 1935, followed by a successful merchandising empire of spin-off products.

Sources: ANB; Duke, 148; Lambiek; Robbins, 17, 42, 70, 114–15, 142; Robbins and Yronwode, 68.

CANNATA, DOLORES

b. ca. 1934, Los Angeles

Father: George Cannata, animator; mother: Dorothy; brother: George Cannata Jr.

Work includes: contributions to designs for seventy-five shorts for *The Boing Boing Show* including *The Trial of Zelda Belle* and *Just Believe in Make Believe*; designed characters for Elektra.

Sources: Michael Sporn, "Delores Cannata," *Splog: Michael Sporn Animation Inc.*, September 13, 2010, http://www.michaelspornanimation.com/splog/?p=2356.

CARRÉ, LILLI ESMÉ

b. 1983, Los Angeles

School of the Art Institute of Chicago, BFA, 2006

Work includes: published graphic narratives *Tales of the Woodsman Pete* (2006); *The Lagoon* (2008); *The Fir Tree* (2009); *Heads or Tails* (2012); *Tippy and the Night Parade* (2014); cofounder/director of Eyeworks Festival of Experimental Animation, Chicago (2010).

Awards include: nominee, Eisner award for Best Writer / Artist / Humor for *Tales of Woodsman Pete*, 2007; included in *The Best American Comics* (2010); nominee for Outstanding Artist, Outstanding Anthology or Collection, 2013, Outstanding Story ("The Carnival"), 2013; Ignatz Award, Outstanding Online Comic ("The Bloody Footprint"), 2015.

Sources: Lambiek; Tom Spurgeon, "A Short Interview of Lilli Carré," *Comics Reporter*, August 2, 2009, http://www.comicsreporter.com/index.php/resources/interviews/21374; www.lillicarre.com.

CHAST, ROZ

1966

b. 1954, Brooklyn

Father: George Chast, teacher; mother: Elizabeth, assistant principal; husband: Bill Franzen, writer; two children

Rhode Island School of Design, BFA, painting, 1977

Work includes: sold first cartoon to the *New Yorker* in 1978; won a contract with the magazine in 1979; over twelve hundred cartoons and twenty cover designs published by the *New Yorker*, many published collections of her cartoons, and her graphic memoir *Can't We Talk about Something More Pleasant?* (2014) that won the inaugural Kirkus Prize for nonfiction, 2014, and National Book Critics Circle Award for autobiography, 2015.

Awards include: honorary doctorate of fine arts, Pratt Institute, 1998; Art Festival Award, Museum of Cartoon and Comic Art, 2004; New York City Literary Award for Humor, 2012; honorary doctorate of arts, Lesley University/ Art Institute of Boston, 2010, and Dartmouth College, 2011; Reuben Award for Best Gag Cartoon, 2013; Reuben Award for Best Cartoonist of the Year, from National Cartoonists Society, 2015; Heinz Award in the arts and humanities category, 2015.

Major solo exhibition, *Roz Chast: Cartoon Memoirs*, at the Norman Rockwell Museum, Stockbridge, MA, and Museum of the City of New York, 2015–2016, featured more than two hundred works.

Sources: Roz Chast, *Theories of Everything: Selected, Collected, and Health-Inspected Cartoons, 1978–2006* (New York: Bloomsbury, 2006); "Roz Chast," *Contemporary Authors Online*, Gale, 2015, *Biography in Context*; Roz Chast, *Cartoon Memoirs*, an exhibition at the Museum of the City of New York, 2016, http://www.mcny.org/exhibition/roz -chast; Donnelly, 13, 16, 20, 126, 130, 132–37, 140–41, 158–59, 170, 174–75, 190, 204; http://rozchast.com.

CHRISTENSEN, BONNIE

b. 1951, Saranac Lake, NY; d. 2015, Williston, VT

Father: Wallace Christensen, forest economist; mother: Theo; one daughter

University of Vermont, theater major; wood-engraving course with John Depol

Taught art, St. Michael's College, 1995

Work includes: freelance children's book illustrator of more than twenty titles, nine of which she also authored; *An Edible Alphabet* (1994); *Rebus Riot* (1997); *Woodie Guthrie: Poet of the People* (2001); *The Daring Nellie Bly* (2003); *I, Dred Scott* (2005); *Pompeii: Lost and Found* (2006); *Ida B. Wells* (2008); *Django Reinhardt: World's Greatest Jazz Guitarist* (2009); *Fabulous: A Portrait of Andy Warhol* (2011).

Awards include: Horn Book-Boston Globe Honor Award, a Parent's Choice Gold Award, "Best Book of the Year" designation by *Publisher's Weekly*, and a New York Book Show Award for *Woody Guthrie*; Oppenheim Toy Portfolio Gold Award for *The Daring Nellie Bly*, 2004; Kirkus "Best Children's Book of 2006" designation for illustrations in *Pompeii*; 2010 Schneider Family Book Award from the American Library Association for *Django*.

Source: "Obituary, Bonnie Christensen," *Burlington Free Press*, January 24, 2015.

CHURCH, MARILYN

b. 1941, New York

Pratt Institute, BFA, 1959; University of Indiana,1959–1960; Art Students League, 1961; School of Visual Arts, 1969–1973

Work includes: freelance illustrations for various publications, 1960s; courtroom artist for the *New York Times* and ABC-TV, beginning in 1976; covered many high-profile subjects on trial including subway vigilante Bernard Goetz, former boxer Rubin "Hurricane" Carter, Jean Harris, "Dapper Don" John Gotti, Martha Stewart, Woody Allen and Mia Farrow in their custody case; published a collection of her courtroom drawings, *The Art of Justice: An Eyewitness of Thirty Famous Trials* (2006).

Church worked with the Library of Congress between 2009 and 2011, to place some four thousand of her drawings, most of her work, at the Library.

Sources: Marilyn Church and Lou Young, *The Art of Justice: An Eyewitness View of Thirty Infamous Trials* (Philadelphia: Quirk, 2006); Mark Hartsell, "Artist Marilyn Church: From Courtroom to Library, a Collection of Sketch Characters," *Library of Congress Information Bulletin* 70, nos. 1–2 (January–February 2011): 292–98 (cover story); John O'Connor, "Courtroom Confidential: Renowned Court Artist Marilyn Church Talks about Life behind the US's Most Iconic Legal Dramas," *Financial Times*, February 4, 2011; Susanne Owens, M. Jessica Rowe, and Barry M. Winiker, *Contemporary Courtroom Artists* (Syracuse: Lowe Art Gallery, College of Visual and Performing Arts, Syracuse University, 1976), 7; Patsy Southgate, "Marilyn Church: Courtroom Artist Seeks Larger Frame," *East Hampton Star*, March 6, 1997.

CIESEMIER, KALI

b. 1986, Glen Ellyn, IL

Maryland Institute College of Art (MICA), BFA, illustration, 2008

Instructor, MICA, 2009–2013; freelance illustrator

Works include: cover designs for the *Progressive* and *Domestic Etch Magazine*; illustrations for articles in the *Boston Globe Magazine*, *Ebony*, and *Parenting Magazine*; book cover design for *Newt's Emerald* by Garth Nix (HarperCollins, 2015); posters for events such as the Small Press Expo (2013).

Sources: Shannon Weltman, "Artist Interview: Kali Ciesemier," *Claw Claw*, June 6, 2014, http://www.clawclaw .com/2014/06/artist-interview-kali-ciesemier/; www.cie semier.com.

CLEAVELAND, BESS BRUCE

b. 1876, Washington Court House, OH; d. 1906

Art Students League; Pratt Institute, 1901

Works include: illustrations published in *St. Nicholas, Little Folks Monthly Magazine*; illustrated children's books, including *Windmills and Wooden Shoes* (1920); *Instructor Jointed Toys: For Coloring, Cut Out, and Construction Work* (1920); *Happy Hour Readers Book Four* (1921); *Standard Bible Story Readers: Book Four* (1927) and *Book Five* (1928).

Source: Bess Bruce Cleaveland Collection, Carnegie Public Library, Ohio Memory, a collaborative project of the Ohio History Connection and the State Library of Ohio, http:// www.ohiomemory.org/.

COE, SUE

b. 1951, Tamworth, Staffordshire, England

Sister: Mandy Coe, writer

Chelsea School of Art, Royal College of Art, London

Work includes: editorial illustrations published first in *Raw*, followed by the *New York Times, New Yorker, Nation, Entertainment Weekly, Time, Details*, the *Village Voice, Newsweek, Rolling Stone, Esquire*, and *Mother Jones*. Published collections include *How to Commit Suicide in South Africa* (1983); *Paintings and Drawings* (1985); *X* (text with Art Spiegelman, 1986); *Police State* (catalog), 1987; *Meat: Animal and Industry* (with Mandy Coe, 1991); *Dead Meat* (1995); (with illustrator Robert Crumb) *Dangerous Drawings: Interview with Comix and Graphix Artists*, ed. Andrea Juno (1997); *Pit's Letter* (2000); *Cruel: Bearing Witness to Animal Exploitation* (2011).

Exhibitions include: *Police State*, Anderson Gallery, Richmond, VA, and Museum of Modern Art, New York, 1987; *The Pit: The Tragic Tale of the Rise and Fall of a Vivisector*, Galerie St. Etienne, New York; *Porkopolis*, Portland, ME, and Bloomington, IN, and St. Louis, MO; Hirshhorn Museum and Sculpture Gallery, Washington, DC, 1994; *The Tragedy of War*, Galerie St. Etienne, New York; *One Hand Washes the Other*, Tyler Art Gallery, SUNY, Oswego, NY; *Commitment to the Struggle, The Art of Sue Coe*, Brown University, Providence, RI, 2002; *The Last 11 Days*, National Museum of Women in the Arts, Washington, DC, 2010; *"Mad as Hell!"* Galerie St. Etienne, New York, 2012.

Sources: Judith Brody, "Sue Coe and the Press: Speaking Out," *Flashpoint Magazine*, http://www.flashpointmag.com/suecoe.htm; "Sue Coe," *Contemporary Women Artists*, Gale, 1999, *Biography in Context*; Sue Coe, *Cruel: Bearing Witness to Animal Exploitation* (New York: OR books, 2011); "Sue Coe," *Graphic Witness: Visual Arts & Social Commentary*, accessed March 13, 2017, http://graphicwitness.org/coe/coebio.htm; Stephen F. Eisenman, "The Art and Politics of Sue Coe—Animal Rights as Anti-Capitalism," *Women's Caucus for Art Honor Awards 2015*, accessed June 8, 2016, https://www.nationalwca.org/LTAcat-pics/LTA/LTA2015.pdf; *"Mad as Hell!" New Work (and Some Classics) by Sue Coe*, an exhibition at Galerie St. Etienne, New York, 2012, exhibition brochure; *Oxford Art Online*.

CONNER, AMANDA

b. 1965, Los Angeles

Father: Al Conner, artist; mother: Eulala, artist; husband: Jimmy Palmiotti, comics artist and writer

Joe Kubert School, Dover, NJ

Work includes: drawing for Archie comics, Marvel Comics, Claypool Comics, DC Comics. Notable titles are *Vampirella, Painkiller Jane*, as well such collaborative projects as *Gatecrasher* (with co-creators Jimmy Palmiotti and Mark Waid), *The Pro* (with co-creators Jimmy Palmiotti and Garth Ennis). Work for DC Comics includes *Birds of Prey*, a run of *Power Girl*, and *Before Watchmen: Silk Spectre*.

Sources: "Amanda Conner, DC Comics Talent Directory," http://www.dccomics.com/talent/amanda-conner; Amanda Conner, *DC Comics: The Sequential Art of Amanda Conner* (New York: DC Comics, 2013); Alex Heigl, "DC Comics Amanda Conner Talks about Her Work, Fantasy-Casting Power Girl, and Being a 'Woman in Comics,'" *People*, October 21, 2014, http://www.people.com/article/amanda-conner-DC-comics; Lambiek; Robbins, 156–57; Conner's website, www.paperfilms.com.

CORY, FANNY YOUNG (COONEY)

b. 1877, Waukegan, IL; d. 1972, Stanwood, WA

Father: Benjamin Sayre Cory, traveling salesman; mother: Jessie McDougall; husband: Fred Cooney, rancher

Work includes: illustrator of children's literature, and later, creator of comics; illustrations for *St. Nicholas, Life, Saturday Evening Post, The Master Key* (1901), *Alice in Wonderland* (1901).

Sources: Bob Cooney and Sayre Cooney Dodgson, "Montana Mother and Artist: Fanny Cory," *Montana: The Magazine of Western History*, June 4, 2013, 1–17; Duke, 60–61; Larson, 127; Reed, 96; Robbins, 8, 10, 21, 55–56; Robbins and Yronwode, 9, 36, 38.

DABAIE, MARGUERITE

b. 1981, San Francisco

School of Visual Arts, BFA, cartooning, 2007; Fashion Institute of Technology, MFA, completed thesis "Women in Middle Eastern Comics," 2013

Work includes: comic, "Ali's House," collaboration with writer Tom Hart, launched 2016; wrote and illustrated *Hookah Girl and Other True Stories, Vol. 1* (2007), and *Vol. 2* (2009); *A Voyage to Panjikant*, historical fictional comic about the seventh-century Silk Road (Rosarium Publishing, 2018)

Sources: "Ali's House," *GoComics*, http://www.gocomics.com/alis-house/; www.mdabaie.com.

DAVIS, GEORGINA A.

b. ca. 1850, New York; d. 1901

Cooper Union; Art Students League; Boston Art Club

Work includes: illustrations, paintings, and etchings; covers and illustrations for McLoughlin Bros., publishers of children's books; works for *Aldine*, *Frank Leslie's Illustrated Weekly*, and the Salvation Army's *War Cry.*

Exhibitions include: the Women's Pavilion of the US Centennial Exposition in Philadelphia, 1876; Boston Art Club, 1876; Pennsylvania Academy of Fine Arts, 1877; "Woman Etchers of America," New York City, 1888; Union League Club, New York City, 1888; Boston Art Club, 1898; National Academy of Design; Salmagundi Club.

Sources: Mary Lynch, "Alumni Profile: Georgina Davis," *Cooper Union Alumni Association*, November 11, 2012, http://cooperalumni.org/alumni-profile-georgina-davis/; Phyllis Peet, *American Women of the Etching Revival* (Atlanta: High Museum of Art, 1988), 54; Petteys, 184; Samuels and Samuels, 126.

DENNY, DIANA (KALMUS)

b. 1923, Highland Park, IL; d. 2015, Mitchellville, MD

Pennsylvania Academy of Fine Arts, BFA, MFA; two Cresson Fellowships

Husband: Henry P. Kalmus, electrical engineer; three children

Exhibitions include: Pennsylvania Academy of Fine Arts, 1945; Indianapolis Museum of Art, 1946.

Sources: Diana Denny Kalmus, [Brief biography with reproduced photographs of herself, examples of caricature], ca. 2006; "News Caricaturist 'Arrives': Diana Denny's Newspaper Drawings Hung at Pennsylvania Academy," *Washington Daily News*, October 29, 1945: 5; "Obituary, Diana Denny Kalmus (1923–2015)," *Washington Post*, February 3, 2015; *Caricatures by Diana Denny*, an exhibition at the Indianapolis Museum of Art, March 27–April 11, 1946, http://www.imamuseum.org/exhibition/diana-denny-caricatures.

DONNELLY, LIZA

b. 1955, Washington, DC

Earlham College (Richmond, IN), BA, 1977

Work includes: first cartoon published in the *New Yorker* in 1979, continued to publish with them for more than thirty years; books include *Funny Ladies: The* New Yorker's *Greatest Women Cartoonists and Their Cartoons* (2005); *Sex and Sensibility: Ten Women Examine the Lunacy of Modern Love in 200 Cartoons* (2008); *Cartoon Marriage: Adventures in Love and Matrimony* (with husband cartoonist Michael Maslin) (2009); *When Do They Serve the Wine? The Folly, Flexibility and Fun of Being a Woman* (2010); *Women on Men* (2013), a finalist for the 2014 Thurber Prize; written and illustrated seven dinosaur books for children, published by Scholastic, Inc.; columnist for Forbes.com; weekly columnist for *Medium*; cartoons and writings published in *Politico*, *Salon*, the *Huffington Post*, and the *Washington Post.*

Cultural envoy for the US State Department, speaking on freedom of speech, cartoons, and women's rights; joined United Nations initiative Cartooning for Peace, 2007; TED talk, 2011; honorary doctorate, University of Connecticut, 2014.

Sources: "Liza Donnelly," *TED: Ideas Worth Spreading*, January 2011, https://www.ted.com/speakers/liza_donnelly; Maslin; "New Yorker Cartoonist," Earlham College, http://www.earlham.edu/feature/?type=Profile&title=Liza%20Donnelly&id=2681&r=4938; www.lizadonnelly.com.

DRAYTON, GRACE (GEBBIE; WIEDERSEIM)

b. 1877, Philadelphia; d. 1936, New York

Father: George Gebbie, art publisher; mother: Mary; sister: Margaret Hays, writer and artist; husband: Theodore E. Wiederseim; second husband: W. Heyward Drayton III

Philadelphia School of Design for Women; Drexel Institute

Work includes: creating the Campbell's kids, ca. 1904; comic strips *Naughty Toodles, The Strange Adventures of Pussy Pumpkin and Her Chum Toodles* (1903); *Dotty Dimple* (1908–1911); *The Turr'ble Tales of Kaptin Kiddo* (with sister Margaret Hays, 1909–1913); *Dimples* (ca. 1911–1918); *Dolly Dingle* paper dolls (1916–1922); *The Pussycat Princess* (1935–1947 partly posthumous).

Founding member of the Plastic Club

Sources: Duke, 85–86; Lambiek; W. E. McGrath, "Grace Drayton, a Children's Illustrator Who Also Painted Young Women—a Biographical Sketch," *International Journal of Comic Art* 14, no. 2 (Fall 2012): 239–63; Robbins, 8, 17–18, 21, 26, 28, 34, 56, 58, 69; Brian Walker, *The Comics before 1945* (New York: Harry N. Abrams, 2004), 107, 293; Robbins and Yronwode, 6, 8, 15–17, 68; Susanna McLeod, "Grace Gebbie Wiederseim Drayton, Creator of the Campbell Kids and Comics Pioneer," *Cartoonists,* 2004, http://the cartoonists.ca/Index_files/2004index.htm.

DRYDEN, HELEN

b. 1887, Baltimore; d. 1981

Pennsylvania Academy of Fine Arts

Work includes: more than ninety cover designs and illustrations for *Vogue* (1911–1923), where publisher Condé Nast allowed her unusual freedom; illustrations for advertising and fashion clients; art director, Dura Company (1930), where she designed decorative chrome objects, textiles, and glassware; involved with redesign of 1937 Studebaker auto (1934–1937).

Influenced by Art Nouveau, Aubrey Beardsley, children's books and Japanese prints, Dryden's colorful, witty cover designs and illustrations for *Vogue* helped define the elegant look of the magazine.

Sources: Duke, 86–87; Petteys, 210; Reed, 189; Christopher G. McPherson, "Helen Dryden," *Plasticliving.com*, http://www.plasticliving.com/dura/hd.html.

DUMM, FRANCES EDWINA

b. 1893, Upper Sandusky, OH; d. 1990, New York

Father: Frank Edwin Dumm, actor, playwright, newspaperman; brother: Robert Dennis, writer

Landon Correspondence School course in cartooning; Art Students League, studied with George Bridgeman and Frank Gruher

Work includes: hired by *Columbus Monitor* (later *Columbus Daily Monitor*) from 1915 to 1917 to contribute comic strips (*The Meanderings of Minnie*), spot drawings, and political cartoons; the first woman known to work as a political cartoonist and endorse women's suffrage in her cartoons; enlisted by the George Mathews Adams Syndicate to do a comic strip about a boy and his dog, debuted *Cap Stubbs and Tippie* in 1918; launched Sunday feature titled simply *Tippie* in 1934, syndicated by King Features, ran until 1963; collections published in *Two Gentlemen and a Lady* (1928) by Alexander Woollcott; *Flush of Wimpole Street and Broadway* (1933) by Flora Merrill; collections of her own series, *Sinbad, a Dog's Life* (1930), and *Sinbad, Again!* (1932), in addition to children's books and illustrations for her brother's verse. Credited as the first woman to create a continuity strip.

Sources: ANB; Lucy Shelton Caswell, "Seven Cartoonists," *1989 Festival of Cartoon Art* (Columbus: The Ohio State University Libraries, 1989), 71–73; Duke, 88–89; Petteys, 214; Robbins, 24, 52–53, 70–71,74; Sheppard, 223.

DURIEUX, CAROLINE (WOGAN)

b. 1896, New Orleans; d. 1989, Baton Rouge

Father: Charles Wogan; husband: Pierre Durieux, export-import businessman

Sophie Newcomb College, BA, design, 1916, BA, art education, 1917, studied with painter and etcher Ellsworth Woodward; Tulane University; Pennsylvania Academy of Fine Arts, studied with painter Henry McCarter, 1917–1919; master printers Dario Mejia and George Miller instructed her in lithography, Mexico

Work includes: "Mexico Series" of lithographs (1934) exhibited in New York; second series "North Americans" (1936); lithographs targeting Creole subculture, ca. 1936–1940s. Became known as a lithographer and social satirist in the tradition of George Grosz and Honoré Daumier. Published collections include Carl Zigrosser, *Caroline Durieux: Forty-Three Lithographs and Drawings* (1942); Richard Cox, *Caroline Durieux: Lithographs of the Thirties and Forties* (1977).

Taught art at Newcomb College, Louisiana State University, 1936–1944; served as director of Federal Art Project for

Louisiana, 1936–1943; honored for national outstanding achievement in the visual arts (with four others) by the Women's Caucus for Art, 1980.

With university science professors, invented a new printmaking process she named electron printing, which involved radioactive ink. Credited with reviving and technically innovating the print process of cliché verre (glass print process in which a print is made by placing photographic paper beneath a glass plate on which a design has been incised through a coating of an opaque substance and then exposed to light) and developed a method to add color to such prints.

Sources: Laura Clark Brown, Finding Aid for Durieux (Caroline Wogan) Papers, Mss. 3827, Inventory, Special Collections, Hill Memorial Library, Louisiana State University Libraries, Baton Rouge, 2009, http://www.lib.lsu.edu/sites/default/files/sc/findaid/3827.pdf; Richard Cox, *Caroline Durieux: Lithographs of the Thirties and Forties* (Baton Rouge: Louisiana State University Press, 1977); Heller,165–66; Petteys, 218; Rubinstein, 215–16, 225–26; Seaton, 122–23.

ELIOT, JAN BUELL

b. 1950, San Jose, CA

Husband: Ted Lay, corporate consultant; two daughters

Southern Illinois State University; University of Oregon, Eugene, women's studies, 1977

Work includes: comic strips that feature a single mother, *Patience and Sarah*, *Sister City*, and finally, *Stone Soup*, syndicated in 1995, ran twenty years as a daily and Sunday strip, and as of 2015 continued as Sunday-only feature. Published eleven collections of her cartoons that include: *Brace Yourself* (2011); *It Seemed Like a Good Idea at the Time* (2014); *Privacy Is for Wussies* (2016).

Awards include: Best Book, B. D. Amadora International Cartoon Exhibition, Lisbon, Portugal (2001); College of Arts and Sciences Alumni Fellow Award from the University of Oregon (2005); Toonie Award for Best Syndicated Cartoonist by Cartoonists Northwest (2008); Women Make a Difference award, International Women's Forum (2009); Distinguished Service Award from the University of Oregon (2010).

Sources: Frank Pauer, "Jan Eliot, Sixteen Years in the Making of Stone Soup," *The Cartoon!st, Newsletter of the National Cartoonists Society*, January–February 2007, 9-11; "Stone Soup Creator Jan Eliot Reflects on Her Semiretirement," *GoComics*, October 1, 2015, http://www.gocomics.com/news/laugh-tracks/1916/stone-soup-creator-jan-eliot-reflects-on-her-semiretirement.

EMMET, LYDIA FIELD

b. 1866, New Rochelle, NY; d. 1952, New York

Father: Thomas Addis Emmet; mother: Julia Colt Pierson Emmet; sister: Rosina Emmet Sherwood

Académie Julian, 1883; Art Students League, 1889–1895

Work includes: illustrations for *Harper's Magazine*; mural of allegorical figures for Women's Building, 1893 World's Columbian Exposition, Chicago (her sister Rosina E. Sherwood also completed a mural); portrait miniatures, 1896; focused on portraiture in latter phase of career.

Awards include: Academician of the National Academy of Design in 1912.

Sources: "Emmet, Lydia Field," National Gallery of Art, http://www.nga.gov/content/ngaweb/Collection/artist-info.1267.html; Charlene G. Garfinkel, "Rosina H. Emmet Sherwood," in Wanda M. Corn, *Women Building History: Public Art at the 1893 Columbian Exposition* (Berkeley: University of California Press, 2011), 24–126, 193–94; Oxford Art Online; Petteys, 229–30; Rubenstein, 123, 140, 154, 164.

FAULCONER, MARY (FULLERTON)

b. 1912, Pittsburgh; d. 2011

Philadelphia Museum School of Art; taught advertising there, 1936–1940

Art director, *Harper's Bazaar*, 1940; art director, *Mademoiselle*, 1945

Work includes: freelance work appeared in *Fortune, House and Garden, Life, Look, Seventeen, Town & Country, Vogue*; commissioned by US Postal Service to design six postage stamps (including rose and love designs), 1982.

Exhibited paintings in New York City galleries to critical acclaim from the 1940s to 1985.

Sources: Duke, 99–100; Falk, 1092; "Mary Faulconer," RoGallery.com auction house and gallery, http://rogallery.com/faulconer_mary/faulconer-bio.html.

FISH, ANNE HARRIET (SEFTON)

b. 1890, Bristol, England; d. 1964, Hayle, Cornwall, England

Father: Benjamin Fish, commercial clerk, accountant; mother, Annie Hitchcock; husband: Walter William Sefton, Belfast linen manufacturer for whom she produced textile designs

John Hassall School of Art (earlier called The New School)

Work includes: humorous illustrations, caricatures, humor cartoons published in *Eve*, *London Calling*, *Printer's Pie*, *The Patrician*, *Punch*, *Tatler*, *Vanity Fair* (more than 130 cover designs), *Vogue*, *Harper's Bazaar*, and *Cosmopolitan*; advertising art for Murad and Abdulla cigarettes, and Eno's Salts; wrote and illustrated *Third Eve Book: Drawings by Fish, Written and Designed by Fowl* (1919); *High Society* (1920); illustrated *World We Laugh In* (1924); *Tatlings* (1922).

Sources: Mark Bryant, "Fish (Harriet) Annie [Anne]," *Oxford Dictionary of National Biography*, Oxford University Press, September 2004, http://www.oxforddddnb.com/view/article/5712; Duke, 103; Simon Houfe, *The Dictionary of British Book Illustrators and Caricaturists, 1800–1914* (Antique Collectors' Club, 1981); Petteys, 248.

FOOTE, MARY HALLOCK

ca. 1874

b. 1847, near Milton, NY; d. 1938, Hingham, MA

Father: Nathaniel Hallock, Quaker, farmer; mother: Anne Burling, Quaker; husband: Arthur De Wint Foote, mining engineer; three children

Cooper Union, 1864–1867, studied with William J. Linton (wood engraving); studied with William Rimmer, Samuel F. Johnson

Work includes: illustrations published in *Our Young Folks* (predecessor of *St. Nicholas*), *Hearth and Home*, *Scribner's Monthly*, *Appleton's Journal*, and *Aldine*; contributed to special gift book editions of *The Hanging of the Crane* and *The Skeleton in Armor* by Henry W. Longfellow, and *The Scarlet Letter* by Nathaniel Hawthorne. Well known for illustrations and writings on her life in the Far West first published in *Scribner's Monthly* in 1878, followed by features in the *Century Magazine* that included her acclaimed series, "Pictures of the Far West," 1888–1889. Gradually shifted to writing novels set in the West.

Exhibitions include: wood engravings in Women's Pavilion, Centennial Exhibition, Philadelphia, 1876; paintings in Columbian World's Fair, Chicago, 1893; a painting in the Armory Show, New York, 1913.

Sources: ANB; Shelley Armitage, "The Illustrator as Writer: Mary Hallock Foote and the Myth of the West," in *Under the Sun: Myth and Realism in Western American Literature*, ed. Barbara Howard Meldrum (Troy, NY: Whitston, 1985), 150–74; Mary Hallock Foote, *A Victorian Gentlewoman in the Far West: The Reminiscences of Mary Hallock Foote*, ed.

Rodman W. Paul (San Marino, CA: Huntington Library, 1972); Kovinick, 95; Sue Rainey, "Mary Hallock Foote: A Leading Illustrator of the 1870s and 1880s," *Winterthur Portfolio* 41, nos. 2–3 (2007): 97–139.

FOSTER, GENEVIEVE (STUMP)

b. 1893, Oswego, NY; d. 1979, Westport, CT

Father: John William Stump, science teacher; mother: Jessie Starin; husband: Orrington C. Foster, engineer; two children

University of Wisconsin, BA, 1915; Chicago Academy of Fine Arts, 1916–1917

Work includes: nineteen children's books, including four that received Newbury Honor citations: *George Washington's World* (1942); *Abraham Lincoln* (1945); *George Washington* (1950); *Birthdays of Freedom* (1953); illustrations for *Mother's Magazine*, *Golfers*, *Women's World*, and some advertising as well for *Child Life*.

Brought attention to lesser known historical figures and sought to make history "alive for children" by telling stories about historical figures' perceptions of the events around them.

Sources: "Genevieve Stump Foster," *Contemporary Authors Online*, Gale, 2002, *Biography in Context*; Guide to the Genevieve Foster papers, 1937–1978, Special Collections and University Archives, University of Oregon Libraries; "Foster, Genevieve," Social Networks and Archival Context, http://socialarchive.iath.virginia.edu/ark:/99166/w6ks6x9h; Larry Peterson, Finding Aid, Genevieve Foster Papers (2004), and Christina Cowan (1998), Part of the Children's Literature Research Collections, University of Minnesota.

FOSTER, LAURA E. (MONROE)

b. 1871, San Francisco; d. 1920, San Francisco

Husband: Donald Monroe

Began career as a newspaper artist; exhibited work at the Mechanic's Institute in San Francisco, 1885–1891, and with San Francisco Newspaper Artists, 1903. Moved to New York after 1906 earthquake in San Francisco; produced illustrations with pro-suffrage imagery for *Life*, *Saturday Evening Post*, *Judge*, and other publications.

Sources: *American Women: A Library of Congress Guide for the Study of Women's History and Culture in the United States*, ed. Sheridan Harvey, Janice E. Ruth, and Barbara Orbach Natanson (Washington, DC: Library of Congress; Hanover: University Press of New England, 2001), 8; Hughes, vol. 1, 391; Sheppard, 223.

FRUHAUF, ALINE

b. 1907, New York; d. 1978, Bethesda, MD

Husband: Erwin Vollner, physiologist; two daughters

Parsons School of Design; Art Students League with Boardman Robinson, Kenneth Hayes Miller

Work includes: caricatures published in the *New York World*, *Musical America*, and drawings in *Vogue*, *Theater Magazine*, and the *Dance Observer*; memoir, *Making Faces: Memoirs of a Caricaturist* (1990).

Sources: *Aline Fruhauf: The Face of Music II*, an exhibition at the Charles Marvin Fairchild Memorial Gallery, Georgetown University, Washington, DC, January 15–May 14, 2002, http://www.library.georgetown.edu/exhibition/aline-fruhauf-face-music-ii; Falk, 1207; Fruhauf; Obituary, *New York Times*, May 28, 1978; Reaves, 161–63, 190–91.

GÁG, WANDA HAZEL

b. 1893, New Ulm, MN; d. 1946, New York

Father: Anton Gág, painter; mother: Elisabeth Beibl; husband: Earle Humphrey

Grew up with customs and fairy tales of parents' native Bohemia; St. Paul Art School, 1913–1914; Minneapolis Art School, 1914–1917; Art Students League, studied with Robert Henri, Frank Vincent Dumond, and Kenneth Hayes Miller

Work includes: children's book author and illustrator and fine artists with talent for woodcut and lithography; *Millions of Cats* (1928); *The Funny Thing* (1929), *Snippy and Snappy* (1931); *ABC Bunny* (1933); *Nothing at All* (1942); translated, illustrated, and published *Tales from the Grimm brothers* (1936), *Snow White and the Seven Dwarfs* (1938), *Three Gay Tales from Grimm* (1943). Pursued fine art projects between publication projects.

Solo exhibitions of her work at Weyhe Gallery, New York, 1926, 1928, 1930, 1940.

Sources: ANB; Wanda Gág papers, Van Pelt Library, University of Pennsylvania, and Minnesota Historical Society; Petteys, 268; Rubinstein, 193; Seaton, 130–31.

GAUERKE, MARY FLANIGAN

b. ca. 1927; d. 1989
Father: Lon Flanigan; husband: Carl Gauerke
Stevens College (Columbia, MO); self-taught
Work includes: comics appeared in *Family Circle, Look, National Observer*, the *New York Times, New Yorker, Playboy*, and regularly from 1966 in William F. Buckley's *National Review* for fifteen years. Created a comic panel entitled, *The Alumnae*, distributed by the Register and Tribune Syndicate in 1969, that featured four women characters with distinct personalities that ran into the early 1970s. Hippies were frequent targets.
Sources: Duke, 121–22; *Geneva Times* (New York), September 8, 1969: 5; Maslin; Robbins and Yronwode, 82.

GETSLER, SYLVIA

b. ca. 1926, Poland; emigrated to United States, ca. 1933; d. 2009, Lambertville, NJ
Husband: Joseph Treceno, artist and writer; one daughter
Work includes: freelancer; made hundreds of gag cartoons that conformed to stereotypes of her time (e.g., men were alcoholics and skirt chasers and women sought only to marry and shop); favorite focus was on the innocence and wit of children; gag cartoons published in *Ladies' Home Journal, McCall's, Playboy, Saturday Evening Post*, and *True Detective*. Posthumous exhibition, *Have Gags Will Travel: The Life and Times of a New York Cartoonist*, March 10–July 1, 2012, Pfundt Gallery, James A. Michener Museum.
Sources: *Have Gags Will Travel* exhibition press release, James A. Michener Museum, February 8, 2012, www.michener museum.org/press/?item=2012-02-08a.

GIBSON, LYDIA

b. 1891, New York; d. 1964
Father: Robert W. Gibson, ecclesiastical architect; husband: Robert Minor, cartoonist
Studied with James Fraser, Pierre Van Parys Bourdelle, Jules Guerin, and Henry Varnum Poor
Work includes: regular contributions to the *Masses* by 1912; after it ceased publication in 1917, published illustrations in the *Liberator, Red Cartoons from the Daily Worker*, and the *Worker's Monthly*; painted portraits and still lifes, and wrote and illustrated a children's book, *The Teacup Whale* (1934).
Exhibitions include: Whitney Museum of Art, 1922–1923; Salons of America, 1922–1926, 1928, 1930–1931, 1933; Society of Independent Artists, 1922, 1928, 1930–1931, 1934–1936.
Member, Society of Independent Artists. Advocated for women's suffrage.
Sources: Doris Ostrander Dawdy, *Artists of the American West: A Biographical Dictionary* (Chicago: Sage Books, 1974), vol. 2, 104–5; Falk, 1279; Hughes, vol. 1, 427; "Lydia Marie Gibson," *Labor Arts*, http://www.laborarts.org/exhibits/themasses/bios.cfm?bio=lydia-gibson-minor.

GILLESPIE, JESSIE

b. Jessie Gillespie Willing, 1888, Brooklyn; d. 1972, Glen Ridge, NJ
Father: John Thomson Willing, art editor, *Associated Sunday Magazine*
Pennsylvania Academy of Fine Arts
Art editor, Keystone Publishing Company, Philadelphia (1922–1931)
Work includes: illustrations for the *Girl Scout Handbook* (1930s–1940s); text and illustrations for *Precious Books: Why and Where They Are Treasured* (1933); magazine illustrations for *Vogue, Life, Associated Sunday Magazine*, and *Ladies' Home Journal*; book illustrations for works by Kate Douglas Wiggin and Dorothy Canfield Fisher. Known for her subtly drawn silhouettes of fashionably dressed figures.
Honorary life member of the National Art Society
Sources: Lansing Moore, "Jessie Gillespie: The Art of the Elegant Silhouette," *Art at the Ocean House: The Good Life through the Artist's Eye* (Bronxville, NY: Dongan Antiques, 2011), 167–71; Petteys, 281; Roger Reed, e-mail to the author, June 29, 2013.

GRAMBS, BLANCHE (AKA GRAMBS MILLER)

b. 1916, Beijing, China; d. 2010, New York

First husband: fellow student Hugh Miller; second husband: James Aronson, one of the founders of the *National Guardian* (the *Guardian*, 1967)

Art Students League, 1934, studied printmaking with Harry Sternberg, printed own etchings, lithographs printed by Will Barnet

Work includes: worked as a printmaker from 1934 to 1939; illustrator for *Woman's Day* after 1939; later in career as an illustrator, used the name Grambs Miller.

Sources: Sara Duke, "Blanche Grambs, 1916," *Life of the People: Realist Prints and Drawings from the Ben and Beatrice Goldstein Collection, 1912–1948*, ed. Harry Katz (Washington, DC: Library of Congress, 1999), 97; Falk, 1344; "Blanche Grambs (1916–1940)," Susan Teller Gallery, http://www.susantellergallery.com/cgi/STG_bio.pl?artist=grambs.

GREATOREX, ELIZA PRATT

b. 1819, Manorhamilton, Ireland; emigrated to United States, ca. 1840; d. 1897, Paris, France

Father: James Calcott Pratt, Methodist minister; husband: Henry W. Pratt, organist, teacher; three children

Studied with Hudson River artists William and James Hart, William Wotherspoon; studied in Paris with Émile Lambinet, Charles Henri Toussaint; traveled to Munich and Colorado

Taught art at Miss Haines School for Girls, New York

Work includes: published collections of prints and drawings, *Homes of Ober-Ammergau* (1872); *Summer Etchings in Colorado* (1873); *Old New York from the Battery to Bloomingdale* (1874), for which she is best known; *Etchings in Nuremburg* (1875). Focused on etching and engraving for most of her career because painting negatively affected her health.

Exhibitions include: Pennsylvania Academy of Fine Arts, Boston Athenæum, American Society of Painters in Water Colors in New York, Philadelphia Centennial Exposition, 1876.

One of first two women elected associate member, National Academy of Design, 1869.

Sources: Kovinick, 117; Katherine E. Manthorne, "The Lady with the Pen: The Graphic Art of Eliza Greatorex," *American Arts Quarterly* 29, no. 4 (Fall 2012); Rubinstein, 71–72, 89, 90.

GREEN, ELIZABETH SHIPPEN (ELLIOTT)

1910

b. 1871, Philadelphia; d. 1954, Villanova, PA

Father: Jasper Green, artist correspondent during the Civil War; mother: Elizabeth Boude; husband: Huger Elliott, professor of architecture

Pennsylvania Academy of Fine Arts, studied with Thomas Anshutz and Robert Vonnoh; studied with Howard Pyle

Work includes: early work published in *Philadelphia Times*, *St. Nicholas*, *Women's Home Companion*, and the *Saturday Evening Post*; exclusive contract with *Harper's Monthly* beginning in 1901; illustrations in Charles and Mary Lamb, *Tales from Shakespeare* (1922).

Member of the Plastic Club; won Mary Smith Prize (1905) for the best work by a Philadelphia woman artist at Pennsylvania Academy of Fine Arts's annual exhibition; known as one of the Red Rose Girls.

Sources: Carter; Harrison S. Morris, "Elizabeth Shippen Green," *The Book Buyer* 24 (March 1902): 111–15; Ann B. Percy, "Elizabeth Shippen Green Elliott (1871–1954)," *Philadelphia: Three Centuries*, 485–86; *A Petal from the Rose: Illustrations by Elizabeth Shippen Green*, an exhibition at the Library of Congress, Washington, DC, June 28–September 29, 2001, https://www.loc.gov/exhibits/petal/; Catherine Connell Stryker, *The Studios at Cogslea* (Wilmington: Delaware Art Museum, 1976); Wagner, 12, 14, 20–21, 23, 34, 45, 52–56.

GROSVENOR, THELMA CUDLIPPE

b. 1892, Richmond, VA; d. 1983

Mother: Annie Ericsson Cudlipp, assistant editor, the *Delineator*; husband: Theodore Grosvenor, attorney

Art Students League; Royal Academy and St. John's Wood School, London

Work includes: illustrations for *Harper's*, *Century*, *Vanity Fair*, *Town & Country*, *Saturday Evening Post*, and *McClure's*; illustrated books, and produced poster designs during World War I.

Exhibited paintings at the Pennsylvania Academy of Fine Arts, the Toledo Museum of Art, and the Art Institute of Chicago, and won an award for her work in 1936 from the National Association of Women Painters and Sculptors.

Sources: Falk, 301; Keith Newlin, ed., *A Theodore Dreiser Encyclopedia* (Westport, CT: Greenwood Press, 2003), 77–78, 105, 326; Petteys, 301.

GUISEWITE, CATHY

b. 1950, Dayton, OH

Mother: Anne; former husband: Chris Wilkinson, screenwriter; one daughter

University of Michigan, BA, English, 1972

Work includes: semiautobiographical comic strip *Cathy*, one of the first strips to feature a single working woman, ran from 1976 to 2012 and inspired a successful merchandising empire of spin-off products. A few among at least thirty-seven published collections of her strips include *The Cathy Chronicles* (1978); *It Must Be Love, My Face Is Breaking Out* (1982); *How to Get Rich, Fall in Love, Lose Weight, and Solve all Your Problems by Saying "NO"* (1983); *Eat Your Way to a Better Relationship* (1983); *Thin Thighs in Thirty Years* (1986); *Revelations from a 45-Pound Purse* (1993).

Awards include: Emmys (1987) for three animated television specials of *Cathy*; Reuben Award (1993) from the National Cartoonists Society.

Sources: "Cathy Lee Guisewite," *Encyclopedia of World Biography* 18, Gale, 1998; Ben Fulton, "It's the End of the Line for 'Cathy,'" *Salt Lake Tribune*, September 28, 2010; Tom Heintjes, "The Cathy Guisewite Interview," *Hogans Alley*, April 12, 2012, http://cartoonician.com/cathy-guisewite-the-goodbye-girl/; Robbins, 152; Robbins and Yronwode,116, 118–19.

HAMEL, JUANITA

b. 1891, De Soto, MO; d. 1939, Hamilton, Bermuda

Father: F. G. Hamel; mother: Lucille Hamel (later Craven); husband: A. Fowle, in shipping business

St. Louis Art School, Washington University

Work includes: drawings published in *St. Louis Times*, *Chicago Herald*, Newspaper Picture Service (based in New York), *Cleveland Plain Dealer*; work included in an exhibition of St. Louis newspaper artists at the St. Louis Press Club, 1915; rare surviving examples of her drawings feature beautiful young women depicted in a fine-lined, Art Nouveau–influenced style that strongly recalls that of Nell Brinkley.

Sources: Duke, 139; Alex Jay, "Ink-Slinger Profiles: Juanita Hamel," *Stripper's Guide*, December 4, 2013, http://strippersguide.blogspot.com/2013/12/ink-slinger-profiles-by-alex-jay.html.

HARDING, CHARLOTTE

b. 1873, Newark, NJ; d. 1951, Smithtown, NY

Father: Joseph Harding; mother: Charlotte Elizabeth Matthews; husband: James Adams Brown, meteorological engineer; one daughter

Philadelphia School of Design for Women; Pennsylvania Academy of Fine Arts; Drexel Institute, studied with Howard Pyle

Work includes: illustrations for many magazines including *Century*, *Collier's*, various *Harper's* titles, *McClure's*, *Ladies' Home Journal*, and *Saturday Evening Post*, and a number of books.

Shared a studio with Alice Barber Stephens from 1899 to 1903; taught at Drexel Institute's School of Illustration; founding member of the Plastic Club; won Silver Medals for work exhibited at Woman's Exposition, London, England, 1900; St. Louis Exposition, 1904, and Panama Pacific International Exposition, San Francisco, 1915. Donated drawings to the Library of Congress in 1934, and burned the rest, telling artist Thornton Oakley she had no reason to keep any of her drawings. While stylistically influenced somewhat by her mentor and friend Stephens, Harding's work stands out for pleasing use of patterning and boldly designed scenes that draw viewers in.

Sources: Ann Barton Brown, *Charlotte Harding: An Illustrator in Philadelphia* (Chadds Ford, PA: Brandywine River Museum of the Brandywine Conservancy, 1982); Reed, 103; Rubenstein, 162; Patricia Smith Scanlan, "'God-Gifted Girls': Women Illustrators, Gender, Class, and Commerce in American Visual Culture, 1885–1925." PhD diss., Indiana University, 2010. ProQuest (AAT 3409785).

HARVEY, ALICE

b. 1894, near Austin, IL; d. 1983, Westport, CT
Husband: Charles H. Ramsey Sr.; two children
School of the Art Institute of Chicago, studied with Wallace Morgan; Parsons School of Design, studied with Howard Giles
Work includes: illustrations for *Life, Judge, Woman's Day, McCall's, Saturday Evening Post, Harper's Bazaar*; work appeared in the *New Yorker* from 1925 to mid-1940s, including three cover designs and at least five cartoons; illustrations for books include *Cherished and Shared of Old* by Susan Glaspell (1940); *"Ask My Secretary": The Art of Being a Successful Business Girl* by Gladys Torson (1940); *Bicycle Commandos* by Wendell Farmer (1944); *Out on a Limbo* by Claire MacMurray (1944); *Applejack for Breakfast* by Alfred S. Campbell and Helen Monteith Campbell (1946); *Innocents from Indiana* by Emily Kimbrough (1950); *Through Charley's Door* by Emily Kimbrough (1952); *Dear Mad'm* by Stella Walthall Patterson (1956).
Sources: Donnelly, 13, 19, 28–29, 36–46, 55–56, 58, 70, 74, 84–86, 108, 114, 203–4; Maurice Horn, *World Encyclopedia of Comics,* vol. 4 (New York: Chelsea House, 1976), 508; Trina Robbins, *The Great Women Cartoonists* (New York: Watson-Guptill, 2001), 47; Thorndike, 35.

HELLER, HELEN WEST (BARNHART)

b. 1872, Rushville, IL; d. 1955, New York
Art Students League; St. Louis School of Fine Arts
Suffered from poor health much of her life and supported her art training by working professionally as a model and taking menial jobs
Work includes: painting, printmaking, writing, and illustrating; author-illustrator of *Migratory Urge: Wood-cut Poems* (1928); *Woodcuts U.S.A* (1947). Employed on the 1933–1934 Public Works of Art Project, then under the Works Progress Administration Federal Art Project (WPA-FAP), she created prints and murals.
Exhibited her work from mid-1920s–1950 at the Chicago Art Institute, Walen Bookshop (Chicago), American Artists' Congress (New York, 1936). Awarded First Purchase Prize, Library of Congress, 1945; elected member, National Academy of Design, 1948. Work is represented in collections of the Brooklyn Museum, New York Public Library, the Metropolitan Museum of Art, Chicago Municipal College.
Sources: Heller, 547–48; Seaton, 154–55; Mantle Fielding, 393; Petteys, 329.

HILL, ALICE AMELIA STEWART

b. 1851, Amboy, NY; d. 1896, Dansville, NY
Father: George H. Stewart, judge; mother: Sarah; husband: Francis B. Hill, businessman
Cooper Union; National Academy of Design
Taught classes in drawing, watercolor, and oil painting in Colorado Springs in 1874; investigated, classified, and painted native flora; illustrated books by Virginia McClurg and most notably, one hundred copies of *The Procession of Flowers* (1886) by Helen Hunt Jackson.
Sources: Edwin and Nancy Bathke, "Alice Stewart Hill, Colorado Springs' First Wild Flower Artist: Her Family & Friends," *Extraordinary Women of the Rocky Mountain West,* ed. Tim Blevins (Colorado Springs: Pikes Peak Library District, with the Colorado Women's Hall of Fame, 2010); Kovinick, 140; Samuels and Samuels, 224–25.

HOGEBOOM, AMY

b. 1891, active 1920s–1950s
Work includes: illustrations for magazines, author and illustrator for children's books; cover art for literary periodicals *Golden Book Magazine* (London: Fleetway Press) and *Magazine of Fiction and True Stories That Will Live*; among nineteen titles she wrote and illustrated from 1939 to 1958, a number treat historical figures or topics such as *Gay Kilties of Cape Breton* (1941), Nathan Hale in *One Life to Lose* (1942), and *Christopher Columbus and His Brothers* (1951); several others are how-to drawing books such as *Dogs and How to Draw Them* (1944).
Sources: Lui Antal Deak, "Biography: Amy Hogeboom," *askART Academic,* http://www.askart.com/artist_bio/Amy_Hogeboom/135973/Amy_Hogeboom.aspx.

HOKINSON, HELEN ELNA

b. 1893, Mendota, IL; d. 1949, Washington, DC
Father: Adolph Hokinson, farm machinery salesman; mother: Mary Wilcox
Chicago Academy of Fine Arts; Chicago Art Institute; Parsons School of Art, studied with Howard Giles
Work includes: fashion illustration for New York department stores; cartoons and covers for the *New Yorker* beginning in 1925; published three collections of her cartoons: *So You're Going to Buy a Book* (1931); *My Best Girls* (1943); *When Were You Built?* (1943). Posthumous collections include *The Ladies, God Bless Them* (1950), *There Are Ladies Present* (1952), and *The Hokinson Festival* (1950).

Sources: Donnelly, 27–40, 42, 44–46, 76–81, 84, 90, 98, 101–9, 112, 114–18, 120, 162, 203–4; "Helen Elna Hokinson," *World Encyclopedia of Biography* 23, Gale, 2003; Thorndike, 55.

HOLLANDER, NICOLE

b. 1939, Chicago

Father: Henry Garrison; mother: Shirley Mazur Garrison

University of Illinois, Urbana-Champaign, BFA, 1960; Boston University, MFA, 1966

Work includes: graphic design for feminist publication *The Spokeswoman*, 1970s; comics for *Mother Jones*, 1980s; comic strips include *The Feminist Funnies*, in which character Sylvia was introduced (late 1970s); *Sylvia* (ca. 1979–2012), syndicated by Field Enterprises in 1981 and which ran in more than sixty daily and weekly papers; published twenty collections of *Sylvia* cartoons, including three anthologies; other publications include *Drawn Together: Relationships Lampooned, Harpooned, and Cartooned* with Skip Morrow and Ron Wolin (1983); *Choices* (1990); *An ABC of Vice: An Insatiable Woman's Guide* with Gina Barreca (2003); *Tales of Graceful Aging from the Planet Denial* (2007); illustrated numerous children's books by Robie H. Harris and Allia Zobel.

Musicals based on her work include *Female Problems* and *Sylvia's Real Good Advice*, winner of a Joseph Jefferson Award in 1991.

Awards include: Wonder Woman Foundation Award for Women of Achievement Over 40 (1983) and Yale's Chubb Fellowship for Public Service (1984–1985).

Sources: Martha H. Kennedy, "Sylvia's World: Nicole Hollander Shares a Spicy Slice of Life," *Library of Congress Information Bulletin* 63, no. 4 (April 2004): 66–67; Robbins, 148, 150; Robbins and Yronwode, 116, 118, 119; Elizabeth Wenning, "Nicole Hollander," *Contemporary Authors Online*, Gale, 2003, *Biography in Context*.

HUGET, VIRGINIA (CLARK)

b. 1899, Dallas; d. 1991, Columbia, SC

Parents: William and Sarah Clark; husband: Coon Williams Hudzietz; three children

School of the Art Institute of Chicago

Work includes: first strip, *Gentlemen Prefer Blondes*, sold to Bell Syndicate (1926), using French-sounding name "Huget"; *Molly the Manicure Girl* (1928); *Campus Capers* (1928); Sunday magazine cover comic strips include *Babs in Society* (1927); *Flora's Fling* (1928); "*Double Dora*" (1929); *Miss Aladdin* (1929); drew strip *Skippy* for Percy Crosby (1937); took over strip *Oh Diana!* from artist Don Flowers (1944), using maiden name, Clark; illustrated two books in the *Boners* series originated by Theodor Seuss Geisel, *Still More Boners* (1931) and *Prize Boners for 1932* (1932).

Sources: Duke, 103; Ron Goulart, *The Funnies: One Hundred Years of American Comic Strips* (Holbrook, MA: Adams Publishing, 1995), 58; Allan Holtz, "Obscurity of the Day: Gentlemen Prefer Blondes," *Stripper's Guide*, October 10, 2011, accessed May 3, 2017, http://strippersguide.blogspot.com/2011/10/obscurity-of-day-gentlemen-prefer.html; Lambiek; Trina Robbins, *The Great Women Cartoonists* (New York: Watson-Guptill, 2001), 28; Robbins, 38–40, 42, 59, 74, 97, 99, 105.

HULME, ETTA

b. 1923, Somerville, TX; d. 2014, Arlington, TX

Husband: Vernon Hulme; four children

University of Texas, Austin, BFA

Work includes: worked in Disney animation studio in California; produced commercial art and taught in an art school in San Antonio; illustrated Red Rabbit comic books in Chicago; freelanced as an editorial cartoonist for the *Texas Observer* in the 1950s before the *Fort Worth Star-Telegram* hired her as a full-time editorial cartoonist in 1972; published collection of her cartoons, *Ettatorials: The Best of Etta Hulme* in 1998.

First woman to win the National Cartoonists Society Editorial Cartoon Award in 1981, awarded again in 1998; served as president of the Association of American Editorial Cartoonists in 1987; documentary, "Trailblazer: The Editorial Cartoons of Etta Hulme," screened at 2004 meeting of the AAEC.

Sources: Hess and Northrop, 139; Tim Madigan, "Etta Hulme, Acclaimed Star-Telegram Cartoonist, Dies," *Fort Worth Star-Telegram*, June 27, 2014; Robbins, 108.

JETTER, FRANCES

b. 1951, New York

Parsons School of Design

Work includes: numerous editorial illustrations (lino-cuts) published in the *New York Times,* the *Village Voice, Time*, and the *Progressive*; artist books; sculpture.

Exhibited work nationally and internationally, including at the Salon de la Jeune Grauvure, Paris, 1995; represented in collections of Stanford University, Fogg Art Museum, New York Public Library, Rhode Island School of Design, and University of Michigan. Since 1979, has taught at the School of Visual Arts, New York.

Awards include: New York Foundation for the Arts Fellowship, Printmaking/Drawing/Artist's Books, 2003; Honorary Mention Award for "Cry Uncle," Pyramid Atlantic Book Arts Fair, Silver Spring, MD, 2010; Puffin Foundation, Ltd. Grant, 2010; New York Foundation for the Arts Fellowship, Printmaking/Drawing/Book Arts, 2011. Additional awards and honors from Society of Newspaper Designers, the Society of Illustrators, American Illustration, Print Annuals, the Society of Publication Designers, Graphics Annuals, Communication Arts Annuals.

Sources: Mantle Fielding, 454; Oxford Art Online; Zina Saunders, "Frances Jetter Profile," *Zina Saunders*, February 15, 2010, http://zinasaunders.buglogic.com/?section =news&article=9810&d=true; www.fjetter.net.

JOHNSON, CAROLITA

b. 1965, New York

Husband: Michael Crawford, cartoonist (d. 2016)

Parsons School of Design, fashion design; studied literature in Paris

Work includes: cartoons for the *New Yorker,* her first cartoon published there October 20, 2003; work published in the *Hairpin, Scratch Magazine*, and *Cosmopolitan*; she has said she gathers ideas on the subway and sometimes develops them as she rides. Launched web comic *Oscarina*, in April 2011, described as Johnson's alter-ego: a pissed-off trailblazer bent on destroying the patriarchy with each sharp rebuke. Became cartoon editor of *Upstart Magazine*, 2016.

Sources: Donnelly, 192–94; Jessica Jones, "On the Cover: Carolita Johnson," *Chronogram*, July 1, 2015, http://www .chronogram.com/hudsonvalley/on-the-cover/Con tent?oid=2315901; Maslin; David Remnick, "Remembering an Adored Cartoonist," *New Yorker: Postscript*, July 25, 2016, http://www.newyorker.com/magazine/2016/07/25/ remembering-an-adored-cartoonist; http://carolitajoh nson.squarespace.com/.

JOHNSTON, LYNN BEVERLY

b. 1947, Collingwood, Ontario

Father: Mervyn Ridgway, jeweler; mother: Ursula, calligrapher; brother: Alan: trumpet player; first husband: Doug Franks, television cameraman; second husband: Roderick Johnston, pilot, dentist; two children

Vancouver School of Art

Work includes: worked in an animation studio, as a medical illustrator, freelance commercial artist and writer before beginning to draw comics; three books of cartoons focused on children and family life; comic strip *The Johnsons*, renamed *For Better or for Worse*, ran from 1979 to 2008, appearing in two thousand newspapers, becoming one of the most extraordinarily successful comics of its type.

Awards include: Member of the Order of Canada (1992); Pulitzer Prize nomination (1994); inducted into International Museum of Cartoon Art Hall of Fame (1997); inducted into Canadian Cartoonists' Hall of Fame (2008); honorary degrees from four Canadian universities.

Selected sources: Michael Cavna, "Lynn Johnston's Long Drawn-Out Adieu to Cartooning," *Washington Post*, August 7, 2008; Harvey, 43; "Lynn Johnston," *Contemporary Authors Online*, Gale, 2011, *Biography in Context*; Don Markstein, "For Better or for Worse," *Don Markstein's Toonopedia*, http://www.toonopedia.com/forbettr.htm; www.fborfw.com.

KALMAN, MAIRA

b. 1949, Tel Aviv, Israel

High School of Music and Art, New York; New York University, literature

Husband: Tibor Kalman, graphic designer and creative director for Barnes & Noble

Work includes: covers for the *New Yorker* (including *New Yorkistan*); illustrated narrative journal (*New York Times*, 2006–2007); children's books *Hey Willy, See the Pyramids* (1988), *Sayonara, Mrs. Kackleman* (1989), *Max Makes a Million* (1990), *Ooh-la-la—Max in Love* (1991), *Max in Hollywood* (1992), *Fireboat: The Heroic Adventure of the "John J. Harvey"* (2002), and *Looking at Lincoln* (2011); illustrated editions of William Strunk and E. B. White's *The Elements of Style* (2005) and Michael Pollan's *Food Rules: An Eater's Manual* (2011); exhibition companion volume *Maira Kalman: Various Illuminations of a Crazy World* (2010); *The Principles of Uncertainty* (2007) and *And the Pursuit of Happiness* (2010).

Sources: "Maira Kalman," *Contemporary Authors Online*, Gale, 2006. *Biography in Context*; www.mairakalman.com.

KARASZ, ILONKA

b. 1896, Budapest, Hungary; d. 1981, Warwick, NY

Husband: Willem Nyland, chemist and teacher; one daughter

Royal Academy of Arts and Crafts, Budapest

Work includes: from 1924 to 1973, created 186 cover designs for the *New Yorker*, the most by any female artist; founder-director of Design Group, Inc., engaged with manufacturers in production of fabrics, rugs, flatware, china, and furniture; created cover designs for the *Masses*, the *New Yorker*, and illustrations for *Playboy* and *Quill*.

Sources: "Ilonka Karasz, 84, Artist-Designer; Drew Covers for the New Yorker," *New York Times*, May 30, 1981; Zurier, 180.

KAY, GERTRUDE ALICE

b. 1884, Alliance, OH; d. 1939, Youngstown, OH

Father: Charles Young, hardware merchant; mother: Gertrude Cantine

Philadelphia School of Design for Women; studied with Howard Pyle, Chadds Ford, PA

Work includes: cover designs and story illustrations for *Ladies' Home Journal*, *Good Housekeeping*, *Outlook*, and other magazines from 1908 to the 1920s; illustrated numerous children's books including some she also wrote. Beginning in 1921, traveled extensively to China, Japan, Ireland, England, and Italy, and wrote and illustrated articles about her travels for *Ladies' Home Journal*.

Exhibitions include: Art Institute of Chicago, American Watercolor Society in New York, and the Plastic Club, Philadelphia.

Sources: "Gertrude Kay," *Illustration Art Solutions*, http://www.illustration-art-solutions.com/gertrude-kay.html; Larson, 135; Petteys, 387.

KENNY, AGGIE WHELAN

Born in Worcester, MA

Work includes: courtroom illustrations for the trial of the Gainesville Eight (1973), Mitchell-Stans trial (1974), for which she won an Emmy, and many other cases including those of political activist Angela Davis, former military leader of Panama Manuel Noriega, James Earl Ray, Oliver North, David Berkowitz, and Jerry Sandusky; during decades of Supreme Court assignments, she has drawn the Warren Burger Court, the William Rehnquist Court, and most recently, the John Roberts Court; clients include NBC News, ABC News, CBS News, Associated Press, ESPN, CNN, and Newsday; produced drawings for CNN series "Death Row Stories," 2014.

Exhibitions include: drawings of World Trade Center recovery operation in 2002 included in *Artist as Witness: The 9/11 Responders*, New York City Police Museum, 2010; illustrations of Justice William J. Brennan featured in show of notable trials at the William J. Brennan Courthouse in New Jersey, 2013.

Sources: Williams and Russell, 232; Williams.

KING, FAY

b. 1889, Seattle; active 1918–1930s

Former husband: Oscar Matthew "Battling" Nelson, lightweight boxing champion

Work includes: comic strips that voiced her personal opinions and advice to women and included figure of herself looking like Olive Oyl; reproduced examples of her panels and strips appeared in *Cartoons Magazine*, the *Denver Post*, and *Kansas City Post*.

In 1939, Chuck Thorndike referred to her as one of the top five women cartoonists in America.

Sources: Allan Holtz, "Ink Slinger Profiles: Fay King," *Stripper's Guide*, January 22, 2013, http://strippersguide.blogspot.com/2013/01/ink-slinger-profiles-fay-king.html; Robbins, 45–48; Robbins and Yronwode, 18, 32; Thorndike, 35.

KIRK, MARIA LOUISE

b. 1860, Philadelphia; d. 1938, Philadelphia

Father: George H. Kirk; mother: Harriet A. Craig

Philadelphia School of Design for Women; Pennsylvania Academy of Fine Arts

Works include: known as a painter of portraits and an illustrator; illustrations for more than fifty books, including *Pioki and Her People: A Ranch and Tepee Story* (1894); *Story of Hiawatha* (1910); *Story of the Canterbury Pilgrims* (1914); *Dog of Flanders* (1915); *Water-Babies* (1917); *Gulliver's Travels* (1918); *Heidi* (1919); *Child's Garden of Verses* (1919); *Cornelli: A Story of the Swiss Alps* (1921); awarded the Mary Smith Prize for best painting by a woman, 1894.

Sources: Mantle Fielding, 493; Petteys, 397.

KUNZ, ANITA

Self-portrait, 2001

b. 1956, Toronto

Ontario College of Art, 1978, studied with Doug Johnson

Work includes: numerous editorial illustrations and cover designs for such leading magazines as *Time, Newsweek, GQ,* the *New York Times Magazine,* the *Washington Post Magazine,* and more than twenty cover designs for the *New Yorker*, in addition to illustrations or cover designs for more than fifty books.

Exhibited work nationally and internationally in solo shows in Toronto, Boston, Cincinnati, Laguna Beach, CA, New York, Philadelphia, Washington, DC, Rome, and Tokyo, in addition to many group shows. Work represented in the Library of Congress; Canadian Archives, Ottawa; McCord Museum, Montreal; Museum of Contemporary Art, Rome; National Portrait Gallery, Washington, DC; Musée militaire en France, Paris.

Awards include: Hamilton King Award, Museum of American Illustration, New York (2007); Office of the Order of Canada, Canada's highest civilian honor, 2010; honorary doctorate from the Ontario College of Art and Design University (2010); recipient of the Queen's Diamond Jubilee Medal of Honour (2012); honorary doctorate from the Massachusetts College of Art and Design (2015); Lifetime Achievement Award, *Applied Arts Magazine*, Toronto (2016); induction into the Hall of Fame, Museum of American Illustration, New York (2017).

Sources: Martha H. Kennedy, *Canadian Counterpoint: Illustrations by Anita Kunz*, an exhibition at the Library of Congress, Washington, DC, 2003–2004, https://www.loc.gov/exhibits/kunz/; Anita Kunz, "The Curious Mirror," *NUVO* 5, no. 2 (Summer 2002): 48–54; Françoise Mouly, *Blown Covers: New Yorker Covers You Were Never Meant to See* (New York: Abrams, 2012), 10, 32, 73, 101, 110, 115, 124; Robert Newman, "Illustrator Profile—Anita Kunz," *AI-AP's Profiles*, November 12, 2015, http://www.ai-ap.com/publications/article/15721/illustrator-profile-anita-kunz-this-is-a-golde.html; Reed, 433; www.anitakunzart.com.

LASKO-GROSS, MISS (MELISSA)

b. 1977, Boston

Husband: Kevin Colden, cartoonist

Pratt Institute, BFA, comic books, illustration, painting

Work includes: comic strip, *Aim* (1993–2001); editor of Pratt Institute's comic anthology, *Static Fish*; two semiautobiographical graphic novels, *Escape from "Special,"* (2007) and *A Mess of Everything* (2009); collection of short stories, *Miss Lasko-Gross 1994–2014* (2014); allegorical graphic novel, *Henni* (2015); collaborated with husband Kevin Coldon on comic book series, *The Sweetness* (2016).

Exhibitions include: New Museum of Contemporary Art; Museum of Comic and Cartoon Art.

Sources: Michael Cavna, "National Book Festival: Miss Lasko-Gross Enchantingly Taps the Art of Our Unease," *Washington Post*, September 4, 2015; Alex Dueben, "The Miss Lasko-Gross Interview," *Comics Journal*, April 13, 2015, accessed May 4, 2017, http://www.tcj.com/the-miss-lasko-gross-interview/; "Miss Lasko-Gross," *Contemporary Authors Online*, Gale, 2010, *Biography in Context*; Kieran Schiach, "I Only Trust People with Weird Haircuts: Miss Lasko-Gross and Kevin Colden on the World of 'The Sweetness,'" *Comics Alliance*, March 28, 2016, accessed May 4, 2017, http://comicsalliance.com/miss-lasko-gross-kevin-colden-the-sweetness-interview/; www.misslaskogross.com.

LEIGHTON, CLARE VERONICA HOPE

b. 1898, London, England; came to United States, 1939; became US citizen, 1945; d. 1989, Waterbury, CT

Father: Robert, writer; mother: Marie Connor, writer; husband: Henry Noel Brailsford

Brighton School of Art, Slade School of Fine Art, London Country Council Central School of Arts and Crafts; Colby College, DFA, 1940

Work includes: fifty-nine wood engravings for 1929 publication of Thomas Hardy's *Return of the Native*; twelve wood engravings for her own volume *The Farmer's Year, a Calendar of English Husbandry* (1933); twenty-four drawings for *Folks Do Get Born* by Marie Campbell (1946). Created designs for Steuben glass, Wedgewood plates, and stained-glass windows.

Sources: Oxford Art Online; Seaton, 182–83.

LINKS, MARTY (AKA MARTHA ARGUELLO)

b. 1917, Oakland, CA; d. 2008, San Rafael, CA

Husband: Alexander Arguello; three children

Fashion Art Institute, San Francisco

Work includes: best known for her teen comic strip *Emmy Lou* that ran for over forty-five years in the *San Francisco Chronicle* and in nearly one hundred newspapers at its peak.

Sources: Duke, 148; Shaenon K. Garrity, "All the Comics #7: Marty Links," Comixology, January 17, 2008, https://pulllist.comixology.com/articles/18/All-the-Comics-7-Marty-Links; Lambiek; Carl Nolte, "Martha Arguello—Bobby Sox, Emmy Lou Cartoonist Dies in San Rafael," *San Francisco Chronicle*, January 9, 2008; Robbins, 96–97, 99.

LOPEZ, PATRICIA ANN

b. 1954, Germany

Southwestern Oklahoma State University, Weatherford, art education and commercial art

Work includes: courtroom drawings on Karen Silkwood case (1979), trials of Timothy McVeigh (1995) and Terry Nichols (1998) for Oklahoma City bombing, Whitewater Inquiry (1996), Abu Ghraib Military Courts Martial (2005), for television news broadcasts.

Sources: Amanda Bransford, "Getty Settles Courtroom Sketch Artist's Copyright Suit," *Law360*, December 7, 2011, http://www.law360.com/articles/291550/getty-settles-courtroom-sketch-artist-s-copyright-suit; "Pat Lopez," *Fine Art America*, 2012, http://fineartamerica.com/profiles/patlopezartworks.html; Rosanna Ruiz, "Artist Highly Sought for Court Depictions: Sketch of Justice," *Houston Chronicle*, June 12, 2002, http://www.chron.com/news/houston-texas/article/Artist-highly-sought-for-court-depictions-2062832.php.

MACDONALD, ROBERTA

b. 1917, San Francisco; d. 1999, Santa Rosa, CA

Husband: W. H. Simon, music critic

Work includes: 103 cartoon drawings published in the *New Yorker* from 1960 to 1952; illustrations for many humor books, adults and children's books, beginning in the late 1940s.

Sources: Donnelly, 92–98, 130; Robert Mankoff, ed., *The Complete Cartoons of the New Yorker* (New York: Black Dog & Leventhal, 2004); Maslin.

MAGAGNA, ANNA MARIE

b. 1938, Wilkes-Barre, PA

Marywood College (Scranton, PA); Art Students League; School of Visual Arts

Work includes: illustrated *Christmas Miniature* (1958) by Pearl S. Buck; illustrated fifteen children's books; selected by groundbreaking fashion retailer Geraldine Stutz to be exclusive fashion illustrator for clothing and accessories store Henri Bendel, ca. 1969–early 1970s; fashion illustrator for Christian Dior, Bloomingdale's, Lord & Taylor, and Abercrombie & Fitch.

Taught fashion illustration at Pratt Institute (1970–1974); Parsons School of Design, 1985–2000.

Exhibited work in solo and group shows, including at the Museum of the City of New York, the New-York Historical Society, and the Society of Illustrators.

Sources: "Anna Marie Magagna," *Madelyn Jordon Fine Art*, http://madelynjordonfineart.com/artist/focus/magagna; Mantle Fielding, 571–72; Swann Auction Galleries catalog entry for Lot 157, Sale 2337, January 23, 2014, http://catalogue.swanngalleries.com.

MALMAN, CHRISTINA (MASTERS)

b. 1911, Southampton, England; d. 1959

Husband: Dexter Masters, writer, editor, nephew of the poet Edgar Lee Masters

Pratt Institute, 1934

Work includes: at least twenty-four cover designs and hundreds of spot illustrations for the *New Yorker*. In a number of the former, she juxtaposes solemn adult figures in dark clothing with the single form of a child dressed in bright colors and uses dark color schemes and ghostly figures in several World War II–era covers to project a somber mood. Illustrated books include *My Own Manhattan* (1946) and *Carol's Side of the Street* (1951).

Sources: "Christina Malman," *Cooper Hewitt, Smithsonian Design Museum*, https://collection.cooperhewitt.org/people/18049679/; *Complete Book of Covers*, 390; Douglas B. Dowd, "Christina Malman (1911–1959)," *Drawing the Social Landscape, Writings on Visual Culture*, May 22, 2016, http://www.dbdowd.com/illustration-history/2015/11/13/christina-malman; Harold C. Schonberg, "Dexter Masters, 80, British Editor; Warned of Perils of Atomic Age," *New York Times*, January 6, 1989.

MATTHEWS, DORIS M.

b. 1919, Spartanburg, SC; d. 2007, New York

Took art classes; Woodstock, NY, art colony

Work includes: cartoons published in the *New Yorker*, 1951–1959; began drawing cartoons to support her pursuit of painting.

Exhibited work at Corcoran Gallery Biennial, 1943.

Sources: Donnelly, 13, 20, 112–13, 118; Falk, 2218; Maslin.

MCKAY, DOROTHY (JONES)

Self-portrait, ca. 1943

b. 1904, San Francisco; d. 1974, New York City

Husband: Donald McKay, cartoonist; one daughter

California School of Fine Arts, San Francisco; Art Students
League

Work includes: secretary at ad agencies; cartoons for the
New Yorker published from 1934 to 1936, and submissions
continued from 1937 to 1938; many cartoons published in
Esquire, the *Saturday Evening Post, Collier's, Life, College
Humor, Ballyhoo*, and *Forum Magazine*.

Best known for her cartoons for *Esquire*, many of which bring
sharp humor to interactions between the sexes.

She said her "'hobby,' was 'scrubbing the floor and her pet
aversion [was] cops . . . which probably accounts for the
number of them you see in her drawings.'"

Sources: Donnelly, 13, 78–82, 98; *Meet the Artist: An Exhibition
of Self-Portraits by Living American Artists* (San Francisco:
M. H. de Young Museum, 1943), 93; Thorndike, 34.

MCMEIN, NEYSA (MARJORIE) MORAN

b. 1888, Quincy, IL; d. 1949

Father: Harry Moran; mother: Isabelle Parker; husband: John
Baragwanath

School of the Art Institute of Chicago

Work includes: posters in support of World War I effort for
YMCA and Red Cross; cover designs for *McCall's* maga-
zine, 1923–1938 (pastel portraits of beautiful young wom-
en); designed Gold Medal Flour's trademark character
Betty Crocker, 1936; drew occasional cover designs for
Women's Home Companion, McClure's, Photoplay, and the
Saturday Evening Post; drew comic strip *Deathless Deer*
written by Alicia Patterson, 1942.

Under the auspices of the YMCA, the musically talented Mc-
Mein went to France during World War I and entertained
with her singing and piano accompaniment to the animated film *Gertie the Dinosaur* created by Winsor McCay.

Sources: Mantle Fielding, 607; Petteys, 465; Reed, 163, 187;
Robbins, 70–72; Rubinstein, 163; Bridget Quinliven, "Once
Upon a Time in Quincy: Local Woman Remembered for
Famous Portraits," *Quincy Herald-Whig*, September 30,
2011; Taraba, 296–305.

MERGEN, ANNE BRIARDY

b. 1906, Omaha; d. 1994, Miami

Father: Frank Briardy, Union Pacific Railroad; mother: Elizabeth, seamstress; husband: Frank Mergen, company executive; two children

American Academy of Art Chicago

Work includes: more than seven thousand editorial cartoons
published in not only the *Miami Daily News*, but also in
such Cox company newspapers as the *Atlanta Journal,* the
Dayton News, and the *Springfield News* (Ohio). Although

retired in 1956, she still published some cartoons as late as 1959.

Wendy Warren Award, 1953

Sources: Joan Mergen Bernhardt and Paul S. George, "Anne Mergen, Miami's Trailblazing Editorial Cartoonist," *South Florida History* 36, no. 3 (2006): 26–33; Stephen Hess and Milton Kaplan, *The Ungentlemanly Art: A History of American Political Cartoons* (New York: Macmillan, 1968), 19; Martha H. Kennedy, "A Self Selected Sisterhood: Women Cartoonists Represented in the Library of Congress Collections," *International Journal of Comic Art* 10, no. 2 (Fall 2008): 62–64; Richard Spencer, *Editorial Cartooning* (Ames: Iowa State College Press, 1949); *Anne Mergen: Editorial Cartoonist*, an exhibition at Ohio State University, 2008, http://library.osu.edu/blogs/library news/2008/01/29/anne-mergen-editorial-cartoonist.

MESSICK, DALE (DAHLIA)

ca. 1941

b. 1906, South Bend, IN; d. 2005, Penngrove, CA

Father: Cephas Messick, artist, sign painter; mother: Bertha, milliner, seamstress; first husband: Everett George; second husband: Oscar Strom; one daughter

Ray-Vogue School of Commercial Art, Chicago

Work includes: comic strips *Weegee* (mid-1920s); *Mimi the Mermaid* (early 1930s); *Peg and Pudy: The Strugglettes* (mid-1930s); *Streamline Babies* (later 1930s); *Brenda Starr Reporter* (1940).

Awards include: Inducted to Will Eisner Hall of Fame (2001); Milton Caniff Lifetime Achievement Award from the National Cartoonists Society (1997); "Brenda Starr" won the National Cartoonist Society's "best story strip" award (1976).

Sources: David Astor, "A 'Starr'-Spangled Evening for Dale Messick," *Editor & Publisher*, May 2, 1998; "Dale Messick," *Gale Biography in Context*, Gale, 2005. *Biography in Context*; Lambiek; Dale Messick, *Brenda Starr Reporter: The Collected Dailies and Sundays: 1940–1946* (Neshonnock, PA: Hermes Press, 2012); Robbins, 26, 30, 58–60, 63–64, 70, 72, 74, 120, 152; Patrick Sullivan, "Cartoonist Dale Messick Dies: Creator of Brenda Starr Strip," *Washington Post*, April 8, 2005: B06.

MILBRATH, DEB

Born in Milwaukee, WI

University of Wisconsin, BFA, graphic design, 1972

Work includes: retail advertising, Minneapolis; art director, Saks Fifth Avenue, New York; political cartoons published in the *New York Times, Newsweek,* the *New York Daily News, Atlanta Journal Constitution, Slate.com,* and on CNN Headline News. Weekly contributor to the *Seattle Post Intelligencer* until its last issue.

Member of the Association of American Editorial Cartoonists

Sources: "Deb Milbrath," Association of American Editorial Cartoonists, http://editorialcartoonists.com/cartoonist/ profile.cfm/MilbrD/; Cartoons & Cocktail, fundraising event for Young D.C., October 20, 2011, auction catalog, 42; www.milbrathdraws.com.

MINNICH, REBECCA (BECKY)

Active since 2001

University of Minnesota, BA, Latin American studies and Spanish; City College of New York, MFA, creative writing; Columbia University, TESOL teaching certification

Taught English as a Second Language at American Language Institute/SPS since 2007, and at Columbia University and Kaplan International Centers

Work includes: drawings contributed to special 9-11 issue of *World War 3 Illustrated*; publications include POZ, Metrosource, Promethean. Received Meyer Cohn Award in Literature for best essay in literary criticism (graduate). Buying and creative assistant, Arnold Worldwide, an advertising agency.

Sources: "Rebecca Minnich," *New York University School of Professional Studies*, https://www.sps.nyu.edu/professional-pathways/faculty/12726-rebecca-minnich.html; "Rebecca Minnich," *School of Visual Arts*, http://www.sva.edu/ faculty/rebecca-minnich.

MITCHELL, SADIE WENDELL

b. Sadie Wendell (or Wendill) MacFarlane, 1884, St. John, New Brunswick; emigrated to United States, 1903; d. before 1923

Father: Foster MacFarlane; mother: Elizabeth Babbet or Bubbet; husband: George Harold Mitchell, illustrator

Work includes: poster series "Girls Will Be Girls," promoting education for young women (1909); posters advertising Hackett-Carhart clothing for boys. In both series, Mitchell fashioned diagonal compositions, rendered figures as flat, strongly outlined forms, and used color effectively, whether vibrant or muted, to create appealing light-hearted scenes with touches of humorous details.

Sources: "Obituary, George H. Mitchell," *New York Times*, June 7, 1951: 33.

NOOMIN, DIANE

b. 1947, Brooklyn

Husband: Bill Griffith, cartoonist, creator of *Zippy the Pinhead*

Brooklyn College; Pratt Institute

Work includes: published in underground comics such as *Wimmen's Comix, Weirdo, Young Lust, Arcade: The Comics Revue, Real Girl, The New Comics Anthology*, and the *Nation*. Work also appeared in anthologies she edited: *Twisted Sisters: A Collection of Bad Girl Art* (1991) and *Twisted Sisters 2: Drawing the Line* (1995). Collected works featuring DiDi Glitz, signature character created in 1973, published in *Glitz-2-Go: Collected Comics* (2012). Musical, "I'd Rather Be Doing Something Else: The DiDi Glitz Story," staged in San Francisco, 1981.

Awards include: Inkpot Award, San Diego Comic-Con, 1992; nominated for Harvey and Eisner awards.

Exhibitions include: La Luz de Jesus Gallery, Los Angeles (1991); solo exhibition, Little Frankenstein Gallery, San Francisco (1994); Museum of Cartoon Art, San Francisco (1995).

Sources: Lambiek; Lightman, 256; Diane Noomin, "I'd Rather Be Doing Nothing Else," *Glitz-2-Go* (Seattle: Fantagraphics Books, 2012), 9–13.

NOSWORTHY, FLORENCE PEARL (ENGLAND)

b. 1872, Milwaukee, WI; d. 1936, Hampton, CT

Boston Museum School of Fine Art, studied with Edmund Tarbell, Kenyon Cox; Cowles Art School, Boston; Art Students League

Work includes: illustrations and cover designs for magazines including *Youth's Companion, Redbook, Associated Sunday Magazine*, and book illustrations including *A Garden of Girls* (1902), a collection of her drawings that reflect her version of the American beauty.

Sources: Falk, 2442; Larson, 144; Petteys, 529.

OAKLEY, VIOLET

b. 1874, Bergen Heights, NJ; d. 1961, Philadelphia

Father: Arthur Oakley; mother: Cornelia Swain, aspired to be a painter; paternal grandfather: George Oakley, elected associate, National Academy of Design; maternal grandfather: William Swain, artist, elected to National Academy of Design

Art Students League; Académie Montparnasse, Paris; studied with Charles Lazar, England; Pennsylvania Academy of Fine Arts; Drexel Institute, studied with Howard Pyle

Works include: illustrations, designs for stained glass; murals for Governor's Reception Room, Capitol Building, Harrisburg, PA, 1927; portraits of participants forming League of Nations, Geneva, Switzerland, 1927.

First woman elected to National Society of Mural Painters; recipient of the Gold Medal of Honor, Pennsylvania Academy of Fine Arts; first woman to receive the Gold Medal of Honor, Architectural League of New York; awarded honorary doctor of law degree, 1948, Drexel Institute; second woman to teach at Pennsylvania Academy of Fine Arts.

Sources: Carter, 30–36, 46–49, 174; Finding Aid, Violet Oakley Papers, 1841–1981, Smithsonian Institution Archives of American Art, http://sova.si.edu/record/AAA.oaklviol; Reed, 110.

O'NEILL, ROSE CECIL

ca. 1907

b. 1874, Wilkes Barre, PA; d. 1944, Springfield, MO
Father: William Patrick O'Neill, bookseller; mother: Alice
  Asenath Cecelia, schoolteacher; first husband: Gray
  Latham; second husband: Harry Leon Wilson, writer,
  editor
Self-trained
Work includes: "The Old Subscriber Calls" (*Truth Magazine*,
  1896), possibly the first comic strip by a woman in America; more than seven hundred cartoons including at least
  five cover designs for *Puck* (ca. 1893–1905); invented the
  Kewpies, 1909 (first appearing in *Ladies' Home Journal*,
  December 1909); patented Kewpie doll, 1913; Sunday
  strip *Kewpies*, 1917–1918 (McClure Syndicate); Sunday
  strip Kewpies, 1934–1937 (self-syndicated); produced illustrations for *Life, Cosmopolitan, Collier's, Harper's Bazaar, Everybody's, Good Housekeeping*, and for novels by
  Wilson (her husband) *The Spenders* (1902), *The Lions of
  the Lord* (1903), *The Seeker* (1904), and her own novels
  including *The Loves of Edwy* (1904), *The Lady in the White
  Veil* (1909), and *The Goblin Woman* (1930).
Exhibitions include: fine art drawings at Devambez Galleries,
  Paris, 1909; Wildenstein Gallery, New York, 1922.
Sources: ANB; Shelley S. Armitage, *Kewpies and Beyond:
  The World of Rose O'Neill* (Jackson: University Press of
  Mississippi), 1994; Linda Brewster, *Rose O'Neill, the Girl
  Who Loved to Draw* (Boxing Day Books, 2009); Helen
  Goodman, "Rose O'Neill (1874–1944)," *The Art of Rose
  O'Neill* (Chadds Ford, PA: Brandywine River Museum,
  1989), 11–39; Petteys, 225; Robbins, 8, 10–11, 17–18, 21, 24,
  34, 55–56, 69; Taraba, 316–27.

ORMES, JACKIE (ZELDA JACKSON)

1946

b. 1911, Pittsburgh; d. 1985, Chicago
Father: William Winfield Jackson; mother: Mary Brown Jack-
  son; sister: Delores, singer; husband: Earl Clark Ormes,
  accountant
School of the Art Institute of Chicago
Work includes: proofreader, reporter, and artist for the *Pitts-
  burgh Courier*; comic strips include *Torchy Brown in
  "Dixie to Harlem"* in the *Pittsburgh Courier* (1937–1938);
  Candy (1945); *Patty-Jo 'n' Ginger* syndicated in the *Pittsburgh Courier* (1945–1956); *Torchy [Brown] in Heartbeats*
  syndicated by the Smith-Mann Syndicate (1950–1954).
  Torchy in Heartbeats accompanied by paper doll with
  outfits, *Torchy Togs*.
Handpainted features on some of the "Patty-Jo" dolls manu-
  factured by Terri Lee doll company (1947–1949).
Ormes interwove her concerns for social justice, bigotry, and
  threats to the environment in comics with engaging characters and storylines.
Active in the NAACP, Chicago Urban League, Clarence Dar-
  row Community Center, DuSable Museum of African
  American History.
Sources: Shelley Armitage, "Black Looks and Imagining Oneself Richly: The Cartoons of Jackie Ormes," *Polish Journal
  for American Studies* 7 (2013): 83–102; Nancy Goldstein,
  *Jackie Ormes: The First African American Woman Car-
  toonist* (Ann Arbor: University of Michigan Press, 2008);
  Robbins, 111–12.

ORR, MARTHA (HASSEL)

b. 1908, Hillyard, WA; d. 2001, Winter Park, FL

Uncle: Carey Orr, Pulitzer Prize–winning political cartoonist for the *Chicago Tribune*; husband: Henry Hassel; two children

Chicago Art Institute

Work includes: best known for comic strip *Apple Mary* that debuted 1934, quickly became popular, and ran until 1939, when Orr sold it so she could spend more time with her daughter Louise. Strip is considered precursor to *Mary Worth*.

Sources: Rich Hepp, "Martha Orr Hassel, 92: Syndicated Cartoonist in the Depression Era," *Chicago Tribune*, July 31, 2001; Holtz, 255–56; Don Markstein, "Apple Mary," *Don Markstein's Toonopedia*, accessed March 3, 2014, http://www.toonopedia.com/applmary.htm; Robbins, 50–51; Robbins and Yronwode, 74, 77.

PALMER, FRANCES (FANNY) FLORA BOND

ca. 1860

b. 1812, Leicester, England; d. 1876, New York

Father: Robert Bond, attorney; mother: Elizabeth Springthorpe; husband: Edmund Seymour Palmer

Work includes: at least two hundred prints (between 1851–1868) published by Currier & Ives.

Sources: Stephanie Delamaire, *Lasting Impressions: The Artists of Currier & Ives*, (Winterthur, DE: Winterthur Museum, Garden & Library, 2016), exhibition catalog; Reed, 10, 14; Rubenstein, 68–70; Charlotte Streifer Rubinstein, *Fanny Palmer: A Long Island Woman Who Portrayed America* (Cold Spring Harbor, NY: Society for the Preservation of Long Island Antiquities, 1997).

PARKER, GLADYS

b. 1906; d. 1966, Glendale, CA

Work includes: comic strip *Gay and Her Gang*, about flappers (1920s); took over one-panel cartoon *Flapper Fanny* from Ethel Hays in 1932, in addition to another one-panel cartoon, Hays's *Ethel*, that she renamed *Femininities*; created her own character, Mopsy, who resembled herself and featured in daily and Sunday strips from 1939 to 1965; took over Russell Keaton's war comic strip *Flyin' Jenny* from 1942 to 1944, replaced by Marc Swayze in 1944.

As a fashion designer, Parker also had her own clothing line in the 1930s.

Sources: Lambiek; Don Markstein, "Mopsy," *Don Markstein's Toonopedia*, http://www.toonopedia.com/mopsy.htm; Robbins, 36–40, 67, 76, 79, 96, 99, 159; Robbins and Yronwode, 26–27.

PECK, ANNA GLADYS

b. 1884, Monmouth Beach, NJ; d. 1867

Studied with John Twachtman, Willard Metcalf, and Benjamin West Clinedinst, New York

Work includes: illustrations for *Harper's Weekly* and the book *Our Language*, 3 volumes, by James P. Kinard (1927); cover designs for books including *Cinder the Cat* (1931) and *Kitten-Kat* (1934). Exhibited work at the Art Institute of Chicago, 1913.

Source: Falk, 2556; Petteys, 552.

PECK, ANNE MERRIMAN (FITE)

b. 1884, Piermont, NY; d. 1976, Tucson

Husband: Frank E. Fite

Studied with Robert Henri, Irving Wiles; Hartford Art School; New York School of Fashion and Apparel

Work includes: illustrations for *Harper's,* for which she specialized in woodcuts and lithographs; illustrated more than forty books and wrote and illustrated more than twenty children's books, including *Storybook Europe* (1929); *Young Americans from Many Lands* (1935); *Pageant of South American History* (1941); *Young Mexico* (1948); *Pageant of Canadian History* (1963).

Exhibited work at Weyhe Gallery, New York, and in Tucson in early 1900s.

Lived in Tucson for extended periods of time and taught at the University of Arizona in the Extension Division.

Sources: Kovinick, 375; Mantle Fielding, 710; Petteys, 552.

PECK, CLARA ELSENE (WILLIAMS)

b. 1883, Allegan, MI; d. 1968

Husband: John Scott Williams, artist, with whom she occasionally collaborated

Minneapolis School of Fine Arts; Pennsylvania Academy of Fine Arts; studied with William Merritt Chase

Work includes: advertising illustrations for Proctor & Gamble, Aeolian Company, and Metropolitan Life; illustrations for magazines, including *St. Nicholas, Collier's,* and *Ladies' Home Journal*; illustrations for books, including *Shakespeare's Sweetheart* (1905); *A Lady of King Arthur's Court* (1907); *In Border Country* (1909). Known mainly for drawing women and children, her work is described as decorative and sensitive. In addition to fiction, she illustrated writings on education, child psychology, and expectant mothers.

Exhibitions include: Art Institute of Chicago, Pennsylvania Academy of Fine Arts, 1913; Women Painters and Sculptors, 1921 (prize); American Watercolor Society traveling exhibition, Metropolitan Museum of Art European traveling exhibition, both 1956–1957; Washington County Museum of Art, Hagerstown, MD, 1958; Gettysburg College (solo), York (PA) Art Center, 1958.

Member of the American Watercolor Society and Society of Illustrators.

Sources: Falk, 2557; Mantle Fielding, 710; Petteys, 552; Reed, 111.

PETTY, MARY (CANTWELL DUNN)

b. 1899, Hampton, NJ; d. 1976, Paramus, NJ

Father: Robert Davison Petty, professor of law, New York Law School; mother: Florence Servis, schoolteacher; husband: Alan Dunn, major cartoonist for the *New Yorker*

Mostly self-taught, learned from husband

Work includes: 273 drawings and thirty-eight cover designs (watercolor and ink) for the *New Yorker*, from 1927 to 1966; illustrated several books and published *This Petty Pace* (a collection of her drawings) (1945).

Exhibitions include: Salons of America, Society of Independent Artists, 1929; Cincinnati Art Museum, 1940; Syracuse University, 1979.

Importance of social consciousness to Petty was reflected in her work. Became known for satirizing the upper class in her cartoons, creating the characters "Fay," a maid, and the old woman she served, "Mrs. Peabody." The beautifully detailed Victorian interiors in her work contrasted with the austere and reclusive life she and husband, Dunn, led.

Sources: ANB; Donnelly, 64–74; Falk, 2593.

PLUMMER, ETHEL MCCLELLAN

b. 1888, Brooklyn; d. 1936, New York

Husband: Norman Jacobsen; second husband: Col. Frederick E. Humphreys

Studied with Robert Henri and Francis Luis Mora

Work includes: cover designs for *Vanity Fair*, illustration and/or cartoon drawings for *Vogue, Life, Women's Home Companion, Shadow-land, New York Tribune,* and the *New Yorker*.

Vice president of the Society of Illustrators and Artists; exhibited at *Exhibition of Independent Artists* (1910) and *Exhibition of Painting and Sculpture by Women Artists for the Benefit of the Women Suffrage Campaign* (1915).

Sources: Duke, 246; "Ethel McClellan Plummer: The Greenwich Bookshop Door," *Harry Ransome Center, University of Texas at Austin*, http://norman.hrc.utexas.edu/bookshopdoor/signature.cfm?item=43#1; "Ethel Plummer, Artist was Wife of Colonel F. E. Humphrey of 102d Engineers," *New York Times*, November 1, 1936: N10; Mantle Fielding, 731.

PRENTICE, PEGGY

Active in the 1920s and 1930s

Worked for King Features Syndicate in 1920s

Examples of her work are rare and show strong stylistic similarities to that of Nell Brinkley. The high quality of her finely detailed drawing and engaging compositions set her work apart from that of many other, less accomplished imitators.

Sources: Duke, 250; *Century of American Illustration*, 79, 150.

PRESTON, MAY WILSON

b. 1873, New York; d. 1949

First husband: Thomas Henry Watkins, artist; second husband: James Moore Preston, Ash Can School painter

Oberlin College, studied art and music; Art Students League, studied with Robert Henri, John Twachtman, William Merritt Chase, 1892–1897; World Art Center, Paris, studied with James McNeill Whistler

Work includes: illustrations published in *McClure's, Scribner's,* and *Saturday Evening Post* for stories by such authors as Mary Roberts Rinehart, Ring Lardner, F. Scott Fitzgerald, and P. G. Wodehouse.

Exhibited work in the Armory Show of 1913, won bronze medal for work exhibited in the Panama Pacific International Exposition of 1915. Member of the Society of Illustrators, Society of Independent Artists. As an activist in the National Women's Party, she worked hard to promote woman's suffrage.

Sources: Larson, 139; Petteys, 576; Reed, 190; Rubinstein, 165, 166–67; Sheppard, 87, 96, 98, 104, 111, 113, 118, 120, 134, 143, 183, 226.

PRICE, HILARY B.

b. 1969, Weston, MA

Stanford University, BA, English literature, 1991

Work includes: cartoons first published by the *San Francisco Chronicle,* while she worked there as a freelance copyeditor; syndicated daily strip, *Rhymes with Orange,* debuted in 1995; work also published in *Parade Magazine, People, The Funny Times,* and *Glamour.* Collections of her work include *Rhymes with Orange: A Cartoon Collection* (1997), *Reigning Cats and Dogs* (2003), and *Pithy Seedy Pulpy Juicy: Eleven Rhymes with Orange Books* (2007).

Awards include: National Cartoonists Society (NCS) Newspaper panel award (2012); NCS Silver Reuben for Best Newspaper Panel Cartoon (2015); Inkpot Award, San Diego Comic-Con (2015); one of five finalists for NCS Reuben Award (2016).

Sources: Kelli Anderson, "Rhymes with Harpoonist," *Stanford Magazine,* May/June 1999, http://alumni.stanford.edu/get/page/magazine/article/?article_id=40671; Lambiek; www.rhymeswithorange.com.

PROVENSEN, ALICE

b. 1918, Chicago

Father: Jay Horace, broker; mother: Kathryn Twitchell, interior decorator; husband: Martin Elias Provensen, writer and illustrator of children's books; one daughter

School of the Art Institute of Chicago; University of California, Los Angeles; Art Students League

Work includes: more than forty picture books including both titles created by herself and those created jointly with her husband; won a Caldecott Medal for *The Glorious Flight: Across the Channel with Louis Blériot, July 25, 1909* (1984); other titles include *Our Animal Friends at Maple Hill Farm* (1974); *A Peaceable Kingdom: The Shaker Abecedarius* (1978); *A Visit to William Blake's Inn: Poems for Innocent and Experienced Travelers,* written by Nancy Willard (1981); *Town & Country* (1985); *The Buck Stops Here: The Presidents of the United States* (1990); *Punch in New York* (1991); *My Fellow Americans: A Family Album* (1995).

After her husband's death in 1987, Provensen observed, "We were a true collaboration. Martin and I really were one artist."

Selected sources: "Alice Provensen," *Contemporary Authors Online,* Gale, 2004, *Biography in Context*; Hughes, vol. 2, 900.

PYLE, KATHERINE

b. 1873, Wilmington, DE; d. 1938

Father: William Pyle; mother: Margaret Churchman Painter; brothers: Howard Pyle, illustrator, Clifford and Walter

Philadelphia School of Design; Art Students League; Drexel Institute, studied with Howard Pyle

Work includes: wrote and illustrated more than fifty books. Although influenced by brother Howard in creating illustrations that capture the drama of texts, she also incorporated elements of illustration styles of Walter Crane and Art Nouveau.

Sources: Katherine L. Miner, *Tales of Folk and Fairies: The Life and Work of Katharine Pyle* (Wilmington: Delaware Art Museum, 2012); Rubinstein, 163.

REED, ETHEL

ROBBINS, TRINA

ca. 1895

b. 1874, Newburyport, MA; d. 1912 in England
Father: Edgar Reed, photographer; mother: Mary Elizabeth (from Ireland); husband: Arthur Sale Whiteley (later known as Warwick), British military officer; two children
Cowles Art School, Boston; studied drawing with Laura Coombs Hill, but mostly self-taught
Work includes: poster designs advertising the *Boston Herald*, books published by Boston firms Copeland and Day, Lamson Wolffe, Louis Prang, as well as cover designs, illustrations, and endpapers for some of these firms' books. Contributed to British Aestheticism's leading journal *The Yellow Book*.
Sources: Oxford Art Online; Petteys, 588; W. S. Peterson, *The Beautiful Poster Lady: A Life of Ethel Reed* (New Castle, DE: Oak Knoll Press), 2013; Rubinstein, 163.

b. 1938, Brooklyn
Father: Max Bear, tailor and writer; mother: Elizabeth Rosenman, teacher; husband: Paul Jay Robbins; one daughter
Cooper Union; Queens College
Work includes: comics published in the *East Village Other* (1970); *It Ain't Me, Babe* (1970); *Wimmen's Comix* (of which she was a founding contributor and sometime editor) (1972–1992); *From Girls to Grrlz* (1994); *The Great Women Superheroes* (1996); *Go Girl!* graphic novels 1–3 (2000–2006); *Nell Brinkley and the New Woman in the Early 20th Century* (2001); *Lily Renee, Escape Artist* (2011); *Marvel's Girl Comics* (2012); *Pretty in Ink: North American Women Cartoonists, 1896–2013* (2013).
Dedicated to creating outlets for and chronicling the careers of women comics artists.
Awards include: Inkpot Award, San Diego Comic-Con, 1977; Parents Choice Award, 1994, for *A Century of Women Cartoonists*; Lulu Award, Friends of Lulu, 1997, for *The Great Women Superheroes*; Lulu of the Year and Friends of Lulu Female Cartoonist Hall of Fame, both 2000; Special John Buscema Haxtur Award for comics published in Spain, 2001; Norton Award, 2010; Inductee, Will Eisner Hall of Fame, 2013.
Sources: "Trina Robbins," *Authors and Artists for Young Adults*, vol. 61, Gale, 2005. *Biography in Context*; Lambiek; Lightman, 266–68.

ROBERTS, VICTORIA

b. 1957, New York

Grew up in Mexico City and Sydney, Australia; attended National Art School, Sydney

Work includes: staff cartoonist for the *New Yorker* since 1988; published cartoons in the *New York Times, Washington Post, Time, Barron's, Boston Globe, Wall Street Journal, Town & Country, Business Week, Real Simple, Ms. Magazine, Healthy Living,* and *Playboy*; "My Sunday," weekly comic strip published in Australia's *Nation Review*, when Roberts was nineteen; books include *My Sunday* (1982), *My Day* (1984), *The Book of Meaningful Relationships* (1985), *Biographees* (1986), *Australia Felix* (1988), and *Cattitudes* (1999); illustrated at least twelve books by other writers.

Roberts performed on stage at the National Museum of Women in the Arts as the cartoon character "Nona Appleby," whom she created. She has also written a number of plays.

Sources: Donnelly, 13, 158–65, 172, 175, 190; Harvey, 87; "Victoria Roberts," *Contemporary Authors Online*, Gale, 2014, *Biography in Context.*

RUNDQUIST, ETHEL CAROLINE

b. 1892, Minneapolis, MN; active 1910s–1920s; d. 1977

Father: August Rundquist; mother: Lina; husband: Emin Cobham; two children

School of the Art Institute of Chicago, 1911–1914

Work includes: illustrations and covers for *Vanity Fair* and *Vogue*; illustrations for James W. Evans and Gardner L. Harding, *Entertaining the American Army: The American Stage and Lyceum in the World War I* (1921).

Sources: *Century of American Illustration* 150; Duke, 272; Falk, 2855.

SAKUGAWA, YUMI

b. 1984, Orange, CA

University of California, Los Angeles

Works include: *I Think I Am in Friend-Love with You* (2014); *Your Illustrated Guide to Becoming One with the Universe* (2014); *There Is No Right Way to Meditate: And Other Lessons* (2014). Selected short stories and minicomics include *Claudia Kishi: My Asian-American Female Role Model of the 90's* (2012); *Moon between the Mountains* (2013); *Ikebana*, Retrofit Comics (2015); *Fashion Forecasts* (2016).

Sources: Wes Woods, "Comic Book Artist Yumi Sakugawa Provides Self-Help in Comic Book Form," *Los Angeles Daily News*, October 1, 2014, http://www.dailynews.com/arts-and-entertainment/20141006/comic-book-artist-yumi-sakugawa-provides-self-help-in-comic-book-form; www.yumisakugawa.com/.

SAWYERS, MARTHA LOUISE (REUSSWIG)

b. 1902, Cuero, TX; d. 1988, Connecticut

Husband: H. William Reusswig

Art Students League

Work includes: designs for stained glass at J & R Lamb Studios, the oldest decorative arts firm in continuous operation in the United States; paintings and drawings primarily of people in Bali, Penang, Singapore, Sumatra, Java, Shanghai, and Peiping; illustrations of "Asiatic lore" for *Collier's*, in addition to books coauthored and illustrated with William Reusswig: *Illustrated Book about the Far East* (1961); *India and Southeast Asia* (1964).

Sources: Ernest W. Watson, "Martha Sawyers: Illustrator of Oriental Lore," *Forty Illustrators and How They Work* (Freeport, NY: Books for Libraries Press, 1946, reprinted 1970), 264–67.

SCHULMAN, NICOLE

b. 1975, New York

Husband: Dustin Chang, writer

Work includes: comics, posters, album covers, and illustrations published in the *New York Times,* the *Progressive, New Politics,* and *World War 3 Illustrated*; coedited with Paul Buhle, *Wobblies: A Graphic History of the Industrial Workers of the World* (2005).

Serves on the editorial board of *World War 3 Illustrated.* Teaching artist and muralist with Groundwell, a community-based organization dedicated to public-art-making, New York. Exhibited in group shows at Exit Art, New York, Three Cities Against the Wall (New York, Tel Aviv,

Hebron), and Municipal Art Museum, Ravenna, Italy. Teaches visual art at public high school in Brooklyn.

Awards include: Best Illustration Award, cover art, *Communique Magazine*, "Breaking Labor's Glass Ceiling," from the International Labor Communications Association AFL-CIO, CTW, CLC, 2008; Puffin Foundation Grant, for development of historical graphic novel, 2008; First prize, Houston Progressive's "Freeman's Town History Contest," for historical comic "Allen Parkway Village," 2001.

Sources: "Nicole Schulman," *Labor and Immigration Artists: A Resource Guide*, ed. Jesse Connor (Haledon, NJ: The American Labor Museum, Botto House National Landmark, 2015), 66; www.nicholeschulman.com.

SELZ, IRMA (ENGELHARDT)

b. 1908, Chicago; d. 1977, New York

Husband: Charles Leonard Engelhardt, major, US Army Air Corps, WWII; one son

University of Chicago; Chicago Art Institute

Work includes: theatrical caricatures for the *Chicagoan*, the *Chicago Tribune*; known as "New York's girl caricaturist," she did many theatrical and political caricatures for the *New York Times*, the *Herald Tribune*, the *New York Post*, the *Daily News*, the *Brooklyn Eagle*, the *New Yorker*, *Vogue*, *Glamour*, and *Stage and Cue* during the 1930s–1950s; illustrated and wrote five children's books.

Sources: Tom Engelhardt, "A Message in a Bottle from My Mother," *TomDispatch*, July 21, 2015, http://www.tomdispatch.com/blog/176025/; Fruhauf, 61–62, 140; Steven Heller, "New York's Girl Caricaturist," *International Journal of Typographics* 11, no. 2 (August 1984): 19–20; Reaves, 42, 191–92, 196, 293n46.

SENGER, RITA

b. 1893, New York; active 1915–1919; d. 1990, Chicago

Father: Adolph Senger; mother: Barbara Ehrlich; husband: Joseph Stein

Gifted designer of cover art for *Vanity Fair* and *Vogue*. Surviving examples highlight a single attractive female figure wearing fashionable or exotic clothing, rendered in a graceful, linear style, with restrained use of color, details, and setting that reflect the influence of Japanese prints or other Asian influence. Examples from both magazines date from 1915 to 1919.

Sources: Duke, 282; Gary Fitzgibbon, Finding Aid, Emily Elliott Collection, Art Gallery of Ontario, https://www.ago.net/assets/files/pdf/special_collections/SC004.pdf; William Packer, *The Art of Vogue Covers* (Bonanza Books, 1985), 42.

SEVERIN, MARIE

b. 1929, East Rockaway, Long Island

Father: Jack Severin, designer for Eve Arden; mother: Peg Severin; brother: John Severin, cartoonist

Work includes: colored *A Moon, A Girl . . . Romance #9* for EC Comics (1949); colored nearly all EC Comics classic titles; worked as colorist for Atlas/Marvel, 1950s; freelance work as commercial artist; penciled *Doctor Strange*, *King Kull*, *Sub Mariner*, and *The Cat*, for Marvel (beginning 1966); Marvel's parody title, *Not Brand Ecch* (1967–1969); penciled *The Incredible Hulk*, *Sub-Mariner*; covers include *The Amazing Spider-Man*, *Iron Man*, *Conan the Barbarian*, *Daredevil*; contributed to *Big Apple Comics* (1976); drew *Fraggle Rock* (1985); drew *Soulsearchers* (2000).

Assigned to Special Projects at Marvel Comics, worked on many non-book licensing jobs, including maquettes and movie costumes.

Awards include: Inkpot Award, San Diego Comic-Con (1988); inducted into Will Eisner Comics Hall of Fame (2001).

Sources: Dewey Cassell with Andrew Sultan, *Marie Severin: The Mirthful Mistress of Comics* (Raleigh, NC: TwoMorrows Publishing, 2012), 7–11, 166–73; Steve Duin and Mike Richardson, *Comics between the Panels* (Milwaukie, OR: Dark Horse Comics, 1998), 396, 404; Katherine Keller, "The Chromatic Queen: Marie Severin," Sequential Tart, 2001, accessed August 20, 2012, http://www.sequentialtart.com/archive/may02/severin.shtml; Lambiek; Trina Robbins, *The Great Women Cartoonists* (New York: Watson Guptill, 2001), 102–3, 107, 120, 122, 124, 132; Robbins, 110–11, 118–20; Robbins and Yronwode, 103–4.

SHAHN, BERNARDA BRYSON

1960

b. 1903, Athens, OH; d. 2004, Roosevelt, NJ

Father: Charles Henry Bryson, editor, publisher of the *Athens Morning Journal*; mother: Lucy Weethee, Latin professor; first husband: Victor Luster Parks; second husband: Ben Shahn, artist; three children

Ohio State University; Case Western Reserve University; New School for Social Research; Cleveland School of Art; John Huntington Polytechnic Institute

Editor for the *South Side Advocate* in Columbus, Ohio; art critic for the *Ohio State Journal*; taught lithography and etching at the Columbus Gallery of Fine Arts from 1930 to 1931.

Work includes: editorial illustrations for *Fortune, Harper's, Life, Atlantic,* and *Scientific American* from the 1940s to the 1970s; wrote and illustrated children's books, including *The Twenty Miracles of Saint Nicolas* (1960) and *Gilgamesh: Man's First Story* (1967), both of which won AIGA book of the year awards; *The Zoo of Zeus: A Handbook of Mythological Beasts and Creatures* (1964); illustrated *The Sun Is a Golden Earring* by Natalia Belting (1962), a Caldecott Honor Book; collaborated with her husband on a fifty-foot fresco mural at Roosevelt Public School, and a mural, "America at Work," in the Bronx Post Office; published a monograph, *Ben Shahn* (1972).

Awards include: Outstanding Achievement in the Visual Arts award from the Women's Caucus for Art, 1989; honorary doctorate from Ohio University in Athens, 1993; retrospective exhibition of her art at the Ben Shahn Galleries, Wayne, New Jersey, 2002.

Sources: "Bernarda Bryson Shahn," *Contemporary Authors Online,* Gale, 2006, *Biography in Context;* Seaton, 224–25; Bernarda Bryson and Jake Milgram Wien, *The Vanishing American Frontier: Bernarda Bryson Shahn and Her Historical Lithographs Created for the Resettlement Adminis-*

tration *of FDR* (Seattle: University of Washington Press, 1995); Jean Fitzgerald, Finding Aid, Bernarda Bryson Shahn Papers, Smithsonian Institution Archives of American Art, September 7, 2011, https://www.aaa.si.edu/files/resources/finding-aids/pdf/brysbern.pdf; "Bernarda Bryson Shahn, Painter, Dies at 101," *New York Times,* December 16, 2004, http://www.nytimes.com/2004/12/16/arts/bernarda-bryson-shahn-painter-dies-at-101.html?_r=0.

SHERMAN, WHITNEY

b. 1949, New Jersey

Maryland Institute College of Art, photography; self-taught in illustration and design

Work includes: illustrations for the *New York Times, Business Week,* and *Forbes;* clients include Tolleson Design, Pentagram, Ronn Campisi Design, and Karnes-Prickett, national institutions such as the Templeton Foundation, Robert Wood Johnson Foundation, and the American Red Cross, and publishers such as Clarkson Potter, Random House, and St. Martin's Press; illustrations for books include *Hear! Here!* (1994), *A Cow of No Color* (1998).

Director of MFA Program in illustration at the Maryland Institute of College Art (MICA); codirector of Dolphin Press & Print @ MICA; editor, The History of Illustration Project

Sources: Hope Katz Gibbs, "Whitney Sherman," *100 Truly Amazing Women Who Are Changing the World and You Can, Too,* http://trulyamazingwomen.com/the-women/

artist-whitney-sherman; Sherman's website, http://www
.whitneysherman.com/bio/; Whitney Sherman, *Playing
with Sketches: 50 Creative Exercises for Designers and
Artists* (Beverly, MA: Rockport Publishers, 2014); Faculty profile, *Maryland Institute College of Art*, https://www
.mica.edu/About_MICA/People/Faculty/Faculty_List_
by_Last_Name/Whitney_Sherman.html.

SHERMUND, BARBARA

Self-portrait

b. 1899, San Francisco; d. 1978, New Jersey
California School of Fine Arts; Art Students League
Work includes: 599 cartoons published in the *New Yorker*;
    eight cover designs in addition to drawings published in
    Esquire; illustrated book *Stuffed Shirts* by Clare Boothe
    Brokaw (1931).
Exhibitions include: San Francisco Art Academy, 1923–1924;
    Salons of America, 1934; de Young Museum, San Francis-
    co, 1943; International Cartoon Exhibition, Belgium, 1964;
    San Diego Exposition, 1964.
Sources: Donnelly, 54–61, 63–64, 70, 81–83, 98–102, 104, 108,
    114, 203–4; Duke, 286; Falk, 3010; Maslin; Thorndike, 35.

SHINN, FLORENCE SCOVEL

b. 1871, Camden, NJ; d. 1940, New York
Father: Alden Cortlandt Scovel, lawyer; mother: Emily Hop-
    kinson; husband: Everett Shinn
Pennsylvania Academy of Fine Arts
Work includes: illustration drawings published in *The Centu-
    ry*, *Harper's Bazar*, *Truth*, *Life*, and books including *Mrs.
    Wiggs of the Cabbage Patch* (1901) and its sequel *Lovely
    Mary* (1903) by Alice Hegan Rice; wrote the following
    philosophical books: *The Game of Life and How to Play
    It* (1925), *Your Word Is Your Wand* (1928), and *The Secret
    Door to Success* (1940).
Exhibited her work at the Kraushaar Gallery, New York, 1906.
Sources: Mantle Fielding, 848; Petteys, 644; Reed, 120; Ru-
    binstein, 165, 167.

SMITH, JESSIE WILLCOX

1917

b. 1863, Philadelphia; d. 1935, Philadelphia
Father: Charles Henry Smith; mother: Katherine DeWitt
Philadelphia School of Design for Women; Pennsylvania
    Academy of Fine Arts, studied with Thomas Eakins; stud-
    ied with Howard Pyle

Work includes: illustrations for hundreds of covers, numerous books, and such magazines as *Harper's, Collier's, Good Housekeeping, Ladies' Home Journal*, and *Women's Home Companion*. Illustrations for *Dream Blocks* (1908) and *The Water Babies* by Charles Kingsley (1916) are some of her most acclaimed drawings.

Member of the Plastic Club; won Mary Smith Prize (1903) for the best work by a Philadelphia woman artist at the Pennsylvania Academy of Fine Arts's annual exhibition; won watercolor medal at the Panama Pacific International Exposition (1915), San Francisco; known as one of the Red Rose Girls.

Sources: Carter; Ann B. Percy, "Jessie Willcox Smith," *Philadelphia: Three Centuries*, 504–5; Reed, 10, 87, 102, 122, 131; S. Michael Schnessel, *Jessie Willcox Smith* (New York: Thomas Y. Crowell, 1977); Wagner, 11–14, 19–21, 25–27, 31–32, 45, 45, 66–72; *The Water Babies: Illustrations by Jessie Willcox Smith*, an exhibition at the Library of Congress, Washington, DC, http://www.loc.gov/rr/print/swann/waterbabies/wb-overview.html.

SMITH, SARAH KATHARINE

b. ca. 1878, Rio Vista, CA
Father: George H. Smith; mother: Rachel Mooar
Wheaton College (Wheaton, IL), 1900; School of the Art Institute of Chicago, studied with William Merritt Chase
Work includes: illustrations published in *Outlook, St. Nicholas*, and *Youth's Companion*; books including *The Wide Awake Reader* by Clara Murray (1914), *The Fun of Cooking: A Story for Boys and Girls* by Caroline French Benton (n.d.), and *The Love Cycle* by Lulu Daniel Hardy (1924).
Taught at Wheaton College from 1906 to 1908 and at Gulf Park College in 1940.
Exhibitions include: Art Institute of Chicago, Southern States Art League, Mississippi Art Association (gold medal), all in 1939; Gulf Coast Art Association, New York Watercolor Club, American Watercolor Society Watercolor Exhibition in Boston, and the Plastic Club.
Sources: Falk, 3090, 3091; Finding Aid, Sarah K. Smith Collection, Wheaton College, https://archon.wheaton.edu/index.php?p=collections/controlcard&id=134; Hughes, vol. 2, 1039; Larson, 141; George Mooar, *Mooar (Moors) Genealogy: Abraham Mooar of Andover and His Descendants* (Boston: Charles H. Pope, 1901), 74.

SORENSEN, JEN

Self-portrait

b. 1974, Lancaster, PA
Father: John Sorensen, public schoolteacher; mother: Linda, public schoolteacher; husband: Scott Johnsen
University of Virginia
Work includes: weekly cartoon *Slowpoke* that began in 1998, became more political in 2000–2001, and was nationally syndicated as of 2017; long-form comics have appeared in *Progressive, Nation, Daily Kos, Austin Chronicle, NPR, Ms. Magazine*, and *Politico*; written and illustrated other long-form comics on health-care reform (commissioned by *Kaiser Health News*), synopsis of Jane Austen's *Pride and Prejudice* for NPR, and illustrations for the *American Prospect, Nickelodeon Magazine, MAD* magazine, and *Women's Review of Books*; published collections of her cartoons include *Slowpoke Comix #1* (1998); *Slowpoke: Café Pompous* (2001); *Slowpoke: America Gone Bonkers* (2004); *Slowpoke: One Nation, Oh My God!* (2008).
Editor of Graphic Culture section of *Fusion*, an online news aggregator from varied sources.
Awards include: numerous Alternative Newsweekly Awards; Xeric Award to publish first collection of strips, 2000; Herblock Prize finalist, 2012; Robert F. Kennedy Journalism Award, 2013; Herblock Prize, 2014; Pulitzer Prize for editorial cartooning, finalist, 2017.
Sources: "2014 Prize Winner," *Herb Block Foundation*, http://www.herbblockfoundation.org/herblock-prize-winner/1072; Michael Cavna, "Jen Sorensen Becomes First Female Winner of Herblock Prize for Political Cartooning," *Washington Post*, April 29, 2014: C1-C2; www.jensorensen.com.

STEPHENS, ALICE BARBER

ca. 1890

b. 1858, near Salem, NJ; d. 1932, Rose Valley, Moylan, PA

Father: Samuel Clayton Barber, farmer; mother: Mary Owen, farmer; husband: Charles Hallowell Stephens, portrait painter; one son

Philadelphia School of Design for Women; Pennsylvania Academy of Fine Arts, studied with Thomas Eakins; Académie Julien, studied with Tony Robert-Fleury, Paris

Work includes: a high volume of illustrations published in *Scribner's Monthly, Century Illustrated Monthly, Collier's Weekly, Cosmopolitan, Country Gentleman, Harper's, Ladies' Home Journal, McClure's,* and *Women's Home Companion*; illustrated books include *Middlemarch* by George Eliot (1899); *The Marble Faun* by Nathaniel Hawthorne (1900); and *Little Women* by Louisa May Alcott (1903).

Sources: Ann Barton Brown, *Alice Barber Stephens: A Pioneer Woman Illustrator* (Chadds Ford, PA: Brandywine River Museum, 1984); Helen Goodwin, "Alice Barber Stephens," *American Artist* 48, no. 501 (April 1984): 46–49, 98–100; Helen Goodwin, "Alice Barber Stephens, Illustrator," *Arts Magazine* (January 1984): 126–29; Phyllis Peet, "Alice Barber Stephens, American Painter, Illustrator, and Graphic Artist, 1858–1932," *Concise Dictionary of Women Artists,* ed. Delia Gaze (London: Fitzroy Dearborn Publishers, 2001), 641–43; Phyllis Peet, "Alice Barber Stephens," *Dictionary of Literary Biography*, vol. 188 (Gale, 2009): 345–51; Reed, 81, 103; Taraba, 393–99.

STORER, FLORENCE EDITH

b. 1881, active ca. 1909–1928, working in Boston, ca. 1913

Work includes: illustrations for *Youth's Companion* and *St. Nicholas*; illustrated *Strawberry Acres* (1911) by Grace S. Richmond; *Christmas Tales and Christmas Verse* (1912) by Eugene Field; *The Colonel's Experiment* (1913) and *June* (1916) both by Edith Barnard Delano; *A Child's Garden of Verses* (1928 edition) by Robert Louis Stevenson, and other books from ca. 1909–1928.

Staff, *Youth's Companion*, Boston.

Sources: Falk, 3193; Petteys, 676.

STOSSEL, SAGE

b. 1971, Boston, MA

Father: Thomas Stossel, physician; mother: Anne Hanford, lawyer; brother: Scott, editor, the *Atlantic* magazine

Harvard University, English, American literature and languages

Work includes: editor and cartoonist for *TheAtlantic.com*; contributes cartoons to the *Boston Globe*, the *Provincetown Banner*; has published cartoons in the *New York Times Week in Review*, *CNN Headline News*, Cartoon Arts International/The New York Times Syndicate, the *Editorial Humor*, and *Copyediting*. Author/illustrator of graphic novel *Starling* (2013) and children's books *On the Loose in Boston* (2009), *On the Loose in Washington, DC* (2013), and *On the Loose in Philadelphia* (2015).

Won New England Press Association Award for work for the *Provincetown Banner*

Sources: "Sage Stossel," *Association of American Editorial Cartoonists*, http://editorialcartoonists.com/cartoonist/profile.cfm/StossS/; Stossel's website, www.sagestossel.com; Julie Bosman, "Enough Anxiety to Fill Two Books: Stossel Family Problems Spelled out in New Releases," *New York Times*, December 22, 2013.

STRATTON, LUCY LADD

b. 1834, Dalton, NH; d. 1936

Father: Hiram Ladd; mother Aurelia Palmer; husband: George W. Stratton, wholesale importer of musical instruments and composer

Private instruction as a child

Work includes: about sixteen hundred paintings in watercolor and gouache based on keen study of her subjects, primarily wildflowers and orchids in New England and mid-Atlantic states, as well as in Europe and Scotland, produced from ca. 1860–1885.

Sources: Kirk W. Steehler, *Erie Arists: A History of Heroes*, unpublished manuscript excerpted with permission from the Erie Museum, published in "Lucy Ladd Stratton," askART Academic, http://www.askart.com/artist_bio/Lucy_Ladd_Stratton/11161660/Lucy_Ladd_Stratton.aspx.

SUBA, SUSANNE (McCRACKEN)

b. 1913, Budapest, Hungary; d. 2012, New York

Father: Miklos Suba, painter, architect; mother: May; husband: Russell McCracken

Pratt Institute

Work includes: five cover designs, one cartoon, and numerous spot drawings for the *New Yorker*, a collection of which she published in *Spots by Suba: From the* New Yorker (1944). Illustrated more than seventy children's books, some of which she also wrote, and contributed regularly to *Publisher's Weekly*.

Sources: *Complete Book of Covers*, 391, 91, 107, 113, 226, 232; Falk, vol. 3, 3215; Finding Aid for the Susanne Suba Papers, de Grummond Collection of Children's Literature, University of Southern Mississippi, Hattiesburg, MS, http://www.lib.usm.edu/legacy/degrum/public_html/html/research/findaids/DG0954.html.

SWEENY, GLYNIS

b. 1962

Rochester Institute of Technology, graphic design, 1984; State University of New York, training in illustration under Alan E. Cober

Work includes: staff designer and illustrator at the *Detroit News*; illustrations and caricatures published by *Time*, *Wall Street Journal*, *Business Week*, *Village Voice*, *New York Times*, *Comedy Central*, *Atlantic*, *Fortune*, *Rolling Stone*, *GQ*, *Entertainment Weekly*, *Los Angeles Times*, and *Boston Globe*.

Awards include: Society of Illustrators, Society of Newspaper Design and the Society of Professional Journalists.

Sources: "Notable Alumni," Rochester Institute of Technology, https://www.rit.edu/alumni/about/notablealumni; www.gsweeny.com.

TAMAKI, JILLIAN

b. 1980, Ottawa, Canada

Husband: Sam Weber, illustrator; cousin: Mariko Tamaki, writer and sometime collaborator

Alberta College of Art, Calgary, BA, design, 2003

Work includes: worked at video game developer Bioware in Edmonton; editorial illustrations for magazines and newspapers; books include *Gilded Lilies* (2006), *Indoor Voice* (2007), short story collection, *Boundless* (2017); collaborated with cousin Mariko Tamaki on young adult graphic novels *Skim* (2008), *This One Summer* (2014), both of which won Ignatz Awards for best graphic novel, and latter also garnered Eisner Award for best graphic novel, Canadian Governor-General's Award, and Caldecott and Printz Honors; online comic *Super Mutant Magic Academy* (2012) won Ignatz award.

Taught at Parsons School of Design and School of Visual Art.

Acclaimed for her superb drawing skills and highly varied subjects that she tackles, Tamaki also stands out among many in her field in terms of impressive productivity and willingness to keep pushing beyond boundaries and categories, creating outstanding work for young adults, portrait drawings, editorial illustration, and stories exploring the surreal and melancholy.

Sources: "Even Superheroes Need Prom Dates: Calgary-Raised Illustrator Jillian Tamaki Has Won High Praise for Chronicling the Typical Dramas of Extraordinary Teens," *Globe & Mail* [Toronto], June 11, 2015: L2; Lambiek; Robbins, 165; www.jilliantamaki.com/about.

TELGEMEIER, RAINA

b. 1977, San Francisco
Husband: Dave Roman, cartoonist
School of Visual Arts, BFA, 2002

Work includes: self-published minicomic *Beginnings* (2002) created in response to her reading *Barefoot Gen* (autobiographical comic by Keiji Nakazawa about bomb dropped on Hiroshima); adapted Ann M. Martin's Babysitter's Club titles, including *Kristy's Great Idea* (2006); *The Truth about Stacy* (2006); *Mary Ann Saves the Day* (2007); *Claudia and Mean Janine* (2008); collaborated with husband, Dave Roman, and Anzu on *X-Men: Misfits 1* (2009); *Smile: A Dental Drama* (2010), which won an Eisner Award for Best Publication for a Teen Audience, Dorothy Canfield Fisher Award, Maine Student Book Award, and was an Honor Book for the Boston Globe-Horn Book Awards and Editor's Choice for the *New York Times* and listed on the Booklist Top Ten Graphic Novels for Youth; *Drama* (2012), which was a Stonewall Honor Book, Editor's Choice for the *New York Times* and Booklist, and was selected for YALSA's Top Ten Great Graphic Novels for Teens; *Sisters* (2014); *Ghosts* (2016).

Awards include: Ignatz Award nominations for Promising New Talent and Outstanding Minicomic for *Take-Out* (2003); The Friends of Lulu's Kim Yale Award for Best New Talent (2003); Eisner Award nomination for Talent Deserving of Wider Recognition (2005); *Smile* on the *New York Times* Graphic Novel Bestseller List for five years, and *Drama* also made the list, which was discontinued in February 2017.

Sources: Michael Cavna, "The *New York Times* Just Killed Its Graphic Novel Bestseller Lists—and Authors Aren't Happy," Comic Riffs, *Washington Post*, January 27, 2017, https://www.washingtonpost.com/news/comic-riffs/wp/2017/01/27/the-new-york-times-just-killed-its-graphic-novel-bestseller-lists-and-authors-arent-happy/?utm_term=.7fe768495d96; Lambiek; "Raina Telgemeier," *Contemporary Authors Online*, Gale, 2013, *Biography in Context*; Robbins, 165; www.goraina.com.

TELNAES, ANN

Self-portrait

b. 1960, Stockholm, Sweden; became a US citizen in 1973
Husband: David Lloyd
Arizona State University; California Institute of the Arts, BFA, animation

Work includes: political cartoons beginning in 1989, syndicated with North American Syndicate, distributed with Los Angeles Syndicate (taken over by Tribune Media Services), and self-syndicated; animated editorial cartoons for the *Washington Post*, beginning in 2008.

Worked for Disney Imagineering from 1987 to 1993; president, Association of Editorial Cartoonists, 2016–2017.

Awards include: Best Cartoonist (Population Institute XVIIth Global Media Awards) and Best Editorial Cartoonist (Sixth Annual Environmental Media Awards), both in 1996; National Headliner Award for Editorial Cartoons, 1997; Pulitzer Prize for editorial cartooning, 2001; Maggie Award, Planned Parenthood, 2002; Clifford Berryman Award for Editorial Cartooning, 2003; Herblock Prize finalist, 2010; finalist for NCS Reuben Award for Outstanding Cartoonist of the Year, 2016; Reuben Award for Outstanding Cartoonist of the Year, National Cartoonists Society, 2017.

Sources: *Humor's Edge: Cartoons by Ann Telnaes*, an exhibition at the Library of Congress, Washington, DC, 2004, https://www.loc.gov/exhibits/telnaes/; Martha Kennedy, "Ann Telnaes, Cartoonist: Singular in Style and Substance," *Humor's Edge: Cartoons by Ann Telnaes* (San Francisco: Pomegranate, 2004), 13–19; Michael Rhode, "Ann Telnaes at the 2011 Small Press Expo," *International Journal of Comic Art* 15 no. 1 (Spring 2013): 251–69; Ann Telnaes, *Dick* (Cartoonist Group, 2010); www.anntelnaes.com.

TIMMONS, ANNE

b. 1955, Milwaukie, OR

Oregon State University, BFA, illustration; Pacific Northwest College, class in sequential art

Work includes: illustration contributions to Eisner-nominated *Dignifying Science: Stories about Women Scientists* (1999); collaborated with Trina Robbins on *Go Girl* (2000–2006), *Northanger Abbey* by Jane Austen (2007), and other titles on Florence Nightingale, Hedy Lamarr, Elizabeth Blackwell, and Lily Renée; freelance work with Lerner Publishing Group, Graphic Classics.

Sources: Lambiek; Robbins, 165, 168, 175; www.annetimmons .com.

TYLER, CAROL ANN

b. 1951, Chicago

Father: Charles William; mother: Hannah Elizabeth Yates; husband: Justin Green, cartoonist; one daughter

Middle Tennessee State University, BFA; Syracuse University, MFA

Work includes: comics appeared in *Weirdo*, *Wimmen's Comix*, and *Twisted Sisters*; wrote and illustrated *The Job Thing: Stories about Shitty Jobs* (1993); *Late Bloomer* (2005); *You'll Never Know, Book I: A Good and Decent Man* (2009); *Book II: Collateral Damage* (2010); *Book III: Soldier's Heart* (2012).

Exhibitions, artist's residencies, exhibition curator, and teaching positions include Tennessee Arts Commission, Davis Art Center, Sacramento History Museum, Ohio Arts Council, Arts Learning Program, adjunct professor in University of Cincinnati School of Art.

Sources: "C. Tyler," *Contemporary Authors Online*, Gale, 2011, *Biography in Context*; "C. Tyler," *The Writers Directory*, St. James Press, 2016, *Biography in Context*; Lambiek.

WEBER, SARAH STILWELL

b. 1878, Concordville, PA; d. 1939, Philadelphia

Husband: Herbert S. Weber

Drexel Institute; studied with Howard Pyle

Work includes: illustration for children's books *Dorothy Deane: A Children's Story* by Ellen Olney Kirk (1898); *Mother's Hero* by Ethel C. Dow (1910); *The Musical Tree: Songs and Pictures* (a music book for children, 1925) also written by Weber; illustrated for *Collier's*, *Harper's*, *St Nicholas*, and the *Saturday Evening Post*, for which she designed more than sixty covers.

Member of the Plastic Club.

Sources: Mantle Fielding, 901; Petteys, 741–42; Reed, 87, 128; "Sarah Stilwell Weber," *Saturday Evening Post*, January 7, 2015, http://www.saturdayeveningpost.com/2015/01/07/ art-entertainment/cover-artists-art-entertainment/sar ah-stilwell-weber.html.

WHITING, GRACE SPAFFORD

b. 1891, Chicago, IL; d. 1964, Jerusalem, Israel

Father: Horatio Spafford, cofounder of American Colony, Christian community of American Swedes and others based in Jerusalem; mother: Anna, cofounder of same; husband: John David Whiting, business manager, artifact dealer for colony; four children; sister: Bertha Spafford Vester (who also produced watercolor drawings of flora)

Privately educated with sister Bertha by tutor

Work includes: drawings of flowers and other plants native to vicinity of Jerusalem in watercolor, ca. 1933 and until ca. 1961.

Sources: Letter from Wendy Whiting Blome to Barbara Bair, December 12, 2008; Visual materials from the Papers of John D. Whiting, Prints and Photographs Division, Library of Congress, Washington, DC, https://www.loc.gov/ rr/print/coll/629_whiting.html.

WILKINSON, SIGNE

Self-portrait

b. 1950, Wichita Falls, TX

Denver University, BA, English; Pennsylvania Academy of Fine Arts

Work includes: editorial cartoonist for the *San Jose Mercury News* beginning in 1982; cartoons for *Ms. Magazine*; editorial cartoonist for the *Philadelphia Daily News* in 1985; comic strip *The Family Tree* ran 2008–2011.

President of the Association of American Editorial Cartoonists, 1994–1995.

Awards include: first woman to win Pulitzer Prize for editorial cartooning, 1993; Thomas Nast Award from the Oversea Press Club, 1996, 2000, 2006, 2015; Robert F. Kennedy Journalism Award, 2002 and 2008; Visionary Woman Award from Philadelphia's Moore College of Art and Design, 2011.

Sources: Harvey, 65; Hess and Northrop, 33, 142–43, 148, 180, 184; Signe Wilkinson, *One Nation under Surveillance: Cartoon Rants on Life, Liberty and the Pursuit of Privacy* (Manhattan Beach, CA: The Cartoonist Group, 2005); Wilkinson's cartoons at http://www.gocomics.com/signewilkinson.

WILLIAMS, ELIZABETH

Parsons School of Design, 1979, focused on fashion illustration; Washington University, St. Louis; Syracuse University; Otis Art Institute, University of California, Los Angeles

Worked in fashion illustration in Hollywood in 1980, but also began working that year as a courtroom artist.

Work includes: published on the front pages of the *New York Times, Wall Street Journal, New York Post, Newsday*, and in the *Los Angeles Times, Washington Post*, and *Times* (London); covered high-profile court cases such as those of John Delorean (1984), John Gotti (1992), Martha Stewart (2004), Bernard Madoff (2009), Dominique Strauss-Kahn (2011), and Abu Hamza (2014).

Exhibited work at the Society of Illustrators, John Jay College of Criminal Justice (both in New York), New York City Police Museum, William J. Brennan Courthouse in New Jersey, and Conejo Valley Art Museum in California.

Sources: Daniel Fitzsimmons, "Reporting by Drawing," *New York Press*, November 6, 2013, http://www.nypress.com/reporting-by-drawing/; Sara Randazzo, "She Draws a Crowd: Chatting with Courtroom Artist Elizabeth Williams," *Law Blog, The Wall Street Journal*, June 10, 2015, http://blogs.wsj.com/law/2015/06/10/she-draws-a-crowd-chatting-with-courtroom-artist-elizabeth-williams/; Julie Shapiro, "Artist Captures the Sketchiest Character of All: Bernie Madoff," *Downtown Express* 22, no. 8, July 3–9, 2009; Williams and Russell, 233; Williams; www.elizabeth williamstudio.com.

WILLIAMSON, ADA CLENDENIN

b. 1880, Camden, NJ; d. 1958, Ogunquit, ME

Father: T. Roney Williamson, architect; mother: Ada Olympia Clendenin

Drexel Institute, 1896–1908, studied with Howard Pyle; Pennsylvania Academy of Fine Arts, studied under William Merritt Chase and Cecelia Beaux

Work includes: illustrations published in *Success* magazine, *Harper's, St. Nicholas, Delineator, Women's Home Companion, Youth's Companion*, and *House and Garden*; illustrated books include *Janey* by Inez Irwin (1911), *A Little Princess of the Stars and Stripes* by Aileen Cleveland Higgins (1915), *Understood Betsy* by Dorothy Canfield (1917), *The Girl from Four Corners* by Rebecca Newman Porter (1920), and *Touring New England on the Trail of the Yankee* by Clara Walker Whiteside (1926).

Exhibited work at the Pennsylvania Academy of Fine Arts in 1922, 1924, and 1941–1945, and with the Painters and Sculptors of Los Angeles, 1929.

Sources: Hughes, vol. 2, 1198; Larson, 144.

WINTER, ALICE BEACH

b. 1877, Green Ridge, MO; d. 1970, Gloucester, MA

Husband: Charles Allen Winter, artist

School of Fine Arts, St. Louis, graduated with highest honors; Art Students League, studied with John Twachtman, Joseph DeCamp, and George de Forest Brush

Work includes: illustrator of schoolbooks, magazines, portrait painter, especially of children, also became known as a sculptor; among the founding editors of the *Masses*, also served at times as its art editor, in addition to contributing her own drawings; published drawings in *Woman Voter* and the *Delineator*.

Exhibited work at Pennsylvania Academy of Fine Arts, Chicago Art Institute, Carnegie Foundation, St. Louis Exposition of 1897; Member of the National Association of Women Arts, North Shore Art Association, Business & Professional Women's Club, and Gloucester Art Association. She and her husband were members of the Socialist Party.

Sources: Hughes, vol. 2, 1206; Sheppard, 228; Zurier, 182.

WIREMAN, EUGÉNIE M.

b. 1875, Philadelphia; d. 1934

Pennsylvania Academy of Fine Arts; studied with Howard Pyle

Work includes: illustrated books for children and adults including, *In Assyrian Tents: The Strange Adventures of Uriel* (1904); *Miss Philura's Wedding Gown* (1912); *Goldfish: A Christmas Story for Children between Six and Sixty* (1912). Examples demonstrate highly accomplished technique in watercolor.

Member, Art Alliance of Philadelphia.

Sources: Falk, 689; Mantle Fielding, 1048; Gary Fitzgibbon, Finding Aid, Emily Elliott Collection, Art Gallery of Ontario, https://www.ago.net/assets/files/pdf/special_collections/SC004.pdf.

WOODWARD, HILDEGARD H.

b. 1898, Worcester, MA; d. 1977, Connecticut

School of Museum of Fine Arts, Boston; studied in Paris; learned about book illustration from illustrator Marguerite Davis

Work includes: illustration for at least thirty-four books and portraits of children; received Caldecott Honor Book awards for *Roger and the Fox* (1947) and *The Wild Birthday Cake* (1949) both written by Lavinia (Riker) Davis; wrote and illustrated children's books including *Everyday Children* (1935) and *The House on Grandfather's Hill* (1961).

Art instructor at private schools in New York; taught design at School of Museum of Fine Arts, Boston.

Sources: Christina Cowan, Finding Aid, Hildegard Woodward Papers, Elmer L. Andersen Library, University of Minnesota, http://special.lib.umn.edu/findaid/xml/CLRC-1719.xml; Finding Aid, Hildegard Woodward Papers, de Grummond Collection, McCain Library and Archives, USM Libraries, The University of Southern Mississippi, Hattiesburg, MS, http://www.lib.usm.edu/legacy/degrum/public_html/html/research/findaids/woodward.htm#bio; Petteys, 767.

SELECTED BIBLIOGRAPHY AND SUGGESTIONS FOR FURTHER READING

Banta, Martha. *Imaging American Women: Idea and Ideals in Cultural History*. New York: Columbia University Press, 1987.

Carter, Alice A. *The Red Rose Girls: Art and Love on Philadelphia's Main Line*. New York: Abrams, 2000.

Chute, Hilary. *Graphic Women: Life Narrative and Contemporary Comics* (Gender and Culture Series). New York: Columbia University Press, 2010.

Cocca, Carolyn. *Superwomen: Gender, Power, and Representation*. New York: Bloomsbury, 2016.

Donnelly, Liza. *Funny Ladies: The* New Yorker's *Greatest Women Cartoonists and Their Cartoons*. Amherst, NY: Prometheus Books, 2005.

Doyle, Susan, Jaleen Grove, and Whitney Sherman, eds. *A History of Illustration*. New York: Fairchild Books, 2018.

Harvey, Sheridan, Janice E. Ruth, Barbara Orbach Natanson, Sara Day, and Evelyn Sinclair, eds. *American Women: A Library of Congress Guide for the Study of Women's History and Culture in the United States*. Washington, DC: Library of Congress, 2001.

Heller, Steven, ed. *Innovators of American Illustration*. New York: Van Nostrand Reinhold, 1986.

Hess, Stephen, and Sandy Northrop. *American Political Cartoons: The Evolution of a National Identity*. New Brunswick, NJ: Transaction Publishers, 2011.

Katz, Harry, ed. *Cartoon America: Comic Art in the Library of Congress*. New York: Abrams, 2006.

Lepore, Jill. *The Secret History of Wonder Woman*. New York: Alfred A. Knopf, 2014.

Lightman, Sarah. *Graphic Details: Jewish Women's Confessional Comics in Essays and Interviews*. Jefferson, NC: McFarland, 2014.

Mankoff, Bob, ed. *The Complete Cartoons of the* New Yorker. New York: Black Dog & Leventhal, 2006.

Mouly, Françoise. *Blown Covers:* New Yorker *Covers You Were Never Meant to See*. New York: Abrams, 2012.

Noomin, Diane, ed. *Twisted Sisters: A Collection of Bad Girl Art*. New York: Penguin Books, 1991.

——, ed. *Twisted Sisters 2*. Northampton, MA: Kitchen Sink Press, 1995.

Robbins, Trina. *The Complete Wimmen's Comix*. 2 vols. Seattle: Fantagraphics Books, 2016.

——. *The Great Women Superheroes*. Northampton, MA: Kitchen Sink Press, 1996.

——. *Pretty in Ink: North American Women Cartoonists, 1896–2013*. Seattle: Fantagraphics Books, 2013.

Rubinstein, Charlotte Streifer. *American Women Artists from Early Indian Times to the Present*. Boston: G. K. Hall & Co. and Avon Books, 1982.

Taraba, Fred. *Masters of American Illustration: 41 Illustrators and How They Worked*. St. Louis, MO: Illustrated Press, 2011.

Wagner, Margaret E. *Maxfield Parrish and the Illustrators of the Golden Age*. San Francisco: Pomegranate, 2000.

Walker, Brian. *The Comics: The Complete Collection*. New York: Abrams, 2011.

Zurier, Rebecca. *Art for the* Masses: *A Radical Magazine and Its Graphics, 1911–1917*. Philadelphia: Temple University Press, 1988.

SPECIFIC ARTISTS

Armitage, Shelley. *Kewpies and Beyond: The World of Rose O'Neill*. Jackson: University Press of Mississippi, 1994.

Barry, Lynda. *Blabber Blabber: Volume 1 of Everything*. Montreal: Drawn & Quarterly, 2011.

——. *The Greatest! Of Marlys!* Seattle: Sasquatch Books, 2000.

Bechdel, Alison. *The Essential Dykes to Watch Out For*. Boston: Houghton Mifflin Harcourt, 2008.

——. *Fun Home: A Family Tragicomic*. Boston: Houghton Mifflin, 2006.

Brown, Ann Barton. *Alice Barber Stephens: A Pioneer Woman Illustrator*. Chadds Ford, PA: Brandywine River Museum, 1984.

Chast, Roz. *Can't We Talk about Something More Pleasant?* New York: Bloomsbury, 2014.

———. *Theories of Everything: Selected, Collected, Health-Inspected, 1978–2006.* New York: Bloomsbury, 2006.

Goldstein, Nancy. *Jackie Ormes: The First African American Woman Cartoonist.* Ann Arbor: University of Michigan Press, 2008.

Goodman, Helen. *The Art of Rose O'Neill.* Chadds Ford, PA: Brandywine River Museum, 1989. Exhibition catalog.

Hollander, Nicole. *The Sylvia Chronicles: Thirty Years of Misbehavior from Reagan to Obama.* New York: New Press, 2010.

Kirtley, Susan E. *Lynda Barry: Girlhood through the Looking Glass.* Jackson: University Press of Mississippi, 2012.

Kraus, Jerelle. *All the Art That's Fit to Print (And Some That Wasn't) Inside the* New York Times *Op-Ed Page.* New York: Columbia University Press, 2009.

Messick, Dale. *Brenda Starr, Reporter: The Collected Daily and Sunday Newspaper Strips.* Vol. 1. Neshannock, PA: Hermes Press, 2012.

Miller, Darlis A. *Mary Hallock Foote: Author-Illustrator of the American West.* Norman: University of Oklahoma Press, 2002.

Robbins, Trina. *From Girls to Grrrlz: A History of [Women's] Comics from Teens to Zines.* San Francisco: Chronicle Books, 1999.

———. *Nell Brinkley and the New Woman in the Early 20th Century.* Jefferson, NC: McFarland, 2001.

Telnaes, Ann. *Humor's Edge: Cartoons by Ann Telnaes.* San Francisco: Pomegranate in association with the Library of Congress, 2004.

Wilkinson, Signe. *One Nation under Surveillance: Cartoon Rants on Life, Liberty, and the Pursuit of Privacy.* Seattle: Cartoonist Group, 2005.

MANUSCRIPTS

Scanlan, Patricia Smith. "'God-Gifted Girls': Women Illustrators, Gender, Class, and Commerce in American Visual Culture, 1885–1925." PhD diss., Indiana University, 2010. ProQuest (AAT 3409785).

Erwin Swann papers, 1946–1976. Library of Congress, Manuscript Division, Washington, DC

IMAGE CREDITS

Unless where noted, images in this book are from the Library's Prints & Photographs Division and can be viewed at www.loc.gov/pictures by using the negative or digital ID numbers listed below.

LIBRARY OF CONGRESS DIVISIONS
GC   General Collections
RBSC   Rare Book & Special Collections
SER   Serial & Government Publications Divisions

PRINTS & PHOTOGRAPHS COLLECTIONS
AWC   Art Wood Collection
CAI   Cabinet of American Illustration

CHAPTER ONE: GOLDEN AGE ILLUSTRATORS

5   LC-DIG-pga-05058.
7   LC-DIG-ppmsca-37431.
8   (top) LC-DIG-ppmsca-37432; (bottom) CAI LC-DIG-cai-2a12522.
9   CAI LC-DIG-cai-2a12521.
10 (left) CAI LC-DIG-cai-2a15122; (right) CAI LC-DIG-ppmsca-38581.
11 CAI LC-DIG-cai-2a15074.
12 CAI LC-DIG-ppmsca-38582.
13 CAI LC-DIG-cai-2a15062.
14 CAI LC-DIG-ppmsc-04729.
15 CAI LC-DIG-ppmsc-04735.
16 (left) LC-USZC4-9395; (right) CAI LC-DIG-cai-2a13037.
18 (left) CAI LC-DIG-ppmsc-05892; (right) CAI LC-DIG-ppmsc-05895.
19 (left) LC-DIG-ppmsca-37435; (right) CAI LC-USZC4-1543.
20 CAI LC-DIG-ppmsca-31858. Purchase, The Alfred Bendiner Foundation, 2010.
21 (top) CAI LC-DIG-ppmsca-31860. Purchase, The Alfred Bendiner Foundation, 2010; (bottom) CAI LC-DIG-ppmsca-31859. Purchase, The Alfred Bendiner Foundation, 2010.

22 (left) LC-DIG-ppmsca-43195; (right) LC-DIG-ppmsca-38282.
23 (top left) RBSC PS3117 .V35 1919; (top right); RBSC PR4218 .A1 1900; (bottom left and right) RBSC PS1556 .C2 1901.
24 (top left, top right, bottom right) RBSC QK150 .J12 1888; (bottom left); John D. Whiting Collection LC-DIG-ppss-00780.
25 (top) LC-DIG-ppmsca-51966; (bottom) LC-DIG-ppmsca-51965.

CHAPTER TWO: EARLY CARTOONISTS

30 AWC LC-DIG-ppmsca-08333.
31 LC-DIG-ppmsca-38579.
32 LC-DIG-ppmsca-19109.
34 AWC LC-DIG ppmsca-23877.
35 AWC LC-DIG-ppmsca-05784.
36 (top) AWC LC-DIG-ppmsca-33577. Photo credit: Woody Kimbrell/Chicago Tribune/TNS; (bottom) AWC LC-DIG-ppmsca-33576. Photo credit: Woody Kimbrell/Chicago Tribune/TNS.
37 AWC LC-DIG-ppmsca-06584.
38 LC-DIG-ppmsca-03341.
39 (top) LC-DIG-ppmsca-51789. Gift and bequest of Caroline and Erwin Swann, 1977; (bottom) LC-DIG-ppmsca-31874.
42 LC-DIG-ppmsca-38597. Gift of Nancy Goldstein, 2010.
43 LC-DIG-ppmsca-38597. Gift of Nancy Goldstein, 2010.
45 (top) AWC LC-DIG-ppmsca-33586. Photo credit: Dale Messick/Chicago Tribune/TNS; (middle) AWC LC-DIG-ppmsca-33587. Photo credit: Dale Messick/Chicago Tribune/TNS; (bottom) AWC LC-DIG-ppmsc-00178. Photo credit: Dale Messick/Chicago Tribune/TNS.

CHAPTER 3: NEW VOICES, NEW NARRATIVES IN COMICS

49 AWC LC-DIG-ppmsca-38595. Courtesy of Rick Camp.

50 (left) AWC LC-DIG-ppmsca-38594. Courtesy of Rick Camp; (right) AWC LC-DIG-ppmsca-38593. Courtesy of Rick Camp.

51 (top) AWC LC-DIG-ppmsca-51788. Courtesy of Lynn Johnston; (bottom) AWC LC-DIG-ppmsca-09130. Courtesy of Lynn Johnston.

52 (top) AWC LC-DIG-ppmsca-33041. Courtesy of Lynn Johnston; (bottom) AWC LC-DIG-ppmsca-33042. Courtesy of Lynn Johnston.

53 (top) LC-DIG-ppmsca-31375. Gift of the artist, 2008. STONE SOUP © Jan Eliot. Reprinted with permission of ANDREWS MCMEEL SYNDICATION. All rights reserved; (bottom) LC-DIG-ppmsca-33047. Gift of the artist, 2011. STONE SOUP © Jan Eliot. Reprinted with permission of ANDREWS MCMEEL SYNDICATION. All rights reserved.

55 (top) LC-DIG-ppmsca-05091. Gift of the artist, 2002. © Nicole Hollander, January 1998; (bottom) LC-DIG-ppmsca-05095. Gift of the artist, 2002. © Nicole Hollander, March 1998.

56 AWC LC-DIG-ppmsca-09131. CATHY © 1987 Cathy Guisewite. Reprinted with permission of ANDREWS MCMEEL SYNDICATION. All rights reserved.

57 LC-DIG-ppmsca-31876. Gift of the artist, 1995. WHERE I'M COMING FROM © 1991 ANDREWS MCMEEL SYNDICATION. Reprinted with Permission. All rights reserved.

58 LC-DIG-ppmsca-38048. Gift of the artist, 1995. WHERE I'M COMING FROM © ANDREWS MCMEEL SYNDICATION. Reprinted with Permission. All rights reserved.

59 LC-DIG-ppmsca-04909 and LC-DIG-ppmsca-04910. Gift of the artist, 2003. Courtesy of Alison Bechdel.

60 LC-DIG-ppmsca-04907 and LC-DIG-ppmsca-04908. Gift of the artist, 2003. Courtesy of Alison Bechdel.

61 (top) LC-DIG-ppmsca-51303. Gift of the artist, 2016. Rhymes with Orange: © 2010 Hilary B Price. Distributed by King Features Syndicate; (bottom) LC-DIG-ppmsca-51302. Gift of the artist, 2016. Rhymes with Orange: © 2015 Hilary B Price. Distributed by King Features Syndicate.

63 LC-DIG-ppmsca-32259 © MARVEL.

64 LC-DIG-ppmsca-01885. Gift of the artist, 2002. "The Sleeping Giant," story by Stan Lee, art and colors by Marie Severin, letters by Ken Bruzenak. Published by DC Comics in 9-11: The World's Finest Comic Book Writers and Artists Tell Stories to Remember vol. 2 © 2002 DC Comics. Used with permission.

65 (left, middle, right) LC-DIG-ppmsca-33044, LC-DIG-ppmsca-33045, and LC-DIG-ppmsca-33046. Gift of the artist, 2002. Courtesy of Anne Timmons.

66 SER. Courtesy of Trina Robbins.

67 SER. Courtesy of Carol Tyler.

68 (left) LC-DIG-ppmsca-51300. Gift of the artist, 2016. Courtesy of Trina Robbins; (right) LC-DIG-ppmsca-51301. Gift of the artist, 2016. Courtesy of Trina Robbins.

69 Collection of the artist. © Diane Noomin. Reprinted with permission.

70 (top left) LC-DIG-ppmsca-51296; (top right) LC-DIG-ppmsca-51297; (bottom left) LC-DIG-ppmsca-51298; (bottom right) LC-DIG-ppmsca-51963. Copyright Lynda Barry, Used with permission by Drawn & Quarterly.

72 (left and right) SER. From SMILE by Raina Telgemeier. Scholastic Inc./Graphix. Copyright © 2010 by Raina Telgemeier. Reprinted by permission Scholastic Inc.

73 (left) LC-DIG-ppmsca-37433. Gift, Small Press Expo, 2011. From BABYSITTERS CLUB GRAPHIX #4: CLAUDIA AND MEAN JANINE by Ann M. Martin, illustrated by Raina Telgemeier. Scholastic Inc./Graphix. Text copyright © 2013 by Ann M. Martin, illustrations copyright © 2013 Raina Telgemeier. Used by permission; (right) LC-DIG-ppmsca-40491. Gift, Small Press Expo, 2015. From BABYSITTERS CLUB GRAPHIX #4: CLAUDIA AND MEAN JANINE by Ann M. Martin, illustrated by Raina Telgemeier. Scholastic Inc./Graphix. Text copyright © 2013 by Ann M. Marti, illustrations copyright © 2013 Raina Telgemeier. Used by permission.

74 (top) LC-DIG-ppmsca-40502. Image copyright Jillian Tamaki; (bottom) LC-DIG-ppmsca-40500 Image copyright Jillian Tamaki.

75 (top) LC-DIG-ppmsca-40505; (bottom) LC-DIG-ppmsca-40506. Gift, Small Press Expo, 2011. Courtesy of Lilli Carré.

76 LC-DIG-ppmsca-40492. Gift, Small Press Expo, 2015. Courtesy of Miss Lasko-Gross.

INTERLUDE: ILLUSTRATIONS FOR INDUSTRY

78 (top) HABS CAL, 43-SARA, 2- (sheet 10 of 10); (middle left) LC-USZ62-114185; (middle right) LC-DIG-ppmsca-31508; (bottom) LC-DIG-ppmsca-31507.

79 (top left) LC-DIG-ppmsca-09504; (top right) LC-DIG-ppmsca-05905. Courtesy Eames Office, LLC, © 2017 Eames Office, LLC (eamesoffice.com); (bottom) LC-USZC4-12796. Courtesy Eames Office, LLC, © 2017 Eames Office, LLC (eamesoffice.com).

80 (top left) LC-DIG-ppmsca-39682. Courtesy Eames Office, LLC, © 2017 Eames Office, LLC (eamesoffice.com); (top

right) LC-DIG-ppmsca-08868. Courtesy Eames Office, LLC, © 2017 Eames Office, LLC (eamesoffice.com); (bottom left) LC-USZC4-4925. Courtesy Eames Office, LLC, © 2017 Eames Office, LLC (eamesoffice.com); (bottom right) LC-USZC4-14217. Courtesy Eames Office, LLC, © 2017 Eames Office, LLC (eamesoffice.com).

81 (left) LAMB, no. 1522 (B size) [P&P]; (right) LAMB, no. 1980 (AA size) [P&P].

82 (left) LC-DIG-ppmsca-51960. Courtesy of the artist, Anna Marie Magagna; (right) LC-DIG-ppmsca-51961. Courtesy of the artist, Anna Marie Magagna.

CHAPTER FOUR: COMMENTATORS AND REPORTERS

84 (left) LC-DIG-ppmsca-05930; (right) LC-DIG-ppmsca-05931.

85 (left) LC-DIG-ppmsca-05932; (right) LC-DIG-ppmsca-05929.

86 (left) LC-DIG-ppmsca-51304. Gift, The Bernarda Bryson Shahn Family, LLC, 2012; (right) LC-DIG-ppmsca-51306. Purchase, The Alfred Bendiner Foundation, 2012.

87 LC-DIG-ppmsca-51305. Gift, The Bernarda Bryson Shahn Family, LLC, 2012.

88 (left) LC-DIG-ppmsca-40496. Gift of the artist, 1995. Sue Coe: *Union Carbide*. Copyright © 1986 Sue Coe. Courtesy Galerie St. Etienne, New York; (right) LC-DIG-ppmsca-40498. Sue Coe: *Haiti*. Copyright © 1986 Sue Coe. Courtesy Galerie St. Etienne, New York.

89 LC-DIG-ppmsca-40497. Sue Coe: *Bothatcher*. Copyright © 1986 Sue Coe. Courtesy Galerie St. Etienne, New York.

90 LC-DIG-ppmsca-37424. Sue Coe: *War*. Copyright © 1991 Sue Coe. Courtesy Galerie St. Etienne, New York.

91 LC-DIG-ppmsca-37425. Gift of the artist, 1995. Sue Coe: *Supreme Cruelty*. Copyright © 1991 Sue Coe. Courtesy Galerie St. Etienne, New York.

92 (top left) LC-DIG-ppmsca-51311. Gift of the artist, 2016. Courtesy of Frances Jetter; (top right) LC-DIG-ppmsca-51312. Gift of the artist, 2016. Courtesy of Frances Jetter; (bottom left) LC-DIG-ppmsca-51309. Gift of the artist 2016. Courtesy of Frances Jetter; (bottom right) LC-DIG-ppmsca-51310. Gift of the artist, 2016. Courtesy of Frances Jetter.

93 LC-DIG-ppmsca-03323. Gift of the artist, 2003. © Anita Kunz.

94 LC-DIG-ppmsca-03313. Gift of the artist, 2003. © Anita Kunz.

95 (left) LC-DIG-ppmsca-03324. Gift of the artist, 2003. © Anita Kunz; (right) LC-DIG-ppmsca-03309. Gift of the artist, 2003. © Anita Kunz.

96 Semi-Postal: Breast Cancer Research Stamp © 1998 United States Postal Service. All Rights Reserved. Used with Permission.

97 (left) LC-DIG-ppmsca-38589. © 2017 Whitney Sherman. Courtesy of the artist; (right) LC-DIG-ppmsca-51962. © 2017 Whitney Sherman. Courtesy of the artist.

98 (top left) LC-DIG-ppmsca-38592. Courtesy of Melinda Beck. Art Director: Matthew Dorfman; (top right) LC-DIG-ppmsca-38590. Courtesy of Melinda Beck; (bottom) LC-DIG-ppmsca-38591. Courtesy of Melinda Beck. Art Director: Matthew Dorfman.

99 LC-DIG-ppmsca-51959. Courtesy of Melinda Beck. Creative Director: Bob Newman.

100 LC-DIG-ppmsca-52056. Courtesy of Melinda Beck.

101 (top) LC-DIG-ppmsca-37417 Purchase/gift, Jillian Tamaki, 2011. Image copyright Jillian Tamaki; (bottom) LC-DIG-ppmsca-12817.

102 RBSC N7433.4.J48 C79. Courtesy of Frances Jetter.

103 LC-DIG-ppmsca-31198. Drawing by Marilyn Church.

104 (top) LC-DIG-ppmsca-31210. Drawing by Marilyn Church; (bottom) LC-DIG-ppmsca-31209. Drawing by Marilyn Church.

105 LC-DIG-ppmsca-39839. Gift/purchase, Pat Lopez, 2014. Courtesy of Pat Lopez.

106 LC-DIG-ppmsca-39832. Gift/purchase, Pat Lopez, 2014. Courtesy of Pat Lopez.

107 (top) LC-DIG-ppmsca-39838. Gift/purchase, Pat Lopez, 2014. Courtesy of Pat Lopez; (bottom) The Thomas V. Girardi Collection of Courtroom Drawings LC-DIG-ppmsca-51124. Artist, Aggie Whelan Kenny.

108 The Thomas V. Girardi Collection of Courtroom Drawings LC-DIG-ppmsca-51137. Courtesy of Elizabeth Williams.

CHAPTER FIVE: COVERS AND CARTOONS

111 (top) AWC LC-DIG-ppmsca-07919; (bottom) LC-USZC4-13008.

112 LC-DIG-ppmsca-25959.

113 LC-DIG-ppmsca-25590.

114 (left) LC-DIG-ppmsca-01591. Gift and bequest from Caroline and Erwin Swann, 1977; (right) LC-DIG-ppmsca-37449. Gift and bequest from Caroline and Erwin Swann, 1977.

115 (left) LC-DIG-ppmsca-01581. Gift and bequest from Caroline and Erwin Swann, 1977; (right) LC-DIG-ppmsca-37418. Gift and bequest from Caroline and Erwin Swann, 1977.

116 (top) LC-DIG-ppmsca-31878. Gift and bequest from Caroline and Erwin Swann, 1977; (bottom) LC-DIG-ppmsca-40483

117 LC-DIG-ppmsca-33572.

118 (left) LC-DIG-ppmsca-52126; (right) LC-USZC4-6781.

119 LC-DIG-ppmsca-01603.

120 (left) LC-DIG-ppmsca-51807; (right) LC-DIG-ppmsca-38577. Helen E. Hokinson/The New Yorker Collection/The Cartoon Bank.

121 (top) LC-DIG-ppmsca-51964; (bottom) AWC LC-DIG-ppmsca-06563. Alice Harvey/The New Yorker Collection/The Cartoon Bank.

122 AWC LC-DIG-ppmsca-05772.

123 LC-DIG-ppmsca-33049. Previously published in *Esquire* magazine, 1960.

124 LC-DIG-ppmsca-33048.

125 (top) New Yorker Cartoon Drawings Collection LC-DIG-ppmsca-40487; (bottom) New Yorker Cartoon Drawings Collection LC-DIG-ppmsca-33574. Roberta Macdonald/The New Yorker Collection/The Cartoon Bank.

126 New Yorker Cartoon Drawings Collection LC-DIG-ppmsca-37437. Roberta Macdonald/The New Yorker Collection/The Cartoon Bank.

127 LC-DIG-ppmsca-51308. Previously published in *Esquire* magazine, March 1954.

128 (left) AWC LC-DIG-ppmsca-07848; (right) LC-DIG-ppmsca-40486. Previously published in *Esquire* magazine, November 1954.

129 LC-DIG-ppmsca-33050. Gift of the artist, 2011. Victoria Roberts/The New Yorker Collection/The Cartoon Bank.

131 LC-DIG-ppmsca-31865. Purchase, The Alfred Bendiner Foundation, 2010. "Mixed marriage. Takes two to tango" by Roz Chast, originally published in The New Yorker. Copyright © 2008 Roz Chast, used by permission of The Wylie Agency LLC. Roz Chast/The New Yorker Collection/The Cartoon Bank.

132 (top left) LC-DIG-ppmsca-31869. Purchase, The Alfred Bendiner Foundation, 2010. "Style" by Roz Chast, originally published in The New Yorker. Copyright © 2009 Roz Chast, used by permission of The Wylie Agency LLC. Roz Chast/The New Yorker Collection/The Cartoon Bank; (top right) LC-DIG-ppmsca-31868. Purchase, The Alfred Bendiner Foundation, 2010. "Mixed marriage. A quiet evening at home" by Roz Chast, originally published in The New Yorker. Copyright © 2002 Roz Chast, used by permission of The Wylie Agency LLC. Roz Chast/The New Yorker Collection/The Cartoon Bank; (bottom) LC-DIG-ppmsca-31373. Purchase, The Alfred Bendiner Foundation, 2009. "April fool" by Roz Chast, originally published in The New Yorker. Copyright

© 2009 Roz Chast, used by permission of The Wylie Agency LLC. Roz Chast/The New Yorker © Conde Nast.

133 LC-DIG-ppmsca-03321. Gift of the artist, 2003. © Anita Kunz.

134 (left) LC-DIG-ppmsca-03330. Gift of the artist, 2003. © Anita Kunz; (right) LC-DIG-ppmsca-03325. Gift of the artist, 2003. © Anita Kunz.

135 LC-DIG-ppmsca-2214. Gift of the artist, 2008. © Anita Kunz.

136 (left) LC-DIG-ppmsca-02127 #10. Gift of the artists, 2002. By Maira Kalman and Rick Meyerowitz; (right) LC-DIG-ppmsca-02120. Gift of the artists, 2002. Maira Kalman/Rick Meyerowitz/The New Yorker © Conde Nast.

CHAPTER SIX: CARICATURISTS AND POLITICAL CARTOONISTS

138 LC-DIG-ppmsca-37434. Courtesy of Kraushaar Galleries, New York.

139 (left) LC-DIG-ppmsc-05877. Gift and bequest from Caroline and Erwin Swann, 1977. Courtesy of Kraushaar Galleries, New York; (right) LC-DIG-ppmsca-52057. Gift and bequest from Caroline and Erwin Swann, 1977. Courtesy of Kraushaar Galleries, New York.

140 (left) Ben and Beatrice Goldstein Foundation Collection LC-DIG-ppmsca-40731. Courtesy of Louisiana State University Press; (right) LC-USZC2-3688. Courtesy of Louisiana State University Press.

141 LC-DIG-ppmsca-38576. Courtesy of Louisiana State University Press.

142 LC-DIG-ppmsca-38580. Courtesy of Deborah Vollmer, daughter of Aline Fruhauf.

143 (left) LC-DIG-ppmsca-40489. Courtesy of Deborah Vollmer, daughter of Aline Fruhauf; (right) LC-DIG-ppmsca-40488. Courtesy of Deborah Vollmer, daughter of Aline Fruhauf.

144 LC-DIG-ppmsca-38578.

145 LC-DIG-ppmsca-31872. Gift of the artist, 2008.

146 (top left) LC-DIG-ppmsca-31871. Gift of the artist, 2008; (top right) LC-DIG-ppmsca-22144. Gift of the artist, 2008; (bottom) LC-DIG-ppmsca-33051. Gift of the artist, 2008.

147 LC-DIG-acd-2a08595.

148 LC-DIG-ppmsca-02940.

149 (left) LC-DIG-ppmsca-40504; (right) LC-DIG-ppmsca-33575. Gift of Matthew Bernhardt and Christine Hoverman, 2006. © Joan Bernhardt.

150 (left) LC-DIG-ppmsca-38599. Gift of Matthew Bernhardt and Christine Hoverman, 2006. © Joan Bernhardt;

(right) LC-DIG-ppmsca-33578. Gift of Matthew Bernhardt and Christine Hoverman, 2006. © Joan Bernhardt.

151 (left) LC-DIG-ppmsca-22147. Gift of Matthew Bernhardt and Christine Hoverman, 2006. © Joan Bernhardt; (right) LC-DIG-ppmsca-333579. Gift of Matthew Bernhardt and Christine Hoverman, 2006. © Joan Bernhardt.

152 AWC LC-DIG-ppmsca-04613. ETTA HULME © The Fort Worth Star-Telegram. Reprinted by permission of ANDREWS MCMEEL SYNDICATION for UFS. All right reserved.

154 (top) LC-DIG-ppmsca-37446. Gift of the artist, 2012. Courtesy of Signe Wilkinson; (middle) LC-DIG-ppmsca-37447. Gift of the artist, 2012. Courtesy of Signe Wilkinson; (bottom) LC-DIG-ppmsca-33053. Gift of the artist, 2007. Courtesy of Signe Wilkinson.

155 LC-DIG-ppmsca-33055. Gift of the artist, 2007. Courtesy of Signe Wilkinson.

156 (top) LC-DIG-ppmsca-04682, LC-DIG-ppmsca-04683. Gift of the artist, 2004. Courtesy of Ann Telnaes; (bottom) LC-DIG-ppmsca-01970. Gift of the artist, 2004. Courtesy of Ann Telnaes.

157 (top) LC-DIG-ppmsca-04690. Gift of the artist, 2004. Courtesy of Ann Telnaes; (bottom) LC-DIG-ppmsca-04712. Gift of the artist, 2004. Courtesy of Ann Telnaes.

158 LC-DIG-ppmsca-04713. Gift of the artist, 2004. Courtesy of Ann Telnaes.

159 (top) LC-DIG-ppmsca-37445. Gift of the artist, 2012. The Washington Post News Service & Syndicate; (bottom) LC-DIG-ppmsca-37444. Gift of the artist, 2012. The Washington Post News Service & Syndicate.

160 (top) LC-DIG-ppmsca-38585. Gift of the artist, 2014. Courtesy of Liza Donnelly; (bottom) LC-DIG-ppmsca-38587. Gift of the artist, 2014. Courtesy of Liza Donnelly.

161 LC-DIG-ppmsca-33059. Gift, Small Press Expo, 2011. Courtesy of Jen Sorensen.

162 (left) LC-DIG-ppmsca-33058. Gift, Small Press Expo, 2011. Courtesy of Jen Sorensen; (right) Courtesy of Jen Sorensen.

188 Photograph by Steve Murray, 2016. Courtesy Galerie St. Etienne, New York.

189 Photograph by Stephan Glidden. Courtesy of Liza Donnelly.

192 (left) LC-DIG-ppmsca-51967. Photograph by Malcolm Arbuthnot. Published in Dorothy Parker et al, *High Society* (New York: G. P. Putnam's Sons, 1920); (right) Portrait of Mary Hallock Foote, ca. 1874, photCL 358, The Huntington Library, San Marino, California.

195 Clayton Stone Harris Studio, photographer. Charles Scribner's Sons Art Reference Dept. records, 1839–1962. Archives of American Art, Smithsonian Institution.

199 (left) Courtesy of Frances Jetter; (right) Photograph by Brian J. Tremblay. Courtesy of Lynn Johnston.

201 LC-DIG-ppmsca-03311. Gift of the artist, 2003. © Anita Kunz

204 (left) LC-DIG-ppmsca-38584; (right) Photograph courtesy of Joan Bernhardt.

205 Courtesy of Trina Robbins.

207 (left) LC-DIG-ppmsca-12045. Photograph by Gertrude Käsebier; (right) Courtesy of Nancy Goldstein.

208 Harriet Endicott Waite research material concerning Currier & Ives, 1923–1956. Archives of American Art, Smithsonian Institution.

210 Photograph by Scout Cuomo. Courtesy of Hilary B. Price.

211 (left) LC-DIG-ppmsca-38271. Photograph by Frances Benjamin Johnston; (right) Photograph by Jessica Christian. Courtesy of Trina Robbins.

214 (left) Harvard Art Museums/Fogg Museum, Gift of Bernarda Bryson Shahn; (right) Courtesy of Whitney Sherman.

215 (left) Courtesy of Art Research Associates; (right) LC-DIG-ppmsc-05901. Published in *Good Housekeeping*, November 1917, p. 32.

216 Courtesy of Jen Sorensen.

217 LC-DIG-ppmsca-38583.

218 Photograph by Reynard Li. Courtesy of Jillian Tamaki.

219 Courtesy of Ann Telnaes.

220 Courtesy of Signe Wilkinson.

BIOGRAPHICAL SKETCHES

181 LC-USZ62-116756.

182 (left) Copyright Lynda Barry, Used with permission by Drawn & Quarterly; (right) Courtesy of Alison Bechdel.

183 Courtesy of Lisa Benson.

185 Courtesy of Trina Robbins.

186 Courtesy of Roz Chast.

187 Courtesy of Marilyn Church.

INDEX

women: as architects, designers, and drafters, 81–82; in cartoons/comics, 52, 53–54; in comic strips, 41–44; as leaders in world of contemporary illustration, xii; limitations and restrictions on, xi–xii; magazines primarily for, 110; in National Cartoonists Society, 33, 49, 124; as newspaper editors and publishers, 169n60; political and editorial cartooning and, 137, 147, 148; in postwar years, 123; in workplace, portrayals of, 38, 41–44, 52, 53–56. *See also* New Woman

Wood, Grant, 85

Woodard Smith, Cloethiel: career of, 79, 81; Harbour Square apartment houses, *78*; Washington Channel Bridge plan and southeast elevation, *78*

Woodward, Hildegard H., 222

Woollcott, Alexander, 33

World War II, 40, 63, 124, 149, *149*

Wright, Frank Lloyd, 20

Wyeth, N. C., 6

Young, Chic, 48

Zigrosser, Carl, 141

Zurier, Rebecca, 148